MW01627331

MUSCLE CAR

SOURCE BOOK

First published in 2015 by Motorbooks, an imprint of Quarto Publishing Group USA Inc., 400 First Avenue North, Suite 400, Minneapolis, MN 55401 USA. Telephone: (612) 344-8100 Fax: (612) 344-8692

quartoknows.com
Visit our blogs at quartoknows.com

Motorbooks titles are also available at discounts in bulk quantity for industrial or sales-promotional use. For details contact the Special Sales Manager at Quarto Publishing Group USA Inc., 400 First Avenue North, Suite 400, Minneapolis, MN 55401 USA.

10 9 8 7 6 5 4 3 2 1

ISBN: 978-0-7603-4857-4

Library of Congress Cataloging-in-Publication Data

Mueller, Mike, 1959-
Muscle car source book : all the facts, figures, statistics, and production numbers / Mike Mueller.
pages cm
Summary: "Muscle Car Source Book is a muscle car buff's encyclopedia that chronicles the how's why's, and when's of American muscle car manufacturers like Dodge, Plymouth, Ford, and more"-- Provided by publisher.
ISBN 978-0-7603-4857-4 (hardback)
1. Muscle cars--United States. I. Title.
TL23.M775 2015
629.2220973--dc23
2015020604

Acquisitions Editor: Darwin Holmstrom
Project Manager: Jordan Wiklund
Art Director: Brad Springer
Cover & Layout Designer: Simon Larkin

On the front cover: 1964 Pontiac GTO, 1970 Z28 Camaro, 1968 Shelby GT500 (top); 1970 Plymouth Superbird (center).

On the back cover: 1971 Plymouth Hemi 'Cuda convertible.

Printed in China

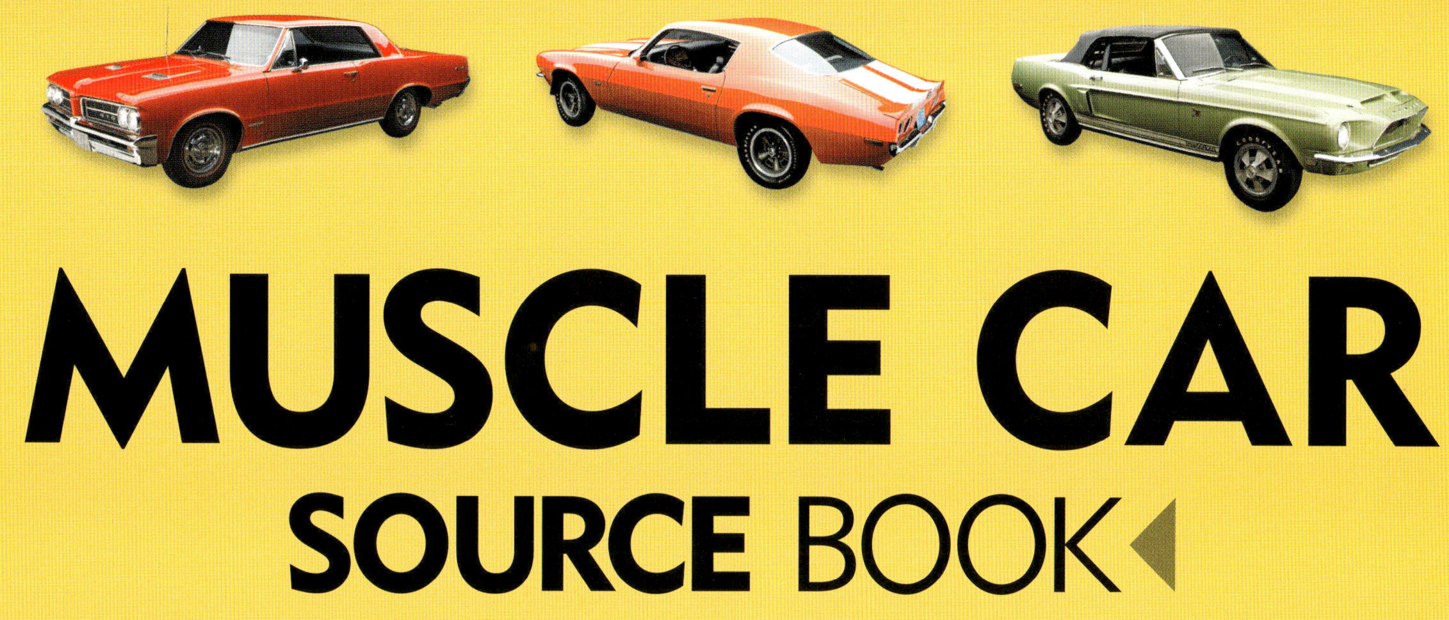

MUSCLE CAR SOURCE BOOK

ALL THE FACTS, FIGURES, STATISTICS, AND PRODUCTION NUMBERS

MIKE MUELLER

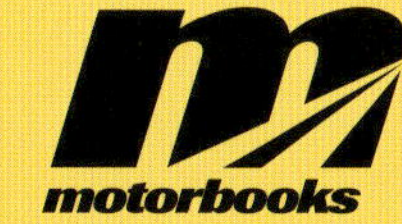

CONTENTS

ACKNOWLEDGMENTS

The latest of more than 30 titles I've produced for Motorbooks, dating back to 1992, this epic easily ranks as the most involved, being some three decades in the making on its own. Much of the following material, both photographic and factual, began filtering into my dust-encrusted library during the 1980s, thanks to the generosity and ample assistance of countless cohorts, friends, and family, some of whom are no longer around to receive their just due. That includes my brother, Jim Mueller, Jr., formerly of Fisher, Illinois. Like the rest of my clan up in the Land of Lincoln, he never once failed to come through for me in the clutch, almost right up until he succumbed to cancer in May 2014. Couldn't have done this without you, Jimbo.

The same goes for another brother, Dave Mueller, who still jumps through hoops upon request despite his soon-to-be-replaced knees (whenever he finally hangs up his hammer). Ma and Pa Mueller (Jim and Nancy) also deserve unending mention and gratitude, as do my sister and her husband (Kathy and Frank Young) and the best-girlfriend-in-the-history-of-girlfriends, Erin Welker, here in Arlington, Texas. Love ya'll more than you know. And trust me—the checks remain in the mail.

A carpenter by trade, the author's brother, Dave Mueller, of Champaign, Illinois, also knows his way around muscle cars. His able assistance during countless photo shoots dating back nearly 25 years rates as priceless, explaining why he has never received a dime for all his hard work—a nickel, maybe, but not one damned dime. *Mike Mueller*

Mucho kudos (and equal remuneration) also go to my boss at Motorbooks, Zack Miller, who has put up with me far longer now than all of my ex-wives combined. Name-dropping Zack's main edit men, Darwin Holmstrom and Jordan Wiklund, is simply a must too, especially considering how little credit (not to mention reward) they receive for dealing with yours truly. Great job, guys. Now you can go sweep up your hair.

As for all the others who helped make these fact-packed pages possible, thanking each of you individually simply cannot be done in 500 words or less. Suffice it to say that almost countless enthusiasts, experts, club officials, archivists, historical figures, media folk, Detroit insiders, and publishing comrades have answered my sometimes-desperate calls over the last 30 years, some amazingly more than once. Among those I've probably bothered the most are three of my former co-workers at good ol' Dobbs Publishing Group (*Muscle Car Review*, *Mopar Muscle*, *Mustang Monthly*, *Super Ford*): Tom Shaw, Steve Statham, and Greg Rager. RIP, DPG. Keep on truckin', Tom, Steve, and Greg.

Veteran automotive journalists Jim McCraw, Joe Oldham, Hilo Bob McClurg, and D. Randy Riggs also found themselves yanked up onto my resource bandwagon for this project, as did fellow Motorbooks author Jim Schild; AMC guru Eddie Stakes (www.planethoustonamx.com); Ford fact guru Kevin Marti (www.martiauto.com); Marcia McCrary of the Points and Condenser Preservation Society in Ypsilanti, Michigan; Mercury Cyclone registry head Robert Day (clubs.hemmings.com/cyclonemontegotorinoregistry); GM Powertrain exec Tom Read; Pontiac historian and former "Copo man" Jim Mattison (www.phs-online.com); Mark Bowden at the Detroit Public Library's National Automotive History Collection; John Kraman and Sam Murtaugh at Mecum Auctions (www.mecum.com); longtime automotive literature dealer Walter Miller (www.autolit.com); and National Chevelle Owners Association co-founder Mark Meekins (www.thechevellereport.com).

Wish I could go on with further well-earned acknowledgments, but page parameters simply won't have it. Last and certainly not least by any means are the few hundred car owners who posed their pride-and-joys for my Hasselblads over these many years. Don't think I don't remember each and every one of you. Hope you like what you see.

Mike Mueller

INTRODUCTION MUSCLE DEFINITION

Even casual witnesses still recognize these three letters, which Pontiac people copped from Enzo Ferrari with nary an apology. More GTOs were sold from 1964 to 1974 than any other American muscle car. *Mike Mueller*

Detroit's original muscle car era, by most definitions, officially opened for business in 1964 following the introduction of a milestone machine from Pontiac Motor Division that, as *Car and Driver's* David E. Davis Jr. later wrote in 1975, "appeared on the American scene like a Methodist minister leaving a massage parlor." No, GTO wasn't this country's first automobile to offer obscene amounts of horsepower. It was the way Pontiac packaged its latest brand of performance that had the congregation swooning.

Before GTO, big cubes in a big car wearing a big price tag represented the only choice for a buyer looking to satisfy a big need for speed. PMD people, on the other hand, determined that less could be more. Their idea was so damned simple: take a relatively lightweight midsize body, stuff it full of engine, and top it off with a bottom line more readily within reach of the younger, power-hungry set. And/or those young at heart.

And wouldn't you know it? As fate would have it, a youthful trend was just starting to make its presence felt in the marketplace when GTO happened. In truth, though, luck had nothing to do with it; anyone with enough fingers and toes

Left: Pontiac promoted the "Tiger" nickname for GTO from the get-go, while the word on the street soon morphed into "Goat." Everything seen in this 1964 ad was standard save for the split exhaust tips, which exited directly behind the rear wheels when installed at extra cost.

First offered by Pontiac in 1957, optional Tri-Power also made its way onto GTO options lists from 1964 to 1966. A single Rochester Quadra-jet four-barrel superseded those three two-barrels when GTO's original 389-cid V-8 grew to 400 cubes in 1967. *David Kimble cutaway*

could've figured it out. Start with 1946, add 16 years, and what did you have? An ever-growing army of eager, newly legalized drivers, offspring of the hundreds of thousands of lonely soldiers who returned home after World War II. The "baby boom" those veterans created promised a flood of young Americans during the 1960s, all ripe for the picking in the eyes of marketing moguls. By 1970, 52 out of 100 Americans were younger than 30, a reality business leaders were well aware of.

"While the kids don't spend all the money in this country, they are the ones everybody is playing to," explained Ford Motorsports director Jacque Passino that year in a *Motor Trend* guest editorial. "The miniskirt wasn't invented because the little old lady from Pasadena wanted one. But she's probably wearing one today, because it's all she can get. Some large chain department stores don't even stock clothes for the over-30 set anymore."

Arguably the first mass-marketing genius in Detroit to embrace baby boomers was Ford's Lee Iacocca, father of the Mustang. Sporty and truly affordable, America's original "pony car" attracted this new breed of buyer with a vengeance in 1964; more than 400,000 came running to jump onto Iacocca's bandwagon during its first year on the road.

Yet as wildly popular as Mustang was, bucket seats and a floor shifter alone didn't quite do it for all customers. Some wanted a sporty car to run like a sporty car, not just look and feel like one. Some also already had noticed just how fun, not to mention fast, moving from point A to B could be.

Countless boomers had watched while teens of the 1950s had scared their families half to death, as naysayers saw it, by hot rodding their way to hell. But despite narrow-minded predictions from parents, priests, and politicians, the

Above: Like Ford's first "flathead" V-8 in 1932, Chevrolet's original small-block, introduced 23 years later, put real power into the hands of Average Joe. This high-winding, short-stroke, overhead-valve V-8 initially displaced 265 cubic inches.

fire-breathing hot rod—along with the paganistic rock 'n' roll that blared from its radio—did not help bring about the fall of civilization as we know it. On the contrary, it inspired an entirely new industry, the aftermarket performance parts biz, which, as the 1960s wound down, was raking in more than $1 billion annually.

"It's the much talked about youth market that has pushed sales to such heights," added Passino in 1970. "Statistics show that today's kids like cars. Economists estimate that teenagers and those just out of their teens spend $3.5 billion annually on automobiles and automotive items. Automobiles are no different than clothes. The kids of today want an 'in' look in the things they wear. They also want the 'in' thing with regard to cars. This has led to the demand for the so-called muscle cars and has helped create the tremendous growth pattern in the accessory business."

Clearly the pump was primed by the time Pontiac introduced its shocking GTO, soon known more affectionately both by its promotional nickname, "Tiger," or its street-slang tag, "Goat." Everything was in place—a young-leaning, thrill-seeking demographic; hip music; good vibrations—and everything was cool, save for the economy, which had heated up considerably. Perhaps most importantly, cars were truly groovy, and the hotter the performance, the groovier the car. It just might have been the best time ever to be young. It certainly was a great time to be building automobiles.

Let's not forget, however, the groundwork laid by the previous generation.

Modern muscle car ancestors included Buick's original Century, created in 1936 by combining the Flint firm's powerful Roadmaster straight-eight engine with its shorter, lighter Special body. The name came from the resulting hot model's ability to hit triple digits on the speedometer, something not at all common before World War II.

Or generations. Again, selling speed was nothing new in 1964, nor were heaping helpings of horsepower. The former practice was every bit as old as internal combustion itself, while the latter quantities had been growing particularly strong dating back to World War II's end. For chrissakes, a young Henry Ford had made a name for himself at a racetrack well before he put the world on wheels. As for stuffing mucho motor into not-so-much car, Buick began planting the big, heavy Roadmaster's powerful straight-eight into the lighter, shorter Special chassis in 1936, with the resulting "Century" named for its ability to peg a speedometer like few other cars of its day.

Then along came General Motors' trend-setting overhead-valve V-8s in 1949. Of innovative, high-winding, short-stroke design, Cadillac's 331-cid OHV V-8 churned out 160 horses, in turn making it Detroit's strongest offering. At the same time, Oldsmobile put its 303-cube, valve-in-head V-8 to work hauling around fewer pounds. With Detroit's top power-to-weight ratio, Olds' 135-horsepower Rocket 88 instantly became the leader of the postwar performance pack—both on the street and the newborn National Association of Stock Car Auto Racing circuit.

Unlike today, stock truly meant stock during NASCAR's first couple decades. And when those "Fabulous Hudson Hornets" fitted with "Twin H-Power" started winning races by the butt-load in 1951, NASCAR fans knew street-going Hudsons were no slouches, either. Armed with two less cylinders than their V-8 rivals, Hornets were still among the hottest things buzzing about on American roads until 1955, the year Chevrolet introduced its "Hot One" and Chrysler unveiled the first of its fabled "letter cars."

Powered by Chevy's own OHV milestone—the brand's first "small-block" V-8—that former machine made real speed available to the masses much like Henry Ford had done with his historic "flathead" V-8 in 1932. Triple digits on the speedometer had never before come this cheap. As for the Chrysler, it featured the first postwar engine to reach the 300-horsepower plateau, hence its name: "C-300." Helping this beautiful brute's 331-cid Fire Power V-8 make all those ponies were cylinder heads incorporating hemispherical combustion chambers, a design that's still making Mopars muscular today.

Chrysler engineers had helped industry watchers forget all about GM's OHV V-8s when they let loose their first "hemi-head" engine in 1951. At 180 horsepower, that year's Fire Power V-8 easily bested the strongest Caddy, making it the talk of the town. "The tremendous power of this V-8 is enough in itself to be a strong selling point," claimed a *Road & Track* review. "When you touch that throttle, you know something mighty impressive is happening under the hood." *Motor Trend's* editors were so impressed they awarded their Car of the Year trophy to 1951's Chrysler. According to *Motor Trend's* Griffith Borgeson, the hemi-head V-8 represented "a major step ahead in American automotive history."

Cadillac took its next step in 1952 with a 190-horsepower V-8 that temporarily put America's luxury leader back in front in Detroit's burgeoning horsepower race. Chrysler then regained the lead two years later with its 235-horsepower Fire Power, and from there hemi-head V-8s dominated the advertised output sweepstakes until they retired—temporarily—after 1958. A 392-cid Fire Power V-8 was making 390 horsepower that last year.

Along with copping *Motor Trend*'s Car of the Year award, Chrysler's new Fire Power V-8 model also was picked to pace the 1951 Indianapolis 500.

Oldsmobile's new-for-1949 Rocket V-8 transformed its 88 models into kings on NASCAR racetracks. According to *Mechanix Illustrated*'s Tom McCahill in 1950, the Rocket 88 was "the best all-around highway-performing production car made in America today."

Like Ford's long-running "flathead" V-8, General Motors' thoroughly modern overhead-valve rivals, introduced just before the 1950s started rolling, were compactly constructed. But contrary to ol' Henry's milestone, Cadillac and Oldsmobile's OHV V-8s also offered considerable growth potential, a key to breeding more and more horses. As all bench racers know, in the absence of any other upgrades, the easiest way to pull more ponies from any engine is by raising displacement.

Suffice it to say further that increasing bore and/or stroke always has and always will equal more cubic inches. But during pre war years, there were rather obvious drawbacks to enlarging either half of the equation too far. All early inline engines used really long strokes to derive needed displacement from small-bore blocks, the latter resulting from a need to keep overall length in line. Too much bore diameter in these blocks, multiplied by however many cylinders were involved, and fitting comfortably between cowl and radiator became an issue.

As for those lengthy strokes, they delivered loads of needed torque, but at what cost? Downsides included excessive piston travel and too much lateral connecting rod motion. This meant more friction, which along with shortening engine life also inhibited higher-rpm operation. Long-stroke engines are inherently low-rpm luggers, various physical laws see to that.

Short strokes, on the other hand, promise less wear because all parts involved don't move around as much through the reciprocating process, at least during normal operation. And because the reciprocating mass (crankshaft, rods, pistons, etc.) has not so far to go as the crank spins around, it can do this dance with far less sweat, meaning much higher rotational speeds are possible. Short-stroke engines are naturally high winders, limited only by their overall ability to rapidly pump air and hold everything together at extremely high revs.

Charles Kettering, the engineering mind behind both the first electric self-starter (1912) and leaded gasoline (1923), also spearheaded development of Cadillac's ground-breaking high-compression OHV V-8, which went into production in November 1948. This short-stroke 331-cid engine produced 160 horsepower.

Along with establishing a new short-stroke trend, GM's postwar V-8s additionally were "oversquare"—that is, bore measured greater than stroke. Long-stroke/small-bore engines, conversely, are "undersquare." As an example, Cadillac's previous 346-cid L-head V-8 featured a bore-to-stroke ratio of 0.78:1, compared to 1.05:1 for its 331-cid 1949 replacement. A ratio greater than 1:1 (latter) is oversquare, less than 1:1 (former) is undersquare.

GM engineers relied on an oversquare layout to produce desired displacements while using shorter strokes. Ample bore diameters in turn translated into more room in the combustion chambers for larger valves, now located directly overhead instead of within the block to the side of each cylinder per L-head designs. Larger valves almost always mean better breathing, hence more power potential.

Improved breathing and a serious increase in volumetric efficiency—how well the fuel/air charge combusts—represented the most important gains inherent to the OHV design. L-heads, by nature, were notoriously bad breathers because fuel/air mixtures and spent gases had to follow such inhibited routes into and out of the combustion-chamber/cylinder arena, which was shaped like an inverted "L" from a longitudinal perspective. Overhead valves, on the other hand, allow much smoother passages into and out of combustion chambers that are located fully atop the cylinder—no sideways extension areas are present to complicate flame propagation and limit compression, as was the case with an L-head.

The OHV layout let engineers design more efficient combustion chambers, as well as increase compression levels to all-new heights. While Cadillac's 1948 L-head and 1949 OHV V 8 both featured industry-leading compression levels—7.25:1 for the former, 7.5:1 for the latter—the potential for even higher ratios for the new engine was promising. Not so for the old maxed-out L-head.

If there was a negative aspect to the valve-in-head design, it involved unwanted pounds. Obviously OHV heads were heavier compared to their L-head counterparts, which were no more than thin, flat (thus Ford's nickname) iron cylinder covers with combustion chambers crudely carved into their undersides. Whatever weight gains encountered, however, were easily overshadowed by a bright future.

Thus armed, Cadillac and Oldsmobile kicked off a horsepower race that didn't start slowing down for more than 20 years.

Hemi heads debuted beneath DeSoto hoods in 1952 then made their way between Dodge fenders the following year. Plymouth never did go Hemi, per se, during the 1950s, but its "polyspherical-head" V-8, introduced to its own raves in 1955, represented ample improvement to drivers who'd only had six cylinders to play with until then. As the name implied, the "poly" V-8's combustion chambers weren't quite hemispherical, but they did feature canted valves like their hemi-head cousins. Valve angles, however, weren't as great, meaning twin rocker shafts (like the Fire Power V-8's; see page 13) weren't required. Poly spark plugs also angled out below the valve covers, making them easily accessible. Hemi plugs were literally buried deep within their valve covers. Maximum poly output came in 1957 via the limited-edition Fury's dual-carb, 318-cid V-8, rated at 290 horsepower.

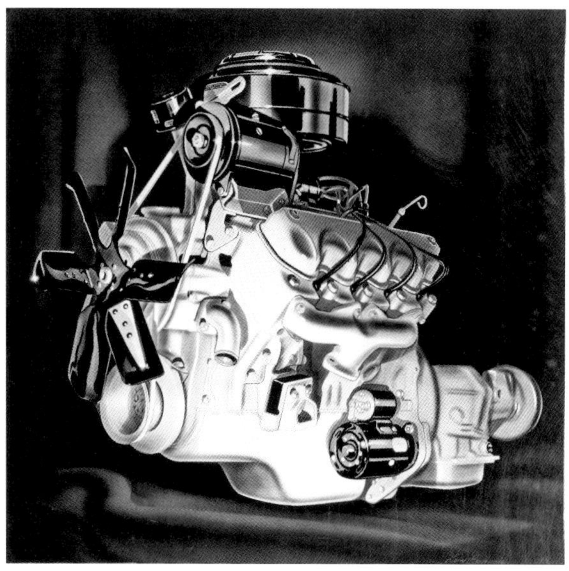

Plymouth's first OHV V-8, introduced for 1955, featured "polyspherical" combustion chambers that required only one rocker shaft per head, as opposed to the two used by Chrysler, Dodge, and DeSoto's Hemi V-8s.

Showcasing the Fire Power V-8 in Chrysler's C-300 resulted in what some old-timers still like to call Detroit's true original muscle car. Debuting in January 1955, the C-300 was, according to promotional paperwork, "America's greatest performing motor car, with the speed of the wind, the maneuverability of a polo pony, the power to pass on the road safely, [and] an all-around performance quite unlike anything you will find available here in America or abroad."

Power brakes and a beefed chassis were standard, as were loads of luxury in a 4,300-pound prestige-mobile able to run right along with Chevrolet's much lighter, far less comfortable Corvette. Fitted with its first V-8 in 1955, Chevrolet's fiberglass two-seater could reach 60 miles per hour from rest in 9 seconds and complete a quarter-mile in 17.2 ticks, topping out at 81.5 miles per hour. With room for the entire family, the palatial C-300 did 0-60 in 9.5 seconds, the quarter-mile in 17.6 seconds at 82 miles per hour. All of these were considered hot numbers for the time.

According to *Mechanix Illustrated's* Tom McCahill, the C-300 was "a hard-boiled, magnificent piece of semi-competition transportation, built for the real automotive connoisseur."

"Semi?" Chrysler's letter-series models made mincemeat of sanctioned stock car racing in 1955 and '56 before retiring to a more civilized existence. The name became "300B" in 1956, kicking off an alphabetical order that continued up through 1965's 300L. Determining why Chrysler's letter legacy ended that year didn't require a rocket scientist's assistance: full-size performance overnight lost its attraction once midsize muscle made the scene.

Those lavish letter cars weren't the only factory hot rods to disappear after 1965, as Chevrolet's real-fine 409 also closed out its short, happy run that year. Honored unforgettably in song by The Beach Boys in 1962, the 409 V-8 traced its roots back to 1958 when Chevy engineers introduced their first W-series big-block, displacing 348 cubic inches, for both car and truck installations. This potent powerplant stood out from the crowd thanks to its unconventional combustion chambers, which resided inside the cylinder bores, not in the heads. Each cylinder bank's deck sloped downward on top at a 16-degree angle off perpendicular (relative to the bores), leaving a wedge-shaped "squish area" between piston and head at top dead center.

Additional performance-enhancing features included staggered valves. Rival "wedge" V-8s at the time all relied on valves laid out in a straight line, this

FACTORY RACING ROOTS

American automakers have been relying on tests of speed and endurance to promote their products for almost as long as autos have been made in America. But competition venues became especially appealing to the factory guys after World War II, thanks to the formation of various sanctioning bodies that promoted various types of racing open to "stock-class" competitors. First came the Sports Car Club of America, founded in Boston in February 1944. The first official SCCA-sanctioned race came in October 1948, at Watkins Glen, New York, and the initial SCCA seasonal championship was decided in 1951. Predictably dominated by European sportsters early on, this circuit became a Corvette playground after 1956. Then in March 1966, SCCA officials staged their first Trans-American Sedan Championship road race, which opened the door for Camaros to battle Mustangs for ultimate supremacy in what was known simply as "Trans-Am" competition.

More appealing to Yankees (though it has operated primarily in the heart of Dixie throughout much of its history) was the National Association of Stock Car Auto Racing league, formed in Daytona Beach, Florida, in February 1948 by Bill France Sr. NASCAR's first "showroom stock" race was held in June 1949, and from then on its top-shelf Grand National circuit would showcase Detroit's hottest passenger cars. Oldsmobiles were the early NASCAR stars, then came Hudson's dominant 1952–54 run. Chrysler garnered much acclaim in 1955 and '56 before the infamous AMA "racing ban" (see pages 14,17) was enacted in 1957 to hopefully curb automakers' involvement at the track.

For a quick background on factory drag racing involvement, see page 21.

Few cars kicked up as much sand on Daytona's old beach/road course than Carl Kiekhaefer's Mercury Marine Chrysler 300s. Here Tim Flock's C-300 speeds around the north turn on the way to NASCAR's 1955 points championship.

Engineer Scott Harvey's Barracuda finished fifth in the SCCA's inaugural Trans-Am championship chase, kicked off in Sebring, Florida, in March 1966.

Various sources still occasionally report that the "C" in C-300 was applied in honor of Briggs Cunningham's Fire Power–equipped Le Mans racers of 1951-54, all of them adorned with the same prefix. But apparently that letter simply stood for "Chrysler." *Mike Mueller*

because their rocker arms were mounted together on long shafts that ran the length of each head. GM's innovative ball-stud rocker arm, introduced by Chevrolet and Pontiac in 1955, allowed the W-engine team to independently position valves where they worked best. In a 348 head, intake valves were positioned up high near the intake manifold runners. Exhaust valves, in turn, were found down close to the exhaust manifolds. All 348s also featured high-compression (9.5:1 or better), all relied on at least a four-barrel carburetor (no single two-barrels; no way, no how), and all had dual exhausts. Maximum posted output during the 348's four-year run was 350 horsepower.

Morphing 348 into 409 for 1961 wasn't simply a matter of boring and stroking the W-series block. Recasting that block with extra iron was required, and countless other modifications meant that parts swaps basically were out of the question. At the heart of the 409 was one of the more radical stock-issue cams of the day, a long-duration bump stick that inherently inhibited low-speed function. As *Motor Trend* explained, "although the [409] will idle at 750 rpm, it will not pull smoothly under 1500 and is 'happiest' when operated over 2000 rpm."

The sum of these parts equaled 360 horsepower for Chevy's first 409, which itself was showcased in the firm's first Super Sport (see page 18), based on 1961's

CHAMBER MUSIC

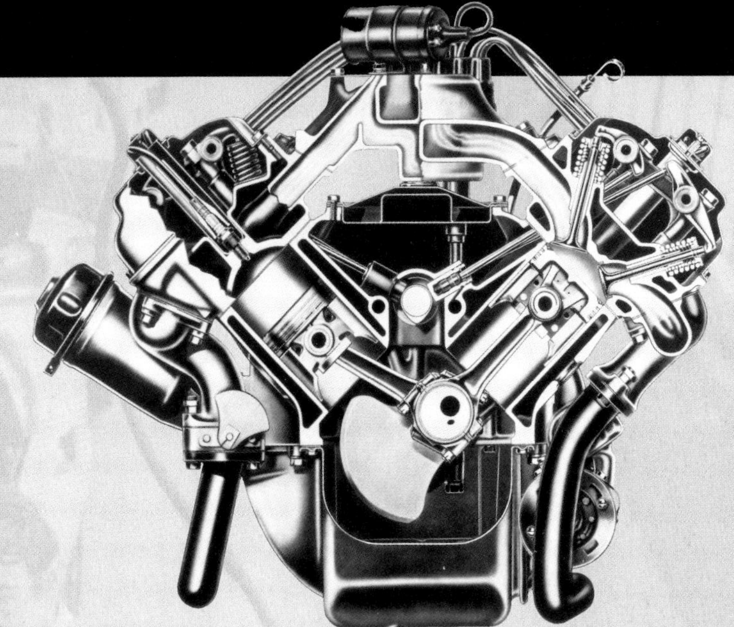

Symmetry is a good thing as far as the internal combustion process is concerned. With its hemispherical combustion chambers and centrally located spark plugs, Chrysler's Fire Power V-8 stood as the state of the art when it debuted for 1951. Canted valves also greatly assisted the good air in, the bad out.

Hemispherical combustion chambers certainly were nothing new when Chrysler rolled out its Fire Power V-8 in 1951. Chelsea Manufacturing, in Chelsea, Michigan, was among the first to try this technology (with two cylinders) in 1903, and France's Peugeot used a similar "pentroof" design for its legendary dual-overhead-cam, 16-valve, four-cylinder racing engine in 1912. "Hemi heads" then found their way into various World War I aircraft, sporting machines from Duesenberg and Stutz, racers from Miller and Offenhauser, and Jaguar's classic XK120 of 1949. But, up to that point, no automaker, foreign or domestic, had gone into mass production with the idea, not like Chrysler.

Fire Power roots dated back to development work originally considered in 1935. Additional experience was gained working with an inverted V-16 hemi-head aircraft engine during World War II, giving Chrysler engineers the confidence to apply this design to their postwar passenger cars.

Hemi advantages are many, beginning with those symmetrical, domed combustion chambers and their centrally located spark plugs. This layout not only enhances volumetric efficiency, the physical nature of those rounded chambers allow more room for bigger valves compared to conventional "wedge" designs. Hemi valves also are inclined in opposite directions to match the chambers' shape, and this means less restriction for both intake and exhaust flow.

Downsides to the original design included its relatively complex valvetrain. Twin rocker shafts were needed to locate the inclined valves atop those hemispherical chambers, as were different-size pushrods and rocker arms—exhaust and intake pieces did not interchange. Size and weight were issues, too, as geometry demanded that these heads be truly big and wide, making for a tight fit between most fenders. On the scales, Fire Power heads weighed as much as 25 percent more than comparable wedge-type units.

This pounds penalty, coupled with all the fuss and muss (not to mention expense) required to engineer and construct these power-packed heads, helped convince corporate officials to drop the design after 1958. As it was, the 413-cid wedge-head that followed released just as many ponies from a lighter, less costly package. But, as drag racers and hot rodders could attest, maximum Mopar muscle just wasn't the same after the first-generation Hemi retired—explaining why a second-gen rendition made its way into competition circles six years later.

Various displacements appeared during that original run, maxing out at 392 cid for Chrysler's top Fire Power. DeSoto's version, "Fire Dome," displaced 276 cubes when it debuted in 1952, while the cubic count for Dodge's first "Red Ram" V-8 was 241 in 1953. Cylinder blocks varied, too, with early Fire Power units featuring an integral flange in back that served as the transmission bell housing's upper half. No DeSoto or Dodge blocks featured this extension, and it was deleted from Chryslers in 1954. A "raised block" (with a 0.75-inch taller deck height) appeared in 1956 when DeSoto and Dodge pushed displacement to 330 and 315 cubic inches, respectively, and this type casting also was required for Chrysler's first 392 in 1957. Maximum first-gen Hemi displacements for DeSoto and Dodge were 345 and 325, respectively.

In a side note, Chrysler's second-edition "letter car," the 300B, became the first American automobile to reach the 1-horsepower-per-cubic-inch plateau in 1956. No, Chevrolet's fuel-injected 283-horsepower, 283-cid Corvette of 1957 does not deserve credit for this milestone, as is commonly claimed. The 300B's optional Fire Power V-8, enlarged to 354 cubic inches, put out 355 horses the year before.

How soon they forget.

CHRYSLER CORPORATION 1ST-GENERATION HEMI V-8s

YEAR	CID	BORE/STROKE	CR	HORSEPOWER	TORQUE	CARBURETOR	VALVE SIZES
1951[1]	331	3.81 x 3.625	7.5:1	180 @ 4,000	312 @ 2,000	Carter 2-barrel	1.81 x 1.50
1952[2]	276	3.625 x 3.344	7.00:1	160 @ 4,400	250 @ 2,000	Carter 2-barrel	1.84 x 1.50
1953[3]	241	3.437 x 3.250	7.00:1	140 @ 4,400	220 @ 2,000	Stromberg 2-bl.	1.75 x 1.41
1955[1]	331	3.81 x 3.625	8.5:1	300 @ 5,200	345 @ 3,200	2 Carter 4-bls	1.94 x 1.75
1957[1]	392	4.00 x 3.906	10:1	390 @ 5,400	430 @ 4,200	2 Carter 4-bls	2.00 x 1.75

NOTE: *CID is cubic-inch displacement; CR is compression ratio; bore/stroke & valve sizes in inches (intake x exhaust).*

1. Chrysler Fire Power V-8

2. DeSoto Fire Dome V-8

3. Dodge Red Ram V-8

HOLD YOUR HORSES!

By 1957, Detroit's battle for horsepower supremacy had grown fierce, to say the least, and factory racing activities also were escalating like nobody's business. New that year were supercharged (Ford) and fuel-injected (Chevrolet) V-8s, both intended to make these arch-rivals' products more competitive on NASCAR tracks. Stock car racing's 1957 season promised to be the most exciting yet, then came a startling rules change. In April, NASCAR officials banned fuel-injection, superchargers and multiple carburetors from Grand National racing, claiming the goal was to level the field for all competitors, big pockets or not.

But NASCAR's reasoning probably was inspired more by current events in Washington, where for about a year congressmen had been asking for limits on the auto industry's unbridled horsepower race. Taxing horsepower and/or regulating automotive safety were proposed, and the Congressional Special Safety Committee decided that racing-themed advertising directly contributed to reckless driving on Main Street USA. The National Safety Council agreed, as did the American Automobile Association, a sanctioning body still reeling after witnessing a 1955 crash at Le Mans that killed at least 82 spectators and left many more than that horribly injured.

Another organization, Detroit's self-policing Automobile Manufacturers Association, also stepped in. AMA chairman Harlow "Red" Curtice recommended that the group's members cut ties with racing. All agreed, and on June 6 the AMA "ban" on factory racing became official. From then on, not only would member companies "not participate or engage in any public contest, competitive event or test of a passenger car involving or suggesting racing or speed," they also would not advertise "the actual or comparative capabilities of passenger cars for speed, or the specific engine size, torque, horsepower or ability to accelerate or perform in any context that suggests speed."

In actuality, the AMA ban was little more than ink, a paper tiger most members only paid lip service to. Not so for Ford and American Motors. Even though the AMA had no enforcement abilities, Dearborn's conservative general manager, Robert McNamara, and AMC's stoic main man, George Romney, followed the resolution to the letter.

General Motors divisions, meanwhile, continued running stronger than ever on both road and track, but with far less flag-waving than before the AMA intervened. Chevrolet was NASCAR's runaway manufacturers points leader from 1958–1961, followed by Pontiac in 1962. Though most witnesses could plainly see what was going on, many corporate officials chose to look the other way as Chevy and PMD parts books began filling up during the late-1950s with an array of heavy-duty, high-performance pieces, some reportedly intended for special use in police cars, taxi fleets and marine applications. That these components also worked well in a competition car apparently was a lucky break, both for purported independent racers and division officials looking for loopholes.

Ford heated up Detroit's horsepower race in 1957 with its supercharged Y-block V-8, introduced for all models that year, including the curious "Retractable" hardtop/convertible (front) and two-seat Thunderbird (rear). *Mike Mueller*

Chevrolet also upped the ante in 1957, adding Rochester-supplied Ramjet fuel injection to its 283-cid V-8. Available for both Corvette and full-sizers, this optional small-block produced 283 horsepower in max form.

Was it just coincidence that the main man behind the ban, Red Curtice, also was GM president? And was it only luck again that the AMA edict came along to help slow Ford in its tracks just as the Blue Oval was preparing to best the Bow-Tie on the yearly sales charts for the first time in two decades?

Chrysler officials also showed little or no respect for the AMA ban and finally came clean about their true feelings right after Henry Ford II denounced the thing (see page 17) in June 1962. GM execs, however, equivocated, claiming they would continue endorsing the resolution as "sufficient time has not been available to evaluate the full implications" of Ford's decision. American Motors didn't leave its AMA-compliant past behind until 1966 or so.

Ironically GM had gone back on the wagon three years earlier, this after top execs finally grew tired of turning a blind eye. In January 1963 Chairman Frederic Donner and President John Gordon issued a memo instructing all divisions to cancel all racing projects, killing off Pontiac's dominant Super Duty, Chevrolet's Z11 lightweight drag car, and Zora Duntov's Grand Sport Corvette. Feeling the axe, too, was Chevy's 427-cid "Mystery Motor," which curiously showed up at Daytona in February and threatened to rewrite NASCAR record books. How were all these outrageous machines built in the first place?

"Ever since the AMA adopted—I think you can term it a recommendation—back in 1957, we have had a policy on our books, and we haven't had any change in it," explained Donner during a February 16 press conference. "Very often you run into interpretations of policies that to an outsider might look like violations—that distance between interpretation and violation is a very delicate one."

What these words smelled like wasn't delicate in the least. And the bull spit continued piling up during the 1960s as General Motors rolled out some of the decade's hottest street racers.

Impala. A dual-carb 409, rated at 409 horsepower, appeared in 1962, and this beast was bumped up to 425 horses the following year. Mightiest of this short-lived breed was the race-only Z11 rendition, created late in 1962. Thanks to an increased stroke, the Z11 actually displaced 427 cubic inches.

By the early 1960s, Detroit clearly had the high-powered big-engine thing down pat. But, discounting a Crosley here, a Rambler there, and a Henry J around the corner, one size generally fit all as far as bodies went prior to 1960. Further ignoring Corvette, Chevrolet didn't begin offering multiple model lines until its rear-engine Corvair debuted that year along with two other new modern compacts, Ford's Falcon and Chrysler's Valiant.

GM's "senior compacts," Buick's Special and Oldsmobile's F-85, appeared in 1961 with a little more size, a lot more prestige, and a bit more engine than the air-cooled, "pancake-six" Corvair. An innovative 215-cid aluminum V-8 (tagged "Rockette" in the Olds' case) was standard for these unit-body cars, which rolled on a 112-inch wheelbase—not exactly a compact stretch. Pushing the definition further were two sporty coupes added into the Special/F-85 mix in the spring of 1961: Skylark and Cutlass.

A third senior compact, Pontiac's Tempest, showed up as well in 1961 but was a true budget buggy powered by a standard "slant-four" engine, created curiously by halving a 389-cid V-8. Additional innovations included independent rear suspension incorporating a transaxle tied to that four-banger by a deflected "rope" driveshaft. An upscale Tempest, Le Mans, debuted in 1962, and an available 326-cid V-8 followed the next year.

High points in American Motors' "prehistory" included Nash's March 1950 introduction of its compact pioneer, Rambler. A curious "convertible" (with a soft top that folded down behind fixed window frames) arrived first, followed by various other body styles, all fitted with two doors until 1954. Ramblers gained size and prestige in 1956, then AMC brought back its original compact ideal two years later in the form of the new Rambler American. Fans of television's classic *Adventures of Superman* series might recognize the show's original Loise Lane, played by Phyllis Coates. Nash was a sponsor of the program, which aired from 1952 to 1958. *courtesy Eddie Stakes, www.planethoustonamx.com*

AMC engineers also tried to pioneer an electronic fuel-injection application in 1957, but the Bendix EFI system they promised as an option for the new Rebel (top) proved problematic and was replaced by a Carter four-barrel in all cases. The ill-fated "Electrojector" 327 V-8 (middle) was rated at 288 horsepower. Chrysler also tried an Electrojector option in 1958 with similar results. Only one Bendix-injected DeSoto is known today.

Introduced in 1958, Chevrolet's 348-cid W-series V-8 featured conventional wedge-shaped combustion chambers. Uncommon, however, was the way those wedges were formed. While almost all engines incorporate combustion chambers formed within their cylinder heads, the 348's chambers were created by cutting the cylinder block deck at an angle, instead of perpendicularly. Notice that the head's face is essentially flat; the combustion chamber itself exists within the cylinder bore. Lincoln-Mercury also tried this trick during the late 1950s.

Right: Chevrolet was offering five different model lines by 1964, lead by Corvette (upper left). Following "America's Sports Car" here is the full-size representative (Impala, Bel Air, Biscayne) and the compact Nova, introduced in 1962. At bottom right is the innovative Corvair, unveiled in 1960 with its air-cooled "pancake" six-cylinder mounted in back. Up front is Chevy's all-new, midsize A-body, Chevelle.

Below: Oldsmobile's "senior compact," F-85, debuted for 1961. In May that year the Cutlass appeared (with sporty bucket seats) as the F-85 line's flagship. And the Jeftire sport coupe (shown here) followed in April 1962 with a turbocharged version of Oldsmobile's 215-cid aluminum V-8.

Originally released in 1960, Ford's compact Falcon (bottom) was joined in 1962 by Detroit's first intermediate model, the midsize Fairlane (top). Both featured unitized body/frame construction, and optional in each case was Dearborn's equally new Windsor small-block V-8.

Also new for 1962 was Chevrolet's Chevy II, a frugal model that shared none of its structure with any other GM product line. Wheelbase was 110 inches and power came from another four-holer, the Bow-Tie brand's first since 1928. Six cylinders were optional for the Chevy II, standard for the top-line Nova. An available V-8 didn't appear until 1964.

It was left to Ford folk to offer Detroit's first modern mid-sizer, this after their new compact had established a rookie-year sales record in 1960. "Not content with the success of Falcon, they've decided that an 'in-betweener'—not as small as a compact and not as big as a [full-size]—would be added to the company lineup," explained *Motor Trend's* Jim Wright. "So it was, and they are calling it Fairlane."

Borrowed from Henry Ford's Dearborn estate (spelled Fair Lane), the moniker wasn't new on Ford cars either, having first adorned top-line models in 1955. "Galaxie" then emerged to fill that role in 1959, leaving the door open to Ford name-callers to simply drop an existing badge down a notch into its new-for-1962 intermediate line. Featuring unit-body construction, Fairlane rested on a 115.5-inch wheelbase—6 inches longer than Falcon's, 3.5 shorter than Galaxie's. V-8 power was available from the get-go.

Riding on a 1-inch-longer wheelbase, Meteor was Mercury's Fairlane running mate for 1962. But it abruptly retired after 1963, leaving the Falcon-based Comet—introduced as a stand-alone model line for 1960—to compete more as a senior compact. Officially labeled a Mercury product in 1962, Comet basically was a stretched Falcon rolling on a 114-inch wheelbase, compared to 109.5 for its Ford cousin. Comet's first available V-8 came in 1963, and the line was restructured into base 202, mid-level 404 and top-shelf Caliente models the next year. Mercury reestablished Comet on the Fairlane platform in 1966, making it a true intermediate.

Over at Chrysler, both Dodge and Plymouth scaled down Dart and Fury, respectively, in 1962, with wheelbases dropping two clicks to 116 inches. But these pioneering B-bodies weren't necessarily considered direct competition for Fairlane. Dodge's resized A-body Dart then appeared for 1963 on an even shorter 111-inch wheelbase, making it more of a match for Chevy II. True intermediate rivals didn't appear from the Mopar camp until Dodge rolled out its new Coronet, on a still lengthy 117-inch wheelbase, in 1965. Trim levels numbered three: base Coronet, Coronet 440, and Coronet 500.

DAMN THE BAN

Despite claims to the contrary, General Motors and Chrysler people for the most part couldn't have cared less about the AMA racing ban, a reality apparent to anyone with eyes. Consider, among other things, Dodge's D500 competition package (introduced the previous year and produced into the 1960s) and Pontiac's Super Duty parts program, initiated in 1959. Ford folk, meanwhile, opted to steer clear of such shenanigans, at least at first.

No longer so willing to stand idly by on the sidelines, Dearborn officials sent a message to their GM counterparts in April 1959 detailing plans to restart performance projects. Revamping the AMA agreement also was suggested, apparently to deaf ears. A reply never came, leaving the Blue Oval gang to proceed as they pleased.

Under the guise of "law enforcement parts development," a three-man team led by engineer Dave Evans set out to put Ford back on track. Chassis man John Crowley and Don Sullivan, whose experience dated back to the flathead V-8's development days, were the other two. As for the fruits of their labor, first came a high-performance rendition of Ford's existing 352-cid Interceptor Special FE-series V-8, rated at 300 horsepower in top form up to that point.

This HP big-block produced 60 more horses, thanks in part to an aggressive solid-lifter cam and a 540-cfm Holley four-barrel on an aluminum intake that weighed half as much as the hulking 80-pound manifold found atop garden-variety 352s. Heavy-duty valve springs (with dampers); a compression boost (from 9.6:1 to 10.6:1); a dual-point, mechanical-advance distributor; and cast-iron header-style exhausts also contributed to the attraction, which was released for public consumption in December 1959. The price was $125, a decent wad at the time.

"It took several years, but we think Ford has the right answer for 1960," wrote *Hot Rod's* Ray Brock after experiencing a 360-horsepower Starliner coupe, which proved capable of more than 150 miles per hour on high-bank test tracks. A beefed clutch and column-shifted, heavy-duty three-speed manual (with overdrive or without) were bolted up behind Ford's new 352 horsepower, and a wide array of optional gear ratios went as low as 5.83:1, just in case pulling tree stumps was part of the plan. An even more challenging clutch and a limited-slip differential were offered, too; an automatic trans wasn't.

Clearly representing the heart of Ford's first modern muscle machine, 1960's 360/352 V-8 was immediately succeeded by even stronger big-blocks; a 401-horsepower 390 topped by three Holley two-barrels in 1961, an even larger 406-cube "6V" V-8, rated at 405 horsepower, in 1962. Ford's supreme FE, the 425-horsepower 427, followed midyear in 1963.

The AMA edict remained in effect then but was obviously inspiring even less respect. A real kick in the teeth came in June 1962, when Henry Ford II—who incidentally was AMA president at the time—issued a short press release explaining how he really felt. After pointing out that his company had initially adhered "to the spirit and letter of the recommendations," he added that "as time passed, some car divisions interpreted the resolution more and more freely, with the result that increasing emphasis was placed on speed, horsepower and racing. As a result, [we] feel that the resolution has come to have neither purpose nor effect. Accordingly, we have notified [the AMA] that we feel we can better establish our own standards of conduct with respect to the manner in which the performance of our vehicles is to be promoted and advertised."

Chrysler issued a similar statement soon afterward calling the AMA ban "inoperative," while GM execs continued their "hear-no-evil, say-no-evil" act. Journalists, on the other hand, were more than willing to speak out, with *Car Life's* editors lauding Henry Ford II for his honesty. In their words, he deserved "a healthy round of applause for being the first industry leader to face the facts as they really are. He has admitted candidly that such things as 406 cubic-inch engines and triple carburetion aren't in keeping with the intent of the [AMA] resolution."

Damn straight.

A low-restriction air cleaner went atop Ford's 360-horsepower 352 V-8 in 1960, as did a Holley four-barrel carburetor. Notice the free-flowing header-type cast-iron exhaust manifolds. *Tom Shaw*

After adhering to the 1957 AMA "racing ban" like glue, Ford broke loose in 1960 with its first modern musclebound model, fitted with a 360-horsepower FE-series big-block V-8. *Tom Shaw*

SO FINE

Although early brochures claimed Chevrolet's Super Sport kit was available for four-door models in 1961, none of the 453 SS Impalas built that first year had more than two doors. Spinner-style wheel covers were included in the package. *Mike Mueller*

Chevrolet engineers knew they had something hot when they built their first 409 V-8 early in 1961. But what a shame it was to hide this much muscle beneath ho-hum Biscayne or middle-of-the-road Bel Air bodies. Even the full-dress Impala, introduced in 1958, wasn't deemed flashy enough to showcase the 409, hence the creation of the "Super Sport kit."

Although early brochures claimed this option was available for four-door models in 1961, none of the 453 Super Sport Impalas built that first year had more than two doors. Priced at a meager $53.80, the Super Sport kit only included spinner wheel covers, SS badges, a Corvette-style glove box grab bar, and a dressy floor plate for four-speed models. It was then left to a long list of mandatory options to complete this sweet deal. Included were power steering and brakes, 8.00x14 narrow-band whitewall tires, and Chevy's "police handling package" (Limited Production Option number 1108), which added a stiffer sway bar up front, sintered metallic brake linings, and heavy-duty springs and shocks. Inside went a 7,000-rpm tachometer (mounted on the steering column) and padded dash.

Only Chevrolet's two W-series big-blocks were allowed beneath an SS hood in 1961. Three 348s were available at 305, 340, and 350 horsepower. Single Carter four-barrel carbs topped the first two, three Rochester two-barrels the latter. A lone Carter also fed the 409, which mandated the installation of a four-speed and 3.36:1 gears. Shorter ratios (running as low as 4.56:1) were available through dealer channels. A Powerglide automatic was optional, too, but only for the 305-horsepower 348.

The famed 409 may have grabbed all the attention, but the majority of those original Super Sports featured 348 V-8s. As it often does, however, size mattered. "Put the big 409 engine into the new Super Sport package and you have one of the hottest test cars of the season," claimed a 1961 *Motor Trend* report. "When I floored it in second I got the impression that Chevrolet had made a mistake in labeling this car a Super anything," added *Motor Trend's* Bob Ames. "They should have called it the Incredible Impala!" With 3.36 gears, *Motor Trend's* test crew managed a 15.31-second quarter-mile in the 409 SS. Switching to optional 4.56 cogs resulted in an alarming 14.02-second pass.

With or without the 409, Impala SS wasted little time becoming one of the 1960s' most popular fun machines. Some 920,000 full-size Super Sports were sold during the decade before the plug was pulled in 1969 as buyers by then apparently no longer cared so much about super-sizing their sporty flights of fancy.

We can thank Pontiac people for that attitude change: midsize muscle became all the rage after GTO hit the ground running in 1964.

Plymouth's counterpart that year wore the company's familiar Belvedere badge and still rolled on the same 116-inch wheelbase introduced three years before. But now an individual model on its own (instead of a trim level package), 1965's Belvedere stood noticeably shorter than Plymouth's revamped, really big Fury and was considerably longer than Valiant—hence it qualified as the firm's first intermediate. Plymouth's midsize pecking order for 1965 also featured three trim levels: Belvedere I, Belvedere II, and Satellite.

GM made big news in 1964 with its new A-body platform, featuring a 115-inch wheelbase and a full frame. Buick, Olds, and Pontiac's existing senior compacts graduated up into full-fledged intermediate ranks on this foundation and were joined by Chevrolet's completely fresh Chevelle, which immediately unseated Fairlane as Detroit's top-selling midsize car. Chevy and the B-O-P trio's newfound midsize form also, of course, morphed into the modern muscle car, led by the LeMans-based GTO.

Hot on GTO's heels came countless copycats, "supercars" as they were called then in the automotive press. Oldsmobile's 4-4-2, Buick's

Looking way too cool wedged between DeSoto, Dodge, and Plymouth fenders in 1960 was the same ram-induction setup that came standard that year beneath the hood of Chrysler's 300F, shown here. A "poor man's supercharger," if you will, this equipment consisted of long tubular manifolds that helped boost horsepower by 10 percent compared to the conventional inline dual-carb design used in 1959. Two types (short- and long-ram) were available, both looking identical on the outside. The short-ram option featured cut-down partitions inside those tubes that shortened the "tuned" runner length from about 28 inches to 18, increasing power in the process. Output was 375 horses for Chrysler's long-ram 413-cid V-8 in 1960, 400 for its short-ram sibling. *Mike Mueller*

Gran Sport and Chevrolet's SS 396 Chevelle all were putting GM's A-body to the test by 1965, inspiring Ford and Chrysler to join the race, the latter with its reborn "street Hemi" in 1966. Two years later, even once-polite American Motors was working down-and-dirty in the supercar business.

So what made Pontiac's pioneering performance car so appealing in 1964? "The message was straight-line speed," continued David E. Davis in his 1975 *Car and Driver* tribute. "And it felt like losing your virginity, going into combat and tasting your first beer all in about seven seconds." As for its milestone status, 1964's GTO was, in his always far-from humble opinion, "the first Muscle Car…a violent, virile catalyst-car that set the pace and tone for five or six years of intense horsepower promotion out of Detroit city, the hallmark of a period that seemed like the culmination of all the dreams of all the enthusiasts on all the back roads in this country, but a period that in reality was nothing more than that—the period at the end of one short paragraph of automotive history."

Short indeed. The great American muscle car reached its zenith in 1970 then even more quickly raced to its demise. The thrill was completely gone by 1975. Why the sudden death?

After briefly marketing Meteor, a midsize Fairlane running mate, in 1962 and 1963, Mercury officials opted to concentrate on its Falcon-based Comet, which rolled on a 114-inch wheelbase. In 1964, the Comet's three-tiered lineup was renamed "202", "404", and Caliente. Pictured is a 1964 Caliente convertible. *Mike Mueller*

FAMILY TIES: CHEVROLET 409 V-8, 1961-65

YEAR	PRODUCTION	RPO	HORSEPOWER	TORQUE	CR	INDUCTION	VALVE SIZES
1961	142	580	360 @ 5,800	409 @ 3,600	11.25:1	Carter AFB 4-barrel	2.07 x 1.72
1962	15,019	580	380 @ 5,800	420 @ 3,200	11:1	Carter AFB 4-barrel	2.19 x 1.72
		587	409 @ 6,000	420 @ 4,000	11:1	2 Carter AFB 4-barrels	2.19 x 1.72
1963	16,902	L33	340 @ 5,000	420 @ 3,200	10:1	Rochester 4-barrel	2.07 x 1.72
		L31	400 @ 5,800	425 @ 3,600	11: 1	Carter AFB 4-barrel	2.19 x 1.72
		L80	425 @ 6,000	425 @ 4,200	11:1	2 Carter AFB 4-barrels	2.19 x 1.72
		Z11*	430 @ 6,000	n/a	13:1	2 Carter AFB 4-barrels	2.19 x 1.72
1964	8,864	L33	340 @ 5,000	420 @ 3,200	10:1	Rochester 4-barrel	2.07 x 1.72
		L31	400 @ 5,800	425 @ 3,600	11:1	Carter AFB 4-barrel	2.19 x 1.72
		L80	425 @ 6,000	425 @4,200	11:1	2 Carter AFB 4-barrels	2.19 x 1.72
1965	2,288	L33	340 @ 5000	420 @ 3,200	10:1	Rochester 4-barrel	2.07 x 1.72
		L31	400 @ 5800	425 @ 3,600	11:1	Carter AFB 4-barrel	2.19 x 1.72

NOTE: *RPO is Regular Production Option code; CR is compression ratio; valve sizes in inches (intake x exhaust; bore & stroke was 4.3125 x 3.50 inches; all 409s used solid-lifter cams except for the 340-horsepower L33.*

** Race-only V-8 that displaced 427 cubic inches thanks to lengthened (3.65 inches) stroke*

Made even more famous by The Beach Boys in 1962, Chevrolet's unforgettable 409 V-8 was a force on the track and the street from 1961 to 1965. Shown here is 1964's L80 rendition, rated at 425 horsepower. *David Kimble cutaway*

A year after GTO's birth, lawmakers in Washington began taking serious notice of environmental issues. Federally mandated "smog controls" then began cramping the muscle car's style in 1968. Horsepower continued running strong for a few more years, but then additional, even tighter emissions controls began strangling the life out of the beast in the 1970s. With the further mandated use of lower octane unleaded fuels awaiting them, engineers in 1971 were forced to make major compression concessions within their engines, effectively ending the road for truly high high-performance V-8s.

Congress in 1965 also kicked off an especially vigorous investigation into automotive safety, changing forever the way cars are built. At the same time, the insurance industry also grew wise to the situation and began raising coverage rates beyond the reach of typical boomers. Skyrocketing fuel costs then hammered the final nails into the coffin in the early 1970s.

Mighty lean years then followed until Detroit's engineering fraternity learned how to effectively combine fuel efficiency, low contaminant counts, and horsepower. The muscle car was then reborn. How long it survives this second time around is anyone's guess.

"Rambler" became the marque name for American Motors' revised 1958 product line, which now rolled on three different wheelbases: 100 inches (for the new compact American), 108 inches (Rambler Six and Rebel), and 117 inches for the full-size Ambassador, a nameplate first applied by Nash to a specially trimmed sedan in 1927, then a complete model line five years later. Rambler Six was renamed Rambler Classic in 1961, and a redesigned American (with a 106-inch wheelbase) debuted for 1964. Rogue, a two-hardtop flagship (upper left), joined the Rambler American lineup in 1966, the year all AMC cars were updated in various areas. A Rebel hardtop (upper right) also joined the Classic clan that year, and the top-shelf Ambassador hardtop (bottom) was rechristened "DPL," short for "Diplomat." Rogue would serve as a base for Hurst's SC/Rambler in 1969, and Rebel would do the same for The Machine in 1970.

SUPER STOCKERS

In 1964, Ford contracted Dearborn Steel Tubing to help fabricate a run of strip-ready Fairlane Thunderbolts (right). Holman-Moody, in Charlotte, North Carolina, then followed that with a handful of altered-wheelbase Factory Experimental (FX) Mustangs (left) in 1965. *Mike Mueller*

Altogether amateurish until *Hot Rod* editor Wally Parks helped establish the National Hot Rod Association in 1951, drag racing really got rolling four years later when the first NHRA Nationals were held in Great Bend, Kansas. The "Nats" moved to Kansas City in 1956, Oklahoma City the following two years, then on to Michigan's Motown, a location chosen for obvious reasons.

"What was undoubtedly the best selling job ever done in behalf of the hot rod sport was accomplished at Detroit this year when [NHRA] members presented the 5th annual National Championship Drag Races there," wrote Parks in his November 1959 *Hot Rod* column. "Among the 80,000 or so who attended were hundreds of representatives from the various auto companies." According to Parks, Chrysler main man Tex Colbert and his Chevrolet counterpart, Ed Cole, stood together wagering whose car would come out on top. Push then morphed into shove, and just like that the Big Three was in the drag car business.

First came hot parts for the garden-variety vehicles that competed in stock-class racing, followed immediately by complete track-targeted V-8s, like Chevy's 409, a dominant force at the drags right from the get-go in 1961. Chrysler responded the next year with its 413 "Max Wedge," and Ford at the same time pushed its FE big-block up to 406 cubes then 427 midyear in 1963. The Bow-Tie boys shot right back with their exotic 409-based Z11 V-8 late in 1962, and Mopar men in 1963 retaliated with a 426-cube Max Wedge, followed by their historic race Hemi (see page 31) in 1964. Ford's response to the Hemi was its 427 "Cammer," detailed further on page 38. Manufacturers also began developing specific models around these engines, full-fledged factory racers that left sanctioning bodies hustling to keep up.

It all had been so simple at Great Bend in 1955 as only four classes existed then for regular-production Detroit iron. By 1968, however, NHRA rules books listed 34 Stock and 12 Super/Stock categories, all created to keep the playing field fair by grouping homologated competitors together based on comparable power-to-weight ratios. Automatic cars gained their own classifications in 1962, and Optional Super/Stock had appeared the previous year. Meant to pick up where S/S limitations left off, the OS/S class became home to factory-direct

Meant to aid weight transfer to the rear wheels during hard launches, altered-wheelbase (AWB) designs became all the rage in drag racing circles in 1964, with Mopar man Dick Landy leading the way. Landy's 1965 AWB Dodge was capable of nine-second blasts down the quarter-mile. *Mike Mueller*

Hurst hooked up with American Motors in 1969 to build 53 AMX Super Stock models, with the first of these going to drag racer Shirley Shahan, the fabled "Drag-On Lady." Under the hood was a specially prepared 390-cid V-8 fitted with Doug Thorley headers and two Holley carbs on a cross-ram intake. *Bob McClurg*

hardware that didn't qualify as "available to the general public." New too in 1962 was the Factory Experimental (FX) category, which soon struggled to contain various Detroit-built ground-pounders that left any and/or all notions of "regular production" in the dust.

OS/S formation was inspired partly by Pontiac, which in 1961 rolled out its 389 Super Duty Catalinas, purpose-built vehicles that among other things featured weight-saving aluminum bumpers. PMD's legendary 421 Super Duty followed in 1962 and was installed in both full-size models and Tempests, both representing unbeatable combinations at the strip. Even more aluminum body parts also appeared that year, as did a "Swiss cheese" frame (drilled out to cut additional pounds) the next. Who knows what more Pontiac engineers might've concocted had GM not pulled the plug on its divisions' competition projects in January 1963?

Ford and Chevrolet announced their own lightweight drag cars in 1962 to help further stretch the definition of "factory-stock," and two years later the Blue Oval gang also rolled out its Fairlane-based Thunderbolt, a mean machine never meant for the street. Manufactured by Dearborn Steel Tubing, T-bolts were fitted with various lightened body parts and chassis beefs along with Ford's full-race 427 "hi-riser" V-8. Meanwhile, the Dodge/Plymouth duo that year went crazy cutting away unwanted pounds, using copious aluminum pieces, acid-dipped steel, and Lexan in place of glass.

Mopar engineers also pioneered altered-wheelbase (AWB) designs, which seriously transferred weight to the rear by relocating all four wheels forward. Such shenanigans initially were condoned by NHRA rules moguls, but only if they didn't differ from stock specifications by more than 2 percent. The resulting "2-percenters" didn't appear all that different at a glance. But when posed next to a stock model, there clearly was something funny going on. Get it—a *funny* car?

This nickname immediately evolved into an accepted reference for an entirely new breed of racer, which still looked like street machines but smoked the quarter-mile like a true dragster. Pioneering funny cars quickly started leaving super-stocks and FX'ers behind in 1965 and were off running in a class all their own within a few years.

Those 2-percent Mopars were followed in 1965 by even wilder AWB machines featuring acid-dipped bodies and wheels relocated 10 inches in front, 15 in back—so wild they were banned by NHRA officials, leaving them to perform on rival circuits. Unaltered Hemi-powered B-bodies, known as "A-990" models, also rolled over from 1964 carrying "W0" and "R0" VIN prefixes, with the "W" designating Dodge, "R" standing for Plymouth, and "0" for super stock. NHRA rules forbade the use of aluminum by these A-990 cars, so they were fitted with various parts stamped specially from lighter gauge steel. Neither Dodge nor Plymouth offered a lightweight drag package for 1966, but the R0/W0 super-stock deal did return the following year, and these were followed in 1968 by race-ready Hemi Barracudas and Darts, built with assistance from the Hurst shifter guys.

Ford followed its Thunderbolt with a handful of AWB Mustangs, created with Holman-Moody's help, in 1965. And a limited run of super-stock 427 Fairlanes (see page 78) appeared in 1966, as did 50 lightweight, race-ready Cobra Jet Mustangs in 1968.

The original muscle car era's last great factory drag car came not from Detroit, but Kenosha, Wisconsin, again with a hand from Hurst. American Motors' 1969 Super Stock AMX featured a 390 V-8 topped by twin Holley four-barrels on an Edelbrock cross-ram intake. Only 53 were built.

Plymouth teamed up with Hurst in 1968 to build 70 Hemi-powered Barracudas for drag racing duty. Dodge also built 80 Hemi Darts that year.

CHAPTER 1

1964 BORN TO RUN

PONTIAC KICKS OFF THE MODERN MUSCLE CAR ERA

The original GTO not only established a sales record for a "rookie" Pontiac model, it also helped mark a new annual production standard for the entire division in June 1964. At left is general manager Elliot "Pete" Estes, the man who made sure this supposedly taboo machine made it past corporate killjoys into production.

HOT OFF THE PRESS: 1964 PONTIAC GTO

"In racing terms, 'G.T.O.' means 'Gran Turismo Omologato.' In Pontiac language, these three letters designate a special, white-hot Tempest."

Bob McVay, Motor Trend, *January 1964*

Talk about your party-poopers. General Motors top officers not only demanded that their divisions get the hell out of racing early in 1963, they followed that up with an additional edict limiting all models (save for Corvette) below full-size ranks to no more than 1 cubic inch of engine displacement per 10 pounds of overall curb weight. This cap was generally reported at 330 cubes, the same count sported by the new downsized V-8 that Oldsmobile made available for its first A-body intermediate in 1964. Buick also rolled out an equally new 300-cid V-8 that year, while Chevrolet's 327 and Pontiac's 326 compliantly carried over for GM's two other modern midsizers.

Apparently not everyone at Pontiac got the memo, however. Or was it simply flushed away?

Corporate paperwork may have plainly mandated how much engine could fit into 1964's A-body Tempest, but it failed to keep a lid on PMD ad man Jim

FAMILY TIES: PONTIAC V-8s

Pontiac engineers were looking well ahead into the future when they created their new-for-1955 V-8, casting in ample iron to allow for some serious growth. Displacement for the first of this family (shown here) was 287 cubic inches. Maximum cube count hit 455 in 1970.

Chevrolet and Pontiac were the last two GM divisions to introduce modern OHV V-8s, with both arriving in 1955. Though noticeably different (Pontiac's was some 2 inches taller and about 75 pounds heavier), the two engines shared one notable innovation: ball-stud rocker arms. Instead of rockers all mounted together on a central shaft, this arrangement featured lighter stamped-steel units that pivoted independently on dedicated studs. Along with saving weight and cost, ball-stud rockers also didn't pass on unwanted motion between themselves via a deflecting central shaft. This idea came from Pontiac, which had started OHV V-8 development in 1946. Engineer Clayton Leach created the ball-stud rocker in 1948, and his design was implemented in a new V-8 initially scheduled for a 1953 release. Various delays, however, pushed that debut back two years, by which time Ed Cole's engineers had copied the individual stamped-steel rocker arm for Chevy's hot, new small-block. Unlike its counterparts from Chevrolet, Buick, and Oldsmobile, Pontiac's V-8 family never branched out into small- and big-block wings—one size basically fit all as far as PMD's long-running main casting was concerned. Peering well into the future, engineers made sure enough iron went into the original cylinder block to allow for ample growth, hence the excess pounds and hefty external dimensions seen in 1955. Displacing 287 cubic inches that year, the Pontiac V-8 maxed out at 455 cubes in 1970. Various bores and strokes were mixed and matched along the way as displacement hit 317 in 1956, 347 and 370 in 1957, then the familiar 389 cid in 1959. The 389 was bumped up to 421 cid late in 1961, first for race-only Super Duty applications then in more civilized fashion as a full-size 1963 option. A 400 replaced the 389 for 1967, and a 428 briefly made the scene from 1967 to '69. A downsized 326 was created for the "rope-drive" Tempest in 1963, followed by a 350 showcased most prominently in Firebirds beginning in 1968. Modifications made as displacements grew consisted mostly of increasing main journal diameters and adding four-bolt main bearing caps in high-perf applications. No recasting for additional deck heights was required. Pontiac's last 455 was offered in 1976, the last 350 in 1977, and the last 400 in 1978.

YEAR	CID	BORE & STROKE	CR	HORSEPOWER	TORQUE	CARBURETOR	VALVE SIZES
1955	287	3.750 x 3.250	7.4:1	173 @ 4,400	260 @ 2,400	Carter/Rochester 2-bl	1.72 x 1.50
1959	389	4.0625 x 3.75	8.6:1	245 @ 4,200	392 @ 2,000	Rochester 2-barrel	1.88 x 1.60
1962	421*	4.0937 x 4.00	11:1	405 @ 5,600	425 @ 4,400	2 Carter AFB 4-bls	2.02 x 1.76
1967	400	4.120 x 3.75	8.6:1	255 @ 4,400	397 @ 2,400	Rochester 2-barrel	2.11 x 1.77
1967	428	4.120 x 4.00	10.5:1	360 @ 4,600	472 @ 3,200	Quadra-jet 4-barrel	2.11 x 1.77
1968	350	3.875 x 3.75	9.2:1	265 @ 4,600	355 @ 2,800	Rochester 2-barrel	1.96 x 1.66
1970	455	4.151 x 4.210	10:1	360 @ 4,300	500 @ 2,700	Quadra-jet 4-barrel	2.11 x 1.77
1973	455*	4.151 x 4.210	8.4:1	290 @ 4,000	395 @ 3,200	Quadra-jet 4-barrel	2.11 x 1.77

NOTE: *CID is cubic-inch displacement, CR is compression ratio; bore/stroke & valve sizes in inches (intake x exhaust)*

**Super Duty V-8*

Wangers' enthusiasm. Like John DeLorean's engineers, Wangers recognized that Pontiac's potentially potent 389 V-8 was externally identical to its mundane 326-cube little brother —why not give it a go in the new A-body regardless of said statutes? DeLorean and Bill Collins had toyed with a 389-powered Tempest in 1963 but predictably found that year's unit-body/rear-transaxle layout to be an uncooperative patient for a high-octane performance infusion. This clearly wasn't the case concerning the A platform with its full frame and solid axle.

As Wangers explained in a 1991 *Automobile Quarterly* account, "I wrote to DeLorean suggesting the creation of a new Super LeMans for 1964 to help make the market forget quickly about the unfortunate slant four, rope driveshaft era. What an image builder! [It] could provide Pontiac with a one-of-a-kind high-performance specialty car that no one else could offer." DeLorean reportedly inked "Has Wangers got something here?" across the top of this message and passed it

GTO was available in three body styles for 1964: a "pillared" coupe (shown here), hardtop, and convertible. Those twin hood scoops were non-functional.

FAMILY TIES: OLDSMOBILE V-8s

A "short-stroke" 400-cid big-block was standard for Oldsmobile's 4-4-2 from 1965 to 1967. In 1966, this L78 V-8 was rated at 350 horsepower. A new 400 appeared in 1968 with a little more stroke, a little less bore.

Oldsmobile's original Rocket V-8 debuted at 303 cubic inches in 1949 then typically went through various expansions: 324 cid in 1954, 371 in 1957, and 394 in 1959. The 394 retired in 1964, the same year a second-generation Rocket was introduced for the company's new A-body intermediates. At 330 cubes, this gold-painted engine retained various first-gen dimensions (valve diameters, bore center, crank/cam axis distance, etc.) but revised main castings translated into weight savings of about 100 pounds, hence the "small-block" reference that later emerged for this downsized mill. This tag made real sense after Olds engineers recast the 330's cylinder block with a raised deck height (10.625 inches, compared to 9.33) to make room for 1-inch longer connecting rods, which in turn made 425 cubic inches possible for the company's first modern "big-block" in 1965. Even though it was taller and wider, this "Super Rocket" still weighed about 30 pounds less than its 394 forerunner. Debuting as well that year for the 4-4-2 was a smaller 400-cid big-block that shared the 425's forged steel-crankshaft (with its 3.975-inch stroke) but relied on a 4.00-inch (instead of 4.125) bore. Increasing the stroke further to 4.250 inches in 1968 resulted in the supreme Rocket V-8, the under-square 455, which became the 4-4-2's heart and soul in 1970. Most 455s used a cast-iron crank, which was shared with a second-edition 400, a seriously under-square engine that paired the 455's lengthy stroke with a 3.87 bore. This big-block replaced its "short-stroke" predecessor in 1968 and was joined by a new small-block running mate, bored from 330 cid to 350. All 330s used forged-steel cranks, while a cast-iron unit was bolted into all 350s.

YEAR	CID	BORE & STROKE	CR	HORSEPOWER	TORQUE	CARBURETOR	VALVE SIZES
1964	330	3.938 x 3.385	9.0:1	230 @ 4,400	325 @ 2,400	Rochester 2-barrel	1.875 x 1.562
1965	400[1]	4.000 x 3.975	10.25:1	345 @ 4,800	440 @ 3,200	Rochester 4-barrel	2.06 x 1.629
1965	425	4.125 x 3.975	9.0:1	300 @ 4,400	430 @ 2,400	Rochester 2-barrel	2.00 x 1.625
1968	350	4.057 x 3.385	9.0:1	250 @ 4,400	355 @ 2,600	Rochester 2-barrel	1.875 x 1.562
1968	400	3.87 x 4.250	9.0:1	290 @ 4,600	425 @ 2,400	Rochester 2-barrel	2.00 x 1.625
1968	455[2]	4.125 x 4.250	10.25:1	400 @ 4,800	500 @ 3,200	Quadra-jet 4-barrel	2.07 x 1.625

NOTE: *CID is cubic-inch displacement; CR is compression ratio; bore/stroke & valve sizes in inches (intake x exhaust).*

1. Standard 4-4-2 V-8

2. Optional Toronado V-8

As the middle digit in its name implied, all 2,999 4-4-2 models built by Oldsmobile for 1964 featured Muncie four-speed manual transmissions. An available automatic transmission entered the mix the following year. *Mike Mueller*

on to Collins. "How soon do you want to drive it, John?" was Collins' reply. At the time a GTO prototype stood by ready to roll. All that remained was to sneak this big-engine intermediate past corporate killjoys.

Well aware of obvious roadblocks, DeLorean opted for an end run. While new models required ivory tower approval, option groups didn't, making it oh-so-simple to create a 389 package for the Tempest and worry about the consequences later. Luckily Pontiac general manager Pete Estes loved the idea and made sure it didn't get shot down from above. His clueless superiors didn't detect the options list ruse until it was too late. Sales were swift from the get-go, and no exec worth his severance package was going to argue against rising revenues.

Credit for the name went to DeLorean, who copped it unashamedly from Enzo Ferrari. While purists cringed, the American public ate it up. Pontiac sales manager Frank Bridge predicted 1964 sales, at best, might reach 5,000. By the time the tire smoke cleared, nearly 32,500 GTOs had rolled out the door, a division sales record for first-year models. Production doubled and then some in 1965.

By then GM officials had raised their A-body displacement limit to 400 cubic inches, opening the door to corporate knockoffs from Buick and Chevrolet, which

PONTIAC COVER STORY, PART I

Suitable candidates were not available for the press late in 1963 when *Hot Rod's* Ray Brock opted to test Pontiac's new GTO, leaving him to examine a fully loaded, 325-horsepower, auto-trans, highway-axled convertible, not exactly the quickest combo. Hence track results were predictably tame. And Jim Wangers was predictably pissed.

"The most involved and aggressive press agent in all of Detroit," as automotive journalism legend David E. Davis Jr. later called him, Wangers described Brock's review as "an insult to all Pontiac's hard work," then set out to do the car justice. First, he had the guys at Royal Pontiac, in Royal Oak, Michigan, tweak two GTO coupes within inches of their lives, and this pair was delivered to *Car and Driver*, governed by Davis at the time. Recognizing a winner when he saw it, Davis put one on his cover, albeit by way of an artist's rendition. Along with a Ferrari GTO ...in a side-by-side shootout... beneath a banner reading "Tempest GTO: 1-100 in 11.8 sec." Irreverent, even irresponsible simply weren't big enough words to describe *Car and Driver's* famous—or infamous—GTO vs. GTO "road test."

"We felt it was a neat idea, even though we knew we didn't belong on the same track," remembered Wangers in 1996. "But if we could just stay with the Ferrari..."

Davis loved the scheme, too, basically because he was searching for a way to vault his newly renamed magazine—it had just been reborn from its *Sports Car Illustrated* roots—into the forefront. "I didn't know then that they were rethinking their entire image," added Wangers. "They had recognized they'd better jump on the Detroit bandwagon and quit that sports car kick."

If only they could get their hands on a Ferrari...

Luigi Chinetti, head of Ferrari's North American dealer works, wasn't keen on the plan at all. The Italian-American road test comparison was, according to Wangers, "a lose-lose situation for Ferrari"—a Prancing Horse surely would gain nothing by trampling a Goat. "Chinetti saw it that way; he wasn't about to make a GTO available to us."

Instead, *Car and Driver's* test crew simply created a fantasy matchup, using the definitely real high banks of Daytona International Speedway as a stage. "We sailed around Daytona like crazy people, had the times of our lives and shared a growing gut feeling that we were really on to something," wrote Davis retrospectively in 1975.

Concocted mostly by Davis, *Car and Driver's* March 1964 cover story did point out the obvious, that such a comparison was very much akin to pairing apples with oranges. If the two GTOs had indeed met, the Pontiac of course would've been no match on a road course. Then again, the Ferrari wouldn't have stood a chance on a drag strip, not after the Royal "Bobcat" machine screamed through the quarter-mile in an unbelievable 13.1 seconds, topping out at 115 miles per hour. "Ferrari never built enough GTOs to earn the name anyway," read *Car and Driver's* classic conclusion. "Just to be on the safe side though, Pontiac built a faster one."

Exactly how much faster was a product of some questionable scientific methodology. "You've got to remember," recalled Wangers with a chuckle, "all timing was done with hand-held stopwatches; there was not a whole lot of accuracy involved. The magazine's [1–100 in 11.8 seconds] cover blurb? That car couldn't have done that rolling off the top of the Empire State Building." Ten years later, Davis remained unrepentant in every way, but also humorously recalled that blurb,

Has any automotive magazine ever raised more eyebrows than the March 1964 edition of *Car and Driver*? The matchup between the two GTOs, Pontiac's and Ferrari's, was mythical, of course, as was the Tempest's performance blurb at the top.

"which the magazine's technical department still hasn't lived down."

Readers in 1964 couldn't get to their corner mailboxes fast enough after seeing his cover. "I am at a loss for words to describe the utter scorn I have for this piece of very bad, very dishonest journalism," wrote Henry E. Payne III, from Charleston, West Virginia. "I would like to protest such irresponsible journalism concerning the Pontiac Tempest," added Texan Courtland Bell. "You boys should really try to do better if you expect to stay in business."

Davis' magazine did stay in business, better than ever, in fact. That controversial cover story, according to its author, "accomplished just what we had been trying to do for months; to get the attention of the audience and clearly establish us as a contender in the automotive publishing biz. *Car and Driver* was finally on its way—and the GTO did it."

The story also helped do it for GTO. "It was absolutely magnificent publicity for us," concluded Wangers. "It was one of the most significant pieces of merchandising we did. People read [Davis'] words then went into a Pontiac dealership and felt it for themselves. It was a thrill."

Davis later founded *Automobile magazine* in 1986. He died, at age 80, on March 27, 2001.

NEW PONY ON THE BLOCK

Lee Iacocca and the rest at Ford knew they had themselves a hot seller even before Mustang started kicking up dust on April 17, 1964. Initial forecasts claimed about 100,000 pony cars would be sold that first year, but Iacocca was far more optimistic. He had greater goals in mind, specifically Detroit's record for new-model first-year sales, set by Ford's own Falcon four years before. Iacocca's battle cry became "417 by 4-17"—the plan was to sell at least 417,000 Mustangs by 4-17-65. No problem. By April 17, 1965, the tally read 418,812.

Of that record-breaking total, 121,538 were so-called "1964-½" models. Introduced as it was in the middle of a model year, the first Mustang experienced an extended 18-month run that typically ended in August 1965. Most sources initially identified Ford's original pony car as a "1965" model. But various running changes differentiated the cars built before August 1964 from those assembled afterwards, thus making it relatively easy to group the Mustang's first production run into 1964-½ and true 1965 categories. Identifying the differences is not possible in 25 words or less, so you'll have to settle for the most readily recognizable clue: 1964-½ Mustangs used generators, '65s used alternators. The production count for the "true" 12-month 1965 model run was 559,451 Mustangs.

Plymouth's pony car rolled through three generations during its career, with the first spanning 1964–66, the second 1967–69, and the third 1970–74. Up front is a 1966 Formula S; in back is the last of the breed, a 360-equipped 1974 model. *Mike Mueller*

Ford's original pony car was also born in 1964. But while Chevrolet's midsize A-body Chevelle retired in 1977, Mustang just kept galloping on and is still kicking up dust a half century later. Contrasting the 1964-½ convertible in front is a 2007 V-6 droptop. *Mike Mueller*

Funny thing, though. Few today remember that Chrysler actually beat Dearborn to the punch in the spring of 1964. Nearly two weeks before *Time* and *Newsweek* editors began stumbling all over themselves to get their scoops on the new Ford, Plymouth's Barracuda debuted to next-to-no fanfare on April 1. So why, then, didn't it inspire the market segment name we all still use without question today?

For starters, consider sheer impact. As mentioned, Ford set all kinds of sales records with its early Mustangs while rolling more than a million off the line by March 1966. Plymouth let about 23,500 Barracudas loose in 1964, followed by 60,000 in 1965, and 36,000 in 1966. Not bad numbers, mind you, but a history-maker this Plymouth clearly wasn't.

Furthermore, a rocket scientist wasn't required to determine that Barracuda was a knock-off. After learning of Ford's plans, Plymouth people had hastily prepared a copy, speeding the Barracuda through short-order development in less than two years to hopefully upstage Iacocca at his own game. Making this rapid response possible was the plain fact that Plymouth's design studio more or less took the division's existing A-body Valiant and melded on a sleek, sloping rear window. From the cowl forward and beltline down, Plymouth's original Barracuda was essentially all garden-variety A-body, complete with a "Valiant" badge on its tail. But setting it miles apart from its plainly dull sibling was that huge rear window, then the largest expanse of glass ever installed on an American car.

Bucket seats came standard up front, but basically all other features were Valiant carryovers, including suspension (front torsion bars, real leaf springs) and powertrain parts. All 1964–66 Barracudas also were sport coupes—a convertible didn't arrive (along with a "notchback" hardtop) until the breed was redesigned for 1967.

in turn helped inspire rival responses from outside the corporation, each of them owing their existence to the muscular mid size Pontiac that first broke the rules and then made new ones for Detroit (and Kenosha) to follow. "All this unabashed copying by Ford and the other GM divisions is the most powerful single proof of the GTO's position of leadership in this very special area of automotive marketing," concluded a *Car and Driver* 1966 Yearbook report.

A new market leader wouldn't take over until 1969.

Pontiac's Tempest debuted with standard four-cylinder power in 1961. GM's aluminum V-8 was optional. Also included was a rear-mounted transaxle tied to the engine up front by a flexible "rope" driveshaft.

PONTIAC

Officially released on October 1, 1963, Pontiac's GTO package (coded W62) was initially offered for top-shelf LeMans sports coupes and convertibles. LeMans hardtop availability then followed soon afterward. W62 gear included a 325-horse 389 V-8 topped with cylinder heads borrowed from the 389's larger sibling, the 421. Stiffer suspension, 7.50x14 US Royal Tiger Paw redline tires, a three-speed manual with a Hurst shifter, and various dress-up items (blacked-out grille, "GTO" identification, and dummy hood scoops) also were part of the deal. Bucket seats were included inside, as was a padded dash.

Popular options included a Muncie four-speed trans, metallic brakes, a limited-slip Safe-T-Track differential, and the coveted Tri-Power 389 topped by three Rochester two-barrel carbs. A four-spoke wood-grained Custom Sport steering wheel, 7,000-rpm tach, and console could've been added to sex up the interior, and snazzy chrome splitter tips were available for the standard dual exhausts.

Witnesses in 1964 couldn't help but notice the all-new Chevelle's close resemblance up front to the full-size Chevy's facade. Overall impressions also hinted at the fabled "Hot One" image of 1955. Chevelle's flagship was the Malibu Super Sport, available in hardtop and convertible forms with either a six-cylinder or V-8.

OLDSMOBILE

Among the B-O-P triumvirate, only Oldsmobile attempted to transform GM's senior compact into a real performer during its brief three-year tour. Wanting more punch behind the prestige, Olds general manager Jack Wolfram asked veteran engine man Gil Burrell to warm up the F-85's 215-cid aluminum V-8, which Burrell did relying on exhaust-driven turbocharging. The resulting 215-horse engine then became the heart of the Cutlass-based Jetfire coupe, introduced in April 1962 at the New York International Auto Show. Jetfire production that year was 3,765, followed by another 5,842 in 1963.

Oldsmobile engineers gave up toying with turbo technology the following year after the A-body F-85 arrived with a full frame that was ready, willing, and able to handle much more engine. In place of the tiny, weight-saving Rockette V-8 came the aforementioned 330 Rocket, cast conventionally of iron and possessing a decent dose of performance potential exploited simply through typical low-tech applications of more cam, more compression, and more carb. Garden-variety 330 V-8s produced 230 horses using a two-barrel carburetor, a 9.0:1 squeeze, and single exhaust. Switching to a four-barrel and twin mufflers helped up the output ante with little fuss and/or muss and at the same time inspired a new Olds nameplate.

Following in the GTO's paw prints, GM's second midsize muscle car showed up in April 1964 wearing a badge not everyone understood, even after magazine ads explained it in full. That "4-4-2" tag translated into 4-barrel, 4-on-the-floor, and dual (as in 2) exhausts. Along with a Muncie four-speed, standard 4-4-2 fea-

1964 PONTIAC GTO

CONSTRUCTION: body on perimeter-rail frame
MODEL AVAILABILITY: LeMans coupe, hardtop & convertible
PRICE: $295.90 for optional GTO package
WHEELBASE: 115 inches
WEIGHT: 3,470 pounds
SUSPENSION: heavy-duty w/coil springs front & rear, 0.94-inch front stabilizer bar
STEERING: manual recirculating all (24:1 ratio), std; 17.5:1 power assist, optional (quicker 20:1steering, optional)
WHEELS: 14x6 stamped-steel
TIRES: 7.50x14 US Royal Tiger Paw redline, std; whitewall rayon-cord tires available at no extra cost
BRAKES: 9.5-inch 4-wheel drums; power-assist optional
ENGINE: 389-cid V-8 w/500-cfm Carter AFB 4-barrel carburetor
TRANSMISSION: Hurst-shifted 3-speed manual, std; M20 wide- & M21 close-ratio Muncie 4-speeds (w/ Hurst shifters) & column-shifted 2-speed automatic, optional (floor shifter w/console, optional for auto trans)
AXLE RATIO: 3.23:1, std; 3.55:1, 3.36:1 & 3.90:1 (M20 4-speed not available w/3.90:1 gears, M21 only available w/3.90:1 gears)

UNDER THE HOOD: 1964'S HOTTEST V-8s*

MODEL	CID	BORE & STROKE	CR	HORSEPOWER	TORQUE
Pontiac GTO[1]	389	4.06 x 3.75	10.75:1	348 @ 4,900	428 @ 3,600
Olds 4-4-2	330	3.938 x 3.385	10.25:1	310 @ 5,200	355 @ 3,600
Chevrolet Malibu SS	327	4.00 x 3.25	10.5:1	300 @ 5,000	360 @ 3,200
Ford/Mercury[2]	289	4.00 x 2.87	10.5:1	271 @ 6,000	312 @ 3,400
Dodge/Plymouth	426	4.25 x 3.75	10.3:1	365 @ 4,800	470 @ 3,200
Studebaker (R-2 V-8)	289	3.5625 x 3.625	9:1	289 @ 4,500	305 @ 2,800
Studebaker (R-3 V-8)	304.5	3.650 x 3.625	9.75:1	335, estimated (supercharged)	

NOTE: *CID is cubic-inch displacement; CR is compression ratio; bore/stroke in inches*

NOTE: *Chevrolet briefly offered the Corvette's 365-horsepower L76 327 V-8 as a Chevelle option early in 1964 before cancelling this deal after only a handful were built.*

**Discounting factory super stocks, full-size model lines & Corvette*

1. Optional Tri-Power V-8

2. Optional High Performance 289 V-8 for Ford Fairlane/Mustang and Mercury Comet

Only two body styles were initially available when Ford's Mustang debuted in April 1964: "notchback" coupe and convertible. A fastback then joined the lineup in 1965. Demonstrated here is the hottest Mustang offered in 1964, featuring the K-code High Performance 289, rated at 271 horsepower. *Mike Mueller*

1964 OLDSMOBILE 4-4-2

CONSTRUCTION: body on reinforced perimeter-rail "police car" frame
MODEL AVAILABILITY: F-85 2-door club coupe & 4-door sedan; F-85 Deluxe 4-door sedan; Cutlass sport coupe, Holiday hardtop & convertible
PRICE: B09 package cost $285
WHEELBASE: 115 inches
WEIGHT: 3,770 pounds
SUSPENSION: heavy-duty coil springs, front & rear; live axle in back; 0.94-inch front stabilizer bar; 0.875-inch rear stabilizer bar
STEERING: manual recirculating ball, std
WHEELS: 14x6 stamped-steel
TIRES: 7.50x15 US Royal Tiger Paw
BRAKES: 9.5-inch drums, front & rear
ENGINE: 330-cid Golden Rocket V-8 w/Rochester 4-barrel carburetor
TRANSMISSION: Muncie 4-speed manual
AXLE RATIO: 3.23:1, std; 2.78:1, 3.36:1, & 3.90:1, optional

tures included a high-compression 310-horse Rocket V-8 and a typically beefed chassis that included a not-so-typical rear sway bar.

As they always do, Oldsmobile's rear stabilizer reduced body lean, which in turn helped keep more rubber on the road for increased sureness in the corners. "Although the car still basically understeers, it is within much more manageable bounds," commented *Car Life's* critics. "There is, in our judgment, hardly a better handling passenger sedan produced in this country."

According to Harold Metzel, who went from chief engineer to general manager after Jack Wolfram retired in June 1964, the original 4-4-2 was "the most alert performer in Oldsmobile's entire model lineup, with three outstanding dimensions of performance: responsiveness, handling and road sense." As Olds public relations man Jim Williams later told veteran automotive writer Jan Norbye, engineer John Beltz had "wanted a street machine, not a hot rod." Hence, overall balance, instead of brute force, became the priority.

Like GTO, Oldsmobile's original muscle car emerged by way of a special options group, coded B09. Priced at $285, this "police apprehender pursuit package" was offered for any V-8 F-85 models except station wagons. "Put this one on your wanted list," wailed early ads for the new 4-4-2. "Police needed it, Olds built it, pursuit proved it!"

Available as it was for all Olds midsize models, and being born of a cop car heritage, the first 4-4-2 showed up in some cases with more than two doors. Reportedly three F-85 four-door sedans and seven F-85 Deluxe four-door sedans were built.

CHEVROLET

Critics couldn't say enough good things about Chevrolet's all-new A-body after general manager Bunkie Knudsen introduced it to the press in August 1963. "Impressed by its clean and handsome styling, Detroit's normally undemonstrative auto reporters broke into spontaneous applause," announced a *Time* magazine report. "The only complaint about the Chevelle was that dealers couldn't get enough of them," added *Automotive News* in September. Within three months Chevelle was the second hottest-selling Chevy, taking up 18 percent of the company's production

FAMILY TIES: CHEVROLET SMALL-BLOCK V-8s

Now in its 60th year and fifth generation, Chevrolet's venerable, vaunted small-block family traces its bloodlines back to December 1951, when plans initially formed for the division's first modern overhead-valve V-8. To aid this cause, former Cadillac man Ed Cole—who had helped GM's luxury line kick off Detroit's OHV craze in 1949—was made chief engineer in April 1952. Cole's team then created a true milestone, a compact 265-cid V-8 that weighed 42 pounds less than the "Stovebolt" six-cylinder, which had kept America's bestselling cars and trucks running since 1929. Throw in a super short stroke, along with Pontiac's ball-stud rocker arms, and Chevy had a real high-winder, hence the "Hot One" nickname mentioned in 1955 ads. Various bore/stroke combinations over the years produced a long list of displacement choices, with the 283 appearing in 1957, the 327 in 1962, and the 350 in 1967. Three years later came the biggest small-block yet, the 400, which simply wasn't suited for performance applications. Nor was the yeoman 307, offered from 1968 to '73. Chevy's 1967–69 302, on the other hand, was intended solely to make Camaro an unquestionably mean machine. A Camaro SS exclusive in 1967, the 350 Turbo Fire became a Chevy II/Nova option in 1968, then joined the Corvette/Chevelle RPO list in 1969. To make 350 cubes, engineers combined the 327's 4.00 bore with a new 3.48-inch stroke in a recast block featuring enlarged (2.45 inches, compared to 2.30) crankshaft journals. That shaft and its rods were beefed, too, and more reinforcement followed in 1968. All 1955–67 small-blocks relied on two-bolt caps to hold the crank's five main bearings in place. Beginning the next year, all high-perf small-blocks with 4.00-inch bores (save for the 327) received stronger four-bolt caps for the three inner bearings. The hottest 350 was 1970's LT-1, rated at 370 horsepower under Corvette hoods, 360 as the exclusive V-8 for that year's Z28.

A big hit in passenger-car ranks, Chevy's new 265-cid V-8 also helped save Corvette from an early grave, injecting 195 warmly welcomed horses into the equation. *David Kimble cutaway*

YEAR	CID	BORE & STROKE	CR	HORSEPOWER	TORQUE	CARBURETOR	VALVE SIZES
1955	265	3.75 x 3.00	8.0:1	162 @ 4,400	257 @ 2,200	Rochester 2-barrel	1.72 x 1.30
1957	283	3.875 x 3.00	8.5:1	185 @ 4,600	275 @ 2,400	Carter/Rochester 2-bl	1.72 x 1.50
1962	327	4.00 x 3.25	10.5:1	250 @ 4,400	350 @ 2,800	Carter 4-barrel	1.94 x 1.50
1967	350[1]	4.00 x 3.48	10.25:1	295 @ 4,800	380 @ 3,200	Quadra-jet 4-barrel	1.94 x 1.50
1970	350[2]	4.00 x 3.48	11:1	360 @ 6,000	380 @ 4,000	Holley 4-barrel	2.02 x 1.60
1970	400	4.125 x 3.75	9.0:1	265 @ 4,400	400 @ 2,400	Rochester 2-barrel	1.94 x 1.60

NOTE: *CID is cubic-inch displacement; CR is compression ratio; bore/stroke & valve sizes in inches (intake x exhaust).*

1. Camaro SS L48 V-8

2. Z28 Camaro V-8

schedule. It ended up tops in 1964's intermediate sales race, besting Ford's Fairlane by more than 60,000 units.

Nearly 23 percent of Chevelles sold that first year were sexy Super Sports, available in Malibu hardtop or convertible forms. Standard for the Malibu SS were bucket seats, a four-gauge instrument cluster, a console with floor shifter for Powerglide and four-speed equipped cars, and stylish SS wheel covers. Popular options included Chevrolet's new Muncie four-speed gearbox, metallic brake linings, heavy-duty suspension and clutch, and a Positraction differential.

Both six-cylinders and V-8s were available for Chevy's first midsize Super Sport, with 67,000 customers choosing the latter variety, equipped in base form with a

HOT OFF THE PRESS: 1964 OLDSMOBILE 4-4-2

"Our [test] Cutlass was the best handling of any GM car we've been exposed to (except the Sting Ray) and far superior to its identical cousins from the other divisions."

Car Life, *August 1964*

FAMILY TIES: FORD WINDSOR V-8s

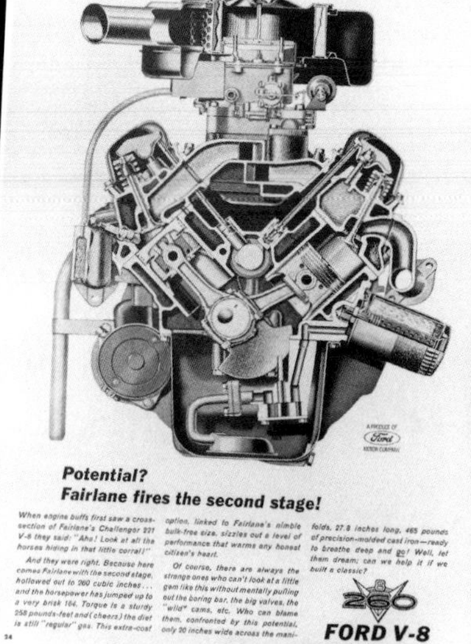

Created using a new thinwall casting technique, Ford's compact Windsor small-block debuted for 1962 in two displacements: 221 and 260 cubic inches. The 260 served as the Mustang's first V-8 before being superseded by an enlarged 289-cid Windsor.

Ford Motor Company's historic "flathead" V-8, born in 1932, was finally superseded by a modern OHV successor in 1952, a 317-cid engine introduced by Lincoln. Called a "Y-block"—because its cross-section spelled "Y," not "V," due to the cylinder block's extended "skirt"—this modernized (albeit heavy) mill debuted beneath Ford and Mercury hoods in 1954 in 239-cid (former) and 256-cid (latter) forms. A 292-cid Y-block was last seen in Ford's passenger-car ranks in 1962, the year Dearborn unveiled a new lightweight V-8 for its equally new midsize Fairlane. Named for the plant where it was built, this "Windsor" small-block was created using the same ultra-precise thinwall casting technique Ford engineers had relied on to cut pesky pounds off Falcon's new six-cylinder in 1960. Even more unwanted iron was left behind by not repeating the Y-block's lowered skirt. Fairlane's first Windsor displaced a tidy 221 cubic inches, same as ol' Henry's original L-head flattie. The Windsor block was bored out to 260 cid midyear in 1962 and again, to 289 cubes, midway in 1963. New too this year was a 271-horsepower High Performance 289, which remained the hottest Mustang option from 1964 to 1966. Overshadowed by Mustang's first available big-block, this "Hi-Po" small-block made one final appearance in 1967, as did the 289 in 1968. A 302 Windsor, was offered concurrently that year then completely replaced its smaller sibling in 1969. An even larger small-block, the 351 Windsor, appeared too for 1969 after engineers raised the existing block's deck height by 1.275 inches to allow room for even more stroke. Both V-8s, 302 and 351, survived up into the 1990s.

YEAR	CID	BORE & STROKE	CR	HORSEPOWER	TORQUE	CARBURETOR	VALVE SIZES
1962	221	3.50 x 2.870	8.7:1	143 @ 4,400	217 @ 2,200	Autolite 2-barrel	1.59 x 1.38
1962	260	3.80 x 2.870	8.7:1	164 @ 4,400	258 @ 2,200	Autolite 2-barrel	1.67 x 1.45
1963	289	4.00 x 2.870	9.0:1	195 @ 4,400	282 @ 2,400	Autolite 2-barrel	1.67 x 1.45
1968	302	4.00 x 3.00	9.0:1	210 @ 4,400	300 @ 2,600	Autolite 2-barrel	1.78 x 1.45
1969	351	4.00 x 3.50	9.5:1	250 @ 4,600	355 @ 2,600	Autolite 2-barrel	1.84 x 1.54

NOTE: *CID is cubic-inch displacement; CR is compression ratio; bore/stroke & valve sizes in inches (intake x exhaust).*

HOT OFF THE PRESS: 1964 CHEVROLET MALIBU SS

"Chevrolet presents a clean new transportation machine of high all-around merit. Sensible dimensions and sparkling performance augur well for its sales future."

Car and Driver, *November 1963*

HOT OFF THE PRESS: 1964 FORD MUSTANG "HI-PO" 289

"We specify the HP Mustang because of its obvious superiority to the more mundane everyday Mustang. Where the latter has a style and a flair of design that promises a road-hugging sort of performance, and then falls slightly short of this self-established goal, the HP Mustang backs up its looks in spades."

Car Life, *September 1964*

195-horse 283 small-block. The strongest option early on was RPO L77, a 220-horsepower 283 topped by a Rochester four-barrel. Two optional 327 V-8s were announced in December 1963: the 250-horsepower L30 and its 300-horsepower L74 running mate. A third 327, the Corvette's smokin' 365-horsepower L76 (see page 32), was briefly mentioned midyear then quickly withdrawn after only a handful were released, leaving Chevelle fans wondering when their rush to market would begin.

FORD

Ford's first Mustang represented various different things to various different drivers. Economical practicality and affordability were there in spades in base six-cylinder form, but also present was a sporty flair all its own. Bucket seats were standard inside, and that unforgettable body with its long hood and short rear deck made it easy to forget that Lee Iacocca's little baby was basically a made-over Falcon beneath that pretty skin.

Initial V-8 choices in April 1964 included the Falcon's 164-horse 260-cid Windsor small-block V-8. A larger Windsor, the 210-horsepower 289 four-barrel V-8 was optional and was joined in June by the supreme rendition of the breed: the High

REBORN TO RACE

Chrysler may have pulled its original hemi-head engines from the streets after 1958 but this by no means signaled the end of the road for this potent technology. Fire Power V-8s continued running strong on NHRA dragstrips, with Emory Cook's 354-cube "rail" becoming the first quarter-miler to best 160 miles per hour in February 1957, a feat many experts had deemed impossible. His 166.97-miles per hour clocking was then topped in October by another 354 Chrysler, Red Greth's Speed Sport Special, which managed 169.11 miles per hour. Next came a young upstart from Florida, Don Garlits, who traded his 354 for a big 392 and blew everyone away in November in the first of his many "Swamp Rat" dragsters, running an incredible 176.40 miles per hour. Hemi power and drag racing remain synonymous to this day.

Hemi-powered machines destroyed drag racing's record book in 1957, with Emory Cook's Cook-Bedwell rail (middle) becoming the first to run 160 miles per hour in February. Red Greth's Speed Sport Special (top) hit 169 miles per hour in October, then Don Garlits blew everyone away the next month in his Swamp Rat (bottom), turning 176 miles per hour in Florida. *Mike Mueller*

Inspired by these ground-pounding pioneers, Chrysler officials opted to reconsider hemi heads five years after they'd dropped them like hot potatoes. Newly appointed corporate president Lynn Townsend put part-time racer, full-time engineer Tom Hoover in charge of his company's competition programs in October 1961, and in December 1962 Hoover's team went to work putting hemispherical combustion chambers back in business. Based loosely on the same RB foundation used by Dodge and Plymouth's existing "Max Wedge" super-stock V-8s, but sharing very few parts, the resulting 426-cid "race Hemi" was, as the name implied, built solely for the track.

Two race Hemi renditions were announced for quarter-mile competition in February 1964: a 415 horsepower version with 11.0:1 compression and its 425-horsepower big brother featuring a 12.5:1 squeeze. Dual four-barrel carbs on a cross-ram intake were included in both cases. A third type, tabbed at 400 horses and topped by a single four-barrel, also went together for the NASCAR circuit. In all cases those "advertised" output figures were jokes; actual power production was more like 550 horses, if not 600.

The single-carb variety debuted just in time to dominate NASCAR's 1964 Daytona 500. Hemis finished 1-2-3, with Richard Petty's winning Plymouth leading five other Mopars in the top 10. Petty eventually copped the NASCAR championship that season by a wide margin, so wide that big Bill France decided to cage this wild animal because it didn't qualify as a "regular-production engine." Chrysler's initial response involved boycotting the 1965 season. Twin-carb Hemis, meanwhile, continued to make big names for themselves at the drags.

Production figures are not complete, but it is known that at least 11 Dodges and 24 Plymouths were released with race Hemis after May 18, 1964. Others surely followed that summer, though it remains unproven whether or not Chrysler's two divisions met the NHRA's minimum production requirement of 50 cars. Another 202 super-stock Hemi Mopars (101 Dodges, 101 Plymouths) followed in 1965.

The next year Chrysler's race Hemi was morphed into a regular-production option, meeting NASCAR homologation standards in the process. Also token rated at 425 horsepower, the garage-friendly "street Hemi" found its way into more than 10,000 Dodge and Plymouth muscle cars from 1966 to 1971—every one of them a true legend.

Token rated at 425 horsepower, the dragstrip-targeted version of Chrysler's 426 race Hemi was fitted with two Carter AFB four-barrels on a cross-ram intake. Note the open air horns, which sealed up to the scooped hood's underside to allow cooler outside air easy access to those Carters. *Mike Mueller*

Other than its fuel-injected 375-horse L84 cousin, there was no Chevy small-block released during the 1960s meaner than the L76 with its solid lifters, loping cam and 11:1 compression. Basically an L84 mounting a Holley four-barrel in place of the Corvette's "fuelie" equipment, the L76 327 initially appeared as a 340-horsepower Sting Ray option in 1963 then returned with 25 more ponies in both 1964 and '65 before it was dropped along with the L84, both being eclipsed by the new 396 Turbo Jet big-block.

While the injected L84 was limited to Corvette installations, the L76 327 was also briefly offered early in 1964 for Chevrolet's first A-body in an attempt to give Pontiac people a run for their midsize money. An L76 Chevelle was first mentioned in assembly manuals in late January 1964, and at least one prototype was built, a roaring road rocket that apparently could hold its own with any muscle machine then running. "The 325-hp GTO and 365-hp Chevelle are very comparable in performance, giving 0-60 times of around six seconds flat," explained the spies at *Motor Trend*. "They're far and away the hottest of the [new intermediates] and quicker than most big cars with high-performance engines."

Full production of the 365-horsepower Chevelle, however, never got rolling. "Don't hold your breath until you can buy a new Chevelle with a 365-hp engine," added a second *Motor Trend* report a month after the magazine first scooped the L76/A-body combo. "Chevrolet jumped the gun a little on the announcement of the '327' Corvette engine option for the Chevelle." Why? "They did this to counter big publicity for the GTO."

Various stumbling blocks influenced this false promise, not the least of which was a shortage of 327s that developed early in 1964 due to unexpected demand from full-size Chevy buyers. But, again according to *Motor Trend*, "the biggest problem is that special exhaust manifolds are needed to clear the suspension in the Chevelle chassis. They're using the same manifolds from the 283 engine for the 250-hp '327' option, so you can order this one right away. But the 300- and 365-hp '327s' need bigger passages, and it's estimated that these manifolds won't be ready for assembly-line installation until May." That delay perhaps explains why the 300-horsepower L74 Chevelle didn't show up until June, although engineers apparently gave up on the better-breathing manifold idea. None were ever cast.

Chevelle enthusiast Scott Gaulter wondered what an ultra-rare 1964 L76 Chevelle might look like in pristine condition, so he built one in exacting detail. While not technically "real," this tribute is an excellent representation of a car we wouldn't be able to enjoy otherwise. *Mike Mueller*

At 365 horsepower, the Corvette-sourced L76 327 small-block surely would've made a Malibu SS a true GTO-killer in 1964 had Chevrolet not axed this option before it found the chance to prove itself on the street. Only a handful of L76 Chevelles were released before the execution order came down. *Mike Mueller*

According to a product update memo (dated March 19) sent to Chevrolet dealers, the 365-horsepower Turbo Fire 327 had "been cancelled and will not be offered" to Chevelle customers. But apparently a few did escape into the wild. Stories of two, maybe three 1964 L76 A-bodies are known.

Recognizing he'd probably never see the real thing, veteran Chevy restorer Scott Gaulter chose to recreate the little-known L76 Chevelle as close as possible to original factory specs, right down to the K66 transistorized ignition—itself also a briefly listed Chevelle option for 1964. Shown here, Gaulter's 365-horsepower Super Sport "reproduction"—Scott felt "clone" didn't do the car justice—is an impressive representation of what might have been had Chevrolet's Corvette-powered Chevelle not been stillborn.

Mercury took its shot at the "youth market" in 1964 with its first Cyclone, which came standard with a 210-horsepower 289 V-8 and simulated chrome reversed-rim wheel covers. The 271-horsepower "Hi-Po" 289 was optional. *courtesy National Automotive History Collection, Detroit Public Library*

Performance 289. Known well by its "K" engine code, Ford's "Hi-Po" V-8 produced 271 horsepower, more than enough to help Detroit's new pony car kick up its heels. Ordering the K-code V-8 also mandated the installation of the Mustang's Special Handling Package (quicker steering and stiffer springs, shocks and sway bar) and a set of 6.95x14 nylon "Red Band" tires, bringing the option's price to $328. A close-ratio "top-loader" four-speed was the only transmission available behind the Hi-Po.

BY THE NUMBERS: 1964 PRODUCTION

PONTIAC GTO			
	coupe	7,384	
	hardtop	18,422	
	convertible	6,644	
	total	**32,450**	(24,205 w/325-hp 389 V-8, 8,245 w/Tri Power)
OLDSMOBILE 4-4-2			
	F-85 club coupe	148	
	F-85 4-door sedan	3	
	F-85 deluxe 4-dr	7	
	Cutlass sport coupe	563	
	Cutlass Holiday	1,842	
	Cutlass convertible	436	
	total	**2,999**	(all w/Muncie 4-speed manual transmission)
CHEVROLET SS V-8			
	hardtop	57,445	(plus 1,551 6-cylinder hardtops)
	convertible	9,640	(plus 8,224 6-cylinder convertibles)
	total	**67,085**	(total, including 6-cylinder models, was 76,860)
MERCURY CYCLONE		**7,454**	(all hardtops)
STUDEBAKER AVANTI		**809**	(sport coupes)

NOTE: *Production data was supplied by various sources, including Christo Datini at the GM Heritage Center, Kevin Marti (Ford material) at Marti Auto Works (www.martiauto.com), and Galen Govier (Mopar material) at Galen's Tag Service (www.galengovier.com).*

1964 CHEVROLET MALIBU SS V-8

CONSTRUCTION: body on perimeter-rail frame
MODEL AVAILABILITY: Chevelle hardtop & convertible
PRICE: $2,646, hardtop; $2,857, convertible
WHEELBASE: 115 inches
WEIGHT: 3,155 pounds
SUSPENSION: coil springs, front & rear; 0.812-inch stabilizer bar in front
STEERING: manual (24.0:1) recirculating ball, std
WHEELS: 14x5 stamped-steel
TIRES: 6.50x14
BRAKES: 9.5-inch drums, front & rear
ENGINE: 283-cid small-block V-8 w/Rochester two-barrel carburetor
TRANSMISSION: 3-speed manual
AXLE RATIO: 3.08:1, std

1964 FORD MUSTANG HIGH PERFORMANCE 289

CONSTRUCTION: unitized body/frame
MODEL AVAILABILITY: hardtop & convertible
PRICE: $327.92 for K-code engine option (Special Handling Package & Red Band tires included in the deal); 4-speed manual transmission ($184.02) specified
WHEELBASE: 108 inches
WEIGHT: 3,000 pounds
SUSPENSION: independent upper A-arms, lower control arms, w/coil springs mounted atop A-arms in front; solid axle w/longitudinal leaf springs in back; Special Handling Package included stiffer springs & shocks, thickened stabilizer bar in front
STEERING: manual recirculating ball w/quicker 22:1 ratio; power-assist, optional
WHEELS: 14x5 stamped-steel
TIRES: 6.95x14 Dual Red Band
BRAKES: 10-inch drums, front & rear; front discs, optional
ENGINE: 289-cid High Performance Windsor V-8 w/600-cfm Autolite 4100-series 4-barrel carburetor
TRANSMISSION: 4-speed top-loader manual
AXLE RATIO: 3.50:1, std; 3.89:1 & 4.11:1, optional

HOT OFF THE PRESS: 1964 MERCURY CYCLONE

"The Cyclone will be immediately recognized in any crowd of Comets by the absence of excess trim, side spears, and other shiny gimcracks so prevalent on the others. In our opinion, it's one of the most tasteful renderings to come out of the Mercury styling studios in many a moon."

Jim Wright, Motor Trend, *August 1964*

TIME SLIPS: 1964

MODEL	¼-MILE PERFORMANCE	SOURCE
Pontiac GTO (Tri-Power)	14.1 seconds at 104.16 mph	*Road & Track*, March 1964
Ford Mustang "Hi-Po" 289	14.68 seconds at 95.03 mph	*Motorcade*, October 1964
Plymouth Sport Fury 426S	15.2 seconds at 95.5 mph	*Motor Trend*, January 1964
Dodge Polara 500 426S	15.2 seconds at 89 mph	*Car Life*, March 1964
Studebaker Lark R-2	15.8 seconds at 90 mph	*Motor Trend*, December 1963
Oldsmobile 4-4-2	15.8 seconds at 89 mph	*Car Life*, August 1964
Mercury Cyclone	16.2 seconds at 80 mph	*Motor Trend*, August 1964
Chevrolet Malibu SS	16.2 seconds at 84 mph	*Car Life*, March 1964

MOTOR OF THE YEAR: 1964 PONTIAC TRI-POWER V-8

Type	OHV V-8 w/chrome dress-up
Displacement	389 cubic inches
Bore	4.0625 inches
Stroke	3.75 inches
Horsepower	348 at 4,900 rpm
Torque	428 at 3,600 rpm
Compression	10.75:1
Fuel Delivery	3 Rochester 2-barrel carburetors w/vacuum-operated linkage
Air cleaner	3 small foam-wrapped open units w/chrome lids
Ignition	Delco-Remy distributor
Cooling	7-blade declutching fan w/heavy-duty (2.625 x 17.5 inches) radiator
Cylinder block	cast-iron
Crankshaft	cast-nodular-iron w/3.00-inch main journals
Connecting rods	cast-iron
Pistons	cast-aluminum
Cam	hydraulic w/273 degrees of duration on intake, 289 on exhaust, 54 degrees of overlap
Rocker ratio	1.5:1
Cylinder heads	cast-iron w/66cc combustion chambers
Valve sizes	1.92-inch intakes, 1.66-inch exhausts
Valve lift	0.406 inch
Exhaust system	cast-iron manifolds, 2.25-inch head pipes, 2.00-inch tailpipes (chrome splitter exhaust tips exiting directly behind rear wheels, optional)

MERCURY

On January 17, 1964, Lincoln-Mercury officials announced various dress-ups for both their full-size lines and the Falcon-based Comet. "We're going to make our classy cars even classier," said general manager Ben Mills. "There's widespread demand for more luxury by today's buyer and we plan to take every possible step to meet this increasing trend."

But less at first appeared like more concerning the newly introduced Comet Cyclone, which was noticeably dressed down compared to its trimmed-out Caliente cousin. "Dechromed" body sides set the Cyclone apart from all other Comets, all the better to attract the younger set, who no longer seemed interested in all the purposeless pizzazz previously favored by their elders.

That's not to say, however, that cool kids then didn't dig shiny stuff. Chrome reversed-wheels were considered particularly groovy by 1960s hot rodders, explaining the standard Cyclone wheel covers that simulated the "chromie" look right down to the plated lugnuts that protruded through them. Extra chrome also came standard beneath the hood for the Cyclone's "Super 289" V-8, rated at 210 horsepower. FoMoCo's super-duper Windsor small-block, the High Performance 289, was optional.

Bucket seats and a console were standard inside, as was a sporty three-spoke steering wheel. Also included in the package was a 6,000-rpm tach, purposefully mounted right where it belonged atop the dash.

DODGE & PLYMOUTH

Neither Dodge nor Plymouth had a direct GTO response early on. No way could their intimidating Max Wedge monster be tamed to go toe to toe with Pontiac's Tiger, though some tried, to the dismay of its creators. "Plymouth was alarmed last year at the way people were snapping up the big Super/Stock '426-R' option to run on the street," began Jim Wright's discussion of the state of Mopar muscle car affairs in *Motor Trend's* January 1964 issue. "We personally know two who ordered the '426-R' for go-to-work cars—and are they sorry!" What part of "R-for-race" did they not understand?

Few noticed Chrysler's initial attempt to jump into Detroit's burgeoning street race in 1964, basically because this first move involved a little-known engine option, not a complete model package. Appropriately tagged the "426-S," this RB-series big-block

FAMILY TIES: CHRYSLER B/RB V-8s

Chrysler's "low-deck" B-series 383 V-8 debuted in 1961 then appeared in various high-perf applications during the 1960s. Shown here is the 280-horsepower 383 Commando V-8 included with 1967's big-block Formula S Barracuda. *Mike Mueller*

Chrysler officials opted to trade their hemispherical combustion chambers for a conventional wedge design in 1959, one year after DeSoto and Dodge introduced the corporation's lighter, far less complex B-series V-8, which required only one rocker shaft per head instead of the two needed for the hemi-head's inclined valves. All B engines from then until this family's retirement in 1978 relied on the same stroke, 3.375 inches, and matching that crank with a 4.06 bore resulted in the 350-cid wedge unveiled by both DeSoto and Plymouth in 1958. Increasing the bore to 4.125 inches produced the 361 V-8 that DeSoto also used that year along with Dodge. Chrysler Division, meanwhile, turned to an even larger B-series variant for 1959. Known as an "RB," this 413-cid V-8 featured a raised (hence the "R") cylinder block that measured 10.725 inches from deck surface to crank centerline, compared to 9.980 inches for its B-series brother. This extra height in turn made room for a 3.750-inch stroke, which also remained constant during the "tall-deck" RB's run up through 1978. Another RB, the little-known 383, appeared briefly for 1959 and '60 and shouldn't be confused with the much more popular "low-deck" 383 that debuted in 1961. This B-series 383 was bored out to 400 cid in 1972. RB displacement hit 426 cubes in 1963, first for race-only "Max Wedge" renditions. The "426-S" then hit the streets the following year. A modified RB cylinder block also served as a base for Dodge/Plymouth's reborn Hemi, which debuted in 426-cid racing form in 1964, followed by its street-going alter-ego in 1966. New too that year was the biggest RB, Chrysler's "440 TNT," a 350-horsepower big-block that at first was little more than a torque-churning beast best suited to turning pulleys on power steering pumps and air conditioning compressors between luxury car fenders. Updated for Dodge and Plymouth B-body applications in 1967, the 440 was treated to better-breathing open-chamber heads, freer-flowing exhaust manifolds, a big Carter four-barrel, and a more aggressive hydraulic cam, resulting in 375 horsepower for what Dodge called its 440 Magnum V-8. Plymouth's counterpart was the 440 Super Commando. A 390-horsepower 440, fed by triple carbs, appeared midyear in 1969 for Road Runner and Super Bee only, then for B- and E-bodies in 1970. Beefier connecting rods were added that year, creating the need for external balancing, a first for a Chrysler engine.

YEAR	CID	BORE & STROKE	CR	HORSEPOWER	TORQUE	CARBURETOR	VALVE SIZES
1958	350	4.0625 x 3.375	10.0:1	280 @ 4,600	380 @ 2,400	Carter 2-barrel	1.95 x 1.60
1958	361	4.125 x 3.375	10.0:1	295 @ 4,600	390 @ 2,400	Carter 2-barrel	1.95 x 1.60
1959	383	4.030 x 3.750	10.0:1	305 @ 4,600	410 @ 2,400	Carter 2-barrel	1.95 x 1.60
1959	413	4.1875 x 3.750	10.0:1	350 @ 4,600	470 @ 2,800	Carter 4-barrel	1.95 x 1.60
1961	383	4.250 x 3.380	10.0:1	325 @ 4,600	425 @ 2,800	Carter 4-barrel	1.95 x 1.60
1963	426*	4.250 x 3.750	13.5:1	425 @ 6,000	480 @ 4,400	2 Carter 4-barrels	2.08 x 1.88
1966	440	4.320 x 3.750	10.0:1	350 @ 4,400	480 @ 2,800	Carter 4-barrel	2.08 x 1.60

NOTE: *CID is cubic-inch displacement; CR is compression ratio; bore/stroke & valve sizes in inches (intake x exhaust).*

NOTE: *Engines with 3.375-inch stroke are B-series V-8s; all RB V-8s used 3.750-inch stroke*

**Dodge/Plymouth Stage 2 "Max Wedge" V-8, race-only*

HOT OFF THE PRESS: 1964 DODGE POLARA 500 426S

"What makes this car so special? Two things: a Paul Bunyon transmission and a big Blue Ox of an engine. Combined into a taut, good-handling chassis, these turn even the most mundane excursions into a Great Adventure."

Car Life, *March 1964*

HOT OFF THE PRESS: 1964 STUDEBAKER LARK R-3

"A new image for Studebaker is being established in the field of performance with custom-built Avanti power and chassis options now available in the Lark."

Ray Brock, Hot Rod, *January 1964*

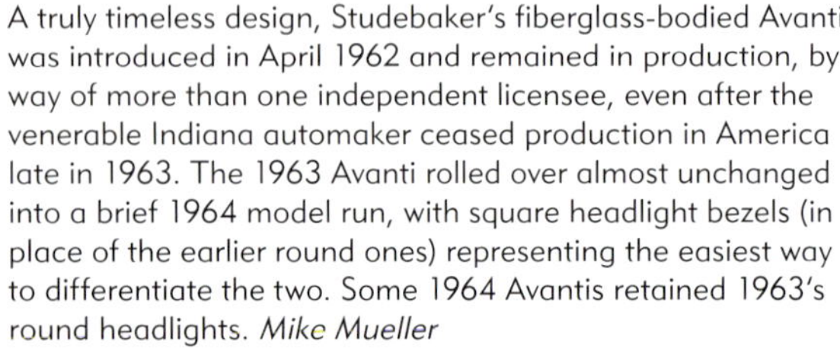

A truly timeless design, Studebaker's fiberglass-bodied Avanti was introduced in April 1962 and remained in production, by way of more than one independent licensee, even after the venerable Indiana automaker ceased production in America late in 1963. The 1963 Avanti rolled over almost unchanged into a brief 1964 model run, with square headlight bezels (in place of the earlier round ones) representing the easiest way to differentiate the two. Some 1964 Avantis retained 1963's round headlights. *Mike Mueller*

While Dodge's 1964 lineup did feature three distinct tiers—compact A-body Dart, 330/440 and Polara, and 880/Custom 880—the middle models didn't really qualify as intermediates due to their lengthy wheelbase, 119 inches, only three short of their full-size running mates. But, although comparatively big and heavy, this 1964 Polara convertible still could run with Detroit's earliest muscle cars thanks to the installation of Dodge's optional 426-S RB big-block, rated at 365 horsepower. *Tom Shaw*

1964 DODGE POLARA 426-S

CONSTRUCTION: unitized body/frame
MODEL AVAILABILITY: all B-body
PRICE: 426-S V-8 cost $482.95 w/4-speed manual, $514.45 w/automatic; heavy-duty suspension & brakes included
WHEELBASE: 119 inches
WEIGHT: 4,040 pounds (convertible)
SUSPENSION: long-arm/short-arm w/longitudinal torsion bars & 0.75-inch stabilizer bar, front; solid axle w/leaf spring, rear
STEERING: manual recirculating ball; power-assist, optional
WHEELS: 14x5 stamped-steel
TIRES: 7.50x14
BRAKES: 11-inch heavy-duty "police" drums, front & rear
ENGINE: 426-cid wedge-head V-8 w/Carter 4-barrel carburetor
TRANSMISSION: 4-speed A833 manual w/Hurst shifter or 3-speed Torqueflite automatic
AXLE RATIO: 3.23:1, std; Sure-Grip differential, optional

was advertised by Plymouth promoters as a "street version of our competition-designed 426 Hemi engine, which holds more records than our competitors care to count." In truth, save for displacement, the 426-S had next to nothing in common with the vaunted race Hemi. Its conventional wedge heads came right out of the 413 passenger-car parts bins, as did its rods, crank, and manifolds. Lifters were civilized hydraulic units and compression was a comparatively calm 10.3:1. A single Carter four-barrel fed the 426-S, rated at 365 horsepower.

The 426-S option was listed for all Dodge and Plymouths, with two doors or four, and included an impressive list of heavy-duty upgrades. A nicely beefed suspension predictably came in the deal along with big, burly police brakes and a choice between Chrysler's excellent three-speed Torqueflite automatic transmission and the corporation's new Hurst-shifted A-833 four-speed manual.

STUDEBAKER

Studebaker's days surely were already numbered when Sherwood Egbert took over in February 1961, but that didn't stop the venerable Indiana firm's new president from giving it his best shot, targeting this country's then-booming youth market with both barrels. Two overnight sensations resulted: the timeless Avanti, created by Ray Loewy's design team, and a thoroughly modernized restyle for the existing Hawk and Lark bodies, the work of Brooks Stevens. Reportedly Stevens' crisp, clean Gran Turismo Hawk was developed in about five months, while the fiberglass-bodied Avanti sport coupe needed only 40 days to go from drawing board to reality. When introduced in April 1962, "America's only 4-passenger High-Performance Personal Car," as brochures called it, stood as this country's first production model to offer caliper-type disc brakes. Standard Avanti power came from a 289-cid V-8. A Paxton supercharger was optional.

As for the updated 1962 Lark, it remained a cost-conscious compact in base form. But an alter ego, named Daytona, was new that year, available in hardtop and convertible forms. Lark Daytona features included bucket seats and an

FAST-LANE FAIRLANE

Few people, including GTO owners, noticed when Ford dropped its K-code High Performance 289 small-block into its midsize Fairlane, mostly due to meager production efforts. Estimates put the 1964 total at about 600. *courtesy Mecum Auctions*

Technically speaking, it was Ford's better-idea guys, not Pontiac people, who first experimented with midsize muscle. But few in the scientific community at the time noticed, basically because a) the focus group was so small, and b) study parameters didn't quite match those of GTO. The model, Fairlane, certainly qualified as an intermediate; it was Detroit's first. But the motor, Ford's 289-cid Windsor V-8, clearly wasn't sizeable at all; they didn't call it a small-block for nothing. Hence it's PMD that takes all the credit for kick-starting that whole big-engine/not-so-big-car thing in 1964.

In December 1962, Dearborn officials introduced "the saltiest little V-8 in the business" for their 1963 Fairlane, an optional mill that "RPM's like an electric fan" and featured "271 muscular horses and a violent urge to show up larger powerplants." This High Performance small-block could handle 7,000 revs with no sweat, and that's where journalists tended to shift on the way to quarter-mile test passes in the 14.6-second range. A four-speed stick was the only choice behind the first "Hi-Po," and available rear gear choices went as low as 4.11:1.

Helping this little engine make big noise was a beefed block featuring stronger main bearing caps cradling a nodular-iron crank, some of which were randomly inspected during assembly for metallurgic content. Cast-aluminum pistons were tied to that crank by reinforced rods clamped down on their big ends by larger 3/8-inch bolts. Up front was a larger (1-13/16-inches thick, compared to the stock 1-inch unit) harmonic balancer and a larger pulley (3.875 inches, compared to 2.75 inches) for alternator-equipped examples, which showed up for 1965. A stronger fan with increased pitch also was added to maximize cooling. Durable valvetrain pieces included stiffer dual valve springs and hardened pushrods, spring retainers, and keepers. Standard cast rocker arms were mounted firmly in place by screw-in rocker studs—other 289s used press-in studs.

The 289 High Performance V-8 was available for all Fairlane models—with two or four doors—save for station wagons. Ford dealers also offered various Cobra kits (labeled "Cobra Tonic" by ads) that among other things added three two-barrel carbs or four Weber two-barrels, with that latter upgrade boosting output up to 343 horsepower. Automatic trans availability was announced for 1965 Hi-Po Fairlanes and again in 1966 for their Mustang cousins.

Estimates put 271-horsepower Fairlane production at about 500 in 1963, 600 in 1964, and 100 in 1965. Apparently a few were built for 1966, too, and a couple Canadian-built Hi-Po Falcons are known as well for 1965.

1964 FORD 289 HIGH PERFORMANCE V-8

Type	OHV Windsor V-8 (K-code) w/special motor mounts
Weight	490 pounds
Displacement	289 cubic inches
Bore	4.00 inches
Stroke	2.87 inches
Horsepower	271 at 6,000 rpm
Torque	312 at 3,400 rpm
Compression	10.5:1 (for early versions; 10:1 for later renditions)
Fuel delivery	600-cfm Autolite 4,100 4-barrel carburetor w/manual choke on a cast-iron intake manifold (Ford published 480-cfm carb for early applications)
Air cleaner	open-element w/chrome lid
Ignition	dual-point mechanical-advance FoMoCo distributor
Cooling	thicker 4-blade fan w/increased pitch; modified water pump (6-blade impellor in place of stock 8-blade)
Cylinder block	cast-iron w/heavy-duty 2-bolt main bearing caps
Crankshaft	nodular-iron w/ "hatchet" counterweight
Connecting rods	forged-steel with 3/8-inch bolts
Pistons	cast-aluminum flat-top
Cam	mechanical w/310 degrees duration, 82 degrees of overlap; thicker 42-tooth cast-iron drive gear (later K-code V-8s used standard "silent chain" aluminum gear w/nylon-coated teeth)
Cylinder heads	cast-iron w/cast-in spring seats, screw-in rocker studs & dual valve springs
Valve spring rate	350 lb/in (standard 289 spring rates was about 250-lb/in)
Combustion chambers	49.2cc, early (54.5cc chambers appeared midyear in 1964, leading to the lower 10:1 compression ratio)
Valve sizes	1.67-inch intakes, 1.45-inch exhausts (1.78-inch intakes appeared midyear in 1964)
Valve lift	0.457 inch, intake/exhaust
Exhaust system	free-flowing cast-iron manifolds

Ford's 271-hp High Performance 289 V-8 is best known for putting the spurs to Dearborn's new pony car in 1964. Along with Fairlane, Mercury's Comet also was fitted with "Hi Po" small-blocks in 1964 and 1965. *courtesy Mecum Auctions*

CHAINED MELODY

Chrysler Corporation countered Ford's 427 SOHC with its own overhead-cam Hemi, which also never made it into regular production.

Taken for granted today, overhead-cam (OHC) engine designs date back to internal-combustion's primordial moments as various automotive pioneers early on discovered that fewer parts and less valvetrain weight meant higher rev capabilities and greater performance potential. Revived OHC trials then proliferated around Detroit during the 1960s, but save for Pontiac's 1966–69 "Sprint" six, none made it into everyday operation.

GM engineers were especially fond of OHC experiments. Pontiac's initial projects (involving V-8s, not sixes) began in earnest in 1963, resulting in various dual-overhead and single-overhead 389s and 421s, one of these using three valves per cylinder. In 1969, John Beltz's team at Oldsmobile took their four-valve-per-cylinder, hemi-head W-43 455 and added dual overhead cams to produce the 700-horsepower OW-43 Can-Am racing engine.

Called "Ford's 90-Day Wonder" by *Hot Rod*, Dearborn's "Cammer" surely came closest to reaching street-legal reality. This 427 SOHC big-block was created in haste (hence *Hot Rod's* label) early in 1964 to hopefully counter Chrysler's new 426 race Hemi. Atop a typical 427 FE block went a pair of cylinder heads featuring hemispherical combustion chambers and a single overhead cam in each. More than 6 feet of timing chain drove those two cams, making sweet music as the twin-carb Cammer churned out 600 real horsepower at a dizzying 7,200 rpm. Reported output was about 580 horses when a single four-barrel shot the juice, just what NASCAR rules specified.

"I wouldn't be surprised to see [the 427 SOHC) dominating stock car racing next summer," wrote *Car Life* contributor Roger Huntington late in 1964. Mopar men, meanwhile, were working hard to trump the Cammer with a wild DOHC Hemi, a monster mill that surely would've trampled everything in its path had it reached running stage. But it didn't. And Ford's 427 SOHC was left all revved up with no place to race after NASCAR's Bill France put his hefty foot down.

Called "Ford's 90-Day Wonder" by *Hot Rod*, Dearborn's 427-cid "Cammer" V-8 was rapidly developed under the watchful eyes of engineers Norm Faustyn, Joe Eastman. Mose Nowland, and Al Rominsky in early 1964. Atop a side-oiler FE block went a pair of cylinder heads featuring hemispherical combustion chambers and a chain-driven single overhead cam in each. *Tom Shaw*

Fearful of where such escalation would lead, NASCAR officials on October 19, 1964, announced a new set of homologation standards scheduled to take effect January 1, 1965. Included was a statement claiming that legal "engines must be of production design only, thus eliminating overhead cams and hemispherical heads."

Chrysler's initial response involved boycotting the upcoming NASCAR season, while Ford simply fell back on its pushrod 427, letting the Cammer instead do its thing in drag racing's factory-experimental classes. The plot, however, soon thickened after Chrysler came back in 1966 with its street Hemi, a fully legal production engine.

Cammer production had continued on into 1965 as Dearborn engineers struggled to bring costs down in hopes of meeting another NASCAR mandate, this one establishing the maximum price of an eligible racing engine at $1,000. Estimates put Ford's early costs at $14,000 apiece for the first 427 SOHCs, and the commonly quoted bottom line for a crated Cammer in 1965 was $4,500. These bloated figures aside, Ford racing men apparently had every intention of letting the SOHC loose on NASCAR tracks in 1966. Again according to Huntington, "a reliable source [told him] as far as Ford is concerned, [the SOHC] is a 'production' engine, and if [Dearborn] has to drop $250,000 selling [them] to racers for $1,000 to prove it, Ford will do so."

In the spring of 1966 Ford leaked news of a planned SOHC option, reportedly priced at $1,963, for its full-size Galaxie. Dearborn then got the go-ahead in April after promising a production run of 50 SOHC Galaxies. The catch? The Cammer could race in NASCAR, but it would be penalized 1 pound per cubic-inch.

Fed up, Henry Ford II immediately announced his company's withdrawal from NASCAR competition. The final hammer blow to the SOHC's coffin came in 1967 when new NASCAR rules stated that "a minimum of 500 of a type of car and engine be titled pursuant to bona fide consumer transactions before they will be made eligible to compete." "Whether a purchase order from Holman and Moody for 500 SOHC V-8s would satisfy Bill France remains to be seen," quipped a *Motor Trend* report on this convoluted tale. All kidding aside, that was that.

While some reports claimed 427 SOHC production was about 75, as many as 300 were probably built, nearly all of them going to Ford's Holman-Moody "racing wing" in Charlotte, North Carolina, where a few were installed in Mustang F/X drag cars in 1965. As for the rest, according to John Holman's son Lee, "when the Dearborn people decided the engine was no longer viable, those Cammers just sat in the warehouse until Ford had us sell them." The younger Holman recalled running magazine ads offering "leftover" SOHC motors for about $975. He also remembered more than one buyer taking home four or five before the supply played out in 1971.

Some garage sale, huh?

One of only 703 Daytona convertibles built for 1964, this topless Lark is fitted with a 240-horsepower 289-cid R-1 V-8. Bucket seats, a 160-miles per hour speedometer, and a 6,000-rpm tachometer also were standard for the Daytona. *Mike Mueller*

optional Borg-Warner T-10 four-speed—just the things that tended to turn John Q. Boomer's head. Race fans also got their looks after a 1962 Daytona convertible paced the 46th running of the Indianapolis 500.

A 210-horsepower 289 V-8 was available for the Daytona, as were the Avanti's R-1 (carbureted) and R-2 (supercharged) engines, designed and tested by Paxton Products' legendary Granatelli brothers—Andy, Joe, and Vince. Although no official output figures were released, informed sources rated the two at 240 and 289 horses, respectively.

In the spring of 1963, the R-series V-8s were made Lark and Hawk options, resulting in the aptly labeled Super Lark and Super Hawk. The Granatellis also developed two other R engines, both displacing 304.5 cubic inches. The blown R-3 put out an estimated 335 horsepower, while the R-4, fitted with dual four-barrels, made something like 290 horses. Egbert apparently had full intentions of offering the R-3 and R-4 V-8s for the 1964 Daytona, as well as that year's Avanti and GT Hawk, and surely would have had terminal illness not intervened—both in his case and his company's.

Demoralized and facing a battle with cancer, Egbert stepped down in November 1963, just one month before his replacement, Byers Burlingame, finally announced the closing of struggling Studebaker's ancient South Bend production plant. Although Lark sedans and wagons would continue rolling out of a facility in Hamilton, Ontario, through 1966, the sporty Daytona hardtop/convertible combo was done for, as were the GT Hawk and Avanti, after a limited run of 1964 models were sold. According to some sources, one Lark two-door sedan and nine Avanti coupes were built with R-3 engines for 1964, and a single Daytona hardtop was fitted with an R-4.

Sherwood Egbert's fight for life ended in 1969.

Along with pioneering modern disc brake installations, Avanti also was available with an optional supercharged 289-cid V-8. *Mike Mueller*

1964 MERCURY CYCLONE

CONSTRUCTION: unitized body/frame
MODEL AVAILABILITY: Comet hardtop
PRICE: $2,655
WHEELBASE: 114 inches
WEIGHT: 3,160 pounds
SUSPENSION: single lower control arms w/stabilizing struts, coil springs & anti-roll bar, front; solid axle w/longitudinal leaf springs, rear
STEERING: manual recirculating ball; power-assist, optional
WHEELS: 14x5
TIRES: 8.00x14
BRAKES: 10-inch 4-wheel drums
ENGINE: 210-hp 289-cid Windsor V-8 w/Autolite 4100-series 4-barrel carburetor, std; 271-hp 289-cid High Performance V-8, optional
TRANSMISSION: 3-speed manual, std (4-speed* & 3-speed Multi-Drive automatic, optional)
AXLE RATIO: 3.25:1
* 4-speed was mandatory option along w/271-hp 289 V-8

1964 STUDEBAKER AVANTI

CONSTRUCTION: fiberglass body (w/integrated steel roll bar) on X-member frame
MODEL AVAILABILITY: sport coupe
PRICE: $4,445
WHEELBASE: 109 inches
WEIGHT: 3,750 pounds
SUSPENSION: coil springs, front; solid axle &leaf springs (w/torque rods), rear; stabilizer bars at both ends
STEERING: manual cam & twin roller (22:1 ratio); 16:1 power-assist, optional
WHEELS: 15-inch stamped-steel
TIRES: 6.70x15 Firestone
BRAKES: power-assisted 11.5-inch Bendix-produced Dunlop front discs, 11-inch Lockheed finned rear drums
ENGINE: 289-cid V-8 w/Carter 4-barrel carburetor, std; supercharger optional
TRANSMISSION: 3-speed manual, std; 4-speed & Borg-Warner automatic trans (w/manual shift capability), optional
AXLE RATIO: 3.73:1, std; 3.31:1, 4.09:1 & 4.55:1, optional

CHAPTER 2

1965 FROM A TO Z

CHEVROLET'S SS 396 ENTERS THE FRAY

Chevrolet rolled out 200 SS 396 Malibu hardtops (plus one convertible) early in 1965, all of them fully loaded, high-priced haulers meant to inspire big-time publicity. Only three colors were offered: Regal Red, Tuxedo Black, and Crocus Yellow. *Mike Mueller*

Doubters in 1964 who figured Detroit's newborn midsize muscle car would end up the latest passing fad had another thing coming 12 months down the road. Sales of Pontiac's GTO and Oldsmobile's 4-4-2 soared by 132 and 733 percent, respectively, for 1965, firmly establishing a true niche market, with room for who knew how many more rivals. Joining the club was simply a matter of mating the right V-8 with the right body. Buick engineers managed the trick in 1965 by dropping their full-size Wildcat's engine between Skylark fenders, resulting in the Gran Sport, the third of General Motor's four A-bodies to make the jump from everyday transport to groovy go-go machine. As for the fourth…

In the sexy Malibu Super Sport, Chevrolet certainly had the right body. A suitable power source, however, was another story. Chevy's 1965 A-body SS continued to feature a thrifty six-cylinder in base form, while the standard V-8 was again the same tame 195-horse 283 used the previous year. Familiar as well

Chevrolet's original 427-cube Mark-series V-8 earned its "Mystery Motor" nickname during record-setting Daytona 500 qualifying sessions in February 1963. Junior Johnson's #3 Impala was one of five Mystery Motor entries that year, all of which failed to impress in the big race on February 24 due to various mechanical troubles. Including Daytona's 100-mile qualifier, held February 22, Johnson won seven races in 1963 and finished 12th in NASCAR's seasonal points standings.

in 1965 was Chevelle's initial top performance option, the carryover 300-horsepower L74 327, a reasonably warm small-block but clearly no match for GTO's 389. Could this be the same Bow-Tie brand that had brought us America's sports car in 1953, "The Hot One" in 1955, and the real fine 409 in 1961?

"When Oldsmobile and Buick jumped onto the big-engine, small-car bandwagon, it was pretty certain that Chevrolet wouldn't be far behind," began a *Car Life* explanation of the situation. "The only surprising part was that Chevrolet wasn't among the leaders in this scheme; after all, [it] has been a respected member of the high-performance club for 10 years now, even if it isn't allowed to say so publicly. The question remained: what would Chevrolet do?"

Finding the right engine early on wasn't easy. The venerable 409 simply wouldn't do, and a counterpart to Pontiac's ceiling-crashing 389 wasn't available, at least at first. Hence, it was back to the Sting Ray parts bin. Not a false promise like 1964's failed L76 offering, the Corvette's 350-horsepower 327 (RPO L79) became an A-body option shortly after 1965's new model introduction and represented a valiant effort to make Chevelle, in *Motor Trend's* words, "more competitive in the booming GTO market." Yet it still wasn't the answer.

Fortunately, patience was. In February 1965, Chevrolet general manager Bunkie Knudsen proudly introduced his historic Tiger-tamer at GM's Desert Proving Ground in Mesa, Arizona. Called "the first of the red-hot Malibus" by *Car Life*, Bunkie's baby was initially identified in press reports by its RPO code, "Z16," or simply "Chevelle 396." But it wasn't long before the word on the street became "SS 396." Those three digits, of course, referred to Chevrolet's equally new Mk IV V-8, which predictably displaced 396 cubic inches and produced 375 healthy horses. "Almighty Malibu" was *Motor Trend's* succinct description for this midsize milestone.

"When Chevrolet Motor Division makes up its mind to do something, it never goes halfway," wrote *Motor Trend's* John Ethridge in praise of the Z16. "While awaiting its new engine, Chevrolet had a chance to watch other [GM] divisions' and competitors' hot performance cars. All were doing well, and some were selling like skateboards, so Chevy decided to come out with one of their own."

In truth, the wait wasn't all that long. Big-block Chevelle roots dated back to April 1963, when Chevrolet Engineering's Product Performance head Vince Piggins proposed a NASCAR-ready Chevelle powered by the same 427-cid "Mystery Motor" (see page 43) that had scorched Daytona's superspeedway in February before GM's anti-racing edict slammed it back onto the shelf. Plainly ignoring the rules, Piggins planned to build 100 Mark-motored 1964 Malibu sport coupes

HOT OFF THE PRESS: 1965 CHEVROLET MALIBU SS 396

"Not merely an engine swap, the Chevelle '396' was re-engineered from the ground up to take Chevy's hot new engine. The wait evidently paid off, because [it] is without a doubt the hottest and finest car of its type ever made."

John Ethridge, Motor Trend, *July 1965*

Chevrolet's L79 327 ranked as one of the company's most powerful carbureted small-blocks before the LT1 350 appeared in 1970. Most witnesses probably remember the L79 most for what it did for Nova performance in 1966. The L79 failed to return to the A-body options list that year but was back for non-SS Chevelles in 1967 and '68.

Basically every option available for early Chevelles also was listed from the get-go for their utilitarian alter egos. Witness the 1965 El Camino shown here, which is powered by an L79 small-block. The 1965 SS convertible at right features the A-body line's base V-8, a 283 rated at 195 horsepower. *Mike Mueller*

with an extended wheelbase to meet NASCAR's minimum standard for Grand National competition. An initial OK was clandestinely given by Knudsen's office and one test vehicle was built, powered by a 396-cube Mystery Motor derivative. Various glitches, however, put the kibosh on Piggins' plan, killing any chance Chevrolet had of releasing a street-worthy 396 Chevelle for 1964. But the delay proved to be a typical blessing in disguise, allowing engineers ample time to perfect the package before the public got its peek.

A year after its introduction, Chevrolet's SS 396 Chevelle would become Detroit's second-best selling high-performance model. It hit #1 in 1969 and stayed there until the original muscle car era wound down.

FAMILY TIES: CHEVROLET'S MARK MOTORS

Casual witnesses commonly mix up the Mystery Motor story today, an understandable situation considering automotive journalists back in the 1960s couldn't keep the facts straight, either. That the two competition V-8s developed in 1962 shared displacements also surely didn't help matters, but here's the straight dope: it was the "porcupine-head" 427-cid Mk IIS, not the 409-based Z11 V-8, that inspired "Mystery Motor" headlines after leaving rivals scratching their heads at Daytona in February 1963. A stroke increase translated into 427 cubes for the Z11 W-series V-8, which was retroactively labeled "Mk I" after the Mystery Motor emerged to wear its Mk II moniker. The Mark-motor legacy went like this:

TYPE	DISPLACEMENT (cu. in.)	DESCRIPTION	NOTES
Mk I	427	409-based "W" V-8	Made hay in super-stock drag racing
Mk II	409	"Porcupine-head" V-8	Precursor to "Mystery Motor"
Mk IIS	427	Stroked "Mystery Motor"	Turned heads at Daytona in February 1963
Mk III	500 [1]	Design study	Never made it off drawing board
Mk IV	396 [2]	375 hp for Z16 Chevelle	Went into regular production in 1965

1. This study involved the feasibility of expanding displacement up to 500 cubes.

2. Displacement increased to 427 cubic inches in 1966 and 454 cubic inches in 1970.

Created late in 1962 for drag racing, the Z11 "409" W-series V-8 (it actually displaced 427 cubic inches) was laughingly rated at 430 horsepower by the factory guys. True output surely exceeded 500 horses. Notice the cowl-induction air cleaner, an idea developed by Chevy engineers early in the 1960s to allow competition engines to breathe easier. *David Kimble cutaway*

Chevrolet's Mk IIS V-8 earned its "Mystery Motor" nickname because NASCAR rivals at Daytona in February 1963 didn't know what had hit them. Displacing 427 cubic inches, this 500-horse V-8 was, according to legendary race car builder Smokey Yunick, "probably the best engine I ever saw come out of Detroit." *David Kimble cutaway*

A MYSTERY NO LONGER

The roots of Chevrolet's Mk IV V-8 ran back to July 1962, when engineer Dick Keinath created a modernized big-block to supersede the fabled 409 in competition circles. Tagged the Mk II, this 409-cid racing mill represented a marked departure from its venerable W-series forerunner, resembling it only slightly on the bottom end and sharing only its bore and stroke dimensions. From there all bets were off.

On top was a pair of superb cylinder heads that breathed better than perhaps anything ever seen before out of Detroit. Nicknamed "porcupines," these castings featured canted valves that protruded up from the combustion chambers at varying angles looking very much like the haphazard quills on the back of a pesky...well, you know. This innovative arrangement was made possible by GM's proven ball-stud rocker arm design, an idea that had helped make The Hot One so hot in 1955. Not only did ball-stud rockers greatly reduce valvetrain weight, they also allowed engineers to place the valves where they would work best. And instead of designing the all-important combustion chamber around a limited, conventional inline valve position, the ball-stud rockers' flexibility gave those engine builders the newfound freedom to shape those chambers almost any way they liked.

Intake valves were located up high near their ports and inclined slightly, making for a straighter flow from intake manifold to combustion chamber. An opposite inclination was applied (to a slightly less degree) on the exhaust end to the same effect. In between, they opened into a "modified wedge" combustion chamber that some classified as a "semi-hemi," and their inclination also allowed for a bit more room in those chambers for truly big valve diameters.

These excellent heads helped the Mk IIS ("S" for stroked after the original Mk II was enlarged to 427 cubes late in 1962) make

After work on Chevy's Mystery Motor began in the summer of 1962, its forerunner of sorts, the Z11 V-8, was retroactively labeled Mk I. Originally displacing 409 cubic inches, the Mystery Motor was tagged "Mark II," then "Mark IIS" after it was stroked to 427 cubic inches. *Mike Mueller*

a whopping 520 horsepower on the dyno, results proven soundly while touring Daytona's superspeedway in February 1963. Too bad the "Mystery Motor" already was doomed by then, a victim of GM's infamous anti-racing edit. But the story didn't end there.

Chevy engineers tamed the Mk IIS for the street, first by reducing bore to make sure displacement stayed in compliance with GM's latest 400-cube A-body limit. The resulting L37 396 Turbo Jet derived for the Z16 Malibu was similar to the 1965 Corvette's L78 counterpart save primarily for a less aggressive hydraulic cam in place of the latter's lumpier mechanical stick. Designed from top to bottom for serious street performance, the L37 featured a truly beefy bottom end with hefty main bearing webs, large bearing surfaces, and four-bolt main bearing caps. The crank and connecting rods were of forged steel, while pistons were impact-extruded (forged to you and me) aluminum.

Top advertised output for the SS 396's Mk IV remained at 375 horsepower up through 1970. According to *Motor Trend's* Roger Huntington, 1965's L37 couldn't "quite match the cubes of the '427' Ford or the '426-S' Dodge/Plymouth option, but breathing may be enough to more than make up the difference." *Motorcade's* Jim Wright made a similar comparison, claiming the 396 wasn't "as spectacular as the all-out racing engines from Ford and Chrysler, but as a high performance street engine it's going to be hard to beat."

Good call.

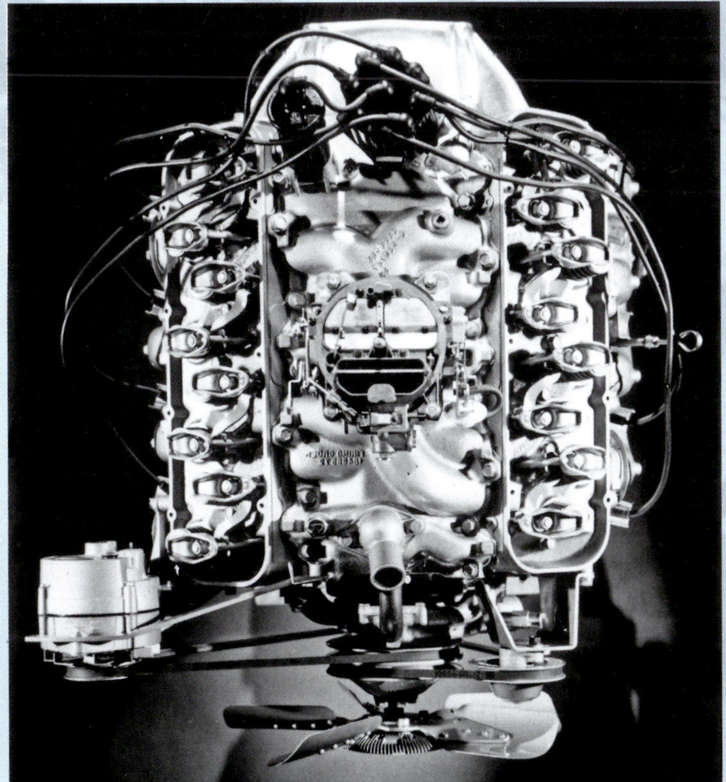

Left: The "porcupine" nickname for Chevrolet's Mk IV big-block referred to its varying valve angles, which protruded upward rather haphazardly, much like the quills on a certain spiny rodent.

Right: Three Mk IV 396 Turbo Jet V-8s were introduced in 1965: the full-size line's 325-horsepower L35 (shown here), the Z16 Malibu's 375-horsepower L37, and the Corvette's 425-horsepower L78. The L78 also was an option for big Chevys in 1965.

HOT OFF THE PRESS: 1965 BUICK GRAN SPORT

"It seems to us that Buick has another winner in the Skylark Gran Sport. The point is that better cars are being built—and Buick is building them."

Bob McVay, Motor Trend, *May 1965*

HOT OFF THE PRESS: 1965 PONTIAC GTO

"'GTO' are the three letters Pontiac has made synonymous with performance and youth. In stock or hot trim, for the road or on the drag strip, the Tiger is a versatile charger, light on its feet, has phenomenal top end potential and, in short, lives up to its reputation."

Eric Dahlquist, Hot Rod, *July 1965*

1965 CHEVROLET MALIBU SS 396

CONSTRUCTION: body on reinforced perimeter-rail convertible frame
MODEL AVAILABILITY: hardtop & convertible
PRICE: RPO Z16 added $1,501.05 to Malibu SS hardtop's $2,647 base price
WHEELBASE: 115 inches
WEIGHT: 3,565 pounds
SUSPENSION: heavy-duty w/coil springs front & rear; 1.06-inch stabilizer bar in front; rear stabilizer between lower control arms
STEERING: recirculating ball w/power-assist & quick 15:1 ratio
WHEELS: 14x6 stamped steel w/riveted rims: mag-style wheelcovers, std
TIRES: 7.75x14 two-ply gold-stripe
BRAKES: 11-inch full-size Chevrolet drums w/power assist front & rear
ENGINE: 396 Turbo Jet Mk IV V-8 w/Holley 4-barrel carburetor
TRANSMISSION: 4-speed Muncie M20 manual
AXLE RATIO: 3.31:1, open differential w/8.875-inch ring gear in special 12-bolt housing

Buick ads in 1965 called the new Skylark Gran Sport "a howitzer with windshield wipers." The 14-inch sport rims seen here were optional. *Mike Mueller*

CHEVROLET

Chevy's original SS 396 Chevelle first found its way into the hands of VIPs, celebrities, or members of the automotive press as part of a plan to obtain as much exposure as possible. Presented with Z16s were high-profile men like Briggs Cunningham, Phil Hill, A. J. Foyt, and Dan Blocker, "people who would be likely to drive them as transportation to Riverside, Watkins Glen, Indy, Daytona, Elkhart, country clubs and the like," according to a Chevrolet memo. Clearly the biggest of these big men was Blocker, who played "Hoss" on *Bonanza*, the popular television western sponsored by Chevrolet.

The star of the Z16 show, of course, was the hydraulic-lifter L37 Turbo Jet, which was backed up by an 11-inch clutch and a Muncie four-speed—no automatic was available. Also included beneath the hood was a high-torque starter, 61-ampere battery, five-blade thermo-modulated viscous-drive fan, large-capacity radiator with fan shroud, and dual-snorkel air cleaner.

Only 200 Z16 Malibu hardtops and one clandestine convertible were built in 1965, all fully loaded and all fitted with a bottom line able to wilt the wallet of most mere mortals. On top of the $2,600 base price for a 1965 V-8 Malibu, the Z16 option added a hefty $1,501.05, a veritable king's ransom a half century back. Additional standard features included bucket seats with console, mag-style wheel covers, power brakes and steering, a reinforced convertible frame, heavy-duty suspension with stabilizer bars front and rear, 7.75x14 gold-stripe high-speed tires on 6-inch wide wheels, 6,000-rpm tach, and Chevrolet's new AM/FM Multiplex stereo radio with four speakers. "There's nothing in this world, Charlie," wrote veteran *Mechanix Illustrated* scribe Tom McCahill, "like slipping down the turnpike being belted in the back by 375 horsepower and in the ear by 4-speed Bach-power!"

Working in concert, the Z16's rigid frame and reinforced, stabilized four-link rear suspension helped make it possible to leave preferred Positraction on the RPO shelf—all SS 396 Malibus in 1965 came with 3.31:1 open differentials. But no worries; Chevy's first SS 396 reportedly put down parallel black rubber patches of equal intensity even with Posi gears missing in action. Rear stabilizer bars are typically

GET-GO COPO CHEVELLE

It's unclear as to when a Chevrolet customer first used Central Office Production Order paperwork (see page 128) to purchase specific equipment or a complete vehicle. As for the first notable, truly high-performance COPO Chevelle, it appeared in 1969, right? Wrong. After COPOs were used in 1964 to create various comparatively mundane Chevelles (like righthand-drive models for export), Chevy's clandestine ordering pipeline pumped out its first super-high-perf A-body the following year. During the first week of June 1965, GM's Kansas City plant rolled out one COPO #9719 300-series sedan fitted with a 425-horsepower L78 396 Turbo Jet, an M22 Rock Crusher four-speed, and stump-pulling 4.88:1 Positraction gears.

While the Rock Crusher didn't officially appear on Chevrolet RPO lists until 1966, prototype installations—mostly in Corvettes—are known for 1965. Muncie plant paperwork showed one M22 (code "XQ") slated that year for a passenger car with 4.88 cogs. And Tonawanda records also clearly substantiated that one L78 396 V-8 (code "IY") was shipped in response to that single COPO 9719 request. Incidentally, "IX" was the designation for the 1965 Z16 Malibu's L37 396 installation.

According to this unique Chevelle's present owner, Mike Smith, COPO 9719 was placed in 1965 by his cousin, Eddy Kantor, a Detroit-area speednik and regular on the Woodward Avenue street-race scene. Kantor reportedly had "connections" at GM, although it's not clear if his friend in high places was fellow drag racer George DeLorean (brother of John Z.) or Bunkie Knudsen himself. Whatever the case, Kantor had no problem buying a ready-to-race Corvette-powered Chevelle. "He ordered the 'post-sedan' because it weighed 200 pounds less than the Z16," Smith explained in April 2014. "The Z16 had all those power options and that stereo, all stuff that added unwanted weight." Kantor's car was delivered sans radio and, being a 300, featured floormats instead of carpet. Flashy N96 mag-style wheel covers were included, though, as was the Z16's boxed convertible frame, riveted wheels, and special 12-bolt rear end. The surviving window sticker shows the 9719A-code "Special Chassis Equipment" added $1,474 to the model #13211 sedan's $2,264 base price.

By the time this unique Chevelle became Smith's first car in November 1968, the entire driveline, engine to axle, was gone, traded for parts Kantor salvaged from a wrecked 1966 Oldsmobile Cutlass. The Olds' interior also was installed, perhaps in an effort to dress up this plain-Janer a bit. "Eddy had taken out the stock bench seat [to save more weight] and it was sitting in his speed shop for customers to sit on," said Smith, who bought his cousin's historic sedan simply because he was just another eager high-schooler ready to roll. "At 17, I didn't really care at all about the car's uniqueness, I just wanted something to drive." And drive it he did. The love of his life, Dot, and he dated in it, and on December 19, 1970, the happily married couple left their church riding on that misplaced Cutlass seat.

Forty-five years later, the Smiths still own their unique 1965 Chevy, though it hasn't been driven for 20 years or so. Why did he keep it? "I still have my first car, my first house, my first farm, and my first wife—they're all still right here where they belong." Don't bother making an offer, he's not interested. "My dream is to have it restored back to showroom condition someday." If he doesn't manage that task, perhaps one of his two sons will.

Only one COPO 9719 Chevelle—a 300-series sedan originally fitted with a 425-horsepower L78 396 V-8 and M22 Rock Crusher four-speed—was built in 1965. *courtesy Mark Meekins*

1965 BUICK GRAN SPORT

CONSTRUCTION: body on reinforced perimeter-rail convertible frame
MODEL AVAILABILITY: Skylark sedan, hardtop & convertible
PRICE: GS package cost $200.53 (bucket seat option also mandatory)
WHEELBASE: 115 inches
WEIGHT: 3,720 pounds
SUSPENSION: heavy-duty w/coil springs front & rear, 0.94-inch front stabilizer bar
STEERING: manual (24:1 ratio) recirculating ball, std; 17.5:1 power-assist, optional
WHEELS: 14x6 stamped-steel, std.; chromed 5-spoke rims, optional
TIRES: 7.75x14
BRAKES: 9.5-inch drums front & rear w/thicker, tougher shoe linings; enlarged wheel cylinders in front; power-assist, optional
ENGINE: 401-cid Wildcat 445 V-8 w/Carter AFB 4-barrel carburetor
TRANSMISSION: 3-speed manual, std; close-ratio 4-speed manual & 2-speed Super Turbine 300 automatic, optional—all featured floor shifters
AXLE RATIO: 3.36:1, std w/manual transmission; 3.08:1 included w/optional automatic; limited-slip differential, optional

The 1964 Tempest's horizontal headlights were traded for stacked units the following year. GTO body styles again numbered three in 1965: coupe, hardtop, and convertible.

added to inhibit body roll, but in the Z16's case the goal primarily involved controlling rear wheel lift due to torque twisting during hard launches.

The costliest muscle car yet—the limited-edition Z16 Malibu—kicked off a high-flying legacy with a high-profile bang. Better late than never, huh?

BUICK

Buick's original recipe for success in this burgeoning market included Skylark, the flagship of the Flint firm's midsize Special line. Finding its way down from full-size ranks, the engine was the "Wildcat 445," a 325-horse mill that traced its roots back to Buick's first modern OHV V-8, introduced a dozen years before. This venerable "nailhead" churned out 445 lbs-ft of torque, hence its official moniker. As for that nickname, it referred to the breed's relatively diminutive valves, which in some minds appeared not much larger than—you guessed it—the head of a nail. For the record, those valves measured 1.875 inches on the intake side, 1.50 on the exhaust—"certainly not the smallest ever seen, [but] not elephantine," according to *Hot Rod's* Eric Dahlquist.

To compensate for those tidy valve diameters, engineers stuffed in a cam with ample lift (0.431-inch) and duration: 302 degrees intake, 295 exhaust. "This combination has led to the famous—or infamous, depending on your persuasion—'rump-rump' Buick idle," added Dahlquist in his May 1965 *Hot Rod* review. Low-restriction dual exhausts also were predictably included, as was a heavy-duty cross-flow radiator for added cooling. A Carter AFB four-barrel supplied fuel/air whenever the hammer went down.

Displacement was 401 cubic inches, 1 more than GM supposedly allowed in intermediate models prior to 1970. Buick promotional people helped make the situation easy enough to overlook by tabbing the first Gran Sport V-8's displacement at "400 cu. in." in all printed references in 1965. *Motor Trend's* Bob McVay fell for this one, repeating the faux figure in his May 1965 road test. But Dahlquist wasn't fooled, nor were his comrades at *Car Life*—in both cases, they reported the correct 401 cubic count.

HOT OFF THE PRESS: 1965 OLDSMOBILE 4-4-2

"We found the 4-4-2 one of the best performance/handling packages on the market, with a price anyone can afford. Here's proof positive that Detroit manufacturers can build cars that perform, handle, and stop, without sacrificing riding comfort."

Bob McVay, Motor Trend, *May 1965*

1965 PONTIAC GTO

CONSTRUCTION: body on perimeter-rail frame
MODEL AVAILABILITY: LeMans coupe, hardtop & convertible
PRICE: $2,787 for coupe, $2,855 for hardtop, $3,093 for convertible (GTO option cost $295.90)
WHEELBASE: 115 inches
WEIGHT: 3,590 pounds
Suspension: heavy-duty w/coil springs front & rear, 0.94-inch front stabilizer bar
STEERING: manual recirculating ball (24:1 ratio), std; 17.5:1 power assist, optional (quicker 20:1 steering optional on its own & w/handling kit)
WHEELS: 14x6 stamped-steel, std; 14x6 Rally wheel, optional
TIRES: 7.75x14 redline, std; whitewall rayon-cord tires available at no extra cost
BRAKES: 9.5-inch 4-wheel drums; power-assist optional
ENGINE: 389-cid V-8 w/500-cfm Carter AFB 4-barrel carburetor
TRANSMISSION: 3-speed Muncie manual w/Hurst shifter[1]; heavy-duty 3-speed*, M20 wide- & M21 close-ratio Hurst-shifted[1] Muncie 4-speeds, & column-shifted two-speed automatic, optional; floor shifter w/console, optional for auto trans
AXLE RATIO: 3.23:1, std; 3.55:1 included with Tri-Power V-8; Safe-T-Track limited-slip differential, optional

1. Some Hurst shifters w/o company stamping on lever were fitted to both 3- & 4-speeds early in 1965 model run

** Top-loader unit sourced from Ford; available after March 1, 1965*

FAMILY TIES: BUICK "NAILHEAD" V-8s, 1953-1966

Buick traded its revered OHV "Fireball" straight-eight for a modern V-8 in 1953, basically in consolation to Flint's body builders, who were no longer allowing room for such tall, long engines beneath their designs' trendy low, low hoods. Also fitted with overhead valves, Buick's new 90-degree bent-eight measured 8.18 inches less from nose to tail compared to its inline forerunner, was 3.38 inches shorter oil pan to air cleaner, and weighed a comparatively scant 625 pounds—a whopping 180 pounds fewer than its big-iron predecessor. Displacement was 322 cubes (up 2 inches) and compression in top form was an industry-leading 8.5:1. Like its history-making GM cousins from Cadillac and Olds, Buick's game changer also featured a rev-conscious short-throw (3.20 inches) crank, and its bore/stroke ratio (1.25) made it Detroit's most oversquare engine to date. Combustion chambers were cone-shaped with spark plugs located centrally overhead, making this mill more of a quasi-hemi-head than a conventional wedge. But, in another concession to overall platform parameters, those cylinder heads were noticeably narrow, the better to fit snuggly between a 1953 Buick's fenders. That slimness in turn forced engineers to position each head's 16 valves inline up high pointing directly skyward on the intake side, a design that made for a rather awkward pushrod/rocker layout (see artwork below) and also limited valve size. To compensate for such small valves while trying to keep up in the 1950s' horsepower race, Buick's better engine designers were soon forced to install some seriously lumpy, long-duration cams, first to help their enlarged 364-cid V-8 reach the 300 horsepower plateau in 1957. Of course the trade-off was a "rumpity-rump" idle that had some mild-mannered customers returning to their dealer to find out what was wrong with their rough-running fine car. Hot rodders and drag racers, on the other hand, considered it sweet music to their ears. Before Chevy's small-block V-8 began turning horsepower hounds' heads away, Buick's relatively light, compact V-8 was a favorite among the hop-up set, who had no problem working around the engine's "nail valves." That term of endearment quickly morphed into "nailhead," a nickname fully entrenched in the gearhead lexicon by the time Buick's Skylark-based Gran Sport debuted in 1965. Buick's nailhead era closed the following year.

YEAR	CID	BORE & STROKE	CR	HORSEPOWER	TORQUE	CARBURETOR	VALVE SIZES
1953	322	4.00 x 3.20	8.5:1	188 @ 4,000	300 @ 2,400	Carter 4-barrel	1.75 x 1.25
1954	264	3.625 x 3.20	8.1:1	150 @ 4,200	240 @ 2,400	Stromberg 2-bl.	1.75 x 1.25
1957	364	4.125 x 3.40	10.0:1	300 @ 4,600	400 @ 3,200	Carter 4-barrel	1.875 x 1.50
1959	401	4.1875 x 3.64	10.5:1	325 @ 4,400	445 @ 2,800	Carter 4-barrel[1]	1.875 x 1.50
1963	425	4.3125 x 3.64	10.25:1	340 @ 4,400	465 @ 2,800	Rochester 4-bl.	1.875 x 1.50
1964	425[2]	4.3125 x 3.64	10.25:1	360 @ 4,400	465 @ 2,800	2 Carter 4-bls	1.875 x 1.50

NOTE: *CID is cubic-inch displacement; CR is compression ratio; bore & stroke and valves size listings in inches.*

1. Or Rochester 4-barrel

2. Optional for Wildcat, Electra 225 & Riviera from 1964 to 1966

NOTE: *Buick offered various nailhead V-8 versions over the years, with compression/output varying depending on transmission application (manual or Dynaflow automatic) or model choice. For example, the 1954–55 264-cid engine was limited to Special models. The engines listed here represent the highest output example built for that year. Topline models (Super/Century/Roadmaster & Invicta/Electra/Wildcat/Riviera) always were treated to higher-powered four-barrel V-8s, while base Buicks (pre-1959 Special & LeSabre) came standard with two-barrels.*

NOTE: *The last 322-cid nailhead, with a maximum of 255 horsepower, was built in 1956.*

NOTE: *The last 364-cid nailhead, with a maximum of 250 horsepower, was built in 1961.*

NOTE: *While not offered direct from Buick, the full-size line's dual-carb setup reportedly was available as a dealer-installed option for the Skylark Gran Sport in 1965 and '66.*

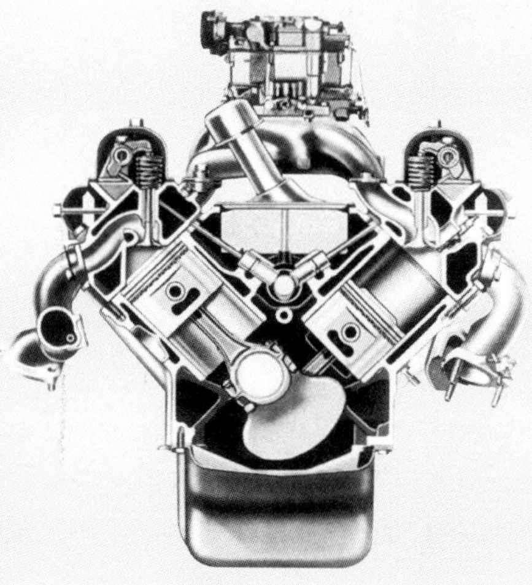

Buick's "nailhead" V-8 featured valves that stood straight up, requiring unconventional rocker arm/pushrod geometry. While that valve angle surely benefited flow on the intake side, it didn't do spent gases any favors. Exhaust flow was forced to take an almost 180-degree turn past those diameter-challenged valves into the ports. Also note the conical combustion chambers and centrally located spark plugs.

Simply saying "Zow!," magazine ads called the Skylark GS a "Superbird," a reference that would take flight again in much more dramatic fashion five years later. According to Buick general manager Edward Rollert, his new muscle machine was "a completely engineered performance car designed to appeal to sports car enthusiasts." And being from Flint, where better cars were built, the classy Gran Sport, in the opinion of *Car Life's* editors, came "off stronger, more distinctive [than standard Skylarks] and with something its owners can appreciate"—that being an incredibly polite asking price. The GS package added a mere $200.53 to the bottom line of a Skylark coupe, sedan, or convertible in 1965.

Along with the Wildcat 445 nailhead, the deal also included beefed suspension and brakes, a boxed convertible frame, and a three-speed manual transmission. A preferred four-speed stick was available, as was Buick's two-speed Super Turbine 300 automatic with its variable-pitch torque converter. Floor shifters were used in all applications, and extra-cost bucket seats were mandated inside. Adding a console with or without a tachometer mounted at its bow was purely optional. All of Buick's typical soft touches were available as well, including air conditioning, power steering, power brakes, and so on. Indeed, "gentleman's hot rod" was a fair description for a fully loaded Gran Sport in 1965.

Oldsmobile cryptologists were forced to rewrite their 4-4-2 code in 1965 after 1964's standard four-speed stick was traded for a three-speed in base applications. Dual exhausts and a four-barrel remained, only this time that carb was bolted atop a new 400 cubic-inch V-8 rated at 340 horsepower. *Mike Mueller*

PONTIAC

A revised Tempest body, now with stacked headlights and revised taillight treatment, appeared this year, and GTO was again available for coupes, hardtops, and convertibles by way of the options list. A truly cool new scoop graced the 1965 hood but was non-functional, at least in most cases. This same style scoop would remain a GTO trademark up through 1967.

Beneath that lid were more horses as an improved intake manifold and revised cylinder heads helped increase standard output to 335 horsepower. Those same improvements translated into 360 horses for the optional Tri-Power 389. New at the corners were larger 7.75x14 standard tires, and optional 14x6 Rally wheels also debuted for 1965. Painted silver, those Rally rims incorporated five cooling slots and were adorned with a center cap and trim ring done in chrome.

In August 1965, dealers began offering a special pan, or "tub," that sealed the Tri-Power V-8's air cleaners to the hood's underside using a large foam gasket. On top, the GTO's previously ornamental hood was modified with replacement trim (installed by the dealer or customer) that unblocked the scoop, allowing cooler, denser air a direct path into the hungry mouths of those three Rochester two-barrels. Although not officially recognized as such at the time, this parts counter option kicked off Pontiac's "Ram Air" legacy (see page 72).

The 1965 4-4-2's 400-cid V-8 was a downsized rendition of Oldsmobile's 425-cube powerplant, also introduced that year for full-size models. *Mike Mueller*

OLDSMOBILE

Olds people changed the code for their second-edition midsize muscle machine, with "4-4-2" now standing for 400 cubic inches, four-barrel carburetor, and dual exhausts. Buyers in 1965 were no longer limited to the Muncie four-speed stick, explaining the main reason for the recoding. A column-shifted three-speed manual was now standard, and joining that carryover Muncie box on the options

HOT OFF THE PRESS: 1965 SHELBY GT350

"All in all, the GT350 is pretty much a brute of a car. There's nothing subtle about it all."
Road & Track, *May 1965*

MOTOR OF THE YEAR: 1965 CHEVROLET 396 TURBO JET

Type	OHV Mk IV big-block, (RPO L37) w/chrome dress-up
Displacement	396 cubic inches
Bore	4.094 inches
Stroke	3.76 inches
Horsepower	375 at 5,600 rpm
Torque	420 at 3,600 rpm
Compression	11:1
Fuel delivery	4150-series Holley 4-barrel carburetor on aluminum intake
Air cleaner	low-restriction dual-snorkel w/chrome-plated lid
Ignition	Delco-Remy distributor
Cooling	5-blade thermo-modulated viscous-drive fan, large-capacity radiator w/fan shroud
Cylinder block	heavy-duty cast-iron w/4-bolt main bearing caps
Crankshaft	forged-steel w/2.75-inch main journals
Connecting rods	forged steel
Pistons	impact-extruded aluminum w/domed head
Cam	hydraulic w/342 degrees duration on intake, 356 degrees on exhaust, 122 degrees of overlap
Rocker ratio	1.70:1
Cylinder heads	cast-iron w/canted valves
Valve sizes	2.19-inch intakes, 1.72-inch exhausts
Valve lift	0.416 inch, intake; 0.500 inch, exhaust
Exhaust system	cast-iron low-restriction manifolds, 2.50-inch main pipes, twin reverse-flow mufflers, 2.25-inch tailpipes

list was the Jetaway automatic transmission, Oldsmobile's version of GM's Super Turbine 300.

A "special duty" Jetaway (also column-shifted) was offered for 4-4-2 applications featuring extra clutches (in forward and reverse) and a recalibrated valve body for more positive shifts. A T-handle floor shifter (with or without a console) was optional for this two-speed auto, as was a Hurst stick for the standard three-speed manual. That Olds made the preferred Hurst linkage available for the mundane three-speed while using its own comparatively clunky gear-changer for four-speeds represented a real head-scratcher not missed by press critics.

Official option nomenclature also changed in 1965 as 1964's B09 police-pursuit deal was exchanged for the aptly named "4-4-2 Performance Package," available for the F-85 club coupe, Cutlass sport coupe, Cutlass hardtop (known in Olds terms as the "Holiday coupe"), and Cutlass convertible—all two-doors. Those 10 four-door 4-4-2 models released in 1964 would be the only examples ever built with such easy rear-seat access.

Included in 1965's Performance Package were all predictable beefs: suspension, frame, driveshaft, and cooling were all treated to heavy-duty upgrades. Those trademark front and rear stabilizer bars returned, and a low-restriction exhaust was installed with "pinched" tailpipes in place of typical resonators.

Truly new in 1965 was a bigger, better power source, which as mentioned fit so well into the latest 4-4-2's reshuffled numbers. Under the hood now was a 400-cube

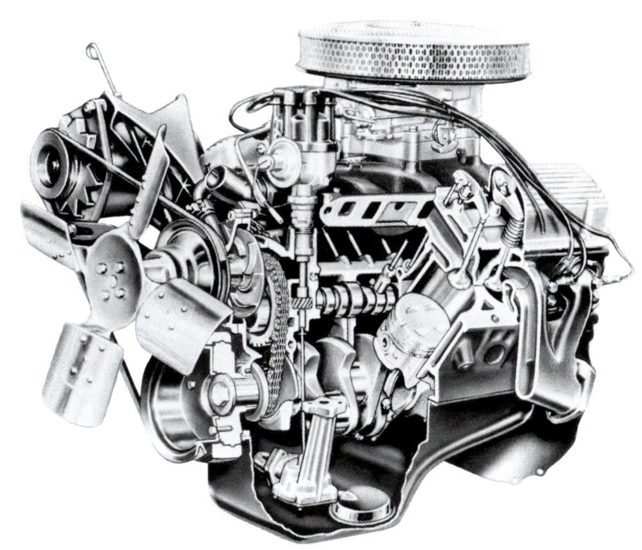

The solid-lifter Hi-Po 289 remained the Mustang's hottest underhood option in 1965. The cam for this 271-horsepower small-block featured 310 degrees duration and 0.460-inch lift on both intake and exhaust. Pistons were cast aluminum and beefed rods featured 3/8-inch bolts with 9/16-inch nuts.

Right: Ford introduced its GT Equipment Group in April 1965, just in time to mark the Mustang's first birthday. Attractive exhaust "trumpets" were included in the GT deal, offered for coupe, fastback, and convertible body styles. Styled steel wheels were optional. *Mike Mueller*

Above: As if the base GT350 wasn't hot enough in 1965, Shelby American also rolled out a full-race version, predictably labeled the "GT350R." Bumpers were deleted and a special front apron was added, as were big front disc brakes. Power came from a modified K-code 289 that produced up to 360 horses. *Mike Mueller*

1965 OLDSMOBILE 4-4-2

CONSTRUCTION: body on reinforced perimeter-rail "police car" frame
MODEL AVAILABILITY: F85 club coupe, Cutlass coupe, Cutlass Holiday hardtop & Cutlass cvt.
PRICE: 4-4-2 Performance Package cost $190.45 for F-85 coupe, $156.02 for Cutlass models
WHEELBASE: 115 inches
WEIGHT: 3,735 pounds
SUSPENSION: heavy-duty w/coil springs front & rear; 0.94-inch front stabilizer bar; 0.875-inch rear stabilizer bar
STEERING: manual (24:1 ratio) recirculating ball, std.; 17.5:1 power-assist, optional
WHEELS: 14x6 stamped-steel
TIRES: 7.75x14 Red-Line
BRAKES: 9.5-inch finned drums, front & rear; power-assist, optional
ENGINE: 400-cid V-8 w/Rochester 4-barrel carburetor
TRANSMISSION: 3-speed w/column shifter, std; 4-speed manual w/floor shifter & 2-speed Jetaway automatic w/column shifter, optional
AXLE RATIO: 3.23:1, std w/manual transmission; 3.08:1 included w/optional automatic; limited-slip differential, optional

little brother to the 425-cid V-8 introduced that year for Oldsmobile's full-size lineup. Fed by a Rochester four-barrel, this developing brute produced a warmly welcomed 345 horsepower, in the process silencing most critics who considered the original 4-4-2's heart to be a bit underwhelming, as well as undersized.

Car and Driver called Oldsmobile's new 400 V-8 "a sweetheart," while others preferred its less amiable side. "This engine gargles and gurgles at idle, thanks to its dual multi-pinch tailpipes, in a manner suggesting a fire in the belly about to be spewed forth," explained a *Car Life* report. "It oozes out 345 bhp without trying, hinting of things to come if this big engine/little car kick lasts." "Keep your eye on Oldsmobile," concluded the *C/D* test crew. "They may surprise us… not to mention their competition."

FORD

It was the Mustang's first birthday, but it was buyers who were treated to gifts. On April 17, 1965, Ford announced two new options packages for its new pony car. One of these was the snazzy "pony interior" with its galloping-horse seat inserts and simulated walnut paneling. The other was the "GT Equipment Group," a sporty addition that helped revive at least some of the fun-loving nature that many critics felt Ford had sadly neglected while transforming the two-seat Mustang I into a more practical regular-production reality.

Priced at $165, the GT package could be added to all three 1965 models; coupe, convertible and the new fastback. The option was only available with one of the 1965 Mustang's two optional four-barrel V-8s, the 225-horsepower 289 Challenger or the 271-horse Hi-Po. Both hot imagery and heavy-duty hardware also were included. Among standard GT fare was the Special Handling Package, which, in typical fashion, simply stiffened things up underneath and added quickened (22:1) steering. All GT Mustangs were fitted with 10-inch front disc brakes and dual exhausts, too.

At the ends of those exhausts were chrome trumpets poking through brightly trimmed cutouts in a special rear valance panel. Further image enhancements came by way of lower bodyside stripes and a unique grille bar framed by fog lamps at each end up front. Completing the GT package was a five-dial instrument panel in place of the standard, rather mundane Falcon-style dashboard.

Suffice it to say that 1965's Hi-Po GT ranked as Ford's hottest, flashiest pony car yet.

Shelby American opened for business in 1962 in Venice, California. Three years later, Carroll Shelby's firm moved into a larger facility adjacent to Los Angeles International Airport (seen here in the background) in order to handle production of GT350 Mustangs, all of which were painted Wimbledon White in 1965. The Cragar wheels seen here were optional, as were blue Le Mans stripes running up and over the body from nose to tail.

SHELBY MUSTANG

Even with the optional K-code small-block, Ford's wildly popular pony didn't exactly thrill everyone in 1964. Some witnesses who had hoped for a true sporting machine, a rival perhaps even to Chevrolet's Corvette, felt jilted. Enter Carroll Shelby, the California-based race car builder who since 1962 had been stuffing Blue-Oval V-8s into those teenie-weenie Britain-sourced AC Ace two-seaters. When Lee Iacocca turned to the Shelby American firm late in 1964 to transform his Mustang into a real racehorse, all was forgiven.

The plan involved building enough street-going GT350 Mustangs to legalize full-race alter egos for Sports Car Club of America (SCCA) B/Production competition, which specified a minimum production run of 100 cars. No problem. Ford supplied the bare-bones 2+2 fastbacks from its San Jose plant in California and Shelby American took care of the rest. GT350 production began in October 1964, with the official public unveiling coming January 27, 1965, to the overwhelming joy of those left disappointed the previous April. "The GT-350 is all that most of us wanted the original Mustang to be in the first place," exclaimed *Car Life* magazine's Jim Wright.

According to *Motor Trend*, what Shelby did was "take a 2+2, inject some Cobra venom, tone up the leg muscles [and] add lightness." Add lightness? Was the tall Texan a magician, too? No, he simply shaved off nearly 200 pounds by, among other things, deleting the back seat (a requirement anyway considering the SCCA B/Production class was for two-seaters) and exchanging Ford's standard steel hood for a scooped fiberglass unit. Beneath was a hopped-up Hi-Po 289 that dynoed at 306 horsepower. On the bottom side was relatively radically modified chassis featuring Koni shocks at the corners and traction bars in back.

All the cars delivered from San Jose to Shelby American showed up wearing Wimbledon White paint, with black appointments inside. Guardsman Blue LeMans racing stripes, running from nose to tail, were optional. All also featured full-size Ford front disc brakes, Borg-Warner T-10 close-ratio four-speeds, burly 9-inch rear ends containing Detroit Locker differentials, and 15x5.5 station wagon wheels.

Shelby American produced an even more limited run of stripped-down GT350R Mustangs for 1965, with the "R" predictably standing for race. R-models quickly proved their worth at the track, with Shelby American driver Ken Miles piloting one to victory in its first SCCA outing in Texas on Valentine's Day 1965. Shelby Mustangs also copped the B/Production title that year.

1965 SHELBY MUSTANG GT350

CONSTRUCTION: unitized body/frame w/fiberglass hood
MODEL AVAILABILITY: 2+2 fastback w/back seat removed
PRICE: $4,311
WHEELBASE: 108 inches
WEIGHT: 2,800 pounds
SUSPENSION: independent upper A-arms, lower control arms, w/coil springs mounted atop A-arms in front & heavy-duty (1.0-inch) stabilizer bar, front; solid axle w/longitudinal leaf springs, back; Koni adjustable shock absorbers & override traction bars (upper A-arms lowered one inch & special lengthened Pitman and idler arms used)
STEERING: manual recirculating ball w/quicker 19:1 ratio
WHEELS: 15x5.5 stamped-steel, std; 15x6 Cragar five-spoke mags, optional
TIRES: 7.75x15 Goodyear Blue Dot
BRAKES: 11.375-inch front discs, 10-inch drums in back; sintered metallic linings
ENGINE: 289-cid Windsor V-8 w/Tri-Y headers, 715-cfm Holley 4-barrel carburetor & glass-packed bullet mufflers exiting through short "cutout" tailpipes
TRANSMISSION: Borg-Warner T-10 4-speed w/aluminum case
AXLE RATIO: 3.89:1 gears in 9-inch housing w/ratcheting Detroit Locker differential

Right: An exclusive grille and extra trim was standard for Mercury's Cyclone in 1965, as were the carryover simulated chrome wheel covers seen in 1964. A Performance Handling Package was optional. *Mike Mueller*

Right: Standard for Mercury's Cyclone in 1965 was a 225-horsepower 289 small-block fed by a four-barrel carb. Although some sources that year claimed this was the only available engine, the 271-horsepower High Performance Windsor V-8 was an option, albeit a rarely seen one. *Mike Mueller*

HOT OFF THE PRESS: 1965 MERCURY CYCLONE

"The Cyclone's 225-horsepower engine had what you'd consider a healthy feeling at any speed between idle and 3000 rpm. Then it felt like four more cylinders were suddenly added and came on very strongly."

John Ethridge, Motor Trend, *May 1965*

1965 MERCURY CYCLONE

CONSTRUCTION: unitized body/frame
MODEL AVAILABILITY: Comet hardtop
PRICE: $2,625
WHEELBASE: 114 inches
WEIGHT: 3,060 pounds
SUSPENSION: single lower control arms w/stabilizing strut & coil springs, front; solid axle with longitudinal leaf springs, back
STEERING: manual recirculating ball; power-assist, optional
WHEELS: 14x5
TIRES: 6.95x14, std; 7.35x14 mandatory option for all Comets equipped with 271-horsepower 289 V-8
BRAKES: 10-inch drums, front & rear
ENGINE: 225-horsepower 289-cid Windsor V-8 w/480-cfm Autolite 4100-series 4-barrel carburetor, std; 271-horsepower 289-cid High Performance V-8, optional
TRANSMISSION: 3-speed manual, std (4-speed* & 3-speed Multi-Drive automatic, optional)
AXLE RATIO: 3.00:1

** 4-speed was mandatory option along w/271-hp 289 V-8*

MERCURY

Mercury's Cyclone whipped its way back onto the scene in 1965 with all the same standard goodies offered the year before plus an exclusive grille treatment. The Super Cyclone 289 also returned, now rated at 225 horses. This four-barrel-fed Windsor was by no means up to the task of taking on GM's big-cube intermediates, but there was help on the options list as the K-code Hi-Po 289 was again available for all 1965 Comets, despite press claims that said the 225/289 was the only engine installed in Cyclones that year.

Among those who reported the 225-horsepower limitation for the 1965 Cyclone, *Motor Trend's* John Ethridge at first called the hydraulic-lifter Super Cyclone small-block "exhilarating" during testing before a burst to 5,000 revs induced valve float, ending the fun. At least the Merc he was testing was fitted with an available favored four-speed stick, as well as an arguably cool fiberglass hood, a new option for 1965.

So what if most of those early Cyclones constituted more hot air than hot performance? At least it was a start.

CHEVY NOT IN RACING?

Chevrolet's read-to-race Black Widow featured various special chassis modifications (including six-lug truck hubs and wheels) and the company's new-for-1957 fuel-injected 283 small-block. *Mike Mueller*

While clearly no match for Pontiac's hottest GTO, the new L79 Chevelle nonetheless had its fans in 1965. "It's hard to believe Chevy's out of racing," wrote *Cars* magazine's Gordon Chittenden after testing the 350-horse A-body. Then along came a true midsize milestone. "While Chevrolet might not be in racing, [it does] build plenty of performance vehicles," explained a *Motorcade* report following the Z16 Malibu's midyear introduction. "It appears that while Chevy doesn't seem to mind if their cars finish far back in the pack at the track, they aren't about to lose any street races."

Say what? The Bow-Tie brand not in racing?

Though this wasn't exactly true, GM execs did discourage their divisions from associating with trackside types during the 1960s, this after the Automobile Manufacturers Association had directed them to do so in 1957. After diving into NASCAR racing two years before with its original small-block V-8, Chevrolet was at the time turning up the heat on the competition, culminating in a complete factory racer, the so-called "Black Widow," the first of Vince Piggins' many contributions to Chevy's revered racing legacy.

The Black Widow tale began in the fall of 1956, when newly promoted Chevrolet general manager Ed Cole gave the go-ahead to newly hired Piggins to organize the Southern Engineering Development Company (SEDCO), an Atlanta-based organization tasked with overseeing the division's stock car racing ventures. SEDCO became home to the race-prepped Widows, fitted with Chevy's new fuel-injected 283 small-block. A Black Widow took NASCAR's Grand National championship in 1957, but the story was cut short by AMA actions that summer. Immediate repercussions included SEDCO's closure, leaving Piggins to work on more mundane engineering projects involving mostly trucks.

Though Black Widows were exterminated, Chevys continued running strong at the track. Pontiacs, too. Bystanders in February 1958 couldn't miss the prominent presence of PMD chief Bunkie Knudsen at Daytona, there celebrating a NASCAR victory by a Pontiac pilot. GM's answer to the obvious question? The wealthy Knudsen was not representing his company, he was fulfilling his own personal need for speed by financing "private" efforts out of his own deep pockets. Right.

The plot thickened further in November 1961 when Knudsen left Pontiac for Chevrolet after Ed Cole was promoted to GM group executive in charge of car and truck divisions. A healthy horsepower hound like Bunkie, Cole had ensured that his company's cars stayed hot during his five-year run as general manager, even going as far as reopening a central office dedicated to assisting racers running Chevys. By 1960, Piggins was back in the race-winning business, this time as head of the Engineering Product Information department.

With an ally on high like Cole, Knudsen had no problem stirring things up at Chevrolet like he had at Pontiac, though he probably needed little help doing so. As former Fleet and Special Services man Jim Mattison explained in March 2014, "Piggins and Knudsen were damned good at begging for forgiveness instead of asking for permission."

What part of "do not race" did Knudsen and crew not understand? "Chevrolet clearly was interpreting the AMA stipulations as they saw fit back then," added Mattison. "As Smokey [Yunick] used to say, if you're not interpreting the rules, you're not winning." It then was left to GM's top brass to define things in 1963, supposedly leaving Chevy racers high and dry. But were the Bow-Tie boys really not racing during the 1960s?

An honest answer was supplied by engineer turned journalist Paul Van Valkenburgh in his 1972 book, *Chevrolet=Racing? Fourteen Years of Raucous Silence!* Based on inside information garnered during the author's days working in Chevrolet's Research and Development department, this epic exposé detailed the Bow-Tie brand's competitive escapades from 1957 to 1970.

"When the [original] book was published, [Chevy general manager] John DeLorean asked, 'Did we really do all this stuff?' " wrote Van Valkenburgh 28 years later. "When assured it was all true, he reportedly decided that all they could do was ignore it." As much as GM execs expected the world to believe they weren't involved in racing, some employees were in it up to their eyeballs.

"In that period, Chevrolet probably acquired more successes and more technical knowledge of high performance than any other company in the world," wrote Van Valkenburgh while introducing his original book, which 25 years later ended up a highly valued collectors' item. All that retroactive demand inspired a 2000 reprint, which even Chevrolet officials wanted to see, demonstrating just how much attitudes can change given a decade or so.

By the 1980s, Chevy people had grown more than proud of their on-track history, so much so that in March 1989 they finally changed the name of Piggins' old "Product Performance" department to Chevrolet Engineering's "Raceshop," which then morphed a few years later into the GM Motorsports Technology Group (MTG), then simply GM Motorsports.

Today Chevy's race-winning legacy commonly stars in advertising campaigns—and the big guys upstairs no longer have to tune out.

Chevrolet wasn't supposed to be in racing at the time, but Roger Penske's dark blue Sunoco Camaros dominated SCCA Trans-Am competition—with ample factory support—in 1968 and 1969.

Zora Arkus-Dunto initially hoped to build 125 lightweight Grand Sport Corvettes for 1963, but GM's anti-racing edict—sent down in January that year—shut the project down after only five were built. The first two of those five coupes were later converted into roadsters. Shown here is Grand Sport #005, owned by Florida collector Bill Tower. *Mike Mueller*

Right: New for 1965 in Plymouth's B-body lineup was the flashy Satellite. Upscale trim was standard for this flagship and included wheel-opening moldings and bright louvers on each rear quarter just ahead of the taillights. *Mike Mueller*

Below: In Plymouth applications, the 426-S V-8 wore the familiar "Commando" name in 1965. Chrome dress-up was just the icing on cake; output again was 365 horsepower. *Mike Mueller*

DODGE & PLYMOUTH

Chrysler's 426-S option returned for an encore in 1965 and again included all the important goodies—transmission choice (Hurst-shifted A-833 four-speed or Torqueflite automatic) and heavy-duty suspension/brakes—along with those 365 horses supplied by the corporation's biggest RB-series V-8 to date. The package was available only for the corporation's B-body intermediates, four-doors or two, with Plymouth's new midsize flagship in the Belvedere line, Satellite, representing the snazziest way to fly. Limited to sporty two-door hardtop and convertible forms, Satellite came standard with extra trim, bucket seats, and a console, heightening the 426-S experience even further. Dodge's B-body also got a new name, Coronet, offered in three trim levels (plus a Deluxe version of the base model), all also delivered with the 426-S V-8 up front in 1965.

Motor Trend's Bob McVay called Dodge's 365-horse, four-speed Coronet 500 hardtop "one of the hottest, most exciting machines we've tested this season." "The 'S' stands for strong," added *Car Life* after testing the same combo. "Perform it does, with a capital 'P'," continued McVay. "In any gear and at any speed, in any traffic situation, the '426' Coronet fairly leaped whenever we gave it the nudge. The special suspension and generous horsepower work very well together, making the car very safe to drive fast."

While other critics typically pined for front discs, McVay was impressed with the notably safe nature of those 11-inch cop stoppers. "The most we can say about the car's husky police brakes is that they're about the best drum units available," he concluded. "They gave stopping power without fading and with a minimum of swerving, even when hot."

Chrysler's 426-S wedge did not return for 1966; in its place was another 426-cube V-8, this one topped by heads featuring hemispherical combustion chambers.

PLYMOUTH BARRACUDA FORMULA S

Detroit's "other" pony car, Barracuda, looked awfully cute to many casual car-watchers but did absolutely nothing to stir the souls of driving-glove-wearing Walter Mitty types early on. "When the sports-oriented variation of Plymouth's Valiant line appeared on the marketplace little more than a year ago, it created a great deal of curiosity and comment," began a *Car Life* review early in 1965. "Close examination and evaluation, however, yielded one conclusion: It was all very much an ordinary Valiant with a new body style. Among others, [we] recommended at the time that Chrysler-Plymouth ought to make some performance-type options available to give it some character and flavor to match its intriguing shape."

Done.

1965 PLYMOUTH BARRACUDA FORMULA S

CONSTRUCTION: unitized body/frame
MODEL AVAILABILITY: fastback sport coupe
PRICE: Formula S package added $258 to the V-8 Barracuda's $2,586 base price
WHEELBASE: 106 inches
WEIGHT: 3,560 pounds
SUSPENSION: independent wishbones w/heavy-duty torsion bars and thickened (0.87-inch) stabilizer bar, front; solid axe w/longitudinal heavy-duty leaf springs, rear; Firm-Ride shock absorbers
STEERING: manual recirculating ball (24:1:1 ratio); 15.7:1 power-assist, optional
WHEELS: 14x5.5J heavy-gauge stamped-steel
TIRES: 6.95x14 Goodyear Blue Streak
BRAKES: 10.0-inch drums, front & rear; power-assisted front discs, optional (dealer-installed)
ENGINE: 273-cid V-8 w/Carter AFB 4-barrel carburetor
TRANSMISSION: 3-speed manual, std; 4-speed A-833 manual w/Hurst shifter & 3-speed Torqueflite automatic, optional
AXLE RATIO: 3.23:1; Sure-Grip differential, optional

COMET CONUNDRUM

When Mercury's second-edition Cyclone stormed the streets, more than one magazine road tester was left mildly disappointed by the apparent lack of any optional oomph under the hood. "The only available engine offered in the Cyclone is the 225-hp, four-barrel-carb powerplant called the 'Comet Cyclone Super 289 V-8,'" wrote John Ethridge in *Motor Trend's* May 1965 issue. "Unfortunately, there's no option like the 271-hp '289' solid-lifter V-8 offered for the Mustang."

Ah, but official Mercury paperwork begged to differ. Features catalogs for 1965 clearly listed an available "Comet Cyclone High-Performance 289 V-8," the aforementioned 271-horse Windsor small-block that had served so well as the original Cyclone's hottest (albeit rare) option. Curiously, Merc men in 1964 had opted to mix up their engine codes, using the "K" reference familiar to Mustangers for the Cyclone's base 210-horse 289 while assigning a "D" tag to their Hi-Po 289s. But all was well again the following year as the now-revered K-code returned for Mercury's High-Performance 289, leaving 1965's 225-horsepower Windsor wearing an "A."

Intriguing as well were 1965's published specs. One Mercury source listed a single exhaust for the K-code 289, while another mentioned the expected duals. That latter publication, a pamphlet titled "Comet Performance for '65," also detailed the complete High-Performance package, which consisted of the 271-horsepower V-8 coupled with various other mandated options: heavy-duty suspension, four-speed top-loader, "low-profile" 7.35x14 rayon tires, and 42-amp heavy-duty alternator. Price for this purpose-built deal was $440.10; $516.10 if optional transistorized ignition equipment was added into the mix. Lastly, this pamphlet explained further, in rather fine print, that the Comet Cyclone High-Performance V-8 was "available now at your Comet Dealer on Dealer Special Order."

Don Watson's mostly original 1965 Comet seen here is one of those dealer-ordered specialties. After watching his brother-in-law, George Pils, take delivery of a similar Hi-Po Comet in April 1965 via Scarritt Motors in St. Petersburg, Florida, Watson decided immediately to buy one of his own; a low-buck, high-performance machine ready to go street racing. Like Pils, he chose a no-frills, lightweight sedan from the lowest rung on the Comet ladder, the 202 series. And, again like his bro-in-law, he was told the 271-horsepower option wasn't available for that model; it would have to be sourced using a Domestic Special Order (DSO) code. Watson's eager-to-please salesman at Scarritt even went so far as to confirm his special request (DSO #8220) personally by phone with assembly plant managers in Mcutchen, New Jersey.

Watson drove his Hi-Po Comet off the Scarritt lot on July 20, 1965. Per additional special requests, it featured 4.11:1 gears out back and a fiberglass hood up front, the latter being a new Cyclone option that year. Pils also had ordered the 'glass hood, and when he took his white sedan (called "The Florida Goose") to Indianapolis for the 1967 NHRA Nationals, he was informed that his lightweight lid wasn't legal; it technically wasn't available from the factory for that car. No problem: he simply went out to the parking lot, found a correct Comet hood stamped out of steel, talked a deal, and traded right there and then.

Watson's Hi-Po Comet also was delivered with a single tailpipe, backing up what some Mercury paperwork reported in 1965. Also odd were the standard 289 exhaust manifolds in place of the better-flowing units bolted up to K-code V-8s in Mustang applications. All other Comet engines, including the Cyclone's A-code 289, used single exhausts in 1965; apparently a suitable dual system for the little-known K-code option hadn't been developed. But again no prob. Jardine headers quickly went on in preparation for some serious stoplight derby action,

Showing barely 25,000 miles on its odometer, this 1965 K-code Comet 202 sedan was bought by Don Watson in July 1965 and remains in his hands today. Notice the fiberglass Cyclone hood, one of this rare Mercury's various special-order features. *Tom Shaw*

as did stump-pulling 5.67:1 gears in a limited-slip differential, labeled "Power Transfer" in Mercury applications.

Once in the wild, Watson's street-racing Merc became a true terror on secluded roads south of St. Pete back in the day. As Don told former *Muscle Car Review* editor Tom Shaw in 2013, "with the tall gear, lots of rpm, and light weight, [my] little Comet got out quick, and the bigger boys couldn't get hooked up quick enough to catch it. I never lost a race."

He also has never let go of his curious Comet, which hasn't been fully restored but was "revived" with the help of good friend Kenny Van Zill. All documentation has survived as well, demonstrating further peculiarities like differing engine codes. The correct "K" appears in the car's papers, but "A" is stamped in various places on the Comet itself, including the door tag.

Additional mystery surrounds the production total for 1965's Hi-Po Comet. According to Van Zill, Scarritt Motors also delivered a third, a Caliente, along with Pils and Watson's 202 sedans. Ford records show that 90 were built that year, but it's unclear as to which models are referenced by that figure. Many Comet fans claim that count refers only to Cyclones, but others aren't so sure.

"I do not know of a solid verification of this number," said Rob Day, who heads the Cyclone/Montego/Torino Registry. "I feel the 90 covers all Comet models, not just Cyclones, though none of the others have turned up with a K engine yet, and may never." Presently the CMT Registry shows only two K-code 1965 Comets, and both are Cyclones.

Day also had a thought or two concerning the K-code Comet confusion witnessed 50 years ago. "It's hard to compare how things worked back then to now," he added in November 2014. "Paper and pencil and rotary phones got things done [in 1965]. Due to the way info spread back then, not every dealer or media person knew the ins and outs."

Like John Ethridge?

All Hi-Po 289 V-8s installed in Mustangs featured free-flowing cast-iron exhaust manifolds. Standard 289 manifolds (backed by a single tailpipe) initially were installed on this engine in 1965 but were quickly traded out for the Jardine headers seen here. *Tom Shaw*

FAMILY TIES: CHRYSLER LA-SERIES V-8s

Chrysler's modern small-block era began in 1964 following the debut of its new LA-series V-8s, with that "L" reportedly standing for "light." Like Ford's Windsor V-8, the LA relied on cutting-edge thinwall casting techniques to slice away as many as 55 pounds from the aging A-series V-8 it was based on. Some also say the L stood for "lower," considering that the LA cylinder block featured a shortened deck height compared to its A-series ancestors. Others (including Chrysler people themselves) occasionally refer to the LA small-blocks as "A" engines, too, but keeping that L in place represents the only correct reference, especially considering the various big differences between the two. Along with contrary measurements, the LA also featured typical wedge-shaped combustion chambers, while the A stuck with the poly-head design that dated back to 1955. Plymouth introduced the first A-series poly, a 277-cid V-8, the following year. A 301-cid version followed in 1957, as did the 318 A-engine that remained a Plymouth staple up through 1966. Dodge traded its hemi-based poly-head for that same 318-cid V-8 in 1960 and also kept it running until '66. A 273-cid LA wedge-head became available for Valiant, Dart and Barracuda in 1964 before also joining the B-body options list the following year. Sometimes confused with its A-series ancestor, a 318-cid LA small-block appeared in 1967 and remained a mundane mainstay (topped into the Seventies by only a two-barrel) in the Dodge/Plymouth lineup for the remainder of the millennium. New for 1968 was a truly hot LA displacing 340 cubes. Only four-barrels fed this 275-horsepower small-block during its all-too-short career, which ended in 1973. The largest LA, displacing 360 cubic inches, appeared in 1971 and eventually sported both two- and four-barrel Carters but was no match for the outgoing 340. The last passenger-car application for the 360 came in 1980.

YEAR	CID	BORE & STROKE	CR	HORSEPOWER	TORQUE	CARBURETOR	VALVE SIZES
1964	273	3.630 x 3.31	8.8:1	180 @ 4,200	260 @ 1,600	Carter BBD 2-bl.	1.78 x 1.50
1965	273[1]	3.630 x 3.31	10.5:1	235 @ 5,200	280 @ 4,000	Carter AFB 4-bl.	1.78 x 1.50
1967	318	3.910 x 3.31	9.2:1	230 @ 4,400	340 @ 2,400	Stromberg 2-bl.	1.78 x 1.50
1968	340	4.040 x 3.31	10.5:1	275 @ 5,000	340 @ 3,200	Carter AVS 4-bl.	2.02 x 1.60
1970	340[2]	4.040 x 3.31	10.5:1	290 @ 5,000	340 @ 3,200	3 Holley 2-bls.	2.02 x 1.60
1971	360	4.000 x 3.58	8.7:1	255 @ 4,400	360 @ 2,400	Carter BBD 2-bl.	1.88 x 1.60
1974	360	4.000 x 3.58	8.4:1	245 @ 4,800	320 @ 3,600	Carter 4-barrel[3]	1.88 x 1.60

NOTE: *CID is cubic-inch displacement; CR is compression ratio; bore & stroke and valves size listings in inches.*

1. A-body option; included in Barracuda's Formula S package

2. Installed exclusively in Plymouth's AAR 'Cuda and Dodge's Challenger T/A

3. Thermoquad carburetor

TIME SLIPS: 1965

MODEL	¼-MILE PERFORMANCE	SOURCE
Pontiac GTO[1]	14.5 seconds at 100 mph	*Car Life,* May 1965
Chevrolet Malibu SS 396	14.60 seconds at 100 mph	*Popular Hot Rodding,* September 1965
Shelby Mustang GT350	14.70 seconds at 90 mph	*Road & Track,* May 1965
Oldsmobile 4-4-2	15.0 seconds at 98 mph	*Car and Driver,* May 1965
Buick Gran Sport	15.3 seconds at 88 mph	*Car Life,* May 1965
Dodge Coronet 426S	15.4 seconds at 89 mph	*Car Life,* May 1965
Mustang "Hi-Po"	15.9 seconds at 89 mph[2]	*Motor Trend,* January 1965
Plymouth Barracuda Formula S	15.9 seconds at 89 mph	*Car Life,* June 1965
Mercury Cyclone	17.1 seconds at 82 mph	*Motor Trend,* May 1965

1. Equipped w/optional 360-hp Tri-Power V-8

2. Car and Driver *published a "questionable" 14.0-second ¼-mile sprint for a 271-hp Mustang fastback (w/optional 4.11:1 gears) in its October 1964 issue undoubtedly relying on a specially "tuned" model, as was this magazine's not-uncommon practice.* Motor Trend's *January 1965 test car, another K-code fastback, used standard 3.89:1 cogs.*

Fortunately Plymouth people opted to distance their newborn pony car from its comparatively mundane beginnings the second time around. First off, the Valiant badge seen on the Barracuda's tail in 1964 was quietly deep-sixed. Snazzy racing stripes and wider 14-inch sport wheels also joined 1965's options list.

Critics who complained of the Barracuda's mild-mannered nature in 1964 were silenced in short order after the Formula S arrived the following year. Though certainly not a GTO-beater, this nimble pony represented a nice start to a proud Plymouth performance legacy.

New on 1965's options list was the Performance Group and the Sports Group, the latter featuring a three-spoke simulated wood-grain steering wheel, whitewall tires, and wheel covers that mimicked bolt-on mags. This package was available with both six-cylinder and V-8 models. The Performance Group added the Rallye suspension and a four-barrel-fed small-block V-8, the "Commando 273." Also listed as a separate option, Rallye underpinnings consisted of predictably beefed-up torsion bars and leaf springs, as well as a stiffened 0.82-inch front stabilizer bar.

Plymouth's Commando 273 V-8 produced 235 horsepower, 55 more than the base small-block, and all those extra ponies instantly transformed the second-edition Barracuda, as *Car and Driver* explained, "from a flabby boulevardier into a rugged middleweight." Zero-to-60 performance was 8 seconds flat, according to *Car Life*, not bad for the time.

As it was, straight-line brute strength wasn't Plymouth's goal during the Barracuda's early years. Witness the effort of engineer Scott Harvey, who spent his free time winning rally championships in SCCA racing. Harvey was the driving force behind a third new 1965 options group, the Formula S package. Though it did include the 235-horse 273, this deal's main focus was handling. Hence, the Rallye foundation, complemented with Firm-Ride shocks, was included, as were widened (to 5.5 inches) 14-inch wheels shod in specially prepared Goodyear Blue Streak 6.95x14 tires. Accenting this wheel/tire combo were those simulated bolt-on wheel covers. A 6,000-rpm tach was standard inside, and a buyer also could've enhanced the image further with an optional racing stripe that ran down the middle of the car from nose to tail. Available on its own without the Formula S option, this stripe was done in five colors, depending on exterior paint choice.

Bam! Just like that Plymouth's pony was in the race.

Also new on 1965's Barracuda options list was Plymouth's solid-lifter, four-barrel-fed "Commando 273" LA-series V-8, rated at 235 horsepower.

UNDER THE HOOD: 1965'S HOTTEST V-8s*

MODEL	CID	BORE & STROKE	CR	HORSEPOWER	TORQUE
Pontiac GTO[1]	389	4.06 x 3.75	10.75:1	360 @ 5,200	424 @ 3,600
Chevrolet SS 396	396	4.094 x 3.76	11:1	375 @ 5,600	420 @ 3,600
Buick GS	401	4.19 x 3.64	10.25:1	325 @ 4,400	445 @ 2,800
Olds 4-4-2	400	4.00 x 3.975	10.25:1	345 @ 4,800	440 @ 3,200
Ford/Mercury[2]	289	4.00 x 2.87	10:1	271 @ 6,000	312 @ 3,400
Shelby Mustang GT350	289	4.00 x 2.87	11.5:1	306 @ 6,000	329 @ 4,200
Dodge/Plymouth	426	4.25 x 3.75	10.3:1	365 @ 4,800	470 @ 3,200
Plymouth Barracuda	273	3.63 x 3.31	10.5:1	235 @ 5,200	280 @ 4,000

NOTE: *CID is cubic-inch displacement; CR is compression ratio; bore/stroke in inches.*
** Discounting factory super-stocks, full-size model lines & Corvette*
1. Optional Tri-Power V-8
2. Optional High Performance 289 V-8 for Ford Fairlane/Mustang & Mercury Comet

BY THE NUMBERS: 1965 PRODUCTION COUNTS

PONTIAC GTO	coupe	8,319	
	hardtop	55,722	
	convertible	11,311	
	total	**75,352**	(54,805 w/335-hp 389 V-8, 20,547 w/Tri-Power)
OLDSMOBILE 4-4-2	F-85 club coupe	1,087	(109 w/3-spd, 736 w/4-spd, 242 w/auto)
	Cutlass spt coupe	5,713	(287 w/3-spd, 3,164 w/4-spd, 2,262 w/auto)
	Cutlass hardtop	14,735	(204 w/3-spd, 8,140 w/4-spd, 6,391 w/auto)
	Cutlass convertible	3,468	(90 w/3-spd, 1,695 w/4-spd, 1,683 w/auto)
	total	**25,003**	
BUICK GRAN SPORT	sedan	2,282	(405 w/3-spd, 614 w/4-spd, 1,263 w/auto)
	hardtop	11,351	(604 w/3-spd, 3,077 w/4-spd, 7,670 w/auto)
	convertible	2,147	(123 w/3-spd, 598 w/4-spd, 1,426 w/auto)
	total	**15,780**	
CHEVROLET SS 396	hardtop	200	
	convertible	1	
	total	**201**	
FORD MUSTANG GT		**15,106**	(includes hardtops, fastbacks & convertibles)
SHELBY GT350	production models	504	
	prototypes, etc.	22	(includes 4 drag cars)
	GT350R competition cars	36	(includes 3 prototypes)
	total	**562**	(all 2+2 fastbacks painted Wimbledon White)
MERCURY CYCLONE		**12,347**	(all hardtops)
PLYMOUTH 426-S	Belvedere I 2-dr sedan	128	(86 w/4-speed, 42 w/auto)
	Belvedere I 4-dr sedan	5	(2 w/4-speed, 3 w/auto)
	Belvedere II 2-dr hrdtp	544	(380 w/4-speed, 164 w/auto)
	Belvedere II, 4-dr sedan	6	(1 w/4-speed, 5 w/auto)
	Belvedere convertible	13	(7 w/4-speed, 6 w/auto)
	Satellite 2-dr hardtop	800	(535 w/4-speed, 265 w/auto)
	Satellite convertible	65	(44 w/4-speed, 21 w/auto)
	total	**1,561**	
DODGE 426-S	Coronet 2-dr sedan	16	(11 w/4-speed, 5 w/auto)
	Coronet 2-dr sedan*	175	(131 w/4-speed, 44 w/auto)
	Coronet 4-dr sedan*	8	(3 w/4-speed, 5 w/auto)
	Coronet 440 2-dr sedan	585	(403 w/4-speed, 182 w/auto)
	Coronet 440 convertible	31	(21 w/4-speed, 10 w/auto)
	Coronet 440 4-dr sedan	9	(2 w/4-speed, 7 w/auto)
	Coronet 500 2-dr hdtp	1,169	(729 w/4-speed, 440 w/auto)
	Coronet 500 convertible	124	(77 w/4-speed, 47 w/auto)
	total	**2,117**	(* Deluxe version)

NOTE: *Production data was supplied by various sources, including Christo Datini at the GM Heritage Center, Kevin Marti (Ford material) at Marti Auto Works (www.martiauto.com), the Shelby American Automobile Club (www.saac.com), and Galen Govier (Mopar material) at Galen's Tag Service (www.galengovier.com).*

SPEED SENSITIVE

A burgeoning sensation in 1965, Detroit's original muscle car hit its peak a scant five years later then rapidly rolled off into the sunset, a victim of multiple assaults, not the least of which coming courtesy of your friendly neighborhood insurance agent. Basically blaming rising insurance costs, a June 1970 *Popular Hot Rodding* article, co-written by Roger Huntington and Lee Kelley, asked the question, "Will there be any '71 super cars?" Reporting payment increases as high as 50 percent, PHR's veteran horsepower hounds pointed out that "insurance rates are slowly strangling high-performance factory cars today." Average muscle car premiums had gone up about $200 over a six month span early in the year, and it was predicted that a young man under the age of 25 would be paying as much as $500 yearly to insure "a late factory super car" by the end of 1970.

Helping the insurance industry hike those rates on high-performance cars was a newfound national focus on highway safety, initially sharpened thanks to the efforts of Connecticut Senator Abraham Ribicoff. A year's worth of congressional hearings kicked off by Ribicoff in May 1965 resulted in the finger of blame for unforgivable traffic death tolls turning away from so-called reckless American drivers (who'd commonly been targeted up to that point), re-aimed instead at reportedly negligent automakers. Those hearings also immortalized East Coast lawyer Ralph Nader, whose legendary literary attack on US car companies (General Motors, most specifically), *Unsafe at Any Speed,* was published in November 1965.

"For over half a century, the automobile has brought death, injury, and the most inestimable sorrow and deprivation to millions of people," began Nader's grim prose. "With Medea-like intensity, this mass trauma began rising sharply four years ago reflecting new and unexpected ravages by the motor vehicle. A 1959 Department of Commerce report projected that 51,000 persons would be killed by automobiles in 1975. That figure will probably be reached in 1965, a decade ahead of schedule."

Nader was present in the gallery on June 24, 1966, when the US Senate voted unanimously to pass a bill that would become the National Traffic and Motor Vehicle Safety Act. Also passed unanimously by the House, this landmark legislation was signed into law on September 8, 1966, by President Lyndon Johnson, who proclaimed that "[automotive] safety is no luxury item, no optional extra; it must be a normal cost of doing business."

One month later, another act of Congress established the US Department of Transportation, which began official operation on April 1, 1967. Various other agencies were born of the same legislation to hopefully help minimize Nader's "mass trauma," under DOT administration, until the National Highway Traffic Safety Administration (NHTSA) was created in 1970 by that year's Highway Safety Act.

Initial NHTSA responsibilities included creating and enforcing various Federal Motor Vehicle Safety Standards (FMVSS), automotive industry regulations originally enacted in 1967. Adopted in March that year, the first of these standards, "FMVSS 209," established minimum seat belt requirements. Among other things, body-side marker lights also began showing up on all American cars in 1968 via the FMVSS process, with the goal being to improve nighttime visibility.

Issued in April 1971, FMVSS 215 specified that 1973 models must feature front bumpers capable of withstanding 5-miles per hour collisions and rear bumpers worthy of 2.5-miles per hour impacts. Also written in 1971, FMVSS 216 dealt with roll-over crash worthiness and was a guiding factor in GM's 1973 Colonnade coupe redesign for its midsize lines, which incorporated Detroit's sturdiest roof to date. Of course, the tradeoff in both cases involved notable gains in both weight and cost, results not missed by more than one press critic.

Fortunately all eventually came out in the wash as American automakers later learned how to build safer cars while keeping pounds and dollars in line. Too bad those lessons had to come the hard way.

HOT OFF THE PRESS: 1965 DODGE CORONET 426S

"Dodge's Coronet 500, equipped with the famous 426-inch V-8, could easily support the title of 'Super/Sleeper of the Year'—there's no exterior indication that's it's anything special. Only when you put your foot in it does the truth come out."

Bob McVay, Motor Trend, *June 1965*

HOT OFF THE PRESS: 1965 PLYMOUTH BARRACUDA FORMULA S

"If any single general observation can be made about the Formula S it might be that it really earned its stripes. The first encounter with twisting roads revealed that corners could be safely negotiated at double or even triple posted limits."

Eric Dahlquist, Hot Rod, *February 1965*

CHAPTER 3

1966 HEADS UP

CHRYSLER TAKES ITS HEMI TO THE STREET

Chrysler's 426 Hemi V-8 surely needs no introduction. More than 10,500 of these monster mills were installed in Dodge and Plymouth muscle cars between 1966 and 1971. A 1968 example appears here. *Mike Mueller*

HOT OFF THE PRESS: 1966 PLYMOUTH BELVEDERE 426 HEMI

"It's big news that in 1966 anyone can buy Plymouth's intermediate-sized Belvedere, right off the showroom floor, with a slightly de-tuned '426-Hemi' and have a darn good chance of winning his class in A/ or AA/Stock right off the bat with only minor modifications."
Bob McVay, Motor Trend, *October 1965*

On January 9, 2014, Chrysler Group LLC's Mopar service, parts and customer-care group announced a year-long birthday celebration for one of Detroit's all-time greatest powerplants. "[We are] proud to mark the 50th anniversary of the introduction of the Gen II 426 Hemi, a revolutionary engine that inspired a long line of quality products in our brand's portfolio," said Mopar president and CEO Pietro Gorlier. "The success of the race Hemi launched a unique brand of sought-after muscle cars, and that is something we are very proud of."

NASCAR officials may have banned the second-generation Hemi after it dominated stock car racing in 1964 (taking 26 checkered flags), but it continued kicking butt on quarter-mile dragstrips the following year, further hammering home a high-performance legacy that continues running strong today—both at the track and on the street. Modern versions of that race Hemi pioneer now power all

UNDER THE HOOD: 1966'S HOTTEST V-8s*

MODEL	CID	BORE & STROKE	CR	HORSEPOWER	TORQUE
Dodge/Plymouth Hemi	426	4.250 x 3.750	10.25:1	425 @ 5,000	490 @ 4,000
Dodge/Plymouth	273	3.63 x 3.31	10.5:1	235 @ 5,200	280 @ 4,000
Pontiac GTO (Tri-Power)	389	4.06 x 3.75	10.75:1	360 @ 5,200	424 @ 3,600
Chevrolet SS 396 (L78)	396	4.094 x 3.76	11:1	375 @ 5,600	415 @ 3,600
Buick GS	401	4.19 x 3.64	10.25:1	325 @ 4,400	445 @ 2,800
Olds 4-4-2 (L69)	400	4.00 x 3.975	10.5:1	360 @ 5,000	440 @ 3,600
Ford/Mercury (GT)	390	4.05 x 3.78	10.5:1	335 @ 4,800	427 @ 3,200
Ford	289	4.00 x 2.87	10:1	271 @ 6,000	312 @ 3,400
Shelby Mustang GT350	289	4.00 x 2.87	10.5:1	306 @ 6,000	329 @ 4,200

NOTE: *CID is cubic-inch displacement; CR is compression ratio; bore/stroke in inches.*

** Discounting factory super-stocks, full-size model lines & Corvette*

Funny Car and Top Fuel NHRA entries regardless of the brand name advertised. And Hemi badges again began showing up in everyday traffic in 2003, first on the fenders of Dodge Ram trucks. Displacing 5.7 liters, Chrysler's latest Hemi began crossing over into passenger-car ranks two years later.

Second-gen Hemi power first hit Main Street U.S.A. in 1966 after Chrysler officials opted to pacify NASCAR rules moguls by offering their so-called "elephant" V-8 in sufficient numbers direct to John Q. Public. More than a little "detuning" was required to transform the 426-cid race Hemi into a regular-production V-8, including an expected compression cut to a still-healthy 10.5:1. A less radical mechanical cam was stuffed in and steel-tube headers were replaced by cast-iron manifolds. On top, a heated aluminum intake manifold mounting two 650-cfm Carter four-barrels superseded the exotic cross-ram. Much of the race Hemi's stout foundation carried over, as did that same token output rating, 425 horsepower.

An understatement? "Most of the street Hemis would make 500 horsepower or better," claimed engineer Tom Hoover to no one's surprise. In his words, that factory figure "was purely an advertising number," and using it "was purely a matter of everybody being in fear that they would be called to Washington to testify before some committee that would say, 'you dirty dogs are out there making more power for cars and that's the un-American thing to do.' We were really worried about that as far back as the early 1960s. We were scared to death."

So was the competition. When wrapped in a Mopar B-body, early street Hemis managed 14-flat sprints down the quarter-mile with no sweat, and this with full exhausts plugging things up, wimpy street tires doing the rolling, and a smoldering Lucky Strike held outside the driver's door. Sticky slicks, unfettered tubular headers and a few other tricks could easily put any Hemi into the low 13s, if not into the 12s, perhaps requiring both hands on the wheel.

By 1970 the Hemi had been squeezed between the fenders of almost everything Dodge and Plymouth built, including a few four-door B-body sedans. Midsize models were the first to feel the joy in 1966, a handful of A-body super-stocks followed in 1968, and they were joined four years later by the ultimate regular-production renditions: E-body 'Cudas and Challengers. Counting those

A rocket scientist isn't required to explain where that "Hemi" name came from. Or is it? If so, what part of "hemispherical combustion chambers" do you not understand? *Mike Mueller*

1966 PLYMOUTH BELVEDERE 426 HEMI

CONSTRUCTION: unitized body/frame
MODEL AVAILABILITY: sedan, hardtop & convertible
PRICE: Hemi V-8 option, $907.60; 4-speed manual, $184.20; Torqueflite automatic, $206.30
WHEELBASE: 116 inches
WEIGHT: 3,940 pounds
SUSPENSION: heavy-duty; long-arm/short-arm w/0.92-inch torsion bars & 0.94-inch stabilizer bar, front; solid axle w/leaf spring, rear
STEERING: manual recirculating ball, std; power-assist, optional
WHEELS: 14x5.5K stamped-steel
TIRES: 7.75x14 Goodyear Blue Streak
BRAKES: 11-inch drums w/metallic linings, front & rear; power-assist, optional
ENGINE: 426-cid Hemi w/dual Carter AFB 4-barrel carburetors
TRANSMISSION: 4-speed manual w/Hurst shifter or Torqueflite automatic
AXLE RATIO: 3.23:1 w/Torqueflite; 3.54:1 w/4-speed

FRAME UP

While hot-to-trot horsepower clearly dominated the show during Detroit's original muscle car era, there was more to this story than simply stuffing mucho cubes into midsize (or smaller) automobiles. Backing up most high-perf V-8s then was a relatively strong supporting cast, although the really heavy heavy-duty stuff more often than not wasn't included in the basic deal, at least early on.

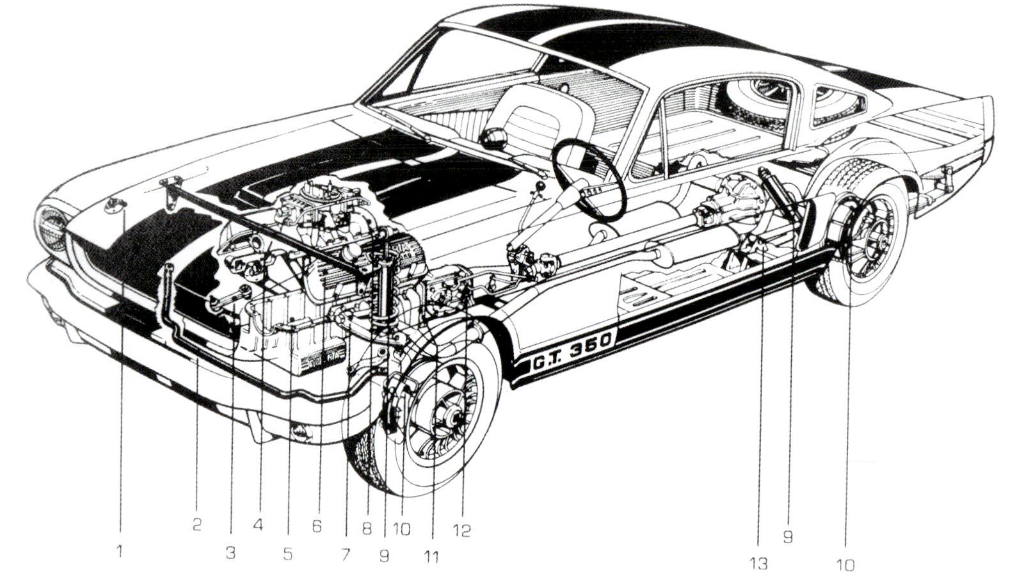

Shelby American's GT350 Mustang featured the most-modified chassis, by far, of any muscle car built during the 1960s. Front geometry was massaged and traction bars were included in back, Koni shocks at the corners. Shock towers also were braced to ensure that geometry remained true during hard cornering.

Consider Chevrolet's ever-popular SS 396 Chevelle. The first of this breed, 1965's high-priced, high-profile Z16, featured a reinforced convertible frame fitted with a stabilizer bar tying the lower control arms together in back. But both that beefy frame and innovative rear stabilizer were dropped from the standard deal the following year in order to bring the basic bottom line down within the reach of Average Joe. A standard rear stabilizer didn't reappear until 1970 after Chevrolet added its excellent F41 sport suspension into the base SS 396 mix. Introduced as an A-body option the previous year, F41 gear also included a seriously thick front stabilizer bar, special-duty bushings, reinforced lower control arms at the tail, and even beefier springs and shocks compared to existing units.

Such was primarily the extent of state-of-the-art muscle car chassis mods back then. Save for the niche-market Corvette's independent rear suspension (IRS), introduced in 1963, and Carroll Shelby's rather radical GT350 Mustang modifications in 1965, no expensively engineered exotic handling upgrades appeared.

Along with an unrelenting 1-inch-thick stabilizer bar up front, Ford's original Shelby Mustang also featured Koni adjustable shocks at the corners and override traction bars and suspension-travel-limiting cables in back. Further handling enhancements included lowering the upper A-arms' mounting points by an inch, which then required special Pitman and idler arms. A one-piece export brace was used in place of the stock Mustang's two-piece arrangement to tie the shocks towers rigidly together for more precise suspension geometry. And a "Monte Carlo" bar tightened things up even more by spanning the gap between shock towers across the engine, thus triangulating underhood bracing. Those time-consuming, costly chassis changes were stopped in 1966, and the Konis moved to the options list, again in the best interests of inviting more buyers by easing up, in this case, on both the wallet and the seat of the pants.

Status-quo basically remained the norm on most muscle cars' dirty sides; typical short/long parallel A-arms with coils (or torsion bars in Chrysler's case) up front and conventional solid axles sprung by either coil springs or longitudinal leafs in back prevailed. Rumors in 1964 did have Ford offering an optional IRS setup similar to the newly introduced Sting Ray's for the Mustang, but such a costly arrangement never appeared.

Much cheaper was an easily installed innovation offered by Oldsmobile in 1964. As part of its new 4-4-2 package, Olds threw in a standard rear sway bar, an understeer-controlling feature that had appeared earlier on American Motors' Rebel in 1957 and Corvette beginning in 1960. Measuring 0.875-inch in diameter—the same as Oldsmobile's standard front unit—this stabilizer helped reduce body lean, which in turn kept the rear treads more firmly planted during hard turns. Long a regular feature from Olds, a rear stabilizer was used in great numbers by AMC as well. Buick also made a rear stabilizer part of its GSX package in 1970.

Arguably one of the best examples of a nicely massaged muscle car chassis came from Ford in 1969 beneath the Boss 302 Mustang. Geometry remained basically unchanged, with the most notable upgrade coming in the size of the car's footprint. Fat F60 Wide Oval tires on big 15x7 Magnum 500 wheels were standard. To make room for all that extra tread, the car's front wheel arches were re-rolled to increase clearance. Engineers additionally had to develop beefier front spindles to handle the increased cornering loads resulting from the Wide Ovals' stronger grip. Upper control arm mounting points also were initially taxed beyond their limits in prototype applications, so extra bracing was added to the shock towers. This bracing soon became a standard feature as well for any Mustang fitted with F60 rubber and Ford's Competition Suspension option.

The rest of the Boss 302's standard foundation typically featured increased-rate springs. Gabriel supplied stiffened shocks, which were staggered (one mounted in front of the axle, the other behind) at the tail to help control axle windup. Staggered shocks also had shown up in 1968 beneath GM's two pony cars, Camaro and Firebird, to cure a troublesome wheel hop problem inherent to the original F-body platform.

By the early 1970s, the best of the muscle car breed was doing a decent job of holding the road for such heavy machines, although it must be mentioned that the nose-heavy big-blocks suffered notably in the turns, their small-block counterparts not so much. Anything more in the way of expensively modified suspensions surely would've ended up hard sells—in more ways than one. No ifs, ands and sore butts about it, supreme-handling high-performance automobiles back then were often as hard on their drivers as they were on the competition.

Appearing on the auto show circuit in November 1962, Dodge's first Charger was a dream machine based on a Polara convertible. The predictive Charger II concept then made the show scene in 1965. Called the "Leader of the Dodge Rebellion," the regular-production Charger was introduced to TV audiences during the Rose Bowl telecast on January 1, 1966—its hideaway headlights were Chrysler Corporation's first since De Soto's in 1942. *Mike Mueller*

Chrysler's street Hemi was available in various Dodge and Plymouth B-bodies—including some four-doors—in 1966. This is as good as it got in Plymouth terms that year: a top-shelf Satellite hardtop fitted with 425 horses worth of Hemi. *Mike Mueller*

racers of 1964 and '65, Dodge and Plymouth rolled out about 10,500 Hemi cars before the end of the line came in 1971.

While exteriors varied, few changes were made beneath the hood during the 426 Hemi's all-too-brief run. Dual inline Carter carbs and that 425-horsepower tag carried over each year. Updates in 1968 included a hotter cam, revised valvetrain, and a windage tray inside a 6-quart oil pan, with the sum of these parts earning a "Stage II" designation. Among other developments were hydraulic lifters, which replaced the maintenance-intensive solid tappets in 1970.

Press critics in 1966 couldn't rave enough about the new Hemi. "If you missed the San Francisco earthquake, reserve your seat here for a repeat performance," began a *Car and Driver* review. "Forget about your GTOs and your hot Fords—if you want to be boss on your block, rush down to your nearest Plymouth (or Dodge) dealer and place your order for a hemispherical combustion chamber 426 V-8. This automobile is the most powerful sedan ever, bar none."

But there was a clear and present downside: price. The engine alone cost about $800. Throw in a long list of "mandatory options"—heavy-duty items such as an 11-inch clutch (with the A-833 four-speed; the A-727 Torqueflite automatic also was available), a Dana rear end with a Sure-Grip differential, 11-inch drum brakes, special tires, higher rate springs, and stiffer shocks—and a Hemi's bottom line took off as quickly as the car itself. Its formidable price tag, combined with a gnarly nature that didn't mix well at all with everyday use, helped make the Hemi a slow seller throughout its career.

That short supply, of course, later inspired great demand on the collector market. Say "Hemi for sale" today, and you'd better get out of the way fast.

DODGE

Dropping the Hemi into a Dodge B-body in 1966 may have instantly set the earth trembling, but it didn't do much to alarm anyone while standing still. After testing a 425-horse Coronet, *Hot Rod* magazine's Eric Dahlquist explained that "people said the hemi package wasn't distinctive enough, lacked uniqueness, needed a hood scoop; in short, it had to look as fast as it went."

1966 PONTIAC GTO

CONSTRUCTION: body on perimeter-rail frame
MODEL AVAILABILITY: LeMans coupe, hardtop & convertible
PRICE: $2,783, coupe; $2,847, hardtop; $3,082, convertible
WHEELBASE: 115 inches
WEIGHT: 3,465 pounds (hardtop)
SUSPENSION: heavy-duty w/coil springs front & rear; 0.94-inch front stabilizer bar
STEERING: manual recirculating ball (24:1), std; 17.5:1 power-assist, optional (quicker 20:1 steering, optional)
WHEELS: 14x6 stamped-steel std; 14x6 Rally wheel, optional
TIRES: 7.75x14 US Royal Tiger Paw redline; whitewall rayon-cord tires available at no extra cost
BRAKES: 9.5-inch drums, front & rear; power-assist, optional
ENGINE: 389-cid V-8 w/Carter AFB 4-barrel carburetor
TRANSMISSION: 3-speed Muncie manual w/Hurst shifter; heavy-duty 3-speed*, M20 wide- & M21 close-ratio Hurst-shifted Muncie 4-speeds, & column-shifted 2-speed automatic, optional; floor shifter w/console, optional for auto trans
* Top-loader unit sourced from Ford
AXLE RATIO: 3.55:1, std w/manual trans; 3.23:1 std w/automatic; 3.55:1 included w/Tri-Power; Safe-T-Track limited-slip differential, optional

HOT OFF THE PRESS: 1966 PLYMOUTH BARRACUDA FORMULA S

"Disc brakes do make a difference. It's good to see American brakes coming along these days. They are well worth their $82 extra cost."
Road & Track, *March 1966*

FAMILY TIES: TRIPLE-CARBURETOR INDUCTION

Able to maximize both muscle and miles per gallon, today's ultra-precise electronic fuel injection technology has long been taken for granted, certainly so by drivers born after 1970. But well before EFI emerged, the best way to bring those polar opposites closer together involved bolting up three carburetors to a high-perf mill. Economy wasn't all that bad during timid operation with just the middle pot shootin' the juice, then power began flowing big-time in progressive fashion as pedal neared metal, bringing the other two into play. Chevrolet was the first to try this trick, adding three single-throat Rochesters to the first Corvette's Blue Flame six-cylinder in 1953. All triple-carb engines to follow were V-8s crowned with a trio of two-barrels, beginning with Oldsmobile's J2 and Pontiac's fabled Tri-Power in 1957, followed by Chevy's "three-deuce" 348 in 1958. Cadillac and Lincoln/Mercury also jumped onto this bandwagon that year to help haul some seriously large bodies around, and Ford's first "6V" FE-series big-block debuted for 1961, first displacing 390 cubic inches. A 406-cid 6V V-8 appeared in 1962, then Ford switched to dual four-barrels for its hottest 427 FE, introduced midyear in 1963. Tri-Power remained a Pontiac option atop 370, 389 and 421 V-8s up through 1966, with the 389 version leading the way in GTO ranks from 1964-66. Olds dropped its original J2 package after only two years then brought a trio of Rochesters back in 1966 for its 400-cid L69 V-8, which became the centerpiece for the first W-30 package. Multi-carb options became taboo at GM after 1966 for all models save for Corvette, leaving the Sting Ray's 1967-69 435-horse L71 427 to close out the corporation's "3x2" legacy. Dodge and Plymouth's 390-horsepower 440, offered from 1969 to '71 with three Holleys, was Detroit's last tri-carb V-8. A triple-carb 340 small-block also appeared for 1970's two E-body Tran-Am racers, Plymouth's AAR 'Cuda and Dodge's T/A Challenger.

Chrysler's 390-hp triple-carb RB big-block debuted midyear in 1969 for two special B-bodies; Plymouth's 440 Six Barrel Road Runner and Dodge's 440 Six Pack Super Bee. Three Holley two-barrels on an aluminum intake were the norm in 1969.

YEAR	MAKE	CID	BORE & STROKE	CR	HORSEPOWER	TORQUE	CARBURETORS
1953	Chevrolet	235	3.56 x 3.93	8:1	155 @ 4,200	223 @ 2,400	3 Carter 1-barrels
1957	Oldsmobile	371	4.00 x 3.688	10:1	300 @ 4,600	415 @ 2,800	3 Rochester 2-barrels
1957	Pontiac	347	3.9375 x 3.25	10:1	290 @ 5,000	n/a	3 Rochester 2-barrels
1958	Cadillac	365	4.00 x 3.625	9.75:1	335 @ 4,800	405 @ 3,400	3 Rochester 2-barrels
1958	Lincoln/Mercury	430	4.30 x 3.70	10.5:1	400 @ 5,200	500 @ 3,200	3 Holley 2-barrels
1961	Ford	390	4.052 x 3.874	10.6:1	401 @ 6,000	430 @ 3,500	3 Holley 2-barrels
1966	Oldsmobile	400	4.000 x 3.975	10.5:1	360 @ 5,000	440 @ 3,600	3 Rochester 2-barrels
1967	Chevrolet	427	4.25 x 3.76	11:1	435 @ 5,800	460 @ 4,000	3 Holley 2-barrels
1970	Dodge/Plymouth	340	4.040 x 3.310	10.5:1	290 @ 5,000	340 @ 3,200	3 Holley 2-barrels
1970	Dodge/Plymouth	440	4.320 x 3.750	10.5:1	390 @ 4,700	490 @ 3,200	3 Holley 2-barrels

NOTE: *CID is cubic-inch displacement; CR is compression ratio; bore/stroke in inches.*

HOT OFF THE PRESS: 1966 PONTIAC GTO

"This is the car that started it all, and in some ways the GTO still has a year's jump on the competition. It is certainly the sportiest looking, and it indicates an awareness on the part of its builders about what this market demands."
Car and Driver, *March 1966*

HOT OFF THE PRESS: 1966 CHEVROLET MALIBU SS 396

"It has just the right measures of ride-handling and acceleration that would make it the nuts for all kinds of driving, especially long trips. It's a fun car for today's dull traffic, and if it helps relieve the tedium of travel, you can't ask for much more."
Eric Dahlquist, Hot Rod, *February 1966*

Barracuda updates for 1966 included revised grille/taillights and new fender-mounted turn signal indicators, and the Formula S (shown here) carried over unchanged from 1965. *Mike Mueller*

Fortunately a major dose of image enhancement came along when a sleek new Dodge started showing up in showrooms in January 1966. Called the "Leader of the Dodge Rebellion" by ad guys, the head-turning Charger was, in division general manager Byron Nichols' words, "a fresh new concept in styling and engineering excellence from bumper to bumper."

"Every style line in metal and glass has been smoothly blended to provide the Charger with a forward-thrusting look and a low silhouette," added chief stylist William Brownlie. "From the swept-back roofline and full-width taillights to the tapering forward-side sculpturing and scoop effect of the frontal area, the Charger is the ultimate in sporty car design."

Of course, most witnesses couldn't help but notice that the first Charger was little more than a Coronet with a trendy fastback roof spliced on. Up front, trendy hideaway headlights helped disguise the fact that the grille surround was the same style used by Coronet. But when those headlights were exposed, Charger's B-body bloodlines were plainly obvious.

A few features may have been familiar on the outside, but customers discovered an interior treatment unlike anything out of Detroit then or now. Standard features included bucket seats and a console, which ran the length of the passenger compartment, splitting the rear seats into twin buckets, too. Those rear seats also folded down, making for some ample cargo capacity once the interior's back panel was opened up into the trunk.

While the 1966 Charger's standard engine—a 318-cid two-barrel V-8—helped keep the bottom line down, a few tasty options were present to help prove the beauty of this beast went more than skin deep. Engine choices included a 361-cid V-8 sporting another two-barrel and a single exhaust—not bad, but still ma-and-pa stuff. Things really started getting hot once the four-barrel 383 fell into place. Output for this premium-fuel big-block was 325 horsepower. At the top of the top was the vaunted Hemi, which became available in February 1966.

1966 CHEVROLET CHEVELLE SS 396

CONSTRUCTION: body on perimeter-rail frame
MODEL AVAILABILITY: Malibu hardtop & convertible
PRICE: $2,776, hardtop; $2,962, convertible
WHEELBASE: 115 inches
WEIGHT: 3,375 pounds (hardtop)
SUSPENSION: heavy-duty w/coil springs front & rear; 0.94-inch front stabilizer bar
STEERING: manual recirculating ball (24:1 ratio), std; power-assist, optional
WHEELS: 14x6 stamped steel w/small hub caps
TIRES: 7.75x14
BRAKES: 9.5-inch drums, front & rear
ENGINE: 396-cid Mk IV V-8 w/Rochester or Holley 4-barrel carburetor
TRANSMISSION: heavy-duty Saginaw 3-speed manual; M20 wide- & M21 close-ratio 4-speed manuals, M22 "Rock Crusher" 4-speed; & Turbo 400 automatic trans, optional
AXLE RATIO: 3.31:1

1966 CHEVROLET NOVA SS L79

CONSTRUCTION: unitized body/frame
MODEL AVAILABILITY: Chevy II hardtop
PRICE: $2,480 (base Super Sport); L79 327 V-8, $198; 4-speed manual, $184; Powerglide automatic, $172.92; heavy-duty springs, $4.75
WHEELBASE: 110 inches
WEIGHT: 3,140 pounds
SUSPENSION: heavy-duty, coil springs & 0.87-inch stabilizer bar, front; solid axle w/leaf springs, rear
STEERING: manual (25.4:1) recirculating ball, std; power-assist, optional
WHEELS: 14x5J stamped-steel w/SS full wheelcovers
TIRES: US Royal 6.95x14
BRAKES: 9.5-inch drums, front & rear
ENGINE: 327-cid V-8 w/Holley 4-barrel carburetor
TRANSMISSION: 3-speed manual, std; M20 wide- & M21 close-ratio 4-speed & Powerglide automatic, optional
AXLE RATIO: 3.07:1, std w/3-speed; 3.31:1 included with 4-speed

HOT OFF THE PRESS: 1966 CHEVROLET NOVA SS L79

"Unlike some samples from the Supercar spectrum, [this one] maintains a gentleness along with its fierce performance potential; its power/weight ratio is second to none and it is definitely better balanced than most."
Car Life, *May 1966*

BY THE NUMBERS: 1966 PRODUCTION

PONTIAC GTO

coupe	10,363	
hardtop	73,785	
convertible	12,798	
total	**96,946**	(77,901 w/335-hp 389 V-8, 19,045 w/Tri-Power)

CHEVROLET SS 396

hardtop	5,429	
convertible	66,843	
total	**72,272**	

CHEVROLET NOVA SS

six-cylinder	4,675	
V-8	16,311	(includes 3,547 w/L79 327 V-8)
total	**20,986**	(all hardtops)

OLDSMOBILE 4-4-2

F-85 club coupe	647	(103 w/3-spd, 456 w/4-spd, 88 w/auto)
F-85 hardtop	1,217	(88 w/3-spd, 798 w/4-spd, 331 w/auto)
Cutlass coupe	3,787	(221 w/3-spd, 2,422 w/4-spd, 1,144 w/auto)
Cutlass hardtop	13,493	(297 w/3-spd, 8,025 w/4-spd, 5,171 w/auto)
Cutlass convertible	2,853	(62 w/3-spd, 1,448 w/4-spd, 1,343 w/auto)
total	**21,997***	

* L69 triple-carb V-8 production (included in above totals)

F-85 club coupe	157
F-85 hardtop	178
Cutlass coupe	383
Cutlass hardtop	1,171
Cutlass convertible	240
total	**2,129**

* W-30 production (included in above totals)

F-85 club coupe	25
F-85 hardtop	8
Cutlass coupe	5
Cutlass hardtop	16
total	**54**

BUICK GRAN SPORT

sedan	1,835	(178 w/3-spd, 308 w/4-spd, 1,349 w/auto)
hardtop	9,934	(450 w/3-spd, 2,199 w/4-spd, 7,285 w/auto)
convertible	2,047	(136 w/3-spd, 431 w/4-spd, 1,480 w/auto)
total	**13,816**	

FORD MUSTANG GT **25,517** (includes coupes, fastbacks & convertibles)

SHELBY GT350

prototypes	5	(includes 1 Paxton-supercharged & 2 Hertz cars)
production models	1,356	
w/Paxton supercharger	10	
Hertz rental cars	999	
drag cars	4	
convertibles	4	
total	**2,378**	

FORD FAIRLANE GT/GTA

hardtop	33,015
convertible	4.327
total	**37,2342**

FORD 427 FAIRLANE **57** (all Wimbledon White Fairlane 500 hardtops)

MERCURY CYCLONE

hardtop	6,889
convertible	1,305
GT hardtop	13,812
GT cvt.	2,158
total	**24,164**

DODGE CHARGER **37,344** (all fastbacks)

DODGE HEMI

Coronet sedan	34	(11 w/4-spd, 23 w/auto)
Coronet 4-dr sedan	2	(both w/automatic trans)
Coronet Deluxe sedan	49	(31 w/4-spd, 18 w/auto)
Coronet 440 hardtop	288	
Coronet 440 convertible	5	(2 w/4-spd, 3 w/auto)
Coronet 500 hardtop	339	(204 w/4-spd, 135 w/auto)
Coronet 500 convertible	21	(12 w/4-spd, 9 w/auto)
Charger	468	(250 w/4-spd, 218 w/auto)
total	**1,206**	

NOTE: Other 4-door Hemi sedans are known; at least 2 Coronet Deluxe and 1 Coronet 440

PLYMOUTH HEMI

Belvedere I sedan	136	
Belvedere II hardtop	531	
Belvedere II convertible	10	(4 w/4-spd, 6 w/auto)
Satellite hardtop	817	
Satellite convertible	27	
total	**1,521**	

PLYMOUTH BARRACUDA

Formula S	**3,702**	(all fastbacks)

NOTE: *Production data was supplied by various sources, including Christo Datini at the GM Heritage Center, Ford Motor Company & Kevin Marti at Marti Auto Works (www.martiauto.com), the Shelby American Automobile Club (www.saac.com), and Galen Govier (Mopar material) at Galen's Tag Service (www.galengovier.com).*

PLYMOUTH

Hemis from Dodge's corporate cousin also inspired a little bad press out of the blocks. "When we tested the 1966 Plymouth, equipped with a street Hemi and four-speed transmission, we were rather upset that [it] didn't look like anything special," complained *Car and Driver's* critics. "A Plain-Jane car sometimes fits well into life's order, but when a buyer forks over extra money for a fast car at the top of the line, he wants it to have a distinctive identification."

Unfortunately, Plymouth customers weren't presented with more distinguished wrappings until 1967, at least in B-body ranks. Sporty small-block fans in 1966 again found Barracuda relatively fun to play with. Updates included revised grille and taillights, new fender-mounted turn signal indicators, and a dash makeover featuring an actual oil pressure gauge in place of an idiot light. A vacuum gauge appeared when the optional tach took its place. Standard bucket seats also were changed to a sportier shell-type.

Making the biggest splash were new front disc brakes, 11.125-inch units supplied by Kelsey-Hayes. Labeled "indispensible" by *Car and Driver*, this option was now available direct from Plymouth; it had been dealer-installed the previous year. All other mechanicals carried over unchanged from 1965, as did the Formula S, still a fine-handling machine that took its sweet time completing a quarter-mile and thus remained mostly overlooked by the youth market.

"No, the Formula S Barracuda, in its present form, won't capture the hearts of teen-age America," continued *Car and Driver*. "It could, provided Plymouth stuffed in its 383 V-8 or even the Hemi, but this would utterly destroy the beautiful balance of the automobile. And in this case, we're four-square behind maintaining the status quo."

For now, that is.

PONTIAC

GTO graduated from options package to full-fledged model status in 1966, and the base 335-horse 389 returned along with its Tri-Power upgrade, which traded the small center carb used in 1965 for one that matched its two mates in throttle bore size. Its optional heavy-duty three-speed and two four-speeds (wide- and close-ratio) each used Hurst sticks, and Pontiac's two-speed automatic transmission again came with a column shift unless a buyer anted up for the optional console and its floor-mounted shifter. Bucket seats (with improved padding) remained standard, but could be superseded by an optional bench for the first time. New too was a mundane column shifter for the standard three-speed manual.

In February 1966, Pontiac introduced a new Tri-Power engine to go along with 1965's dealer-offered induction tub. Along with that functional hood, this XS-code 389 featured a stronger cam and stiffened valve springs. Mandatory XS options also included an M21 close-ratio four-speed, heavy-duty fan, metallic brake linings, and a 4.33:1 limited-slip differential. Though not labeled in any factory papers as such, 1966's XS 389 was the division's first "Ram Air" V-8.

GTO was treated to its third facelift in three years for 1966. Body contours were now smooth and mildly curvaceous. The optional Rally wheels seen here were introduced the previous year. *Mike Mueller*

More than one bit of promotional paperwork depicted a blacked-out rear cove area for the 1966 Chevelle SS 396, but nearly all models sold that year featured body-matching tail panels.

1966 OLDSMOBILE 4-4-2 W-30

CONSTRUCTION: body on perimeter-rail frame
MODEL AVAILABILITY: F-85 club coupe & Deluxe Holiday hardtop; Cutlass sport coupe & Holiday hardtop
WHEELBASE: 115 inches
SUSPENSION: heavy-duty; coil springs & stabilizer bar, front; solid axle w/coil springs & stabilizer bar, rear
STEERING: manual recirculating ball
WHEELS: 14x6 stamped-steel
TIRES: 7.75x14 red line
BRAKES: 9.5-inch drums, front & rear
ENGINE: 400-cid L69 V-8 w/3 Rochester 2-barrel carburetors
TRANSMISSION: 4-speed manual
AXLE RATIO: 4.11:1

1966 FORD FAIRLANE GT/GTA

CONSTRUCTION: unitized body/frame
MODEL AVAILABILITY: hardtop & convertible
PRICE: $2,891, GT hardtop; $3,152, GT convertible
WHEELBASE: 116 inches
WEIGHT: 3,315 pounds, GT hardtop; 3,595 pounds, GT convertible
SUSPENSION: heavy-duty w/coils, front, solid axle w/leaf springs, rear ; 0.85-inch sway bar in front
STEERING: manual recirculating ball (29.4:1 ratio), std; 21.6:1power-assist, optional
WHEELS: 14x6J stamped-steel
TIRES: 7.75x14 Firestone Super Sport
BRAKES: 10-inch drums, front & rear; power-assist, optional
ENGINE: 390-cid Thunderbird Special FE-series V-8 w/Holley 4-barrel carburetor
TRANSMISSION: 3-speed manual (std. w/GT); Sport Shift Cruise-O-Matic automatic (std. w/GTA); 4-speed manual, optional for GT
AXLE RATIO: 3.25:1

1966 SHELBY MUSTANG GT350

CONSTRUCTION: unitized body/frame w/fiberglass hood
MODEL AVAILABILITY: 2+2 fastback, convertible
PRICE: $4,428
WHEELBASE: 108 inches
WEIGHT: 3,158 pounds
SUSPENSION: heavy-duty; coil springs & stabilizer bar, front; solid axle w/leaf springs, rear
STEERING: manual recirculating ball
WHEELS: 15x5.5 stamped-steel or 15x6 Cragar 5-spoke (for 1965 "rollovers"); 14x6 Magnum 500, std for 1966; 14x6 10-spoke, optional
TIRES: 7.75x15 Goodyear, early cars; 14-inch Goodyear
BRAKES: 11.375-inch front discs, 10-inch rear drums; sintered metallic linings
ENGINE: 289-cid High Performance Windsor V-8 w/Holley 4-barrel carburetor
TRANSMISSION: Borg-Warner T-10 four-speed; C-4 automatic, optional
AXLE RATIO: 3.89:1 w/manual trans; 3.50:1 w/automatic

Updated styling enhanced the Super Sport Nova's appeal in 1966, as did the optional L79 327 V-8, a 350-horse small-block first offered to Corvette buyers in 1965. This SS coupe is one of 5,481 Chevy II models built with the 350-horsepower 327 in 1966. *Mike Mueller*

CHEVROLET

Chevy's Malibu-based SS 396 also gained individual model-line status in 1966. No more sixes or small-blocks were offered for the Super Sport Chevelle, it was big-block or no block at all until 1971. Affordability also arrived as much of the Z16's standard makeup was dropped in favor of widening this midsize muscle car's scope. Gone were the rigid convertible frame, 11-inch full-size brakes, and rear stabilizer. A three-speed manual was now the base trannie, and features like the Z16's tach, fake mag wheel covers, and bucket seats became options. No more standard Multiplex stereo, either. In place of the Z16's L37 Turbo Jet was a 325-horsepower 396, listed as RPO L35 for El Camino applications. Early brochures showed a blacked-out rear cove panel, but apparently few models received this treatment.

Options included a beefed suspension, four-speed stick, and two Mk IV V-8s, the L34 and L78, rated at 360 and 375 horsepower, respectively. According to *Motor Trend*, the L78 "should put the Chevelle SS right up front in the supercar market."

In compact ranks, a squeaky clean Chevy II restyle arrived for 1966 while the engine lineup stayed the same—at least until a customer reached the optional 327 listings. The L30 327, listed at 250 horsepower the previous year, was bumped up 25 ponies, and 1966's 300-horsepower L74 was dropped in favor of the truly tough, Corvette-sourced L79, rated at 350 horses. The L79's appearance signaled a coming of age for Nova as it now could claim full-fledged muscle car status.

Left: A totally restyled body appeared for Oldsmobile's 4-4-2 in 1966. Also new was the W-30 option, which featured the 400-cid L69 triple-carb V-8 and special induction equipment. This W-30 F-85 club coupe wears incorrect F-85 Deluxe trim, installed by the dealer who originally sold the car. *Mike Mueller*

1966 MERCURY CYCLONE GT/GTA

CONSTRUCTION: unitized body/frame
MODEL AVAILABILITY: hardtop & convertible
PRICE: $2,891 (GT hardtop), $3,152 (GT convertible)
WHEELBASE: 116 inches
WEIGHT: 3,595 pounds (hardtop)
SUSPENSION: heavy-duty w/coils, front, solid axle w/leaf springs, rear ; 0.85-inch sway bar in front
STEERING: manual recirculating ball; power-assist, optional
WHEELS: 14x5.5 stamped-steel
TIRES: 7.75x14
BRAKES: heavy-duty fade-resistant 4-wheel drums; power-assist, optional
ENGINE: 390-cid Thunderbird Special FE-series V-8 w/Holley 4-barrel carburetor
TRANSMISSION: 3-speed manual (std. w/GT); Sport Shift Merc-O-Matic automatic (std. w/GTA); 4-speed manual, optional for GT
AXLE RATIO: 3.25:1

OLDSMOBILE

Standard power rose slightly to 350 horsepower for Oldsmobile's latest 4-4-2 package, now found under option code L78. L78 availability expanded to five models this year as the F-85 Deluxe Holiday coupe entered the fray.

New too was an optional engine, announced on November 24, 1965. Available only for the 4-4-2, this L69 400 V-8 was topped by three Rochester two-barrel carburetors wearing small "maximum-flow" air filters. Beneath those Rochesters was a unique manifold featuring a clever trick drag racers immediately appreciated: an adjustable baffle that closed off the heat crossover passage that normally enhanced engine warm-up during typical operation. Closing this baffle meant everyday cold starts would suffer. On the other hand, opening it kept the fuel/air mixture inside the manifold cooler longer. A cooler mixture is denser, and a denser mixture generates more horses on the top end—just what was needed to beat other Saturday-night warriors through those lights a quarter-mile away.

FAMILY TIES: CHEVY NOVA SS

A decision was made to insert a fourth model into the Chevrolet lineup just two months after the air-cooled Corvair was introduced on October 2, 1959. This new unit-body compact then went from drawing board to reality in a scant 18 months, making this one of the quickest development sagas in GM's storied history. New-for-1962 Chevy II models started rolling off assembly lines in August 1961. The new breed's flagship was Nova, which ended up shining on alone after the Chevy II nameplate was dropped in 1969. New in 1963 was a Nova Super Sport, available with only one power source, a purely practical 194-cid six. Customers who noticed that the Chevy II engine bay had been designed all along to accept the Bow-Tie small-block could swap in a 283 or 327 V-8 themselves or pay big bucks to have their local dealer install Chevrolet's own V-8 conversion kit—the going rate was $1,500 plus labor, or more than half of what an entire Chevy II cost. Fortunately a factory-direct V-8 option debuted in 1964, as did an optional Muncie four-speed stick. That 283 small-block then was joined by two optional 327s in 1965. And when a fresh restyle followed for 1966, Nova was ready to run.

Chevrolet's Super Sport Nova debuted for 1963 and remained on the scene up through 1976. A convertible version was offered that first year only; all others were coupes.

FOUR ON THE FLOOR

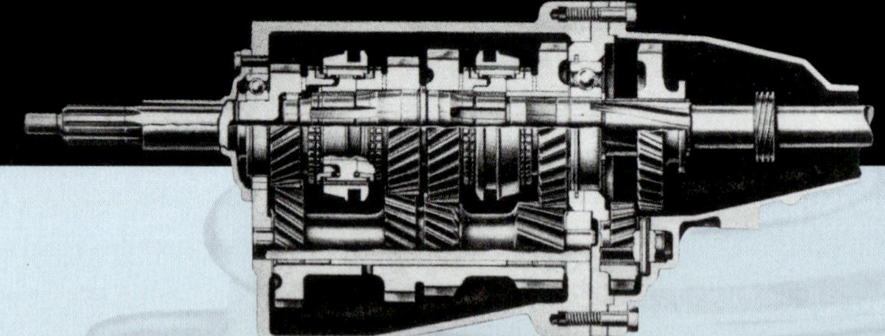

Introduced midyear in 1963, Chevrolet's Muncie four-speed featured an aluminum case and was offered in wide- and close-ratio forms. As *Car and Driver* critics saw it in 1964, it "stands out as the most pleasant of all high-torque gearboxes in production."

The primordial roots of the modern four-speed stick run all the way back to 1880, when Frank and Everett Morse began manufacturing bicycle chains in Trumansburg, New York. Morse Chain was, by 1906, dealing its wares to fledgling automakers, and its timing links later stood as state of the art during the 1920s. Ten years after Morse opened for business, the Mechanics Machine Company was formed in Rockford, Illinois, and by 1911 was busy manufacturing transmissions, axles, and differentials. The name became Mechanics Universal Joint Company in 1925 in honor of its main claim to fame.

Meanwhile, in Batesville, Indiana, farmer George Schebler and his friend Burt Pierce began investigating efficient ways to feed fuel/air to internal combustion engines, with Schebler patenting a carburetor design in 1902, Pierce in 1909. Schebler teamed up with one of the Indianapolis Motor Speedway founders, Frank Wheeler, in 1905 to manufacture his carburetor, and three years later Pierce opened his Marvel Carburetor Company in Flint, Michigan. Wheeler-Schebler remained in business in Indianapolis—with the name remaining even after Schebler sold out in 1912—until 1928, when it was acquired by Marvel.

Sixty miles northeast of Indy in Muncie, brothers Tom and Harry Warner started manufacturing their innovative differentials in 1901, and Warner Gear produced its first transmission eight years later. To the northwest, in Moline, Illinois, furniture-maker Charles Borg went into the tool manufacturing business with Marshall Beck in 1904. Borg's son George then helped create the company's ground-breaking single-plate clutch in 1910, and by 1918—the year the firm moved east to Chicago—Borg & Beck had produced 200,000 clutches, salting away its leadership in the field.

What do these convoluted tales have in common? In May 1928, Borg & Beck merged with Warner Gear, Marvel-Schebler Carburetor, and Mechanics Universal Joint to form the Borg-Warner Corporation, [illegible] Warner, of course, then quickly became the name in transmissions, and not just manuals. Introduced for 1951, Dearborn's first auto trans, "Ford-O-Matic," was developed in cahoots with Borg-Warner, and American Motors also relied on B-W automatics from 1957 to 1971.

But Borg-Warner did manual operation best. And in 1957, the corporation's transmission division supplied Chevrolet with Detroit's first performance-oriented four-on-the-floor, the fully synchronized T–10, announced as a Corvette option in April that year. "Swift and smooth response" and "easy downshift" were the T–10's strong points, according to press releases.

"When you can whip the stick around from one gear to any other the way you'd stir a can of paint, that's a gearbox that's synchronized," added *Motor Trend's* Walt Woron. "And when you can downshift from second to first at 40 mph without double clutching, that's slightly more than just an 'easy downshift.' "

T-10 four-speeds showed up in all brands of supercars into the 1960s, with American Motors relying solely on the Borg-Warner unit right up until Kenosha built its last Javelin in 1974. GM divisions used T-10s exclusively until mid-1963 and began offering a B-W box (the upgraded Super T-10) again in 1974. Ford began bolting in T-10s in 1960 and kept them around for certain applications even after Dearborn engineers developed their own four-speed in 1964. Chrysler [illegible] in-house as well.

The supplier in that latter case was New Process Gear, originally known as the New Process Rawhide Company when founded in 1888 in Baldwinsville, New York. This firm soon relocated to nearby

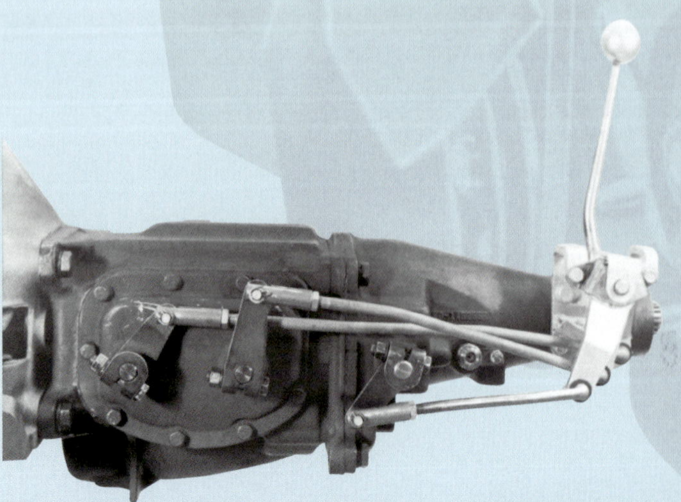

Borg-Warner pioneered high-perf four-speed manual applications with its beefy T-10 in 1957, first for that year's Corvette. T-10s were used across the board in Detroit (and Kenosha) during the original muscle car era.

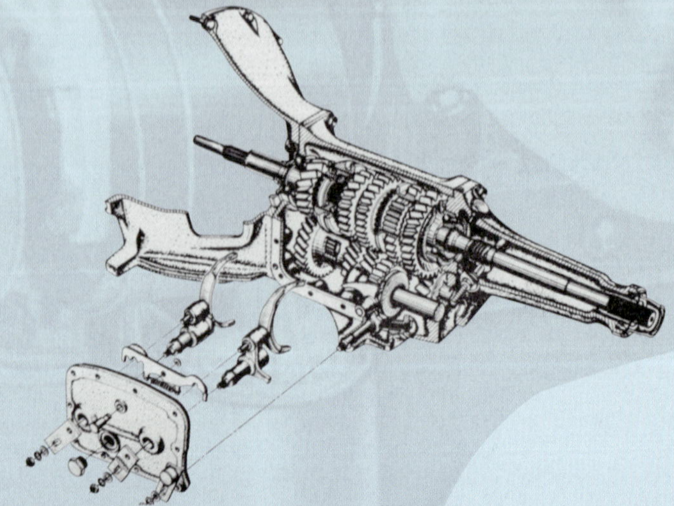

Supplied by New Process, Chrysler's A833 four-speed was a cumbersome beast, but that heft resulted from its battleship-tough construction. A truly beefy A833 was created specifically for high-performance big-blocks and hence became known as a "Hemi four-speed."

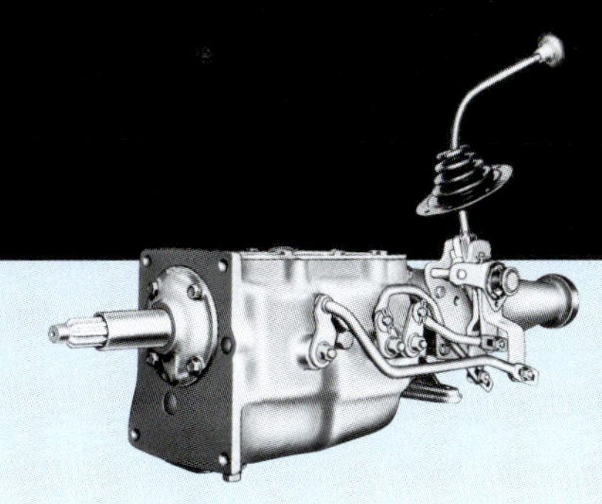

Unlike its rivals, Ford's new-for-1964 four-speed featured a case that allowed access to internals through its "roof," hence its 'top-loader" moniker.

Syracuse, and in 1913 "Rawhide" was dropped in favor of "Gear" on the company shingle. It was a division of the Willys Corporation when purchased in 1921 by GM, which then resold it to Walter Chrysler 13 years later. Known best for its heavy-duty four-wheel-drive systems, New Process also developed the beefy A833 four-speed transmission that became available in all Chrysler cars, slant-six or V-8, in 1964.

Recognized as perhaps the strongest, most durable four-speed sold during the 1960s, the A833 appeared in two different lengths (incorporating a short or long tail-shaft) depending on body application. Early A833s also used a flanged output shaft, while 1966-up versions switched to modern slip-yoke tail-shafts. Two basic gearset configurations appeared, one with a 23-spline input shaft, the other featuring 18 splines. The heavy-duty 18-spline A833 became known as the "Hemi four-speed" due to its specified mating to Dodge and Plymouth's meanest big-blocks. A cast-iron case was the norm until an overdrive-equipped A833 appeared, wrapped in aluminum, in 1975. At about 120 pounds, the iron-cased New Process four-speed certainly was no lightweight.

Based on the T–10 design—and apparently created with Borg-Warner's help—GM's aluminum-cased Muncie four-speed began showing up in place of the B-W product in full-size Chevrolets in February 1963. Corvette installations followed about three months later, as did midsize applications in 1964. After driving a four-speed Chevelle in the fall of 1963, *Car and Driver's* critics called the Muncie unit "light and quick, and certainly one of the very best transmissions now on the market."

Various mechanical changes were made before the Muncie trans was itself pushed aside in favor of Borg-Warner's Super T-10 in 1974, with the most notable involving gear ratios. Three variations were offered: the wide-ratio M20, close-ratio M21, and the super-heavy-duty M22, nicknamed "Rock Crusher" in honor of its unmistakable whine. First seen in rare prototype installations in 1965, the M22 incorporated truly beefy gears with heavier teeth cut at a lesser angle compared to the other two Muncies, hence all the noise.

Unlike its rivals, Ford's new four-speed for 1964 was a "top-loader," in that its access plate was located above, not to the side—an arrangement that reportedly translated into a significantly rigid case. This cast-iron housing appeared in three different lengths during the 1960s and 1970s, and total variations (considering mounting bolt counts, shifter attachments, shaft/gearset specifications, etc.) amounted to more than 130.

Early examples used a wimpy 25-spline output shaft, soon superseded by a stronger unit incorporating 28 splines. The 10-spline input shaft in typical applications measured 1.0625 inches in diameter. At 1.375 inches, the 10-spline shaft used behind 427, 428, and 429 big-block V-8s was the thickest ever installed in a passenger-car gearbox. These supreme top-loaders also were fitted with enlarged 31-spline output shafts. Both wide- and close-ratio top-loader four-speeds (with 2.78:1 and 2.32:1 lows, respectively) were offered, and that "big-shaft" version was only available with those latter tightly grouped gears.

Fitted with a special cam and ram-air ducting, the W-30's L69 V-8 was rated at 360 horsepower. W-30 models also featured trunk-mounted batteries. *Mike Mueller*

Introduced as well late in the year was Oldsmobile's first "W-machine," the W-30 4-4-2, targeted directly at drag racers. Available only with the L69 V-8, the W-30 deal included ram-air ductwork that fed outside air into those three Rochesters via two large plastic scoops situated in the openings in the front bumpers normally reserved for turn signals. Allowing room for that ductwork to run alongside the L69 meant that the battery had to be relocated to the trunk—a fortunate turn considering that's just where drag racers put theirs for improved weight transfer to the rear wheels during hard acceleration.

Additional special equipment included a four-bladed fan without a clutch, a heavy-duty three-core radiator, and a close-ratio four-speed manual transmission. A unique high-lift, long-duration cam (with high-tension chrome vanadium steel valve springs and dampers) was stuffed inside an L69 400 ordered with the W-30 option. Though both this cam and the cool-air equipment obviously enhanced power potential, no rating change was listed. An unknown number of "Track-Pak" 4-4-2s, featuring a dealer-installed W-30 package, also were released for both 1966 and 1967.

HOT OFF THE PRESS: 1966 OLDSMOBILE 4-4-2 W-30

"[Because] this package is stock according to the book, it would be a wise move to pick up on one if you run at the drags once in a while. If you don't and still want a better running engine, it's still a smart move. Once that engine starts to breathe better, you'll not only feel the difference, but you'll help cut down on smog emission problems. Then at least you'll be accomplishing something if you're not setting drag records."
Bud Lang, Car Craft, *August 1966*

HEAVY BREATHING

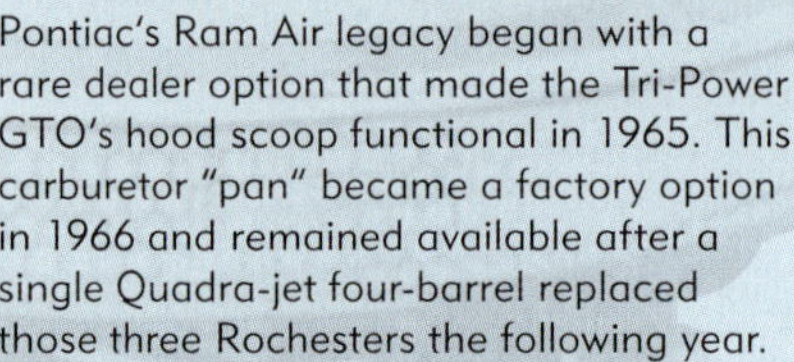

Pontiac's Ram Air legacy began with a rare dealer option that made the Tri-Power GTO's hood scoop functional in 1965. This carburetor "pan" became a factory option in 1966 and remained available after a single Quadra-jet four-barrel replaced those three Rochesters the following year.

So close yet so far. Three different Ram Air V V-8s were planned for 1969: a 303-cid version for Trans-Am racing; 366 cid for NASCAR; and 400 cubes for the street. While the Ram Air V never made it into regular production, some were sold in crates via dealers.

By 1967, Pontiac fans in the know knew that their favorite firm's hottest V-8 was a "Ram Air" engine, even though that label appeared nowhere in PMD nomenclature at the time. The term first was coined on the street, then morphed into an official factory-direct title. And the original tag retroactively became "Ram Air I" after an even hotter Ram Air II appeared in March 1968, followed by Ram Air III and IV V-8s in 1969. A race-ready Ram Air V also was built in small numbers but never made it into regular production.

Those Roman numerals didn't begin appearing abundantly in factory literature until 1970, when "Ram Air III/IV" began receiving full exposure in shop manuals and on order forms. Prior to that, a service bulletin sent out in February 1968 did specifically mention "Ram Air II," as did a magazine ad that year. Decals first showed up on Pontiac hoods in 1969 but simply read "Ram Air" in the III's case. Appropriate numerals only appeared when the Ram Air IV was installed.

The roots of the Ram Air V-8 legacy run back to the August 1965 release of the GTO's air-scoop accessory package, a $49.50 dealer option for the Tri-Power 389. Available again over dealer counters in 1966, this functional hood was joined in February by Pontiac's XS-code 389 V-8, a factory option that rolled over into the first of the Ram Air 400s in 1967. Revised heads (with round- instead of D-shaped exhaust ports), forged pistons and lightweight valves keyed the switch to Ram Air II production early in 1968. Like its forerunner, the Ram Air II used a Quadra-jet four-barrel carburetor.

Standard for both 1969's new GTO Judge and Firebird Trans Am, the Ram Air III 400 switched back to D-port heads, but was fitted with free-flowing cast-iron exhaust headers and a Power Flex fan. Advertised output (in GTO applications) remained the same as the Ram Air II: 366 horsepower. The Firebird's Ram Air III was rated at 335 horses, down 5 from the F-body's Ram Air II. Both the Ram Air III and IV appeared one more time in 1970 before the realities of upcoming compression cuts led to their cancellations.

Though rarely seen, Pontiac's high-priced Ram Air IV certainly made a lot of noise during its short stay, inspiring more than one critic to class it among the original muscle car era's meanest mills. Conservatively rated at 370 horsepower under 1969–70 GTO and 1970 Firebird hoods (345 in 1969 Firebird form), this bully featured a heavy-duty four-bolt block; exceptionally free-breathing heads with round ports; revamped exhaust manifolds; an enlarged Rochester Quadra-jet four-barrel carb on an aluminum intake (in place of the Ram Air III"s cast-iron piece); and a serious cam that produced a race-car-like idle that, according to *Car Life*, was "a rough, rolling bark, music to the driver's ears and a warning to people in the next lane."

The Ram Air V story began in 1967 after Pontiac chief John DeLorean turned Malcolm MacKellar's engineering team loose on various competition projects, including plans to take the Firebird SCCA road racing. To meet the Trans-Am league's 5-liter displacement limit, Special Projects Group engineer Steve Malone de-stroked Pontiac's 400-cid V-8 to 303 cubes and added tunnel-port heads to created the Ram Air V. Special Projects' engineers also developed two other Ram Air V engines: a 366-cid version targeted for NASCAR competition and a 400-cid running mate originally aimed at GTO buyers as a street/strip power choice. All three featured extra-heavy-duty block, rods and crank; free-flowing, individual-runner exhaust manifolds; and a big 780-cfm Holley four-barrel carb on a special aluminum high-rise intake manifold.

The NASCAR 366 reportedly made 585 horsepower, while its 400-cid cousin produced about 85 less. Initial plans called for installing at least 1,000 of the 430-horse (estimated) 303-cube tunnel-ports into 1969 Firebirds to meet SCCA homologation requirements. But tightened budgets and changing corporate attitudes shut all three engines down before they got the chance to prove themselves. While no Ram Air V Pontiacs rolled off a production line, at least 80 tunnel-port V-8s reportedly were sold in crates in 1970, in exchange for about $2,000.

1970 PONTIAC RAM AIR IV

TYPE	OHV V-8; coded L67 in GTO applications, LS1 in Firebird
DISPLACEMENT	400 cubic inches
BORE	4.120 inches
STROKE	3.750 inches
HORSEPOWER	370 at 5,500 rpm
TORQUE	445 at 3,900 rpm
COMPRESSION	10.5:1
FUEL DELIVERY	750-cfm Rochester Quadra-jet 4-barrel carburetor on 2-piece aluminum intake w/separate cast-iron heat crossover
AIR CLEANER	cable-operated ram-air unit sealed to functional hood scoops w/foam "doughnut"
IGNITION	single-point distributor
COOLING	heavy-duty radiator
CYLINDER BLOCK	cast-iron w/4-bolt main bearing caps
CRANKSHAFT	cast-nodular-iron w/3.00-inch main bearing journals
CONNECTING RODS	cast Armasteel (an iron alloy w/steel-like qualities)
PISTONS	forged-aluminum
CAM	hydraulic w/308 degrees of duration on intake, 320 on exhaust, 87 degrees of overlap
ROCKER RATIO	1.65:1 (adjustable w/double locking nuts)
CYLINDER HEADS	cast-iron w/round exhaust ports, 71cc combustion chambers
VALVE SIZES	2.11-inch intakes, 1.77-inch exhausts (w/dual valve springs)
VALVE LIFT	0.520 inch, intake & exhaust (w/limit-travel lifters that required manual lash adjustment)
EXHAUST SYSTEM	free-flowing cast-iron head-style manifolds

BUICK

Additional distinctiveness characterized 1966's Buick Gran Sport, courtesy of black-out treatments for the grille and rear cove panel, simulated vents on the hood and fenders, and body-side paint stripes. Gone was the somewhat "square" Buick hood ornament that appeared, in some opinions, out of place at the nose of the supposedly groovy '65 GS. All mechanicals carried over more or less unchanged for 1966 save perhaps most notably for the addition of finned-alloy iron brake drums, created to help cool things down quicker after hard stops.

FORD

All 1966 Mustangs received minimal updates, including a revised grille and re-arranged trim. Inside, 1965's simple, Falcon-based instrument panel was replaced with the sportier five-dial layout offered the previous year as part of both the Interior Decor and GT packages. Making that five-dial dash standard helped lower the price for the second-edition GT, which featured most of the same stuff offered the previous year.

Most options repeated, too, including Rally-Pac instrumentation, originally introduced one month after Ford's first Mustang debuted. Also notable was automatic-trans availability behind the Hi-Po 289 for the first time. When ordered with the K-code V-8, the Rally-Pac's basic 6,000-rpm tach was traded for an 8,000-rev unit.

Truly fresh in 1966 was Ford's restyled intermediate, which, according to *Motor Trend's* John Ethridge, "put Fairlane into a class it's never seen before." Beneath its critically acclaimed skin was a reinforced, resprung unit-body platform, just the thing to allow big-block entry into Ford's midsize mix for the first time. Two 390-cid FE "Thunderbird" V-8s were available for Fairlane, Fairlane 500 and Fairlane 500 XL models, one rated at 270 horsepower, the other (tabbed "Thunderbird Special") at 315. A second Thunderbird Special 390, dressed up with chrome extras and rated at 335 horses, was reserved for the new GT Fairlane and its GTA running mate.

HOT OFF THE PRESS: 1966 SHELBY GT350

"Through experience in knowing what it takes to make a good sports cars, Shelby-American has come up with an almost perfect result—the 1966 GT-350."
Steve Kelly, Motor Trend, *August 1966*

In 1966, Shelby American supplied Hertz with a special run of rental GT350 Mustangs, all tagged with an appropriate "H." Hertz's rates for the GT350H were $17 a day, $70 a week, plus 17 cents a mile in the New York area. According to Carroll Shelby, many of these hot rentals were wrecked that first winter in New York, and others were returned to Hertz offices with mundane 289 V-8s installed in place of the original Hi-Po small-blocks. After all was said and done, Shelby bought the entire Hertz rental run back at a "reduced price."

TIME SLIPS: 1966

MODEL	¼-MILE PERFORMANCE	SOURCE
Oldsmobile 4-4-2 (W-30)	13.80 seconds at 105.2 mph	*Car Craft,* August 1966
Plymouth Satellite Hemi	13.80 seconds at 103.8 mph	*Car and Driver,* April 1966
Mercury Cyclone GT[1]	13.98 seconds at 103.8 mph	*Car and Driver,* March 1966
Shelby Mustang GT350[2]	14.0 seconds at 92 mph	*Car Life,* July 1966
Pontiac GTO	14.05 seconds at 105.14 mph	*Car and Driver,* March 1966
Ford Fairlane GTA	14.26 seconds at 99.0 mph	*Car and Driver,* March 1966
Dodge "D-Dart"	14.33 seconds at 94.2 mph	*Car Craft,* August 1966
Chevrolet Malibu SS 396	14.42 seconds at 100.2 mph	*Popular Hot Rodding,* June 1966
Ford 427 Fairlane	14.5 seconds at 102 mph	*Hot Rod,* July 1966
Buick Gran Sport	14.92 seconds at 95.13 mph	*Car and Driver,* March 1966
Chevrolet Nova SS (L79)	15.10 seconds at 93.0 mph	*Car Life,* May 1966
Plymouth Barracuda Formula S	17.6 seconds at 81 mph	*Car and Driver,* June 1966

1. Specially "tuned" for this road test; clearly not factory-stock models

2. w/supercharged 289 V-8, rated at 390 horsepower

The not-cool hood ornament seen in 1965 was deleted in 1966 on Buick's second-edition Gran Sport, which also featured a new blacked-out grille. Coupe, hardtop and convertible GS models were again offered this year. *Mike Mueller*

FAMILY TIES: FORD FE-SERIES V-8s

Ford Motor Company's new Edsel lineup was introduced to the public on September 4, 1957, and along with these ill-fated cars came two new big-block engine families, the FE- and MEL-series V-8s. Big was an understatement. Like their Y-block forerunners, both of these brutes featured cylinder blocks with lowered skirts encasing the crankshaft, a design that later allowed cross-bolted reinforcement for the inner main bearing caps in high-perf applications. Mucho iron also was cast into those blocks with significant future expansion in mind: maximum FE displacement hit 428 cubic inches, a whopping 462 for the MEL. Ford's heavyweight featured "skinny" cylinder heads; a huge, wide intake; and valve covers that bolted over both at their top edges—because pushrods protruded up through that manifold, not the heads. Reportedly "FE" stood for "Ford-Edsel," though some sources say it simply represented "Ford Engine." Either way, "MEL" apparently was short for "Mercury-Edsel-Lincoln," so you be the judge as to the true meaning of FE. As we all might guess, Fords relied on the FE, Mercurys and Lincolns the MEL, and Edsels shared the two—so there. Discounting Mercury's 430-cid, triple-carb Super Marauder of 1958 (Detroit's first 400-horse V-8), no MEL even remotely resembled a high-performer during this breed's 1958–68 run, leaving Ford's upscale corporate cousin no choice but to install an FE whenever a need for speed arose. Home to some of the hottest horsepower churns offered during the early 1960s, the FE group debuted at 332 and 352 cubic inches (plus Edsel's 361) in 1958, and that latter Ford V-8 was boosted up to 360 horses in 1960 to become Dearborn's first modern muscle mill (see page 17). FE displacement hit 390 cubes in 1961, and adding three Holley two-barrels to this V-8 resulted in 401 horsepower. A 405-horsepower 406 "6V" (Ford nomenclature: "V" for "venturii") followed midyear in 1962, then came the king of the kings, the fabled 427, midway into 1963's Ford/Mercury model run. Although the actual cube count was more like 425, image-conscious engineers bumped displacement up on paper to make sure no rivals one-upped them. NASCAR rules at the time limited production engines to no more than 7 liters, which translated roughly into 427 cid. Chrysler and GM might've matched Ford's max-performance big-block in size, but they couldn't possibly surpass it and remain in the race. Fitted with an aluminum intake to cut some serious weight, the 427 was offered in two forms from 1963 to '67: a 410-horsepower 4V unit and a 425-horsepower 8V. A single-carb 390-horsepower 427 was offered in 1968 before this rolling legend was superseded by Ford's first Cobra Jet big-block, based on the enlarged 428-cid FE. The last passenger-car FE installations came in 1971.

YEAR	CID	BORE & STROKE	CR	HORSEPOWER	TORQUE	CARBURETOR	VALVE SIZES
1958	332	4.000 x 3.300	9.5:1	265 @ 4,600	360 @ 2,800	Holley 4-barrel	2.04 x 1.57
1958	352	4.002 x 3.500	10.2:1	300 @ 4,600	395 @ 2,800	Holley/Carter 4-barrel	2.04 x 1.57
1961	390	4.052 x 3.784	9.6:1	300 @ 4,600	427 @ 2,800	Motorcraft 4-barrel	2.04 x 1.57
1962	406	4.130 x 3.784	11.4:1	405 @ 5,800	448 @ 3,500	3 Holley 2-barrels	2.09 x 1.66
1963	427	4.232 x 3.784	11.5:1	425 @ 6,000	480 @ 3,700	2 Holley 4-barrels	2.09 x 1.66
1966	428	4.132 x 3.980	10.5:1	345 @ 4,600	462 @ 2,800	Motorcraft 4-barrel	2.04 x 1.57

NOTE: *CID is cubic-inch displacement; CR is compression ratio; bore/stroke & valve sizes in inches (intake x exhaust).*

Introduced midyear in 1963, Ford's 427 FE big-block was offered in two forms up through 1967: 425 horsepower with dual carbs, 410 with a single four-barrel. A single-carb version, rated at 390 horsepower (shown here), also was briefly offered in 1968.

Ford's 428-cid FE big-block, introduced in 1966, was morphed into a 335-horsepower mean machine early in 1968. The first of Dearborn's Cobra Jet V-8s, this engine was offered in Ford and Mercury's midsizers and pony cars that year. A "Shaker" ram-air hood scoop became available in 1969. *Mike Mueller*

SWEET MUSIC

Racing-style "cutout" exhausts were standard in 1970 for Dodge's Challenger T/A (shown here) and Plymouth's AAR 'Cuda. Unique mufflers were included with inlets and outlets both at the front, making for a rather convoluted trip for spent gases. *Mike Mueller*

Knowing that internal combustion engines are basically big air pumps, it only follows that making one function in fast fashion depends partly on its ability to vent the bad stuff out with relative rapidity. The least complicated way around this horsepower-hindering roadblock always has involved reducing overall restriction by increasing the number of mufflers and pipes. Simple, cost-conscious single muffler/tailpipe systems represented the overwhelming norm around Detroit prior to 1955. Then higher-volume dual exhausts started showing up more commonly as part of various "Power Pak" options, which also typically included four-barrel carburetors. Hot engines like Chevrolet's 348 V-8 never used anything but duals, and the same also could be said for any succeeding performance powerplant worth its salt. Larger diameter pipes began appearing as well during the 1960s to allow more exhaust volume to flow through more easily.

When Oldsmobile's 4-4-2 debuted for 1964, ad copy made it clear what that last digit stood for. Plainly put, no model could join the muscle-bound fraternity without at least two exhaust tips sticking out in back. Pontiac people even went so far as to offer too-cool-for-school chrome "splitters" that doubled the tip count and exited downward directly behind a 1964 GTO's rear wheels. Ford also introduced "quad" tips for its 1967 Mustang GT, this after previous GT's had featured prominent exhaust "trumpets" exiting proudly through their rear valances. Witnesses furthermore couldn't help notice the 1968 4-4-2's exclusive rear bumper, which featured indentations that made room along its lower edge for another set of high-profile trumpets.

But not all high-perf exhausts exited at the tail. Chevrolet began adding optional "sidemount" exhausts below Corvette doors in 1965, labeling them "off-road" pieces, undoubtedly to shirk any liability for violating local noise ordinances. This country's other two-seater, American Motors' AMX, built from 1968 to 1970, also could be fitted with dealer-installed sidepipes, as could Javelins.

Carroll Shelby's first GT350 Mustang featured competition-style "cutouts" that protruded just ahead of each rear wheel. "Shorties" also appeared in 1970 for Dodge's Challenger T/A and Plymouth's AAR 'Cuda, though the path taken by exhaust flow this time was not necessarily decreased. The Mopar system remained essentially stock back to the mufflers then all bets were off. Spent gases entered each muffler in typical fashion in front, made a U-turn inside to come back out the same end they went in, and finally arced rearward through unique tailpipes to meet the rear rubber—all this just so street versions of Dodge and Plymouth's Trans-Am pony cars could look like the real racers.

Chevrolet engineers also tried dumping mufflers entirely, replacing them with "chambered exhausts" consisting of specially crimped pipes (featuring 11 baffles running their 45-inch lengths) followed by two smaller baffled tubes farther back. Chambered exhausts were reportedly street legal, though more than one police officer probably begged to differ. This little-known, definitely loud option was offered to Chevelle and Camaro customers during 1969 only.

The next year Pontiac introduced its Vacuum Operated Exhaust (VOE) option for GTO. Controlled by an underdash knob, the VOE system reduced back pressure by using engine vacuum pressure to open special baffles in the mufflers, making a bit more horsepower in the process. VOE predictably also raised the exhaust note, along with the ire of upper office killjoys, who cancelled it in January 1970.

Aftermarket-supplied tubular headers, of course, represented the quickest way to relieve much of the back pressure installed at the factory a half century ago and were commonly bolted up by muscle car customers often before stock cast-iron manifolds had a chance to cool down following their maiden voyage from dealership to driveway. Shelby's GT350 came standard with "Tri-Y" headers in 1965 and '66, but cost considerations and durability issues ruled out similar mainstream installations. While dealer-delivered headers were available for Chevrolet's first Z/28 Camaro in 1967, few customers paid attention, undoubtedly because the price was more than twice that of similar pipes offered at speed shops.

Tube headers from the factory may have been out of the question, but recasting iron manifolds wasn't. Mopar engineers were responsible for some of the more notable pieces, which featured individual upward curving passages instead of one single downward dump. Chevrolet's 409 used nicely streamlined cast-iron manifolds that looked a lot like headers, as did Ford's hottest FE-series big-blocks. Pontiac's 421 Super Duty V-8 was fitted with so-called "long-branch" manifolds, done in either traditional iron or unconventional weight-saving aluminum.

For the most part, however, factory manifolds remained among the weakest links in the typical muscle mill's makeup during the 1960s and 1970s—leaving Hooker, Hedman, and the rest to reap the rewards.

Supplied by Trend Setter Products, Sidewinder exhausts were optional for American Motors' Javelin and AMX from 1968 to 1970. These sweet-sounding sidepipes were priced at $170 in both cases. *Mike Mueller*

TARGETING THE TRACK

Open to factory hot rods sporting a pounds-per-advertised-horsepower ratio that fell between 10.60:1 and 11.29:1 (per NHRA specs), drag racing's D/Stock class fit many supercars to a T during the 1960s—models like Dodge's aptly named "D/Dart," released rather quietly in 1966. Published weight for this A-body hardtop was 2,946 pounds; beneath its hood was a hopped-up LA small-block rated at 275 horsepower. For the calculator-challenged, that was a ratio of 10.71:1—presto, welcome to the club!

Inducing 40 more horses out of Dodge's 273-cid V-8 was simply a matter of stuffing in a more serious cam and bolting (by way of a special adaptor) a big 4160-series Holley four-barrel (with manual choke) on top. Supplied by Camcraft, that long-duration (284 degrees) bumpstick featured mucho lift—0.495-inch on intake, 0.505-inch on exhaust—and was accompanied by Racer Brown heavy-duty valve springs. A dual-point distributor (minus vacuum advance) was added, too, as were Doug Thorley steel-tube headers.

Remaining powertrain features included a Weber clutch, a Hurst-shifted A833 four-speed, and an 8.75-inch Sure-Grip rear end fitted with 4.86:1 gears. Suspension components were predictably beefed, wheels were the Formula S Barracuda's 14x5.5 units, and standard-issue tires were 6.95x14 plain black-sidewallers. According to *Car Craft's* Dick Scritchfield, the sum of these parts "puts the D/Dart about as close as you can get to the top of D/Stock class."

Created to make Dodge's A-body Dart a force in D/Stock drag racing, the aptly named "D-Dart" also was campaigned in SCCA Trans-Am competition, as this vintage racer attests. *David Newhardt photo, courtesy Mecum Auctions*

Stoplight to stoplight was another story, an obvious conclusion considering that burbling cam and those shorter-than-short cogs. "Driving the 'D' on the street becomes a bit un-nerving," added Scritchfield. "Getting a smooth start by feather-footing gets you a series of jerks until the rpm picks up a thousand or so. Too much gas and you burn the tires."

"The 273 maximum performance engine equipped Dart is designed for use in supervised acceleration trials and other racing and performance competition," added Dodge service manager Robert Kline. "It is not recommended for general everyday driving because of the compromise of all around characteristics which must be made for this type of vehicle." Factory paperwork right off the bat made it clear that D/Darts would be sold "as is" sans any warranty whatsoever.

Some sources claim Dodge built 50 D/Darts in 1966, but only two were known at last check. And not all went to the drags, as the road-racing example shown here attests. D/Darts also proved to be nice fits in the SCCA's newborn Trans-American Sedan Championship series (see page 84), controlled early on by Ford Mustangs.

Standard for the D-Dart was a warmed-up 273-cid small-block fitted with a Racer Brown cam, Holley four-barrel carb, and Doug Thorley headers. *David Newhardt photo, courtesy Mecum Auctions*

As that last letter implied, Fairlane GTA featured a standard automatic, Ford's three-speed Cruise-O-Matic, labeled "Sports Shift" due to its split personality. "It's actually two transmissions in one," claimed brochures, "a manual for 'him' and an automatic for 'her.' " Sexist commentary aside, this C6 auto-box could operate in conventional shiftless mode or be manually controlled via an attractive chrome T-handle. A console, with bucket seat accompaniment of course, was standard, for both GTA and GT. A three-speed manual was included in the base GT's case.

That standard 390 featured more cam and more carb to make those 20 extra horses. Atop its Holley four-barrel was a chrome low-restriction air cleaner, and also included were stiffer valve springs

HOT OFF THE PRESS: 1966 BUICK GS

"The Gran Sport is in many ways good in spite of itself. Its springing is soft to the point of absurdity, but this is partly offset by an excellent suspension and chassis. You are given the impression that Buick isn't really attuned to what this performance market is all about and they aren't about to find out."
Car and Driver, *March 1966*

Left: Ford's Fairlane received a truly fresh body for 1966, and two sporty versions debuted: GT and GTA. The "A" stood for "automatic," a reference to the only type transmission available in this case. As expected, all GT Fairlanes featured manual gearboxes. *courtesy National Automotive History Collection, Detroit Public Library*

and a viscous-drive fan. An expectedly beefed suspension and 7.75 Firestone rubber on 14x6 wheels further sweetened the GT/GTA deal, which Ford people hoped would put their Pontiac counterparts in their place. "How to Cook a Tiger," was the headline for magazine ads touting the new GTA, a clear poke at GTO.

SHELBY MUSTANG

Ford opted to tone down the rough-as-a-cob GT350 for 1966. A back seat was added along with an optional C4 automatic transmission. Full tailpipes were hung, suspension mods were discontinued, and those stiff Koni shocks and gnarly Detroit Locker were sent to the options list. Paint choices too were offered: blue, red, green, and black joined the existing Wimbledon White.

Such changes were made in running fashion during the year, with the first 252 '66 GT 350s being 1965 "leftovers" still fitted with many of the previous year's features. Plain-Jane 15-inch rims remained standard for those 252 cars, as did the Koni shocks before they became a dealer-installed option. Five-spoke Magnum 500 wheels became standard from then on. The Cragar-supplied 15-inch five-spokes remained available for the early leftovers, while new 14-inch aluminum-alloy 10-spoke wheel, were optional for later cars.

Reportedly about 82 of those leftovers also arrived at Shelby American as two-seaters, with some of these cars apparently fitted with a rear seat as a dealer option. Another 1965 standard, the override traction arms with their welded-on brackets, continued in place until their supply ran out, apparently after about 800 1966 models were built. Traction-Master bolt-on traction bars were used from there.

A Paxton supercharger was a new option for 1966 and reportedly boosted output by 46 percent. And a GT350 convertible also appeared in 1966, although all six built either stayed with Shelby or went to valued friends.

Late in 1965, Shelby American general manager Peyton Cramer also proposed a special run of rental cars for Hertz, and 1,002 GT350s ended up in its fleet. About 80 percent of those cars wore traditional gold on black exteriors, but as many as 200 models came in typical Mustang colors. A few also were built using steel hoods in place of Shelby's fiberglass lids, and some wore Cragar mags instead of the more familiar Magnum 500 wheels. Most used C4 automatic transmissions and, like all 1966 GT350s with auto boxes, were fitted with a 595-cfm Autolite four-barrel carburetor. Four-speed GT 350H models stuck with the 715-cfm Holley four-barrel.

MOTOR OF THE YEAR: 1966 DODGE/PLYMOUTH HEMI

Type	OHV V-8 w/black-painted valve covers
Displacement	426 cubic inches
Bore	4.250 inches
Stroke	3.750 inches
Horsepower	425 at 5,000 rpm
Torque	490 at 4,000 rpm
Compression	10.25:1
Fuel delivery	2 Carter AFB 4-barrel carburetors on aluminum intake
Air cleaner	chrome-plated w/18-inch-diameter filter
Ignition	dual-point Prestolite distributor
Cooling	high-speed water pump &stretch-resistant drive belt
Cylinder block	stress-relieved cast-iron
Crankshaft	shot-peened & nitrided forged-steel w/2.75-inch main journals
Connecting rods	forged-steel
Pistons	impact-extruded-aluminum
Cam	mechanical w/276 degrees duration (intake & exhaust) and 52 degrees of overlap
Rocker ratio	1.57:1, intake; 1.52:1, exhaust
Cylinder heads	cast-iron w/machined hemispherical combustion chambers; 168–177cc chamber volume
Valve sizes	2.25-inch intakes, 1.94-inch exhausts
Valve lift	0.480 inch, intake; 0.460 inch, exhaust
Exhaust system	streamlined cast-iron manifolds, 2.25-inch pipes

Mercury's Comet graduated up into intermediate ranks for 1966 after adopting Fairlane's updated unit-body platform. This year's Cyclone also served as the prestigious pace car for the 50th running of the Indianapolis 500.

MERCURY

"Lincoln-Mercury people are all smiles when the subject of 1966 Comets comes up," announced an October 1965 *Motor Trend* report. "With good reason, too, because they now have an expanded line of true intermediates (instead of quasi-compacts) to go after that fat market." A Falcon-based model in 1965, Comet began sharing corporate cousin Fairlane's updated foundation the following year, meaning it was now far better suited to go hunting for tigers or goats or such. But with its base 200-horsepower 289 two-barrel, 1966's Cyclone—now offered in hardtop and convertible forms—was clearly no match for Pontiac's leader of the muscle car pack. Two optional 390 big-blocks, a two-barrel at 265 horsepower and a four-barrel at 275, were no real help, either.

Trying to take a big cat by the tail required a Cyclone GT, modeled of course after its Fairlane counterpart. A 335-horsepower 390—Mercury's Cyclone GT V-8—was standard, as was a three-speed stick. A four-speed and the Sport Shift C6 (tagged "Merc-O-Matic") were optional. Cyclone GT also was treated to a twin-scoop fiberglass hood that weighed 16 pounds less than the steel unit included in the basic Cyclone deal. That lightweight lid was optional for non-GT Cyclones.

HOT OFF THE PRESS: 1966 MERCURY CYCLONE

"The Comet came off the line like a Super Stock, surging up on its haunches under power exactly like a specially modified NHRA stocker."
Car and Driver, *March 1966*

UN-FAIRLANE

Ford's famed 427 V-8 was primarily intended to make left turns around NASCAR super speedways and cut straight, quick lines down dragstrips. Early examples became known as "low-risers" after race-only "hi-riser" heads appeared in 1964. "Hi-riser" referred to these heads' huge rectangular intake ports, which were much "taller" than stock and completely unsuitable for the street, a fact that didn't amuse NASCAR rules moguls in the least. They banned hi-riser heads in 1965, but that didn't stop Ford from coming right back with a compromise, the "medium-riser" 427.

Another important design change made in 1965 involved keeping the 427 together at sky-high rpm. Engineers had discovered a weakness in the FE block's bottom end three years before, leading them to redesign it with "cross-bolted" main bearing caps. Cross-bolted caps consisted of the standard two-bolt units reinforced with two additional bolts run in horizontally through the side of the block's extended lower skirt. Although the cross-bolted block did help keep the crankshaft where it belonged, there still existed an inherent oiling problem.

Early FEs were "top-oilers"—lubrication went to the cam bearings on top first, then trickled down to the crank's more thirsty main bearings. Any oil pressure restrictions in the cam area meant sure failure below. Ford engineers solved this problem by casting in an additional oil gallery—which appeared as an exterior bulge running down the left side of the cylinder block—specifically for the main bearings. And thus, the 427 "side-oiler" was born.

Most side-oiling medium-riser 427s found their way into full-size Galaxies and Mercurys during the 1960s. Exceptions included 1966's 427 Fairlane, which appeared in April that year with little fanfare and next to no warning. *Hot Rod's* ever-present horsepower hound, Eric Dahlquist, received a call about the same time inviting him to take a peek at one of three "prototypes" assembled for evaluation and press purposes. A full-dress GT teaser painted Nightmist Blue, the Fairlane Dahlquist tested surely would've left *Hot Rod* readers disappointed once they saw the real thing.

Few, however, got the chance. With NHRA drag-racing rules for Super Stock competition demanding a production minimum of at least 50 cars, Ford rolled out only 57 427 Fairlanes off its Atlanta production line for 1966, and all were middle-of-the-road Fairlane 500 hardtops done in Wimbledon White paint. Ho-hum "dog dish" hubcaps were the norm outside, as were a bench seat and block-off plate in place of a radio inside.

No external imagery was applied save for "427" fender emblems and a special hood with a functional scoop. That hood, in Dahlquist's opinion, offered "instant status." It also fed cooler outside air into the two big Holleys hiding beneath. It saved weight too both because it was made of fiberglass and didn't incorporate hinges. Accessing the 427 Fairlane's engine compartment in 1966 was easy as pulling four pins and lifting the lid off with the help of a co-pilot. If this reminds you of a race car it should.

Stock-class drag racing was the 427 Fairlane's main reason for being in 1966. Ford's approach softened a bit the following year as customers were allowed to chose their own paint and install a 427 in Fairlane sedans, convertibles and the top-shelf XL hardtop. Both the 410-horse single-Holley and 425-horsepower dual-carb were available in 1967, but the functional fiberglass hood was optional, as were flashy styled-steel wheels in place of those small center caps.

1966 FORD 427 FAIRLANE
CONSTRUCTION: unitized body/frame w/lift-off fiberglass hood
MODEL AVAILABILITY: Fairlane 500 hardtop; Wimbledon White paint only
PRICE: R-code 427 engine option alone cost $1,725.20
WHEELBASE: 116 inches
WEIGHT: 3,355 pounds
SUSPENSION: independent upper/lower control arms, front; solid axle w/leaf springs, rear; heavy-duty springs, shock absorbers, and front sway bar
STEERING: manual recirculating ball
WHEELS: 14x5.5 w/small hubcaps
TIRES: 7.75x14
BRAKES: 11.375-inch Kelsey-Hayes 4-piston front discs, 10-inch rear drums (no power assist)
ENGINE: 427-cid medium-riser FE-series V-8 w/dual Holley 4-barrel carburetors
TRANSMISSION: top-loader 4-speed w/11.5-inch clutch
AXLE RATIO: 3.89:1 gears in 9-inch differential w/31-spline axles (4.11:1 and 4.86:1 ratios, optional)

1966 FORD 427 V-8

TYPE	OHV R-code "medium-riser" FE-series
DISPLACEMENT	427 cubic inches
BORE	4.232 inches
STROKE	3.784 inches
HORSEPOWER	425 at 6,000 rpm
TORQUE	480 at 3,700 rpm
COMPRESSION	10.5:1 (various ratios published in 1966)
FUEL DELIVERY	dual Holley 4-barrels on aluminum intake
AIR CLEANER	low-restriction open-element, oval housing
IGNITION	transistorized
CYLINDER BLOCK	cast-iron "side-oiler" type w/cross-bolted main bearing caps
CRANKSHAFT	forged-steel
CONNECTING RODS	cap-screw type
PISTONS	forged-aluminum
CAM	solid w/324-degrees duration, intake/exhaust
ROCKER RATIO	1.76:1
CYLINDER HEADS	cast-iron with 1.34x2.34 intake ports ("hi-riser" ports measured 1.34x2.72 inches)
VALVE SIZES	2.19-inch intakes, 1.72-inch exhausts
VALVE LIFT	0.542 inch, intake/exhaust
EXHAUST SYSTEM	cast-iron head-style manifolds, dual 2.25-inch pipes

Though nowhere near as exotic as its Thunderbolt forerunner, 1966's 427 Fairlane was still a purpose-built super-stocker equipped to go right to the strip. A lift-off fiberglass hood was standard, and all 57 built were painted Wimbledon White. *Mike Mueller*

When topped with twin Holley four-barrels, Ford's R-code 427 medium-riser V-8 was rated at 425 horsepower. *Mike Mueller*

HOT OFF THE PRESS: 1966 FORD FAIRLANE GTA

"We feel this new [Sport Shift] transmission's bound to become popular…simply because there's been nothing quite like it before. Howard Freers, executive engineer for Fairlane, thinks many who'd normally go for 4-on-the-floor will choose this automatic. It's much more than just a compromise between a manual and an automatic."
John Ethridge, Motor Trend, *October 1965*

HOT OFF THE PRESS: 1966 FORD 427 FAIRLANE

"In today's titlist play, the national sales championship is decided both on and off the course. The new 'street Fairlane' puts Ford right next to the pin."
Eric Dahlquist, Hot Rod, *July 1966 (article was titled "427 Wedge Shot")*

CHAPTER 4

1967 WILD HORSES

GM & MERCURY OPEN UP THE FIELD

Disc brakes were standard for Chevrolet's Z28 Camaro in 1967, meaning the division's new Rally wheels also were included—in this case, measuring 15 inches across. Other than these bright rims, the only other outward sign of a 1967 Z28's presence were twin racing stripes on the hood and rear deck. That legendary "Z/28" emblem didn't appear until midway through 1968. *Mike Mueller*

Let's be honest: classing any Mustang as a muscle car prior to 1967 was a bit of a stretch. The majority of the 1965–66 GT models featured only 225 humble horses. And though by no means a plow-puller, the 271-horsepower K-code rendition was simply no match for GM's best (nor Mopar's meanest) big-engine intermediates in this country's hi-perf street race. No matter how you sliced it, a small-block was still a small-block.

Then along came Ford's third-edition pony car, a notably enlarged machine rebuilt with the express goal of allowing Ford's hulking FE-series V-8 between its flanks. Increasing interior room and trunk space definitely was part of the plan, too, but Dearborn's idea guys (save for Lee Iacocca, who was no fan of the bigger, supposedly better Mustang) clearly were hoping to see their latest horse run with Detroit's sizeable dogs—in more than one field, as it turned out. What Ford

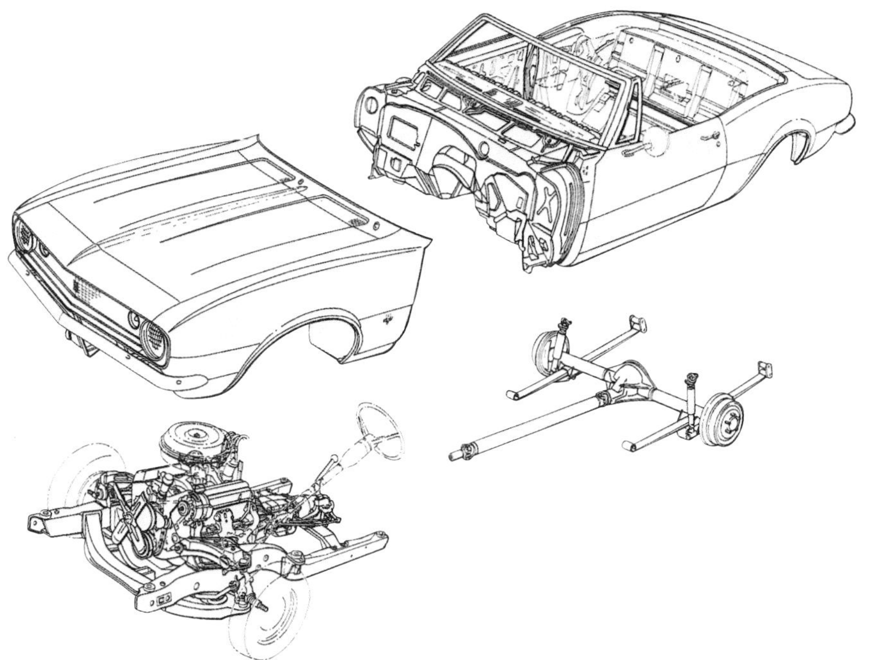

Contrary to the Mustang's fully welded unitized body/frame platform, Camaro's foundation featured an independent front subframe that bolted up to its body structure. Single-leaf springs were standard in back in 1967.

designers didn't know when they first began refashioning Mustang in 1964 was that their counterparts at General Motors would soon be hard at work hammering out their own sporty pony cars, also with an eye toward incorporating ample room up front for mucho cubes.

Chevrolet chief designer Irv Rybicki had proposed a small, sexy Chevy—a model similar to Ford's original two-seat Thunderbird—early in 1962, but general manager Bunkie Knudsen shot it down. Knudsen then changed his mind two years later after Iacocca and crew forced his hand. Chevrolet people were instructed to breed their own pony in August 1964, and they responded with their "F" platform, which mimicked Mustang in every way. Pete Estes, Knudsen's

1967 FORD MUSTANG GT/GTA

CONSTRUCTION: unitized body-frame
MODEL AVAILABILITY: coupe, fastback & convertible
PRICE: GT Equipment Group alone cost $205.05; 200-hp 289-2V V-8 cost $105.63; 225-hp 289-4V V-8 cost $158.48; High Performance 289 V-8 (available only with GT option) cost $433.55; 320hp 390-4V V-8 cost $263.71
WHEELBASE: 108 inches
WEIGHT: 3,255 pounds (GT fastback w/390 V-8)
SUSPENSION: heavy-duty; upper A-arms, lower control arms, w/coil springs mounted atop A-arms, 0.84-inch stabilizer bar, front; solid axle w/longitudinal leaf springs, rear
STEERING: manual (25.3:1) recirculating ball, std; quick-ratio (20.3:1) power-assist, optional (quick 20:1 steering also included w/optional Competition Handling package)
WHEELS: 14x5 stamped-steel w/289 V-8s; 14x6 w/390 V-8
TIRES: F70x14 Wide Oval white-sidewall
BRAKES: power-assisted 11.38-inch front discs; 10-inch rear drums
ENGINE: GT/GTA package available w/all V-8s (289- or 390-cid, 2- or 4-barrel carburetor); bright quad exhaust tips included w/4-barrel V-8s
TRANSMISSION: floor-shifted 3-speed manual, std; 4-speed & Cruise-O-Matic automatic optional (heavy-duty 3-speed required w/390 V-8)
AXLE RATIO: 3.00:1, std

UNDER THE HOOD: 1967'S HOTTEST V-8s

MODEL	CID	BORE & STROKE	CR	HORSEPOWER	TORQUE
Dodge/Plymouth Hemi	426	4.250 x 3.750	10.25:1	425 @ 5,000	490 @ 4,000
Dodge/Plymouth	440	4.320 x 3.750	10:1	375 @ 4,600	480 @ 3,200
Dodge/Plymouth	383	4.250 x 3.380	10:1	325 @ 4,800	425 @ 2,800
Pontiac GTO Ram Air	400	4.120 x 3.75	10.75:1	360 @ 5,400	438 @ 3,800
Pontiac Firebird Ram Air	400	4.120 x 3.75	10.75:1	325 @ 5,200	410 @ 3,600
Chevrolet SS 396 (L78)	396	4.094 x 3.76	11:1	375 @ 5,600	415 @ 3,600
Chevrolet Camaro Z28	302	4.00 x 3.00	11:1	290 @ 5,800	290 @ 4,200
Chevrolet Camaro SS (L48)	350	4.00 x 3.48	10.25:1	295 @ 4,800	380 @ 3,200
Olds 4-4-2	400	4.00 x 3.975	10.5:1	350 @ 5,000	440 @ 3,600
Buick GS-400	400	4.04 x 3.90	10.25:1	340 @ 5,000	440 @ 3,200
Buick GS-340	340	3.75 x 3.85	10.25:1	260 @ 4,000	365 @ 2,800
Ford/Mercury (8V)	427	4.23 x 3.78	11.1:1	425 @ 6,000	480 @ 3,700
Ford/Mercury (4V)	427	4.23 x 3.78	11.1:1	410 @ 5,600	476 @ 3,400
Ford/Mercury	390	4.05 x 3.78	10.5:1	320 @ 4,800	427 @ 3,200
Ford	289	4.00 x 2.87	10:1	271 @ 6,000	312 @ 3,400
Shelby Mustang GT350	289	4.00 x 2.87	10.5:1	306 @ 6,000	329 @ 4,800
Shelby Mustang GT500	428	4.13 x 3.98	10.5:1	355 @ 5,400	420 @ 3,200

NOTE: *CID is cubic-inch displacement; CR is compression ratio; bore/stroke in inches.*

**Discounting factory super-stocks, full-size models, & Corvette*

TIME SLIPS: 1967

MODEL	¼-MILE PERFORMANCE	SOURCE
Dodge Coronet 500 Hemi	13.90 seconds 104 mph	*Rodder & Super/Stock,* March 1967
Oldsmobile 4-4-2 W-30	13.92 seconds at 104 mph	*Hot Rod,* April 1967
Pontiac Firebird 400 (Ram Air)	14.03 seconds at 103.6 mph	*SSDI,* March 1967
Pontiac GTO (Ram Air)	14.09 seconds at 101 mph	*Motor Trend,* January 1967
Plymouth Barracuda Formula S w/383 V-8	14.53 seconds at 97 mph	*SSDI,* April 1967
Buick GS-400	14.70 seconds at 97 mph	*Car Life,* January 1967
Chevrolet Camaro Z28	14.9 seconds at 97 mph	*Car and Driver,* March 1967
Chevrolet Malibu SS 396 (L78)	14.9 seconds at 96.5 mph	*Motor Trend,* July 1967
Dodge Coronet R/T	14.91 seconds at 93.16 mph	*Hot Rod,* February 1967
Shelby GT500	15.0 seconds at 95 mph	*Car and Driver,* February 1967
Plymouth GTX	15.20 seconds at 97 mph	*Car Life,* March 1967
Chevrolet Camaro SS 350	15.40 seconds at 90 mph	*Motor Trend,* December 1966
Shelby GT350	15.5 seconds at 92.2 mph	*Popular Hot Rodding,* February 1967
Ford Mustang GT (390 V-8)	15.6 seconds at 94 mph	*Motor Trend,* December 1966
Mercury Cougar GT	15.9 seconds at 89.1 mph	*Car Life,* July 1967

NOTE: *SSDI is* Super Stock & Drag Illustrated.

1967 CHEVROLET CAMARO SS

CONSTRUCTION: unitized body/frame
MODEL AVAILABILITY: sport coupe & convertible
PRICE: RPO L48 alone cost $210.65, L35 cost $263.30, L78 cost $500.30
WHEELBASE: 108 inches
WEIGHT: 3,269 pounds (SS 350 coupe)
SUSPENSION: heavy-duty; coil springs & stabilizer bar, front; solid-axle w/leaf springs & right-side trailing link, rear
STEERING: manual (24:1) recirculating ball; 17.5:1 power-assist, optional
WHEELS: 14x6 stamped-steel
TIRES: D70 red-stripe Wide Oval
BRAKES: manual 9.5-inch drums, front & rear; 11-inch front discs & power-assist, optional
ENGINE: 350-cid Turbo Fire V-8 w/4-barrel carburetor (L48 SS 350); 396-cid L35 or L78 Turbo Jet V-8s available w/SS 396 package
TRANSMISSION: 3-speed manual, std (L48); close-ratio 3-speed included w/L35 & L78; 4-speed, optional, all; Powerglide automatic, optional (L48); Turbo Hydra-matic, optional (L35)
AXLE RATIO: 3.31:1, std (L48 350); 3.07:1 included w/L35 & L78; Positraction, optional

successor, then introduced Chevrolet's all-new F-body, Camaro, to the automotive press on September 12, 1966.

Estes called the 1967 Camaro a "four-passenger package of excitement." Like Mustang, it was meant to represent various different cars to various different drivers, a fact not missed by admiring journalists. "The problem is not whether to buy the Camaro," began a *Car Life* report, "but what kind of Camaro, for [this model] probably wears more faces than any other single car now made." A budget-conscious base model featured six cylinders, again mirroring Detroit's original pony car. At the top of the heap predictably was a Super Sport rendition, initially offered only with an exclusive 295-horse 350 small-block V-8 early in the 1967 model run. Chevrolet's 396 Turbo Jet big-block was announced for the Camaro SS in November 1966, allowing this newcomer to show off a truly menacing facade.

Chevrolet also rolled out its legendary Z28 Camaro a few weeks later to stir pony car riders' blood even further. Early press references commonly repeated the RPO list code, "Z-28," then badges that showed up in 1968 morphed the tag into "Z/28." The official name later became simply "Z28," which appears mostly on these pages in the best interests of consistency. Whatever the moniker, no Mustang would come remotely close to competing with the Z28 as far as open-road excitement was concerned, at least not until Dearborn's first Boss 302 arrived two years later. Suddenly it seemed the horseshoe was on the other hoof.

New as well for 1967 was Pontiac's first F-body, Firebird. This long-running tale dated back to early 1963, when engineer John DeLorean began toying with his two-seat "Banshee" dream machine. DeLorean continued promoting this sports car ideal after taking over the division's general manager post following Pete Estes move over to Chevrolet in July 1965. Chevy's F-car was already in process by then, but Pontiac's tall, thin g.m. would have nothing to do with it. He

Continued on page 86

SHOOT THE JUICE

Early carburetor evolution was slow, with true "modern" units—using adjustable jet metering and vacuum controls in place of the archaic "air-valve" system that had previously dominated the field—not appearing until the late 1920s. Showing up about the same time were pressurized supply systems (incorporating mechanically operated fuel pumps) that allowed engineers to replace gravity-fed updraft carbs with superior downdraft units. Downdraft pioneer Stromberg made headlines after one of its earliest designs showed up atop Chrysler engines in 1929.

Advances made the following decade included the "duplex" design, which predictably doubled the number of carburetor throats from the single venturi widely used until then. Also enhancing the "two-barrel" duplex carb's attraction was a new "180-degree" manifold that allowed each barrel to work independently through its own segregated passages, sending its mixture to distant cylinders to avoid cyclic conflicts inherent to previous designs. Typical wide-open manifolds of the day tended to let a cylinder rob mixture from a nearby bore during intake-stroke surges. By segregating those suction pulses, the 180-degree intake greatly improved performance—witness Henry Ford's "flathead" V-8, which went from 65 horsepower to 85 in 1934 after adopting this new technology.

Making more horses from there simply became a matter of installing more carb. If two throats were better than one, it only followed that four outdid two, hence the arrival of the modern four-barrel. A precursor to this muscle car staple was a Buick idea seen in 1941–42 that involved a pair of two-barrel carbs tied together with a progressive linkage. Only the front carb operated up until about 75 miles per hour. Once the throttle went beyond that point, the rear two-barrel chimed in to help make Buick's straight-eight one of Detroit's hottest mills of the day.

Buick straight-eights also pioneered the use of conventional four-barrels right after World War II. Buick's earliest choice was the "WCFB," short for "Will Carter Four Barrel." Founded by the same Will Carter in 1909, the Carter Carburetor Company initially was the main four-barrel source during the 1950s, with WCFB units crowning some of the decade's strongest V-8s. Carter later developed its popular "AFB" (aluminum four-barrel), and this was the carb that helped make Chevy's 409 so fine in 1961. Carter AFBs went atop nearly every Mopar muscle mill built during the 1960s.

Chrysler Corporation engineers mostly preferred Carter carbs, with two AFBs mounted atop every 426 street Hemi V-8 installed by Dodge and Plymouth between 1966 and 1971. *Mike Mueller*

But far more famous were the carbs manufactured by the company named after George and Earl Holley. These two brothers introduced their first carburetor, the "iron pot," in 1904 to kick-start a proud legacy that's still running strong in aftermarket circles a century later. Carters may have dominated the 1950s horsepower race, but that didn't stop Ford from planting a Holley four-barrel atop its Y-block V-8 to help put the thunder in those early two-seat T-birds.

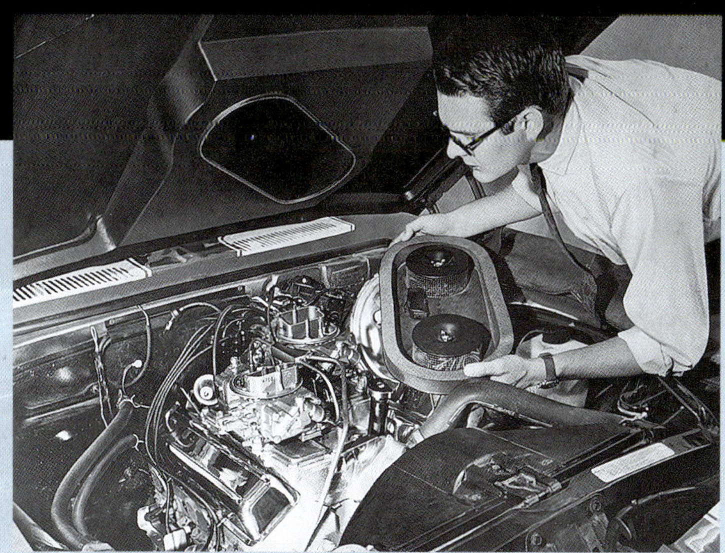

A cross-ram intake sporting two Holley four-barrels was offered over the counter as a service package option for Chevrolet's Z28 Camaro from 1967 to 1969.

While clearly representing progress compared to their two-barrel brethren, early four-barrels still fell a bit short when it came time to develop real horsepower. All 1950s examples were small, flowing about 400 to 450 cubic feet per minute—nowhere near enough to properly feed all the horses hiding within Detroit's biggest V-8s. Engineers were then forced to double, or even triple the number of carbs bolted atop their hottest engines to maximize muscle. Two Carter four-barrels were standard for Chrysler's C-300 in 1955, and various other optional dual-carb packages soon showed up in other camps. All of the race-ready super-stock V-8s that began showing up in 1962 relied on a pair of four-holers.

Pontiac and Oldsmobile introduced triple-carb induction (in V-8 applications) in 1957. Switching from two four-barrels to three two-barrels represented the wisest choice available as far as simultaneously maximizing efficiency and performance was concerned a half century ago.

But the logic behind multi-unit designs began fading as carburetor companies began developing bigger, better four-barrels. Once one large carb became capable of doing the job of two or three smaller ones, the case was closed.

Hence GM's decision in 1967 to drop 2x4 and 3x2 options for all its cars save for Corvettes and full-size models. In place of the three Rochesters seen atop Pontiac GTO and Olds 4-4-2 V-8s in 1966 was 1967's Quadra-jet four-barrel, first seen in a high-performance application atop Chevrolet's new 396-cube big-block V-8 in 1965. Also supplied by Rochester, the sometimes loved, sometimes hated Q-jet was used by Ford as well on its 429 Cobra Jet in 1971.

Holley was the firm most responsible for the four-barrel's major growth during the 1960s after first developing a big super-soaker for NASCAR applications in 1963. Compared to the popular Carter AFB, which flowed at 600 cfm, the new Holley maxed out at 750 cfm. Not long afterward, Holley came out with its Model 4150 four-barrel, able to suck in at 780 cfm. These big four-barrels, with their vacuum-controlled secondaries, then became the state of the art in the high-performance realm, and it was no coincidence that Chevrolet engineers bolted one atop their impressive 454-cid LS6 V-8 in 1970.

NASCAR speedways have long served as Detroit's proving grounds, at least as far as main model lines are concerned. But when it came to pitting pony car versus pony car during the 1960s, the trials and tests all came on Sports Car Club of America road courses. Originating in grassroots fashion right after World War II, SCCA-sanctioned competition really got rolling in 1956 when Chevrolet's Corvette entered the fray, giving flag-waving Yankees something they could really root for. Nothing else built in the U.S.A. qualified as a sports-racer until Carroll Shelby joined forces with Ford six years later. Shelby's little Cobra copped an SCCA Class A Production championship in 1964, and his GT350 Mustangs followed with three consecutive B/Production titles beginning in 1965.

In November 1965, SCCA officials inked plans for a new series, the Trans-American Sedan Championship, with the goal being to feature less exotic (aka, less costly) machines that Average Joe Racefan could relate to more readily. And so it was that a Dodge Dart finished 1st in its class (2nd overall) at the culmination of the inaugural "Trans-Am" event, the Four Hour Governor's Cup Race for Sedans, held in Florida on March 25, 1966, as a prelude to that year's running of the 12 Hours of Sebring. Six more sedan races followed that first season.

Factory-backed Darts and Plymouth Barracudas proved formidable early on before independent Mustangs moved to the forefront, attracting the attention of the Blue Oval boys in Dearborn, who again turned to Carroll Shelby. Shelby American's involvement then iced the first Tran-Am seasonal championship for Ford's pony car, and Shelby's two "Terlingua Racing Team" (named so to disguise factory ties) Mustangs made it back-to-back SCCA titles in 1967.

Although supposedly "not in racing," Chevrolet began thickening the Trans-Am plot that year with its new Z28 Camaro, a purposeful pony bred specifically with SCCA competition in mind. A Z28 finished 2nd behind a Dart its first time out at Daytona to kick off the 1967 Trans-Am season. And Mark Donahue, driving a Camaro for Roger Penske, managed three victories that year, including two straight to complete the 12-race schedule. Ford won the war, sure, but Chevrolet gained some serious battle experience.

Penske Racing's beautiful blue Sunoco Camaros then won 10 of 13 Trans-Am events in 1968, with Donahue taking eight consecutive checkered flags after finishing fourth at Daytona in February. A Shelby Racing Mustang was the Daytona winner, but Ford's pony car stumbled badly from there, allowing Chevrolet to clinch its first SCCA title upon completion of the season's 9th race.

Bunkie Knudsen helped put Ford back on track in 1969 after demanding that his people outdo the Z28, resulting in the Boss 302 Mustang. Facing off this time against Roger Penske's formidable Sunoco cars were two Boss Mustang teams, the existing Shelby Racing group, and a second shepherded by Bud Moore, who had built Mercury's Trans-Am Cougars in 1967 and 1968. The two Bud Moore Engineering Mustangs made the most hay in 1969, and by year's end it was relatively clear that Shelby's time in Trans-Am competition was coming to a close. Too bad the same couldn't be said for Penske dominance. Z28s won 8 of 12 Trans-Am races in 1969, with Donahue claiming 6 of those flags.

Bud Moore's Mustangs returned for the 1970 season but Shelby Racing's didn't. Penske, meanwhile, jumped from GM to American Motors, leaving Jim Hall to run Chevrolet's Trans-Am program. And Chrysler returned to SCCA tracks with its AAR 'Cuda from Plymouth and T/A Challenger from Dodge. Not to be denied this year, Moore's Mustangs closely battled Penske's Javelins, not Hall's Camaros, before finally clinching the championship in September.

Ford withdrew from motorsports two months later, and Chrysler and Chevrolet dropped their SCCA support in 1971, leaving AMC to have its way with what was left of the road racing field. Kenosha people touted their 1971–72 Trans-Am successes big-time before the series closed with a dull thud, foretelling a similar fate for American high-performance cars waiting just around the corner.

Ford Motor Company jumped into SCCA racing big-time in 1967, supporting both Mustang, and Cougar teams. Jerry Titus' Ford lines up here against Parnelli Jones Mercury.

The Big Three dropped out of SCCA road racing after 1970, leaving American Motors to run away with Trans-Am laurels in 1971 and 1972. Shown here is an inside look at 1971's Trans-Am Javelin, campaigned by former Chevy man Roger Penske.

BY THE NUMBERS: 1967 PRODUCTION

PONTIAC GTO

coupe	7,029	
hardtop	65,176	
convertible	9,517	
total	**81,722**	(64,177 w/335-hp 400 V-8, 2,967 w/280-hp 400, 13,287 w/400 HO, 751 w/400 Ram Air

PONTIAC FIREBIRD 400

	18,635*	(includes hardtops & convertibles)
*Ram Air production		(included in above total)
hardtop	63	
convertible	2	
total	**65**	(42 w/manual trans, 3 w/manual trans & air conditioning, 20 w/auto)

CHEVROLET SS 396

hardtop	59,685	
convertible	3,321	
total	**63,006**	

CHEVROLET CAMARO SS

L48 (350 V-8)	29,270	
L35 (396 V-8)	4,003	
L78 (396 V-8)	1,138	
total	**34,410**	(includes hardtops & convertibles)

CHEVROLET Z28 **602** (all hardtops)

CHEVROLET NOVA SS

six-cylinder	1,856	
V-8	8,213	
total	**10,069**	(all hardtops)

OLDSMOBILE 4-4-2

Cutlass coupe	4,750	(422 w/3-spd, 2,535 w/4-spd, 1,793 w/auto)
Cutlass hdtp	16,998	(409 w/3-spd, 7,661 w/4-spd, 8,928 w/auto)
Cutlass cvt.	3,079	(87 w/3-spd, 1,185 w/4-spd, 1,807 w/auto)
total	**24,827***	
* W-30 production		(included in above totals)
Cutlass coupe	129	
Cutlass hardtop	373	
total	**502**	

BUICK GRAN SPORT

GS-340 hdtp	3,692	(California Special, sold in California only)
GS-340 sedan	1,577	(all with automatic trans)
GS-400 sedan	1,014	(116 w/3-spd, 168 w/4-spd, 730 w/auto)
GS-400 hdtp	10,659	(373 w/3-spd, 2,280 w/4-spd, 8,006 w/auto)
GS-400 cvt.	2,059	(9 w/3-spd, 422 w/4-spd, 1,628 w/auto)
total	**19,001**	(another 544 GS-adorned Special coupes also were built; another 194 more export models are also known)

FORD MUSTANG GT/GTA

	24,078	(includes coupe, hardtop, and convertible)

FORD FAIRLANE GT/GTA

hardtop	18,670	
convertible	2,117	
total	**20,787**	

FORD 427 FAIRLANE

	229*	(includes all models w/R-code & W-code V-8s)

*Of these, reportedly 72 were Fairlane 500XL models.

SHELBY MUSTANG

prototypes	4	(includes 1, GT350 fastback, 1 GT500 fastback, 1 GT500 notchback & 1 GT500 convertible)
GT350	1,135	
GT350	35	(w/Paxton supercharger)
GT350	4	(w/dealer-installed Paxton supercharger)
GT500	2,044	
"Super Snake"	1	(first 427-equipped GT500)
GT500 w/427	1	
GT500 w/427	1	(drag car)
total	**3,225**	

MERCURY COUGAR GT

hardtop	5,791	
XR7 hardtop	2,673	
total	**8,464**	

MERCURY COUGAR DAN GURNEY SPECIAL

hardtop	15,166	
XR7 hardtop	4,617	
total	**19,783**	

MERCURY CYCLONE

hardtop	2,682	
GT hardtop	3,419	
convertible	431	
GT convertible	378	
total	**6,910**	

MERCURY 427 COMET

	60*	(includes 202, Comet & Cylone w/W- or R-code V-8s)

*Of these, reportedly 19 were Cyclones, 22 were Comet sedans.

PLYMOUTH BARRACUDA FORMULA S

273 V-8	5,352	
383 V-8	1,841	
total	**7,193**	

PLYMOUTH GTX

hardtop	12,010	
convertible	680	
total	**12,690**	

DODGE DART GT

hardtop	34,496	
convertible	3,729	
total	**38,225**	

DODGE DART GTS **457** (includes hardtops & convertibles; 229 w/manual transmission, 228 w/auto)

DODGE CHARGER **15,788** (all fastbacks)

DODGE CORONET R/T

hardtop	10,109	
convertible	196	
total	**10,305**	

NOTE: *Production data was supplied by various sources, including Christo Datini at the GM Heritage Center, Ford Motor Company & Kevin Marti at Marti Auto Works (www.martiauto.com), the Shelby American Automobile Club (www.saac.com), and Galen Govier (Mopar material) at Galen's Tag Service (www.galengovier.com).*

1967 CHEVROLET CAMARO Z28

CONSTRUCTION: unitized body/frame
MODEL AVAILABILITY: sport coupe
PRICE: Z28 option alone cost $358.10; mandatory options included $184.35 M21 4-speed, $79 J52 front discs & $42.15 J50 power brakes
WHEELBASE: 108 inches
WEIGHT: 3,250 pounds
SUSPENSION: heavy-duty w/coil springs & stabilizer bar, front; solid axle w/leaf springs & right-side trailing link, rear
STEERING: manual (24:1) recirculating ball; quicker 20:1 ratio & 17.5:1 power steering, optional
WHEELS: 15x6 Rally
TIRES: 7.35x15 Goodyear red-stripe
BRAKES: power-assisted 11-inch discs, front; 9.5-inch drums, rear
ENGINE: 302-cid V-8 w/800-cfm Holley four-barrel carburetor
TRANSMISSION: close-ratio M21 4-speed w/Muncie shifter
AXLE RATIO: 3.73:1 (Positraction, optional)

1967 PONTIAC FIREBIRD 400

CONSTRUCTION: unitized body/frame w/dual-scooped hood
MODEL AVAILABILITY: sport coupe & convertible
PRICE: $2,777, hardtop; $3,177, convertible
WHEELBASE: 108.1 inches
WEIGHT: 3,549 pounds, hardtop; 3,885 pounds, convertible
SUSPENSION: heavy-duty w/coil springs & stabilizer bar, front; solid axle w/leaf springs and trailing links, rear
STEERING: manual recirculating ball
WHEELS: 14x5J stamped-steel
TIRES: E70x14 Firestone Wide Oval
BRAKES: 9.5-inch drums, front & rear; front discs & power-assist, optional
ENGINE: 400-cid W66 V-8 w/Rochester 4-barrel carburetor
TRANSMISSION: heavy-duty floor-shifted 3-speed manual, std; 4-speed and automatic, optional

Continued from page 82

was still working on his beloved Banshee in February 1966, leaving GM executive vice president Ed Cole no choice but to step in.

In March 1966 Cole directed DeLorean to forget the Banshee and "make a car out of the Camaro." Pontiac's Mustang-beater then debuted on February 23, 1967, and, like its Bow-Tie-clad running mate, was available with some serious cubic inches. The hot-looking, hot-running Firebird 400 was also more than capable of leaving Ford's big-block pony car in the dust in 1967.

As if GM's newborn thoroughbreds weren't competition enough, Ford Motor Company even created its own in-house copycat, Cougar, a slightly longer, more prestigious pony car from Mercury. Initial plans for this "upscaled" Mustang, code-named T-7, dated back about a year before Iacocca rolled out his record-setting milestone, with the final design nod coming in February 1965. Introduced on September 30, 1966, Cougar initially was offered only in hardtop form, and, unlike its Mustang cousin, was not available with a six-cylinder. It was V-8 power only for the machine *Motor Trend* called its "Car of the Year" in 1967. Both small- and big-blocks were installed from the get-go.

Plymouth people also recognized that building a bigger Barracuda better suited to big-cube installations was in order for 1967. Led by former Studebaker man Milt Antonick, the division's design team opted for a totally blank sheet of paper, and their bold efforts paid off with a sleek body that overnight changed the way critics looked at Plymouth's previously demure pony car. Sure, the second-generation Barracuda still shared its A-body foundation with Valiant and Dodge's Dart, but the connection was no longer visible, not even if you squinted.

"The new Barracuda is unquestionably the best-looking car out of Detroit in 1967," crowed a December 1966 *Car and Driver* review. "It has tautness of line and integrity of design matched by few American cars of any vintage. It's been several years since either division of the Chrysler Corporation has produced a notably handsome car; Plymouth's old Barracuda was hardly the exception."

Up front was an enlarged engine bay that allowed Chrysler's 383-cid B-series big-block, previously reserved for B- and C-bodies, to make its first appearance as an A-car option. Now Barracuda was officially entered in Detroit's muscle car race.

CHEVROLET

Chevy's new 350 small-block and Camaro SS equipment went hand-in-hand in 1967; one couldn't be had without the other, hence the whole package was listed under RPO L48, identified as the "Camaro SS w/295hp Turbo-Fire 350 cubic-inch engine." The model was called the "SS 350," though that nomenclature only appeared in the grille and on the fuel filler cap.

Coveted options included Chevy's new front disc brakes (complemented by the division's first Rally wheels) and the Z22 Rally Sport group, which among other things added trendy hideaway headlights. Appropriate badges were included, too, though these were superseded whenever RPO Z22 was applied to a Super Sport Camaro—"SS" took precedence over "RS."

The Z22 option was available for either Super Sport, small- or big-block. Like the SS 350, the SS 396 was identified on the options list by its engine code, beginning with RPO L35, the tag for the 325-horse hydraulic-lifter 396 V-8. Chevy's bodacious

375-horsepower L78 Mk IV V-8 also was offered, transforming Camaro into the undisputed leader of 1967's pony car performance pack.

The Z28 Camaro offered its own brand of performance, a road-hugging nature best demonstrated on SCCA tracks. But hold your horses—weren't all GM divisions restricted from direct racing involvement per that infamous executive decree sent down early in 1963? Certainly. That reality, however, didn't stop Vince Piggins, Chevrolet's ever-present performance products guru, from taking Camaro to the SCCA Trans-Am circuit.

On August 17, 1966, Piggins issued a memo to his bosses outlining his plan to build an SCCA-legal Camaro, a car possessing "performance and handling characteristics superior to either Mustang or Barracuda." While his proposal was accepted, with no regard to ivory tower instructions, his suggested name, "Cheetah," was ignored in favor of the aforementioned RPO reference.

To meet SCCA homologation standards, the Z28 had to use an engine no larger than 305 cubic inches. No problem: engineers simply bolted a 283 crank into a 327 block, resulting in a 302-cid small-block that made 290 horsepower—on paper, that is. In the real world, that advertised number fooled almost no one. "The 290-hp figure quoted for the Z-28 seems ridiculously conservative," went a *Car and Driver* claim. "It feels as least as strong as the 327, 350-hp engine offered in the Corvette."

Chevrolet's original Z28 was introduced to the automotive press on November 26, 1966, at Riverside, California. Along with its exclusive small-block, the race-ready package also included power-assisted front disc brakes. Thrown in along with those preferred stoppers were 15x6 Corvette-type Rally wheels.

The new front disc option (RPO J52) for 1967's Chevelle also included Rally wheels, but these were 14x6 units. Debuting as well for that year's A-body SS 396 was GM's three-speed Turbo Hydra-matic transmission, an option finally made

In May 1967, a blue-striped, white-painted Camaro SS/RS convertible paced the Indianapolis 500, and Chevrolet then followed that up with an unknown number of pace car replicas, all colored similarly with either 350 small-block or 396 big-block V-8s. An SS 396 Camaro served as Indy 500 pace car again two years later.

HOT OFF THE PRESS: 1967 CHEVROLET CAMARO SS 350

"Some finesse with the gas pedal was needed to get the SS 350 off to a good start. High-rpm runs produced excessive wheelspin and slow times. Coming out with the tack needle resting just below 3000 rpm, and then stabbing it, produced the best times in the acceleration runs."

Steven Kelly, Motor Trend, *December 1966*

HOT OFF THE PRESS: 1967 CHEVROLET CAMARO Z28

"With the Z-28, Chevy is on the way toward making the gutsy stormer the Camaro should have been in the first place. [It] is Chevrolet's version of the Shelby Mustang—a Gran Turismo disguised as a Detroit sporty car."

Car and Driver, *March 1967.*

Updated at both ends and featuring revised "Super Sport" script, 1967's SS 396 Chevelle definitely was adorned with the blacked-out cove panel promised the previous year. As in 1966, the 325-horsepower L35 396 Turbo Jet was standard again, as were mundane "dog dish" hubcaps.

available behind Chevy's mightiest Mk IV big-blocks. SS 396 mechanicals were near-complete carryovers, save for less output (350 horsepower) for the optional L34 396. Super Sport trim was typically updated and included the blacked-out rear cove treatment promised in 1966.

Nova SS returned for 1967 looking essentially identical to its predecessor. With the L79 small-block (now rated at 325 horsepower for this application) dropped early on, it was left to the 275-horse 327 to carry the load.

HOT OFF THE PRESS: 1967 CHEVROLET CHEVELLE SS 396

"The SS 396s were the first GM intermediates we've driven that were free of the rear-end jello-roll blues that make life so hard for backseat passengers, and give the driver a few 'moments' as well."

Robert Schilling, Motor Trend, *July 1967*

Next to no changes were made to the Super Sport Nova for 1967—in back, the "SS" identification seen the previous year was lengthened to "Nova SS." Optional front disc brakes were new this year.

PONTIAC

Though not exactly John DeLorean's dream, Pontiac's new pony car still impressed critics with a sporty flair all its own. "It may be the first step toward a true four-passenger GT car in the best European sense," claimed a *Road & Track* report. "With the introduction of the Firebird we hope to attract new car buyers who want to step up to something extra in styling as well as performance in this segment of the market," added DeLorean while introducing Firebird.

"You'd expect Pontiac to come up with a nifty new sports car like this," announced magazine ads. "But did you expect five?" Pontiac's "Magnificent Five" for 1967 included two Firebirds fitted with the division's innovative overhead-cam six. A base V-8 (326-cid) Firebird was next up the pecking order, followed by the "light heavyweight," Firebird HO, powered by a warmed-up 285-horse 326. PMD's biggest V-8 went into the Firebird 400, which came standard with a beefed suspension and a hood sporting two non-functional scoops.

The base Firebird 400 featured the 400-cid W66 V-8, rated at 325 horsepower. Adding the optional L67 Ram Air 400, also advertised at 325 horses, made those two scoops fully functional, which in turn allowed those ponies to breathe a little easier. Maximum output for the Ram Air 400 arrived at 5,200 rpm, 400 revs above the W66's power peak.

The 1966 GTO's plastic egg-crate grille was replaced by a wire-mesh layout the following year. Engine displacement also went from 389 cubic inches to 400 in 1967. *Mike Mueller*

Firebird Ram Air V-8s all produced less horsepower compared to their GTO counterparts until 1970 due to a carburetor restriction that kept the two rear throttle plates on those Rochester four-barrels from opening fully when pedal met metal. This allowed Pontiac's pony car to remain within another GM-mandated limit, this one involving a maximum power to weight ratio, specified at 10:1.

Standard GTO power remained at 335 horses in 1967 even after Pontiac's venerable 389 was bored out to 400 cubic inches. New that year was an economy-conscious two-barrel 400, rated at 255-horsepower. Compression was 8.6:1 for this lo-po no-cost option, compared to 10.75:1 in all other cases. An automatic was the only available option behind the 255-hp 400, but this transmission was now GM's Turbo Hydra-matic 400. When ordered along with an interior console, the TH-400 also was fitted with Hurst's Dual Gate shifter, which allowed a choice between manual control of those three speeds or conventional automatic operation.

Engine options included the 400 HO and 400 Ram Air, both rated at 360 horsepower. HO features included free-flowing exhaust manifolds, a lumpier cam, and an open-element air cleaner with chrome lid. The Ram Air option added the functional hood and, late in the year, revised heads with stronger valves springs. While the HO was available with a standard three-speed, its Ram Air brother was limited to either a four-speed or TH-400 automatic. "King of the Supercars!" was *Car Life's* description for 1967's Ram Air GTO.

Front disc brakes were new on 1967's options list, as were attractive Rally II five-spoke wheels. Optional Rally I rims also carried over from 1966.

HOT OFF THE PRESS: 1967 PONTIAC GTO

"The Ram Air GTO provided a level of acceleration beyond belief to anyone not accustomed to Supercars. The GTO may be the eldest of the current Supercars, but it remains a worthy target for would-be competitors. Performance brakes and styling continue to set the pace for other manufacturers. By anyone's Supercar yardstick, the GTO is the standard of the U.S."

Car Life, *October 1967*

HOT OFF THE PRESS: 1967 PONTIAC FIREBIRD 400

"Another candidate for the Mustang's sporty-car crown hits the pavement. Will it succeed? Only the Youth Market knows for sure."

Car and Driver, *March 1967*

Twin hood scoops were standard for the 1967 Firebird 400, available in both hardtop and convertible forms. *Mike Mueller*

Like Fairlane beginning in 1966, Ford's 1967 Mustang was offered in both GT and GTA forms, with the latter again signifying the installation of an automatic transmission. GT/GTA Mustangs were fitted with both small- and big-block V-8s. *Mike Mueller*

HOT OFF THE PRESS: 1967 FORD MUSTANG GT

"People are just more aware of [this] machine than almost anything you can think of being made in American today. Whisking along the freeway at speed or slipping through downtown traffic, heads turn and there is a knowing recognition of being with a winner."

Eric Dahlquist, Hot Rod, *March 1967*

All of Ford's 427 Fairlanes were built the same way in 1966: Wimbledon White hardtops with functional fiberglass hoods and humble dog-dish hubcaps on steel rims. In 1967 a 427 fan could order his Fairlane in any color and with various options, including Ford's classy styled-steel wheels. That 'glass hood with its big scoop became an option in 1967. Body style choices were expanded as well to include sedans, convertibles, and the top-shelf XL hardtop. *Mike Mueller*

FORD

Critics were mostly in favor of the Mustang's 1967 redesign, with *Hot Rod* magazine's Eric Dahlquist doing his best to help keep the pony car faithful faithful. "Detroit has cobbled up so many fine designs in the last twenty years that when Ford decided to change the Mustang, everybody held their breath," he wrote. "But it's okay people, everythin's gonna' be all right." Save for wheelbase, nearly all dimensions and measures (including price) increased, but at least the bottom line remained less than a dollar a pound.

Adding more than 260 extra bucks into the mix was the new optional big-block, Ford's 320-horse 390-cid Thunderbird Special V-8, available with or without GT equipment, which rolled over almost unchanged from 1966 save for the addition of F70-14 Wide Oval rubber. For 1967 only, Ford folk also opted to set their hottest Mustangs apart, Fairlane-style, depending on transmission choices: manual-trans models now wore GT badges, while automatic cars were adorned with "GTA." GT engine availability doubled in 1967 as the 390 big-block was joined by the mundane 289 two-barrel, sandwiching 1966's rollover 289 four-barrel and Hi-Po 289. Four-barrel V-8s again were fitted with dual exhausts when ordered for the GT/GTA package, while the two-barrel 289 retained its single exhaust.

Also new for GT/GTA Mustangs in 1967 was an LPO (limited production option) available only with the Hi-Po small-block or 390 big-block. Called the Competition Handling Package, this group included a 0.94-inch-diamter front sway bar, Gabriel adjustable shocks, quick 16:1 steering gear, a 3.25:1 limited-slip differential, and big 15x6 wheels shod in Goodyear Blue Dot racing rubber.

Encoring in 1967, the mildly updated Fairlane's GT/GTA rendition this time came standard with front disc brakes and F70-14 Wide Ovals. But the really big news involved engine availability. The base V-8 this year was a two-barrel small-block, Ford's 200-hp 289. Two 390 big-blocks were optional: the 320-horsepower Thunderbird Special and a two-barrel version rated at 270 horsepower.

Also returning was an available 427 FE for non-GT 1967 Fairlanes. Apparently a few High Performance 289s were installed, too.

A big-block GT500 joined Shelby American's carryover GT350 (shown here) in 1967, and both featured an extended fiberglass nosepiece that stretched overall length by 3 inches compared to a garden-variety 1967 Mustang. Recessed deep in that nose was a grille sporting twin driving lights that were mounted in differing positions, together in the middle or at opposite ends of the grille, depending on the state in which the car was originally delivered. Statutes in some states required minimum distances between headlights, explaining the variation. Cougar sequential taillights and a fiberglass deck lid incorporating a large ducktail spoiler were added in back. *Mike Mueller*

SHELBY MUSTANG

Shelby American introduced a GT500 running mate for its existing GT350 in 1967. A 355-horsepower 428 FE big-block, topped by twin Holley four-barrels, was standard for the GT500, while Ford's Hi-Po 289 carried over for the GT350. Both also were treated to various body modifications, including an extended fiberglass nose, functional rear-quarter scoops, a fiberglass deck lid incorporating a large ducktail spoiler, and Cougar sequential taillights.

GT500s outsold GT350s in 1967 on the way to a Shelby Mustang production high. Two GT500 prototypes, one a notchback coupe, the other a ragtop, also were toyed with this year. These were the last California-built Shelbys as production was transplanted from Los Angeles to the A. O. Smith works in Livonia, Michigan, for 1968. Shelby's LAX lease was up, and Dearborn officials needed no other excuse to bring the GT350/500 "home."

MERCURY

The wildest Cougar in 1967 was the GT, powered by the 320-horsepower 390 backed by (in *Car and Driver's* words) "a pair of loud mufflers." All the stuff you'd expect—toughened chassis, power front discs, and Wide Oval skins on wide 14x6 rims—were included in the GT deal. Mercury's most luxurious cat, the midyear Cougar XR7, also could be fitted with GT equipment. Standard XR7 fare included leather bucket seats, full instrumentation and posh interior accouterments. *Motor Trend's* critics were especially fond of the XR7 buckets, claiming they were "in the same class with those in the more expensive Mercedes sedans, which are justly famed for having comfortable seats."

BABY GRAN

Standard for the GS-340 was a 340-cid small-block topped by a four-barrel carburetor. Output was 260 horsepower. *Mike Mueller*

Buick's big-block Gran Sport was joined in 1967 by a small-block running mate, "designed for enthusiasts who want the GS brand of excitement at a lower price than the GS-400." Unveiled in February 1967 in hardtop form only, the GS-340 may have targeted budget-minded buyers but at the same time was, again in Buick's words, "a lot of car for any car buff." Standard under the hood was the 260-horse 340-cid V-8 introduced the year before, and behind that was a column-shifted three-speed manual trans, which could be traded for Buick's two-speed Super Turbine automatic at extra cost. Helping keep the base price down inside was a taxi-cab-bare bench-seat interior.

Offsetting those cost-cutting measures was an exterior that was far from plain. Broad rally stripes done in red graced the lower body sides, and red accents also appeared at the nose and tail. The hood's twin dummy scoops also were red, as were the standard Rallye wheels, adorned with "deep" chrome trim rings and bright center caps. Standard tires were 7.75x14 rayon-cord tires. F70 redline Wide Ovals were optional. Available as well on the options list were power front discs and Buick's Sport Pac suspension, consisting of quicker 15:1 steering, stiffer springs and shocks, and a rear stabilizer bar.

Offered for 1967 only, the GS-340 was based priced at $2,845, $175 less than that year's GS-400 hardtop. Paint choices were limited to two: Platinum Mist or Arctic White.

Buick's budget-conscious GS-340 joined the existing GS-400 in 1967. Only two GS-340 exterior colors were offered: Platinum Mist or Arctic White. All were hardtops. *Mike Mueller*

HOT OFF THE PRESS: 1967 SHELBY GT350

"[GT500 is] a grown-up sports car for smooth touring. No more wham-bam, thank-you-ma'am, just a purring, well-controlled tiger. Like Shelby says, 'This is the first car I'm really proud of.' Right."

Car and Driver, *February 1967*

1967 SHELBY GT500

CONSTRUCTION: unitized body/frame w/fiberglass body panels front & rear
MODEL AVAILABILITY: Mustang fastback
PRICE: $4,395
WHEELBASE: 108 inches
WEIGHT: 3,286 pounds
SUSPENSION: heavy-duty; upper A-arms, lower control arms, w/coil springs mounted atop A-arms, 0.94-inch stabilizer bar, front; solid axle w/longitudinal leaf springs, rear; adjustable Gabriel shock absorbers (Koni shocks, optional)
STEERING: power-assisted (20.3:1) recirculating ball
WHEELS: 15x6.5 Shelby
TIRES: E70x15
BRAKES: power-assisted 11.38-inch front discs; 10-inch rear drums
ENGINE: 355-hp 428-cid V-8 w/2 Holley four-barrel carburetors
TRANSMISSION: 4-speed manual, std; heavy-duty Cruise-O-Matic automatic, optional
AXLE RATIO: 3.50:1 std w/manual trans; 3.25:1 w/automatic
AXLE RATIO: 3.08:1, std

HOT OFF THE PRESS: 1967 MERCURY COUGAR GT

"The 390-equipped Cougars should be able to say out in front of [SS] Camaros as the latter weigh almost the same and their biggest engine is 40 inches smaller and 25 hp shy."

Motor Trend, *October 1966*

Like Fairlane, Mercury's Cyclone rolled over unchanged into 1967 and again included a 200-horsepower 289 in base form. This Cyclone is fitted with the optional single-carb 427, rated at 410 horsepower. *Mike Mueller*

Mercury's upscale pony car, Cougar, joined Mustang in 1967. The hottest Cougar was the GT, powered by a 320-horse 390 FE big-block. GT equipment also could be added to the prestigious XR7, introduced midyear. *Mike Mueller*

Introduced midyear as well was the Dan Gurney Special, honoring the famed driver who helped promote Mercury's pony car on the 1967 Trans-Am circuit. This package included a chromed-up 289 V-8, turbine wheel covers, and appropriate decals bearing Gurney's signature.

Like its Fairlane corporate cousin, Mercury's Cyclone carried over from 1966 in nearly identical fashion. The 200-horsepower 289 was again included in the basic Cyclone deal, but this year's big-block, the Marauder 390 GT V-8, was down rated to 320 horsepower. Power front discs and Wide Ovals also became standard Cyclone GT features this year. The 410- and 425-horse 427s were available for Comet/Cyclone, too.

PLYMOUTH

Reportedly Plymouth engineers originally planned to incorporate an enlarged small-block into the 1967 Barracuda's supreme performance package. While designers were busy widening the rebuilt breed's engine bay by 2 inches, engineers were preparing to modify Chrysler's existing 318-cid LA-series V-8 for this application. Then came word of the really big engines scheduled for upcoming rival pony cars.

As *Car and Driver* told the tale, "Plymouth pushed aside the 318 and set about wedging their big, fat 383 into the 'Cuda. Tight fit, but—whew!—they made it." A power steering pump, however, didn't make it, due to the fact it couldn't coexist with the driver's side exhaust manifold. That tight fit also contributed to a noticeable power outage. A-body big-block applications required the use of a more restrictive exhaust system, which in turn inhibited horsepower. A tamer cam helped cut advertised output as well, resulting in a 280-horsepower rating for the 1967 Barracuda's optional 383 Commando V-8.

While the big-block option, at $52, surely looked affordable in 1967, the true price actually was a little higher thanks to two mandatory installations: the Formula S suspension package and Kelsey-Hayes front disc brakes. Firestone D70 Wide Oval redline tires were added to 1967's Formula S package, which was offered along with the 383 big-block or 273 small-block.

Former Studebaker designer Milt Antonick garnered most of the credit for the A-body Barracuda's highly acclaimed 1967 makeover. The carryover fastback was joined by a new "notchback" coupe and convertible this year, and the Formula S was offered with both small- and big-block power. *Mike Mueller*

B-body Plymouth muscle also received a boost in 1967 after product planning manager Jack Smith decided it was high time to roll out a midsize factory hot rod that truly looked the part. His first move involved a few doodles on a legal pad, this after noting that a zinger of name was in order, preferably one with three letters to mimic Pontiac's choice. His experiments began with the classic "GT," but how to make this a triplet? "O," of course was already taken, Ford had beaten him to "A," and "S" was slated for a new Dodge A-body you'll read about soon enough. Hence he scrolled down to "X," a letter that always has exuded its own particular coolness. "GTX." Yeah, that was the ticket.

Once he named his baby, Smith caught the ear of design studio chief Richard McAdams, who proposed that they go right to the head of the Belvedere class and use the trimmed-out, top-shelf Satellite as a base for the GTX. Along with a full load of exterior flair, Satellite featured standard bucket seats and was offered only in sporty hardtop and sexy convertible forms.

Making a heavy-duty chassis standard was a no-brainer. A big-block also was a slam-dunk, but which one? The street Hemi surely would've worked, but the better choice was the new 440 Super Commando, an RB that offered ample oomph (375 horsepower) for fewer bucks. What the 440 lacked in advertised output, it made up for in overall ease of use compared to its 425-horse solid-lifter cousin. As *Hot Rod* magazine's Dick Scritchfield explained, the heart-and-soul of GTX was "a street engine with racing ability without the problems of the finely tuned racing mill."

While some buyers did chose the optional Hemi, the majority stuck with the standard Super Commando, losing little in the deal, face or otherwise. Transmission choices numbered two: Torqueflite automatic or four-speed manual. Trading the standard Torqueflite for the no-cost stick mandated the installation of a few options, including a dual-point distributor, viscous-drive fan, and a windage tray in the oil pan to prevent horsepower loss as the crankshaft whipped up the lubricant supply. Four-speed GTX models also were fitted with a heavy-duty Dana rear axle containing 3.54:1 gears in a Sure-Grip differen-

1967 MERCURY COUGAR GT

CONSTRUCTION: unitized body/frame
MODEL AVAILABILITY: base hardtop & XR7 hardtop
PRICE: GT Performance Group alone cost $323
WHEELBASE: 111 inches
WEIGHT: 3,530 pounds
SUSPENSION: heavy-duty; upper A-arms, lower control arms, w/coil springs mounted atop A-arms, 0.84-inch stabilizer bar, front; solid axle w/ longitudinal leaf springs, rear
STEERING: quick-ratio (20.3:1) recirculating ball; power-assist, optional
WHEELS: 14x6
TIRES: F70x14 Firestone Wide Oval
BRAKES: power-assisted 11.38-inch front discs; 10-inch rear drums
ENGINE: 390-cid GT V-8 w/four-barrel carburetor
TRANSMISSION: 3-speed manual, std; 4-speed & Merc-O-Matic automatic, optional
AXLE RATIO: 3.25:1

1967 PLYMOUTH BARRACUDA FORMULA S

CONSTRUCTION: unitized body/frame
MODEL AVAILABILITY: coupe, fastback & convertible
PRICE: Formula S package cost $177.50
WHEELBASE: 108 inches
WEIGHT: 3,310 pounds (273 V-8)
SUSPENSION: heavy-duty; torsion bars & 0.88-inch stabilizer bar, front; solid axle w/leaf springs, rear
STEERING: manual (24:1) recirculating ball; power-assist, optional
WHEELS: 14x5.5 inches
TIRES: D70 Firestone Wide Oval
BRAKES: 10-inch drums, front & rear; 11.125-inch front discs, optional (mandatory w/383 V-8)
Engine: 273-cid LA small-block V-8 or 383-cid big-block V-8
TRANSMISSION: 4-speed manual or Torqueflite automatic
AXLE RATIO: 3.23:1

HOT OFF THE PRESS: 1967 PLYMOUTH GTX

"GTO owners had better look to their defenses. Plymouth has given the GTX strong good looks and one of the best-handling sedan chassis we have ever driven."

Car and Driver, *November 1966*

Though described as a "Belvedere GTX" in Plymouth promotional paperwork in 1967, the original GTX technically was based on the supreme Belvedere variation, the Satellite—both shared the same top-shelf trim, various standard features, and the division's "CR2-P" model series code. The 440-cid RB wedge and 426 Hemi were the only engines used by GTX during its five-year run. *Mike Mueller*

HOT OFF THE PRESS: 1967 PLYMOUTH BARRACUDA

"The new Barracuda is unquestionably the best-looking car out of Detroit in 1967. It has tautness of line and integrity of design matched by few American cars of any vintage. It's been several years since either division of the Chrysler Corporation has produced a notably handsome car; Plymouth's old Barracuda was hardly the exception."

Car and Driver, *December 1966*

1967 PLYMOUTH GTX

CONSTRUCTION: unitized body/frame
MODEL AVAILABILITY: hardtop or convertible
PRICE: $3,178, hardtop; $3,418, convertible
WHEELBASE: 116 inches
WEIGHT: 3,830 pounds (hardtop)
SUSPENSION: heavy-duty; 0.92-inch torsion bars & 0.94-inch stabilizer bar, front; solid axle w/leaf springs, rear
STEERING: manual recirculating ball; power-assist, optional
WHEELS: 14x5.5K stamped-steel
TIRES: 7.75x14 red-stripe
BRAKES: 11-inch drums, front & rear; power-assisted 11-inch front discs, optional
ENGINE: 440-cid Super Commando V-8 w/Carter 4-barrel carburetor, std; 426 Hemi, optional
TRANSMISSION: Torqueflite automatic, std; 4-speed optional at no extra cost
AXLE RATIO: 3.23:1 w/Torqueflite; 3.54:1 Sure-Grip Dana rear end w/4-speed

tial. The Dana unit's ring gear measured 9.75 inches, compared to the standard axle's 8.75-inch gear.

The sum of these parts equaled what Plymouth ads called "a machine of many talents … the most well-rounded Supercar to come out of Detroit (or anywhere, for that matter) in a long time."

DODGE

Dodge's first big-block A-body showed up clandestinely midyear in 1967, thanks to a little help from speed merchant Norm Kraus. Kraus' team at his Grand-Spaulding Dodge dealership in Chicago stuffed a 383 V-8 into a Dart and drove it to Detroit to show Dodge division chief Robert McCurry just how easily this combo went together—and how well it ran. Suitably impressed, McCurry suggested to his engineers that if the Grand-Spaulding guys could pull this one off, they could too. Enter Dart GTS.

The GTS was fitted with a 325-horsepower 383 topped by a low-restriction air cleaner that, as ad copy explained, emitted "a low moan that your mother-in-law won't understand and your wife will eventually get used to." Also included was Dodge's heavy-duty Rallye chassis with its front discs and Red Streak rubber. Save for a low-profile black-and-white magazine ad, no official announcement came from Dodge concerning the Dart GTS's debut, explaining why press reports later erroneously claimed 1968's GTS was the first of the breed. Production reportedly began in February 1967.

Up in B-body ranks, Charger pushed on into 1967 with minor changes. New under the hood was the optional 440 (tagged "Magnum" in Dodge parlance), which again offered a major portion of the Hemi's might at a fraction of the cost. Both the 440 and Hemi options were expectedly supported by a heavy-duty suspension, which featured stiffer 0.92-inch torsion bars and a thicker 0.94-inch

Dodge's big-block Dart GTS appeared rather quietly midyear in 1967. A 280-horsepower 383 Magnum V-8 was standard. *Mike Mueller*

sway bar up front. Six-leaf springs went underneath in back. Hemi-powered Chargers in 1967 also were fitted with a rear-deck spoiler.

Charger was joined in 1967 by Coronet R/T, Dodge's response to Plymouth's GTX. Once fitted with a 440 Magnum and a similarly beefed foundation, GTX's corporate cousin needed only a neato name to complete the deal. Quick-thinking product planner Burt Bouwkamp handled that task, coming up with "R/T," short of course for "road & track." Ad guys then took it from there, announcing that the new Coronet R/T was a "dual purpose machine" that was as "sweet as can be on the road… Hot as you want it on the track."

Being based on the Coronet 500, the decked-out flagship in Dodge's B-body lineup, R/T came standard with sporty bucket seats and the Torqueflite automatic. On the outside, the 1967 Coronet R/T was set apart from the B-body pack with prominent badges, simulated hood louvers, and a Charger-style grille that featured fixed headlamps instead of hideaway units.

Popular options included the ever-prominent Hemi, still priced well above the reach of Average Joe. A box-stock R/T, however, represented (in *Super Stock* magazine's words) "one of the best all-around performance packages being offered, [featuring] as much or more performance per dollar than any other car currently available."

Along with its wallet-wilting bottom-line, a Hemi R/T of course promised supreme straight-line performance. The choice was yours. "If you like to play it safe and economical, the Magnum's your baby with its friendly price tag and full 5/50 warranty," wrote *Motor Trend's* John Etheridge. "On the other hand, if you're the type that likes to live a little, be the envy of every service station attendant, attract admirers of both sexes when you show up at the local drive-in, and have roughly $600 extra to invest; go ahead and get the Hemi. The warranty is limited, but the dividends are high and paid promptly."

FAMILY TIES: DODGE DART

Dodge first stuck Dart badges on a futuristic show car unveiled in 1956. The nameplate then entered the mainstream in 1960, crowning the division's new downsized B-body line. Less was the name of the game again in 1963 when Dart was reborn on Chrysler's A-body platform, superseding Dodge's first compact, Lancer, introduced two years prior. While Lancer had relied on a definitely diminutive 106.5-inch wheelbase, the 1963 Dart's foundation measured 111 inches from hub to hub. Relative affordability remained the main selling point, hence all 1963 Darts, even the top-shelf GT, were powered by frugal six-cylinders. An optional 273-cid two-barrel V-8 appeared for the Dart GT in 1964, followed by a four-barrel 273 in 1965. Outward imagery was enhanced noticeably the next year, then came an optional big-block V-8 midyear in 1967, allowing Dart GT entry into Detroit's muscle car fraternity.

Dodge's compact A-body Dart was introduced for 1963 in three series, 170, 270 and GT, all powered by Chrysler's slant-six engine. An available V-8, the 273-cid LA small-block, then arrived the following year.

Right: Dodge's Charger continued into 1967 almost unchanged—on the outside. Inside, 1966's center console was shortened considerably and moved to the options list. Optional Hemi power remained, as this rare model attests. *Mike Mueller*

Right: Like Plymouth's GTX, Dodge's Coronet R/T only came with standard 440 or optional Hemi V-8s during its short 1967–70 run. Body side paint stripes were included in 1967 but could be deleted on request. Six stripe colors were offered: white, black, dark red metallic, dark blue metallic, light tan metallic, and medium copper metallic. *Mike Mueller*

1967 DODGE CORONET R/T

CONSTRUCTION: unitized body/frame
MODEL AVAILABILITY: hardtop or convertible
PRICE: $3,199, hardtop; $3,438, convertible
WHEELBASE: 117 inches
WEIGHT: 3,830 pounds (hardtop)
SUSPENSION: heavy-duty; torsion bars & 0.94-inch stabilizer bar, front; solid axle w/leaf springs, rear
STEERING: manual recirculating ball; 19:1 power-assist, optional
WHEELS: 14x5.5 stamped-steel
TIRES: 7.75x14 Red Streak
BRAKES: 11-inch drums, front & rear; 11-inch front discs, optional
ENGINE: 440-cid Magnum V-8 w/Carter four-barrel carburetor, std; 426 Hemi, optional
TRANSMISSION: Torqueflite automatic, std; 4-speed optional at no extra cost
AXLE RATIO: 3.23:1

HOT OFF THE PRESS: 1967 DODGE CORONET R/T

"Perhaps the R/T's mystique can be understood by the comments of a young parking attendant at the Century Plaza Hotel, where the to-and-from lot route represents a combination of Nurburgring and the Pikes Peak Hillclimb: 'Hey, I like this better than my GTO.' That's got to be the endorsement of the year."

Eric Dahlquist, Hot Rod, *February 1967*

OLDSMOBILE

The L78 4-4-2 Performance Package was limited to Cutlass Supreme models this year, and while the 350-horsepower 400 V-8 remained the star of the show, the optional auto trans was now the Turbo Hydra-matic. Apparently the new L66 Turnpike Cruisier option could've been combined with the L78 package to create a more fuel-efficient 4-4-2. Included in the L66 deal was a two-barrel-fed 300-horsepower 400 and the TH-400.

Officially known as the "Outside Air Induction" (OAI) option, W-30 equipment was revised this year, most noticeably on top, where a single four-barrel replaced 1966's triple Rochesters. New too were weight-saving red plastic inner fenderwells and revised air intakes, the latter required due to styling changes. The Turbo Hydra-matic transmission also became available for the second-edition W-30.

A pair of Air Injection Reactor (A.I.R.) cylinder heads, introduced as part of the K19 option (designed to meet California's tough emission standards), were added to the 1967 W-30 as well. But while the heads were included, the A.I.R. air-pump plumbing wasn't, meaning that the air-injection ports located just behind the spark plugs had to be covered for the W-30 application.

Oldsmobile's L78 4-4-2 Performance Package was limited to Cutlass Supreme models (sport coupe, Holiday hardtop, and convertible) in 1967. Strato bucket seats were a no-cost option inside. *Mike Mueller*

MOTOR OF THE YEAR: 1967 CHEVROLET CAMARO Z28 V-8

TYPE	OHV V-8 w/chrome dress-up
BORE	4.00 inches
STROKE	3.00 inches
HORSEPOWER	290 at 5800 rpm
TORQUE	290 at 4200 rpm
COMPRESSION	11:1
FUEL DELIVERY	800-cfm Holley 4-barrel carburetor on aluminum intake
AIR CLEANER	open-element w/chrome lid (cowl-plenum unit, optional)
IGNITION	dual-point distributor (transistorized ignition, optional)
COOLING	5-blade viscous-drive fan, heavy-duty radiator & deep-groove pulleys
CYLINDER BLOCK	cast-iron w/2-bolt main bearing caps, high-capacity oil pump & baffled oil pan
CRANKSHAFT	forged-steel w/2.299-inch main journals; tuftrided
CONNECTING RODS	forged-steel w/2.0-inch journals & 11/32-inch bolts; shot-peened, heat-treated & magnafluxed
PISTONS	forged-aluminum domed w/"half-moon" valve reliefs & press-fitted wrist pins
CAM	mechanical w/346 degrees duration (intake & exhaust) &118 degrees of overlap
ROCKER RATIO	1.5:1
CYLINDER HEADS	cast-iron L79 w/pressed-in rocker studs & heavy-duty valve springs; 66cc chamber volume
VALVE SIZES	2.02-inch intakes, 1.60-inch exhausts
VALVE LIFT	0.485 inch, intake/exhaust
EXHAUST SYSTEM	cast-iron manifolds w/2.25-inch pipes & low-tone mufflers (tubular headers, optional)

HOT OFF THE PRESS: 1967 OLDSMOBILE 4-4-2

"Sure-footed balance at speed is 4-4-2's forte. Wide Oval tires, handling package, [and] beefy drive train is the winning formula."
Motor Trend, *October 1966*

HOT OFF THE PRESS: 1967 OLDSMOBILE CUTLASS TURNPIKE CRUISER

"Without hesitation we rate the TC-packaged car above the 4-4-2 as an all-around road car. This goes for all kinds of roads—not just turnpikes—because with an identical suspension , it gives away nothing to the 4-4-2 in this department."
Motor Trend, *February 1967*

1967 BUICK GS-400

CONSTRUCTION: body on perimeter-rail frame
MODEL AVAILABILITY: Skylark coupe, hardtop & convertible
PRICE: $2,956 (coupe), $3,019 (hardtop), $3,167 (convertible)
WHEELBASE: 115 inches
WEIGHT: 3,439 pounds (coupe), 3,500 pounds (hardtop), 3,505 pounds (convertible)
SUSPENSION: heavy-duty, coil springs & 0.937-inch stabilizer bar, front; solid axle w/coil springs, rear
STEERING: manual (24:1) recirculating ball; 17.5:1 power-assist, optional
WHEELS: 14x6 JK stamped-steel
TIRES: F70x14 Wide Oval; red-stripe Wide Oval, optional
BRAKES: 9.5-inch drums, front & rear; power-assisted 9.83-inch front discs, optional
ENGINE: 400-cid V-8 w/Rochester Quadra-jet four-barrel carburetor
TRANSMISSION: 3-speed manual, std; 4-speed & 3-speed Super Turbine automatic, optional
AXLE RATIO: 3.36:1, std; 2.93:1 included w/automatic transmission; 3.50:1 & 3.90:1, optional

Buick's Gran Sport Skylark was officially renamed "GS-400" in 1967, and this time the numbers didn't lie. New beneath the hood was a thinwall-cast big-block that actually displaced 400 cubic inches, not 401. Also introduced this year was the small-block GS-340.

BUICK

Buick's midsize muscle car took on a new name, "GS-400," in 1967, and this time the numbers didn't lie. In place of the venerable Wildcat 445 nailhead was a modern big-block that actually did displace 400 cubes. Advertised output was 340 horsepower. F70 rubber was new for 1967, as were optional front discs and Buick's three-speed Super Turbine automatic transmission.

Debuting as well was the GS-340 hardtop (see page 91), a less costly variation on the Gran Sport theme using a 340-cid small-block V-8. A third Skylark Gran Sport also appeared in 1967, but for California customers only. Appropriately named "California GS," this cost-conscious sedan came standard with the GS-340's small-block (backed by an automatic trans), a bench seat, and vinyl top.

HOT OFF THE PRESS: 1967 BUICK GS

"The new GS 400 is more of an enthusiast's car than ever and will deliver more satisfaction performing any task than any of its predecessors."
John Ethridge, Motor Trend, *October 1966*

FAMILY TIES: BUICK SMALL- & BIG-BLOCK V-8s

General Motors truly put the "small" in small-block in 1961, rolling out a 215-cid V-8 for its three new "Bopettes," "senior compacts" to you. Weighing a mere 320 pounds thanks to its all-aluminum construction, this innovative mini-mill was standard for Buick's Special and Oldsmobile's F-85 that year, optional for Pontiac's Tempest. PMD people then replaced it in 1963 with a conventional iron-block V-8 that was more than half again larger, and the Buick/Olds duo followed suit the next year when its compacts graduated up into intermediate ranks. While F-85 featured Oldsmobile's aluminum "Rockette" engine exclusively prior to 1964, the folks in Flint opted to complement their 215 V-8 with a ground-breaking (in US passenger-car terms) V-6, done in iron, for 1962, and this pioneer then served as a base for the 300-cid V-8 that emerged as an A-body option two years later. Yes, Buick's new-for-1964 small-block was created simply by recasting that six-holer with two extra cylinders. Deck height was raised in 1966 to make room for a longer stroke, which in turn translated into 340 cubic inches. Next came more bore, resulting in the 350 V-8 that replaced the 300/340 pair in 1968 and remained on the market until 1977.

SMALL-BLOCKS

YEAR	CID	BORE & STROKE	CR	HORSEPOWER	TORQUE	CARBURETOR	VALVE SIZES
1961	215	3.50 x 2.80	8.8:1	155 @ 4,400	220 @ 2,400	Rochester 2-barrel	1.625 x 1.313
1964	300	3.75 x 3.40	9.0:1	210 @ 4,600	310 @ 2,400	Rochester 2-barrel	1.625 x 1.313
1966	340	3.75 x 3.85	9.0:1	220 @ 4,000	340 @ 2,400	Rochester 2-barrel	1.8175 x 1.38
1968	350	3.80 x 3.85	9.0:1	230 @ 4,400	350 @ 2,400	Rochester 2-barrel	1.88 x 1.50

NOTE: *215-cid V-8 featured aluminum construction; other engines detailed here were cast-iron.*

Buick's modern big-block era began in 1967 after the venerable "nailhead" finally retired. Replacing the Wildcat 445 V-8 beneath Gran Sport hoods this year was an engine that actually did displace 400 cubic inches, while big Buicks used a bored version of this new powerplant displacing 430 cubes. Primarily the work of engineer Clifford Studaker, this family was created using weight-conscious thinwall casting techniques, which saved more than 100 pounds compared to Chevrolet's Mk IV big-block. Additional improvements included better breathing heads with bigger valves and a beefier lower end featuring a crankshaft with 3.25-inch main bearing journals—main journal diameters in the nailhead measured only 2.5 inches. Another bore job pushed displacement up to 455 cubic inches in 1970.

BIG-BLOCKS

YEAR	CID	BORE & STROKE	CR	HORSEPOWER	TORQUE	CARBURETOR	VALVE SIZES
1967	400*	4.04 x 3.90	10.25:1	340 @ 5,000	440 @ 3,200	Quadra-jet 4-barrel	2.00 x 1.625
1967	430	4.1875 x 3.90	10.25:1	360 @ 5,000	475 @ 3,200	Quadra-jet 4-barrel	2.00 x 1.625
1970	455	4.312 x 3.90	10.0:1	370 @ 4,600	510 @ 2,800	Quadra-jet 4-barrel	2.00 x 1.625

NOTE: *CID is cubic-inch displacement; CR is compression ratio; bore/stroke & valve sizes in inches (intake x exhaust).*

** Exclusive GS-400 V-8*

Buick's cast-iron small-block V-8 debuted for 1964 at 300 cubic inches. It was stroked up to 340 cid in 1967 then bored out to 350 cubes the following year. Shown here is the 1969 GS-350's standard V-8 with "cool dual" induction.

Buick's first modern big-block V-8 appeared in 1967 in two forms: 400 cubic inches for the GS-400 and 430 cid (shown here) for full-size models. Notice the unusual air cleaner.

CHAPTER 5

1968 BACK TO BASICS

PLYMOUTH'S COST-CUTTING ROAD RUNNER DEBUTS

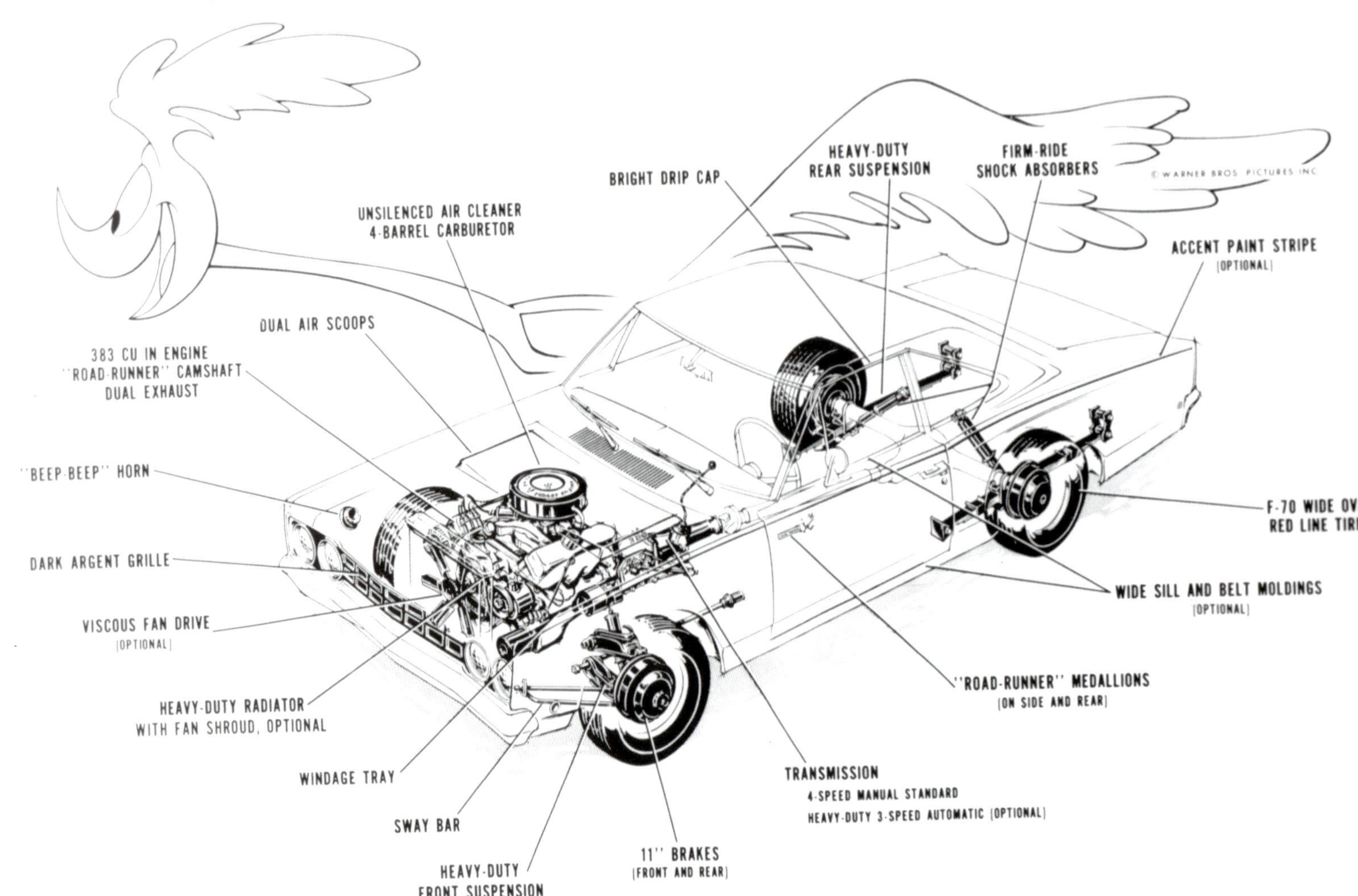

Though the phrase didn't come into vogue until years later, Plymouth's Road Runner surely represented Detroit's "biggest bang for the buck" in 1968. Demonstrated here is everything buyers got for their twenty-nine-hundred dollars, plus a few things they could spend extra for. Not shown is the optional Hemi, which raised the bottom line by 33 percent or so, defeating that whole "Econo-Racer" (*Car and Driver*'s words) ideal big-time.

By 1967 Plymouth execs had recognized that there were plenty of factory hot rods stickered at $3,300 or more that could do 100 miles per hour in the quarter-mile, but not one below that price that could score triple digits in 1,320 feet. Thus became their "frugal" goal: "100 miles per hour in the quarter for less than three G's."

To meet this end, Plymouth designers kept non-essentials to a minimum. A bare-bones Belvedere sedan, with swing-out rear windows instead of roll-up units, was initially chosen as the base for the project. That foundation then was typically upgraded with a stiffened suspension and F70 rubber mounted on rims adorned only with low-buck "dog-dish" hubcaps. Inside, the basic interior was taxicab spartan save for that tall floor shifter. As expected, a four-speed stick was standard. Image-conscious bucket seats were not offered, and frivolity was limited to a blacked-out grille, a GTX hood, and a couple of decals printed up with

Warner Brothers' express permission. "Road Runner" was the name; speeding away from wily Goats was the game.

Many monikers were considered, but it was timing more than anything that helped make the final decision. According to product planner Joe Sturm, "the name Road Runner had shown up on lists off and on for a couple of years, but apparently neither the product was right, nor had the correct 'sell' job been done to get it considered." Sturm then determined the speedy bird's moment had finally arrived after fellow planners Jack Smith and Gordon Cherry sent him home to watch Saturday morning cartoons.

"We were amazed to find that we could put a hold on the name Road Runner for a car," he said in 1969. "That started the process which eventually led to the Plymouth Division adopting the name for the new car. Subsequently, [an] agreement was reached with Warner Brothers to use their copyrighted cartoon character instead of our own, which we had under development."

Along with their gregarious TV star, Warner Brothers also licensed Plymouth to recreate the Road Runner's iconic "beep-beep" sound, achieved by adding a special horn modified with copper windings instead of normal aluminum strands. Comedic value also carried over into advertisements, which referred to this new automotive species by its reputed Latin name, "acceleratii rapidus maximus."

Beneath the Road Runner's hood was a clever combination of passenger-car power source and hot hardware. Its standard 383-cid V-8 shared cylinder heads, crankcase windage tray, intake manifold, and cam with Chrysler's big-bully 375-horsepower 440. The sum of these parts amounted to 335 rather cheaply corralled horses, just what the original budget-conscious plan called for. Spot-on too was the bottom line: roughly $2,900.

"Plymouth's idea is to give lots of performance for the money," concluded a *Car Life* review. "And it does this partly by putting gobs of go-goodies into the car, partly by not charging tremendous amounts for it, and partly by keeping things simple." Calling the new Road Runner "the world's fastest club coupe," *Car and Driver* pointed out that "this is the first car since GTO to be aimed directly at American youth and it very probably is dead on target."

Warner Brothers people were more than happy to share their cartoon character with Plymouth, at a price of course. The deal even allowed Road Runner designers to create a horn that mimicked the Saturday-morning TV star's iconic "me-meep!"

HOT OFF THE PRESS: 1968 PLYMOUTH ROAD RUNNER

"Road Runner emulates what a young, performance-minded driver might do on his own, if properly experienced and motivated. Take a basically light, inexpensive, stripped model and load it to the hilt with equipment to make it run and handle."

Car Life, *May 1968*

BY THE NUMBERS: 1968 PRODUCTION

PONTIAC GTO

hardtop, std V-8	64,586	(25,371 w/manual trans, 39,215 w/auto)
hardtop, 400 2-bl	2,841	(all w/automatic trans)
hardtop, 400 HO	9,337	(6,197 w/manual trans, 3,140 w/auto)
hardtop, 400 RA	940	(757 w/manual trans, 183 w/auto)
hdtp subtotal	77,704	
cvt., std V-8	8,207	(3,116 w/manual trans, 5,091 w/auto)
cvt., 400 2-bl	432	(all w/automatic trans)
cvt., 400 HO	1,227	(766 w/manual trans, 461 w/auto)
convertible, 400 RA	114	(92 w/manual trans, 22 w/auto)
cvt. subtotal	9,980	
total	**87,864**	

PONTIAC FIREBIRD 400 **8,714**[1] (includes hardtops & convertibles)

[1]Ram Air production (included in above total)

Ram Air I	413	(321 w/manual trans, 92 w/auto)
Ram Air II	110	(98 w/manual trans, 12 w/auto)
total	**523**	(511 hardtops, 12 convertibles)

CHEVROLET SS 396

hardtop	55,309
convertible	2,286
El Camino	5,190
total	**62,785**

CAMARO SS

L48 (350 V-8)	12,496	
L35 (396 V-8)	10,773	
L34 (396 V-8)	2,579	
L78 (396 V-8)	4,575	
L89 (396 V-8)	272	(added aluminum heads to L78 V-8)
total	**30,695**	(includes hardtops & convertibles)

CAMARO Z28 **7,199** (all hardtops)

CHEVROLET NOVA SS

SS 350	4,670	
w/L34 (396 V-8)	234	
w/L78 (396 V-8)	667	
total	**5,571**	(all sedans)

OLDSMOBILE 4-4-2

sports coupe	4,282
Holiday hardtop	24,183
convertible	5,142
total	**33,607**[1]

[1]W-30 production (included in above totals)

Cutlass coupe	315
Cutlass hardtop	1,426
Cutlass cvt.	170
total	**1,911**

OLDSMOBILE W-31

F-85 club coupe	38
Cutlass	674
Cutlass Supreme	30
total	**742**

HURTS/OLDS

club coupe	64	
hardtop	451	
total	**515**	(includes 153 cars w/optional air conditioning)

BUICK GRAN SPORT

GS-350 sedan	4,831	(California Special, all w/automatic trans)
GS-350 hardtop	8,317	(106 w/column-shifted 3-spd, 349 w/floor-shifted 3-spd, 844 w/4-spd, 7,018 w/auto)
GS-400 hardtop	10,743	(242 w/floor-shifted 3-spd, 1,632 w/4-spd, 8,869 w/auto)
GS-400 cvt.	2,454	(79 w/floor-shifted 3-spd, 351 w/4-spd, 2,024 w/auto)
total	**26,345**	

FORD MUSTANG GT **17,458** (includes coupes, fastbacks & convertibles)

FORD MUSTANG 428 COBRA JET

coupe	221	
fastback	1,044	(includes 50 specially prepared super-stock drag cars)
convertible	34	
total	**1,299***	

FORD TORINO GT

coupe	23,940
fastback	74,135
convertible	5,310
total	**103,385**

SHELBY MUSTANG

GT350 fastback	829	
GT350 Hertz	224	
GT350 convertible	403	
GT350 cvt. Hertz	1	
GT500 fastback	1,019	
GT500 Hertz	1	
GT500 convertible	401	
GT500 cvt. Hertz	1	
GT500KR fstbk	1,053	
GT500KR cvt.	517	
GT500KR cvt. Hertz	1	
total	**4,451***	(includes 1 GT500 notchback prototype)

MERCURY COUGAR GT

hardtop	955
XR7 hartdtop	1,845
total	**2,800**

MERCURY COUGAR GT-E

w/427 V-8	**357**	(101 base hardtops, 256 XR7 hardtops)
w/428 CJ V-8	37	(14 base hardtops, 23 XR7 hardtops)
total	**394***	(includes 3 428 CJ XR7 models w/4-spd trans; all others featured Select-Shift automatics)

MERCURY COUGAR DAN GURNEY SPECIAL

hardtop	11,899
XR7 hardtop	1
total	**11,900**

MERCURY COUGAR XR7-G

619 (all hardtops; includes 188 Hertz rental cars)

** These statistics are copyrighted Ford Motor Company and Marti Auto Works material; Marti Auto Works has the entire production database of all Ford vehicles from 1967 to the present—visit www.martiauto.com for more details.*

NOTE: *Production data was supplied by various sources, including Christo Datini at the GM Heritage Center, Galen Govier (Mopar material) at Galen's Tag Service (www.galengovier.com, the Shelby American Automobile Club (www.saac.com), and American Motors enthusiast Eddie Stakes at www.planethoustonamx.com.*

MERCURY CYCLONE

hardtop	1,034	
GT hardtop	334	
fastback	6,165	
GT fastback	6,105	
total	**13,638**	

PLYMOUTH ROAD RUNNER

coupe w/383 V-8	28,138	(13,707 w/4-spd, 14,431 w/auto)
coupe w/426 Hemi	840	(449 w/4-spd, 391 w/auto)
hdtp w/383 V-8	15,166	(6,686 w/4-spd, 8,480 w/auto)
hdtp w/426 Hemi	169	(108 w/4-spd, 61 w/auto)
total	**44,313**	(includes US deliveries only; total including deliveries outside US was 44,599)

PLYMOUTH GTX

hdtp w/440 V-8	16,673	
hdtp w/426 Hemi	410	
cvt. w/440 V-8	881	
cvt. w/426 Hemi	36	
total	**18,000**	(includes US deliveries only; total including deliveries outside US was 18,940)

PLYMOUTH BARRACUDA FORMULA S

hdtp w/340 V-8	867	(351 w/4-spd, 516 w/auto)
hdtp w/383 V-8	252	(complete breakdown n/a)
fstbk w/340 V-8	2,857	(complete breakdown n/a)
fstbk w/383 V-8	963	(complete breakdown n/a)
cvt. w/340 V-8	193	(60 w/4-spd, 133 w/auto)
cvt. w/383 V-8	64	(40 w/4-spd, 24 w/auto)
total	**5,196**	

DODGE CHARGER R/T

hdtp w/440 V-8	17,109	(2,743 w/4-spd, 14,366 w/auto)
hdtp w/426 Hemi	475	(211 w/4-spd, 264 w/auto)
total	**17,584**	

DODGE SUPER BEE

coupe w/383 V-8	7,716	(2,933 w/4-spd, 4,783 w/auto)
coupe w/426 Hemi	125	(31 w/4-spd, 94 w/auto)
total	**7,841**	

DODGE CORONET R/T

hdtp w/440 V-8	9,734	(1,983 w/4-spd, 7,751 w/auto)
hdtp w/426 Hemi	219	(complete breakdown n/a)
cvt. w/440 V-8	519	(88 w/4-spd, 431 w/auto)
cbt. w/426 Hemi	9	(1 w/4-spd, 8 w/auto)
total	**10,481**	(includes US deliveries only; total including deliveries outside US was 10,849)

DODGE DART GTS

hdtp w/340 V-8	5,513	(1,281 w/4-spd, 4,232 w/auto)
hdtp w/383 V-8	2,112	(complete breakdown n/a)
cvt. w/340 V-8	315	(44 w/4-spd, 271 w/auto)
cvt. w/383 V-8	80	(40 w/4-spd, 40 w/auto)
total	**8,202**	(includes US deliveries only; total including deliveries outside US was 8,745)

AMC AMX

w/290 V-8	1,009	(525 w/4-spd, 484 w/auto)
w/343 V-8	1,317	(415 w/4-spd, 902 /w/auto)
w/390 V-8	4,399	(2,112 w/4-spd, 2,287 w/auto)
total	**6,725**	(all hardtops)

1968 PLYMOUTH ROAD RUNNER

CONSTRUCTION: unitized body/frame
MODEL AVAILABILITY: coupe & hardtop
PRICE: $2,896, coupe; $3,034, hardtop
WHEELBASE: 116 inches
WEIGHT: 3,405 pounds, coupe; 3,400 pounds, convertible
SUSPENSION: heavy-duty; torsion bars &0.94-inch stabilizer bar, front; solid axle w/leaf springs, rear
STEERING: manual (24:1) recirculating ball, std; 15.7:1 power-assist, optional (power steering mandatory w/optional Hemi V-8)
WHEELS: 14x5.5 (15-inch wheels w/optional Hemi)
TIRES: F70x14 Wide Tread
BRAKES: 11-inch drums, front & rear, std; 11.19-inch power front discs, optional
ENGINE: 383-cid Commando V-8 w/Carter 4-barrel carburetor, std; 426 Hemi, optional
TRANSMISSION: 4-speed manual
AXLE RATIO: 3.23:1

Demand for Plymouth's muscle-car-for-the-masses quickly skyrocketed, with 1968's run surpassing 44,300. Sales for 1969 nearly doubled, making Road Runner Detroit's second-best-selling high-performance model behind that year's new segment leader, Chevy's SS 396 Chevelle. Pontiac people, meanwhile, surely were left wondering what had just hit them.

No, it wasn't an ACME anvil.

PLYMOUTH

The original Road Runner coupe was joined in January 1968 by a comparatively upscale hardtop rendition that featured roll-up rear windows. Mechanical options included a Sure-Grip differential, Torqueflite automatic, and a High Performance Axle Package consisting of a heavy-duty 3.55:1 Sure-Grip rear end, a Slip Drive (viscous) fan with shroud, and a heavy-duty radiator.

The only optional power source was the Hemi, backed by either a Torqueflite or four-speed, both beefed when bolted up behind those 425 ponies. Mandatory for manual-trans Hemi models (it was optional with automatics), was a super-heavy-duty Dana 60 rear axle with 3.54:1 Sure-Grip gears. All Hemi Road Runners also featured their own special "K-member" subframe and extra-heavy-duty suspension, improved cooling, and bigger 15-inch wheels/tires.

Though it clearly defeated Plymouth's original cost-conscious purpose, a Hemi Road Runner ranked right up with the hottest muscle cars ever released to date. According to *Motor Trend's* Eric Dahlquist, this machine represented "probably the fastest production sedan made today."

A new B-body shell and official recognition in the grille appeared for Plymouth's second-edition GTX in 1968. Hardtop and convertible models—fitted with the standard 440 or optional Hemi—again were offered. Bucket seats and a 150-miles per hour speedometer remained standard inside. *Mike Mueller*

Plymouth's Formula S package remained available for all three Barracuda body styles in 1968. Both small- and big-block versions carried over, too, only this time the former was the new 340 LA V-8, conservatively rated at 275 horsepower. *Mike Mueller*

A step up from Road Runner in 1968 was Plymouth's second-edition GTX, again available with either the standard Super Commando RB V-8 or optional Hemi. "This is the winner," claimed *Car Life* in reference to the 425-horse GTX. "The most powerful standard car built in America. And the 440 is not far behind."

Down in A-body ranks, Plymouth's Barracuda got a new engine as the 273 Commando was dropped in favor of a 340-cid LA small-block conservatively rated at 275 horsepower. Topping off the options list was the carryover 383 big-block, which was pumped up to 300 horsepower thanks to the addition of better-breathing heads and an improved intake manifold.

Created solely for performance applications, the 340 featured beefy rods, a forged-steel crank, free-flowing heads, and a superb cam grind. Called a "giant killer from Hamtramck," it quickly established itself as one of Detroit's hottest small-blocks, and would remain so into the 1970s. Its relative light weight meant there was no compromising the Formula S Barracuda's original road-hugging intentions. As in 1967, the Formula S package was required when the 383 was ordered, and the same was true for the new 340. One minor change involved standard rubber, which now consisted of E70 Red Streaks.

HOT OFF THE PRESS: 1968 PLYMOUTH GTX

"As a performance car, the GTX has few equals. The standard 440 GTX should appeal to the man who wants a very fast passenger car with sporty styling and reasonable smoothness and economy. The Hemi GTX will appeal to the acceleration enthusiast who wants the ultimate."

Car Life, *February 1968*

DODGE

As exciting as Dodge's first Charger looked, it didn't sell well at all. But the tide began to turn after a stunning restyle appeared for 1968. William w Brownlie's team had this beautiful body well in the works almost before the clay had dried on the 1966 model—just in time, in other words. Many still feel the 1968 Charger ranks as the best-looking of the breed, if not one of the original muscle car era's overall best.

Car and Driver gave Charger top styling honors for the year going away. Enhancing the appeal further in 1968 was the new R/T package, announced boldly by a set of soon-to-be familiar stripes added out back. This tail treatment honored

THE AMERICAN WAY

343 CUBES

American Motors builds your kind of car

Like Ford, American Motors also followed the 1957 AMA anti-racing edict to the letter, and the Wisconsin-based firm was last of the US automakers to refute it. Instead of promoting performance during the early 1960s, AMC proudly put all its efforts into giving customers practical, sensible, safe transports, as this 1964 advertisement demonstrates. But two years later, company officials finally figured they'd better start catering to the "youth market" or go home.

Magazine ads in 1967 officially announced that American Motors would no longer watch Detroit's muscle car race from across Lake Michigan. New that year was the so-called "Super American," a compact stuffed full of AMC's 280-horsepower 343-cid V-8. A four-speed stick was mandatory. Though by no means a sales success (some stoic dealers simply refused to even offer it), it was a start.

In what represented this country's largest corporate merger to date, George Mason's Nash-Kelvinator group officially teamed up with Hudson in May 1954 to form the American Motor Corporation, based in Nash's existing works in Kenosha, Wisconsin. Mason hoped to keep "independent" automaking alive by combining forces to better battle Detroit's entrenched Big Three, and to this end he also planned to hook up with fellow outsiders Studebaker and Packard once the latter formalized a deal to purchase the former. While Packard did buy out Studebaker in June 1954, the four-part deal never coalesced for various reasons, not the least of which involved Mason's death four months later. His replacement atop AMC, George Romney, wanted no part of the two obviously ailing firms, leaving Studebaker-Packard to limp on towards eventual death in the 1960s.

Romney's American Motors, meanwhile, was born again in 1958 after the decision was made to unceremoniously dump the Nash and Hudson nameplates in favor of the Rambler line, first offered in compact form only in 1950. New for 1958 was the Rambler American, an affordable, economical model that remained an AMC mainstay into the 1960s.

In 1963, the entire Rambler line, from the low-priced American to the top-shelf V-8 Ambassador, earned *Motor Trend's* "Car of the Year" award for "outstanding design achievement and engineering leadership." But those laurels didn't last long enough to rest on, as American Motors' fortunes quickly waned. Dealers began jumping ship in droves two years later, and 1966's stockholders report was awash in red ink. Renewed hope, however, was right around the corner.

Roy Abernethy became AMC president after Romney won Michigan's governorship in 1962, and he reportedly spent $300 million trying to right the ship. Truly fresh model line retooling for 1967 alone cost $75 million, with $40 million of that going into the new speed-conscious 290-cid V-8 (introduced midyear in 1966), a modernized power source that in the minds of many Kenosha-watchers, including Romney himself, didn't exactly mix well with the company's real bread and butter. Trustworthy economy, not frivolous sportiness, was AMC's strong suit, a fact apparently demonstrated by the ill-fated Marlin. Unveiled in February 1965, this swoopy fastback never did sell and was gone after only three years on the market.

The first sign that American Motors was changing its tune came in February 1965 in the form of the fastback Marlin, a reasonably sporty "upsized" response of sorts to Ford's Mustang based on AMC's midsize Classic. Marlin followed in the tire tracks of the Tarpon show car, created a year before by melding a similar sloping roofline to the smaller Rambler American. A regular-production, more compact Tarpon would've represented a far better match for Mustang; Marlin never did find a following and was history by 1968. A 1966 Marlin is shown here.

American Motors continued trying to run with Detroit's big dogs on their turf, jumping onto the pony car bandwagon late in 1967 with its all-new Javelin, a sporty machine that offered performance potential unknown to American Motors customers since Nash's rambunctious Rambler Rebel came and went in a flash in 1957. Javelin was then followed in February 1968 by the two-seat AMX, which Kenosha officials called "the Walter Mitty Ferrari." According to *Mechanix Illustrated's* Tom McCahill, AMX was "the hottest thing to ever come out of Wisconsin." He stood corrected the following year when AMC teamed up with Hurst to create the SC/Rambler, perhaps the greatest "sleeper" of the muscle car era. Done up in a similar patriotic red, white, and blue finish, the Rebel Machine debuted for 1970 to help keep Kenosha's performance legacy standing proud—proud but not necessarily strong.

AMC's decline in the early 1960s primarily resulted from a major demographic shift as younger, image-conscious buyers began flooding the marketplace. Abernethy and crew apparently had little choice but to chase this new trend, then more or less found themselves without a chair once the groovy tunes stopped playing. Horsepower was already trotting into the sunset when gas prices began soaring in 1973, leading to newfound demand for affordable, fuel-efficient compacts. After spending so much hard-to-come-by cash shifting its focus from just such machines to muscle cars, AMC then found itself eating dust even further behind the Big Three in a field it had first plowed well before any of its rivals.

Although the subcompact Gremlin, introduced in 1970, did temporarily find its niche, the too-weird Pacer, born in 1975, basically followed in the disappointing Marlin's tire tracks. Fortunes then faded again, leading AMC stockholders to give up 46 percent of controlling interest to France's Renault in December 1980. The end of the road in Kenosha finally came in 1987 when Chrysler took over AMC.

More than one interested bystander over the years since has blamed the muscle car, at least partially, for AMC's eventual demise. Among these is former American Motors' public relations man John Conde. "I actually believe, especially in the case of AMC, that performance cars were a deterrent to sales," Conde said in 1997. "They stimulate a lot of interest, kids say wow, but almost always they sell poorly. I subscribe to the strong opinion of George Romney that AMC would still be in business if it had not spent valuable tooling money on poor-selling cars like the Javelin, AMX, Marlin and Pacer. I always will believe if they had spent that money developing a good four-cylinder engine, they would still be around. Instead, they worked on a V-8. Oh well."

UNDER THE HOOD: 1968'S HOTTEST V-8s*

MODEL	CID	BORE & STROKE	CR	HORSEPOWER	TORQUE
Dodge/Plymouth Hemi	426	4.250 x 3.750	10.25:1	425 @ 5,000	490 @ 4,000
Dodge/Plymouth	440	4.320 x 3.750	10:1	375 @ 4,600	480 @ 3,200
Dodge/Plymouth	383	4.250 x 3.380	10:1	335 @ 5,200	425 @ 3,400
Dodge/Plymouth	340	4.040 x 3.310	10.5:1	275 @ 5,000	340 @ 3,200
Pontiac GTO Ram Air II	400	4.120 x 3.75	10.75:1	366 @ 5,400	445 @ 3,800
Pontiac Firebird Ram Air II	400	4.120 x 3.75	10.75:1	340 @ 4,800	430 @ 3,700
Chevrolet SS 396 (L78)	396	4.094 x 3.76	11:1	375 @ 5,600	415 @ 3,600
Chevrolet Camaro Z28	302	4.00 x 3.00	11:1	290 @ 5,800	290 @ 4,200
Olds 4-4-2	400	3.87 x 4.25	10.5:1	360 @ 5,400	440 @ 3,600
Olds W-31	350	4.057 x 3.385	10.5:1	325 @ 5,400	360 @ 3,600
Buick GS-400	400	4.04 x 3.94	10.25:1	340 @ 5,000	440 @ 3,200
Buick GS-350	350	3.80 x 3.85	10.25:1	280 @ 4,600	375 @ 3,200
Ford/Mercury	427	4.23 x 3.78	10.9:1	390 @ 5,600	460 @ 3,200
Ford/Mercury (CJ)	428	4.13 x 3.98	10.6:1	335 @ 5,400	445 @ 3,400
American Motors	390	4.165 x 3.574	10.2:1	315 @ 4,600	425 @ 3,200

NOTE: CID is cubic-inch displacement; CR is compression ratio; bore/stroke in inches.

**Discounting factory super-stocks, full-size models, & Corvette*

TIME SLIPS: 1968

MODEL	¼-MILE PERFORMANCE	SOURCE
Mercury Cougar (428 CJ)	13.23 seconds at 103.4 mph	*SSDI*, August 1968
Dodge Charger R/T Hemi	13.50 seconds at 105 mph	*Car and Driver*, November 1967
Ford Mustang 428 Cobra Jet	13.56 seconds at 106.6 mph	*Hot Rod*, March 1968
Chevrolet Malibu SS 396 (L78)	13.60 seconds at 105 mph	*Popular Hot Rodding*, June 1968
Hurst/Olds	13.71 seconds at 102.2 mph	*SSDI*, August 1968
Chevrolet Camaro Z28*	13.77 seconds at 107.4 mph	*Car and Driver*, July 1968
Oldsmobile Cutlass W-31	13.85 seconds at 107.8 mph	*Car Craft*, August 1968
Plymouth GTX Hemi	13.85 seconds at 104 mph	*Popular Hot Rodding*, March 1968
Chevrolet Nova SS 396 (L78)	13.85 seconds at 104 mph	*Popular Hot Rodding*, March 1968
Oldsmobile 4-4-2 W-30	14.00 seconds at 99 mph	*Popular Hot Rodding*, May 1968
Dodge Coronet R/T (440)	14.01 seconds at 102.6 mph	*SSDI*, August 1968
AMC AMX (390 V-8)	14.06 seconds at 98.4 mph	*Hot Rod*, August 1968
Pontiac Firebird 400	14.20 seconds at 100.3 mph	*Car and Driver*, March 1968
Pontiac GTO	14.25 seconds at 99 mph	*Hot Rod*, February 1968
Plymouth Road Runner	14.27 seconds at 92 mph	*SSDI*, March 1968
Dodge Dart GTS (340 V-8)	14.38 seconds at 97 mph	*Hot Rod*, April 1968
Mercury Cyclone (428 CJ)	14.40 seconds at 99.4 mph	*Car Life*, July 1968
Dodge Dart GTS (340 V-8)	14.40 seconds at 99.0 mph	*Car and Driver*, September 1968
Dodge Super Bee (383 V-8)	14.60 seconds at 99 mph	*Speed & Supercar*, October 1968
Buick GS-400	14.78 seconds at 94 mph	*Hot Rod*, January 1968
Shelby GT350	14.90 seconds at 96 mph	*Hi-Performance Cars*, September 1968
Plymouth'Cuda 340	14.97 seconds at 95.4 mph	*Car Life*, December 1967
AMC Javelin (343 V-8)	15.10 seconds at 93 mph	*Motor Trend*, January 1968
Ford Torino GT (390 V-8)	15.10 seconds at 91 mph	*Motor Trend*, December 1967
Mercury Cougar GT-E (427 V-8)	15.12 seconds at 93.6 mph	*Car Life*, July 1968

NOTE: SSDI *is Super Stock & Drag Illustrated* magazine   * w/optional dual-carb cross-ram V-8

New for 1968 was Charger R/T, one of the three founding members of Dodge's Scat Pack. Like Plymouth's GTX, this bodacious B-body could be equipped with two engines only: the standard 375-horsepower 440 Magnum or optional 426 Hemi. And, per Scat Pack specs, it was adorned with trademark "bumblebee" stripes in back. *Mike Mueller*

Charger R/T's membership in Dodge's equally new Scat Pack, made up of, in promotional people's words, "the cars with the bumblebee stripes."

"Dodge's stripes scooped the industry," claimed *Car Life* about the Scat Pack touch. "Others had stripes down the center, down the driver's side, across the hood and down the front fenders. But only Dodge has 'bustle stripes.' As one observer put it, 'Those cars must really be fast—they almost got past the striper.' "

The 440 Magnum was standard for the R/T, the Hemi was optional. A new Charger option, the High Performance Axle Package, also appeared in 1968, but only for 383 Magnum models. This deal added a 3.55:1 Sure-Grip axle, a high-capacity radiator, and a seven-blade Slip Drive fan with shroud.

Dodge's Scat Pack included three members when first announced in the fall of 1967: Charger R/T, Coronet R/T, and Dart GTS. A fourth then appeared shortly after the turn of the year: yet another B-body that, according to those ever-present ad guys, offered "Scat Pack performance at a new low price." First seen in showrooms in February 1968, Dodge's latest muscle machine was meant to follow in Road Runner's tracks and thus echoed many of its tightwad touches. A rather mundane Coronet coupe, with flip-open rear quarter windows, was used as a base. Even chrome exhaust tips were optional.

"[Plymouth] realized it wasn't doing its big engines any favors by stuffing them into cars already overweight with gadgets and glitter, and after much introspection it produced Road Runner," explained a *Car and Driver* review of this newborn breed. "Dodge, which is always somewhere on the same lap with Plymouth, [then] joined the movement."

Like Road Runner, Dodge's counterpart also was given a cartoonish name, this one obviously intended to play up on that whole Scat Pack thing. If a bumblebee could use V-8 power to run around on drag slicks instead of legs, it definitely was no mere mortal insect, right? It was a "Super Bee." Curbside critics, however, weren't quite so sure. "A kind of inverse kinky name, but no less a real car" read *Car and Driver's* initial impression.

Though a bit glitzier than its desert fowl cousin, Super Bee was similarly equipped, starting with its standard 335-horsepower 383 and optional Hemi.

1968 DODGE CHARGER R/T

CONSTRUCTION: unitized body/frame
MODEL AVAILABILITY: hardtop
PRICE: $3,480
WHEELBASE: 117 inches
WEIGHT: 3,650 pounds
SUSPENSION: heavy-duty; torsion bars & 0.94-inch stabilizer bar, front; solid axle w/leaf springs, rear
STEERING: manual (24:1) recirculating ball, std; 15.7:1 power-assist, optional (power steering mandatory w/optional Hemi V-8)
WHEELS: 14x5.5
TIRES: F70x14 Red Streak Wide Tread
BRAKES: 11-inch drums, front & rear, std; 11.19-inch power front discs, optional
ENGINE: 440-cid Super Commando V-8 w/Carter 4-barrel carburetor, std; 426 Hemi, optional
TRANSMISSION: 4-speed manual or Torqueflite automatic
AXLE RATIO: 3.23:1

HOT OFF THE PRESS: 1968 DODGE CORONET R/T

"The old saw about no substitute for cubic inches certainly fits the 440 Magnum. Acceleration is very rapid, yet the engine never seems to be laboring. The 440's brute torque makes high revving completely unnecessary."

Car Life, *April 1968*

HI-PERF HAULER

Introduced in 1959, Chevrolet's original half-car/half-truck rolled into temporary retirement in 1960, but was reborn on GM's new A-body platform in 1964. Initially available with nearly every option that helped make its Chevelle running mate a main attraction, this downsized El Camino could play as hard as it worked, a fact not lost on potential buyers. Chevrolet sold 36,615 that first year, more than twice the number of 1964 Rancheros unloaded by Ford.

Like Chevelle, El Camino could be fitted with a host of hot small-blocks in 1964 and '65 right up to the 350-horse L79. But unlike Chevelle, the early A-body El Camino couldn't wear Super Sport garb. Even the 396 big-block was an option in 1966, as were bucket seats, a console and the SS 396 Chevelle's mag-style wheel covers. Yet the complete SS image remained unavailable.

All that changed in 1968 when Chevrolet introduced an honest-to-goodness SS 396 El Camino, complete with those revered badges, attractive blacked-out grille and bulging hood. "Fancier than a truck, more utilitarian than a passenger car, able to leap past sports cars in a single bound, the [SS 396] El Camino will fill needs that the owner never knew he had"—or so claimed a *Car Life* report, which announced an impressive 14.80-second quarter-mile pass for the latest member of Chevy's Super Sport fraternity. After a little tweaking, *Hot Rod* managed a 14.49/98.79 time slip, serious moving for a machine *HRM's* Steve Kelly called "the near-perfect 'Gentleman's hauler.' "

Chevrolet rolled out 5,190 SS 396 El Caminos for 1968, the only year this high-performance utility vehicle was offered as a distinct model on its own. SS 396 equipment became an options package the following year.

The El Camino's turn to put on an SS face finally came in 1968, by which time it was obvious that work had given way at least partially to play in the car-truck field. El Camino SS 396 production that first year was 5,190.

1968 396 TURBO JET V-8s

	L34	L35	L78
Maximum Horsepower	350 at 5,200 rpm	325 at 4,800 rpm	375 at 5,600 rpm
Maximum Torque	415 at 3,200 rpm	410 at 3,200 rpm	415 at 3,600 rpm
Compression	10.25:1	10.25:1	11.0:1
Carburetor	Rochester 4-barrel	Rochester 4-barrel	780-cfm Holley 4-barrel
Intake Manifold	cast-iron	cast-iron	aluminum
Cylinder Heads	cast-iron oval-port	cast-iron oval-port	cast-iron rectangular port
Combustion Chambers	97cc, closed	97cc, closed	109cc, closed
Pistons	cast aluminum	cast aluminum	forged aluminum
Main Bearing Caps	two-bolt	four-bolt	four-bolt
Lifters	hydraulic	hydraulic	solid
Valve Lift (inches)	0.398	0.480	0.520
Valve Sizes (int./exh.)	2.06/1.72 inches	2.06/1.72 inches	2.19/1.72 inches

"Rumble Bee" was the nickname Dodge ads used in1968 for the new Super Bee, offered only in Coronet coupe (with flip-out rear quarter windows) form. No convertibles were offered during the Super Bee's short flight, which came to rest in 1971.

Dodge's Coronet R/T again appeared in hardtop and convertible forms for 1968. At 208 inches, 1968's new Coronet body was some 5 inches longer than its predecessor.

Inside was a snazzy Charger-sourced Rally dash, an inclusion that plainly represented a paradox paired up with the Coronet's yeoman bench-seat interior.

Overshadowed a bit by the cost-conscious Super Bee, 1968's pricier Coronet R/T carried on with few changes, save of course for its restyled body, which measured some 5 inches longer compared to its predecessor. Exterior enhancements included an aggressive bulging hood that did nothing but look mean—no functional scooping was available for either the standard 440 Magnum or optional Hemi.

As expected, the rare Hemi obviously offered more potential, but not all witnesses were convinced it was the best choice. *Car Life's* critics touted the wedge over the 426, which in their humble opinion required too much fine tuning to perform at its expected best. With no careful handling at all, they concluded, a 440-powered Coronet "ran like the Hemi should have."

New for 1968's fourth Scat Pack member, Dart GTS, was a sporty hood with parallel vents (simulated) facing each fender. The heavy-duty Rally suspension was included, as were Dodge's new Scat Pack tail stripes, which could've been deleted on request. Two V-8s were available this time: the proven 383 and the new 340, which again had bystanders doubting its 275-horse tag. As a *Car and Driver* report explained, "we'd be the last to accuse anyone of 'underrating' but the underground isn't kidding when they say 340s shoot Darts down the road in a 350-hp fashion. "

PONTIAC

A sensationally contoured GTO body appeared this year with trend-setting hideaway windshield wipers, optional headlights that also could be hidden away, and an innovative energy-absorbing Endura front bumper. Color-keyed to the body, this steel-backed synthetic bumper regained its shape after low-speed impacts. An optional chrome unit was available for those who simply couldn't warm up to the new monochromatic look.

Honored with *Motor Trend's* "Car of the Year" award, Pontiac's latest GTO was available only in hardtop and convertible forms. Both the base 400 and two-barrel V-8 (a no-cost option) received slight power boosts for 1968, up to 350 and 265 horsepower, respectively, and both the HO and Ram Air options rolled over from 1967. A 366-horsepower Ram Air II V-8 appeared in March

1968 DODGE SUPER BEE

CONSTRUCTION: unitized body/frame
MODEL AVAILABILITY: coupe
PRICE: $3,027
WHEELBASE: 117 inches
WEIGHT: 3,765 pounds
SUSPENSION: heavy-duty; torsion bars & 0.94-inch stabilizer bar, front; solid axle w/leaf springs, rear
STEERING: manual (24:1) recirculating ball, std; 15.7:1 power-assist, optional (power steering mandatory w/optional Hemi V-8)
WHEELS: 14x5.5 stamped-steel
TIRES: F70x14
BRAKES: 11-inch drums, front & rear, std; 11.19-inch power front discs, optional
ENGINE: 383-cid Magnum V-8 w/Carter 4-barrel V-8, std; 426 Hemi, optional
TRANSMISSION: 4-speed manual, std; Torqueflite automatic, optional
AXLE RATIO: 3.23:1

1968 DODGE DART GTS

CONSTRUCTION: unitized body/frame
MODEL AVAILABILITY: hardtop & convertible
PRICE: $3,189 (w/340 V-8)
WHEELBASE: 111 inches
WEIGHT: 3,480 pounds (hardtop w/340 V-8)
SUSPENSION: torsion bars & stabilizer bar, front; solid axle w/leaf springs, rear
STEERING: manual recirculating ball
WHEELS: 14x5.5 stamped -steel
TIRES: D70x14 Red Streak Wide Tread
BRAKES: 10-inch drums, front & rear; 10.8-inch power front discs, optional
ENGINE: 340-cid LA-series V-8 or 383-cid Magnum B-series V-8
TRANSMISSION: 4-speed manual or Torqueflite automatic
AXLE RATIO: 3.23:1

Dual hood scoops reappeared on GTO's hood for 1968 and again were non-functional in standard form. Truly new was this year's energy-absorbing monochromatic Endura nose, hidden wipers and optional hideaway headlights. *Mike Mueller*

HOT OFF THE PRESS: 1968 DODGE DART GTS

"The latest word from the underground is that the little Mopar 340 is the hot set-up. A giant killer from Hamtramck. We're believers."

Car and Driver, *September 1968*

HOT OFF THE PRESS: 1968 PONTIAC GTO

"The '68 breed of cat is highly improved over the '67—which made a tough act to follow—in terms of style, body and innovations, The new Endura front bumper is the most significant and appealing innovation."

Motor Trend, *December 1967*

1968, backed by either a four-speed or TH-400. A Hurst floor shifter returned as standard fare for the base three-speed manual—no more three-on-the-trees—but a column shifter did remain standard for the automatic.

Performance-oriented upgrades for the second-edition Firebird included staggered shocks and multi-leaf springs in back. Output went up to 330 horsepower for the W66 400, 335 for the Ram Air I. Another option, the L74 400 HO, also rated at 335 horses, appeared in 1968, as did the midyear Ram Air II, advertised at 340 horsepower in F-body applications. F70 tires were standard for 1968's Firebird 400.

CHEVROLET

Like all GM's two-door A-bodies, the SS 396 Chevelle was treated to a new "Coke-bottle" body riding on a shortened 112-inch wheelbase in 1968. Exterior treatment carried over in similar fashion with two exceptions: gone was rear-quarter "Super Sport" script, and engine identification was now relegated to a tiny tag incorporated within the side marker lamp bezels up front, new features for 1968 inspired by ever-tightening federal safety standards. Mechanicals too were familiar, with three 396 Turbo Jets offered again at the same output levels.

Refitted with staggered rear shocks like its F-body cousin, 1968's Camaro again could be dressed up in Rally Sport garb, and this package once more was available along with Super Sport equipment. Most notable SS changes involved the deletion of "350" identification from the grille and gas cap on small-block models. New too were the SS 396's simulated hood vents, which now contained four equally fake carburetor stacks.

Firebird 400 buyers could pick from four V-8s in 1968: the base 330-horsepower W66, the 335-horsepower Ram Air I, the new L74 400 HO (demonstrated here, also pegged at 335 horses), and the midyear Ram Air II, rated at 340 horsepower in F-body applications. *Mike Mueller*

Chevrolet's restyled A-body for 1968 featured a pronounced long-hood/short-deck profile, as well as trendy "Coke-bottle" contours. All SS 396 Chevelles (save for dark-colored models) received black-painted lower body sides. Adding optional pinstripes (RPO D96) deleted that treatment, although some early models apparently included both.

Big-block Super Sport Camaro hoods in 1968 received unique simulated vents featuring four fake carburetor stacks in each. Chevrolet's popular Rally wheel was fitted with a larger center cap this year. *Mike Mueller*

Super Sport drivetrains too rolled over with one new addition as Chevy's 350-horserpower L35 396 joined its L34 and L78 big-block brothers. Limited to the L34 only in 1967, the TH-400 trans was made available as well behind the L35 in 1968, as was a four-speed. Weight-saving L89 aluminum heads debuted, but their heavy price tag ($868.95) inhibited their popularity—only 272 sets were sold.

Basically the same Z28 package rolled over as well, with minor updates including switching from single-leaf springs to four-leaf units with staggered shocks in back. New larger center caps graced this year's Rally wheels, now shod in Goodyear Wide Tread E70 tires. New too was a third transmission choice, the gnarly M22 "Rock Crusher" four-speed. A dealer-installed option—four-wheel disc brakes—showed up in 1968, this after Trans-Am race teams demonstrated their merits on SCCA road courses. Four-wheel discs returned in 1969 with an official RPO code: JL8.

Nova's 1968 revamp included both a new body and foundation, the latter shared with Chevy's pony car. Though curbside kibitzers liked to claim the new Nova was little more than a Camaro in disguise, it was the other way around. Engineers had this platform in the works already when GM's F-car project got rolling; Camaro then did the borrowing before appearing one year earlier than the updated Chevy II. Notable too this year was badge merging as all models were simply called "Chevy II Novas." Even the Super Sport wore Chevy II identification in 1968.

Replacing the retired 283 as the Nova's standard V-8 in 1968 was Chevrolet's new 307-cid Turbo Fire, one of the few small-blocks to never see a high-

1968 CHEVROLET CHEVELLE SS 396

CONSTRUCTION: body on perimeter-rail frame
MODEL AVAILABILITY: hardtop & convertible
PRICE: $2,875, hardtop; $3,102, convertible
WHEELBASE: 112 inches
WEIGHT: 3,844 pounds (hardtop)
SUSPENSION: heavy duty; coil spring & 0.937-inch stabilizer bar, front; solid axle w/coil springs, rear
STEERING: manual recirculating ball
WHEELS: 14x6 stamped-steel
TIRES: F70
BRAKES: 9.5-inch finned drums, front & rear; 11-inch power-assisted front discs, optional
ENGINE: L35 396 Turbo Jet V-8 w/Rochester four-barrel carburetor, std; L34 & L78 396 Turbo Jet V-8s, optional
TRANSMISSION: 3-speed manual, std; 4-speed & Turbo Hydra-matic, optional
AXLE RATIO: 3.31:1 (3.07:1, 3.55:1, 3.73:1 available; 4.10:1, 4.56:1, 4.88:1, by special order); Positraction differential, optional

FAMILY TIES: CHEVROLET'S L79 327 V-8

Before the Z16 Malibu debuted early in 1965, Chevrolet's hottest A-body engine option was the Corvette's 350-horsepower L79 327, offered up through 1968. This mighty mouse returned as a Sting Ray option in 1966 and also debuted on Nova's RPO list that year, still carrying "350 HP" identification in each case. But it oddly went missing from the 1966 Chevelle lineup. Why? While no official answer to this mini-mystery is available, simple logic surely will suffice: no way was Chevrolet going to offer non-SS customers an optional small-block V-8 that was more powerful than the SS 396's standard 325-horse L35 big-block. Okay, so increased demand for this smokin' small-block (thanks to Nova applications) also might have helped preclude A-body availability. But conspiracy theorists were quick to note that when the L79 327 unapologetically returned as a Chevelle option in 1967, it was conveniently down-rated to 325 horsepower, same as the L35 396. Coincidence? We think not.

L79 PRODUCTION

	1965	1966	1967	1968
Corvette	4,716	7,591	6,375	9,440
Chevelle/El Camino	6,021	0	4,048	4,082
Chevy II/Nova	0	5,481	6	1,274
Acadian	23	83	6,375	0

NOTE: *Acadian was the marque name for the Chevelle/Chevy II derivatives marketed by GM of Canada.*

Chevrolet ads promoted 1968's Z28 Camaro as the "closest thing to a Corvette yet." Soon-to-be-familiar "Z/28" fender badges appeared this year. *Jeremy Cliff photo, courtesy Mecum Auctions*

performance transformation. More to a leadfoot's liking was the optional L79 327, which apparently reappeared midyear in 1968. Again rated at 325 horsepower, this rather mysterious mill differed from earlier renditions in that it used a Quadrajet four-barrel carb (topped by a Corvette-style open-element air cleaner) on a cast-iron intake.

Very few L79 V-8s found their way into Novas in 1968, the last year for the 327 in Chevy II ranks. None were bolted into 1968 Super Sports as they at first were limited to one power source: the L48 350 Turbo Fire introduced the year before for Camaro SS. Like its pony car counterpart, 1968's Nova SS was created by checking off that L48 code. And just as the L48 small-block carried over from Camaro, so too did the 396 Turbo Jet later in the year. Two big-blocks were offered for the Nova SS: the 350-horsepower L34 and 375-horsepower L78.

HOT OFF THE PRESS: 1968 CHEVROLET CAMARO Z28

"Chevrolet obviously achieved what they set out to do—namely, build a race-winning Trans-Am sedan."

Road & Track, *June 1968*

HOT OFF THE PRESS: 1968 CHEVROLET NOVA SS 396

"All docile and innocent…the vestal virgin image pales slightly when you turn on the engine."

Car and Driver, *August 1968*

A bigger, better Chevy II body appeared for 1968, just in time to serve as a home for Chevy's first big-block Nova SS. The 295-hp L48 350 small-block was the compact Super Sport's base V-8 this year. Two 396 Turbo Jet Mk IV big-blocks were optional: the 350-horsepower L34 and 375-horsepower L78.

SHIFTY BUSINESS

George Hurst (left) began marketing his slick floor shifters in 1958; by 1965 his Hurst-Campbell company was raking in $20 million a year offering everything from wheels, to brakes, to clutches. Hurst also teamed up more than once with Detroit's automakers to produce specialty models. Make that America's automakers. In 1969 Wisconsin's AMC and Hurst cooperated on the SC/Rambler, based on Kenosha's compact Rogue. At right is American Motors vice president in charge of product R. William McNeally. George Hurst died in May 1986.

Hands down, nobody built precise, lightning-quick shifters like George Hurst. Factory hot rods have come and gone over the years, and come back again. But the ever-popular Hurst shifter always has been there at arm's reach whenever a need for speed shifting has risen.

The roots of this legendary legacy run back to 1954, when 27-year-old Hurst was discharged from the navy. His first business was George Hurst Automotive in Philadelphia, a small shop that did repairs and hop-ups. Popular hot rodding engine swaps quickly became his forte, and he started designing various motor mounts to make these conversions a snap.

He also hand-crafted a fool-proof floor shifter for his 1956 Chevrolet, a durable unit featuring much shorter throws than stock units. Right after Christmas in 1958 he set out in his floor-shifted Chevy in search of buyers for this top-notch performance upgrade. In Detroit, Gratiot Auto Supply immediately ordered as many slick sticks as he could supply, and a *Hot Rod* magazine report soon had gearheads across America clamouring for one. Back home in Philadelphia Hurst took out a $20,000 loan to begin manufacturing his shifters big time.

Earlier in 1958 he had made an existing partnership with cohort Bill Campbell official, resulting in the Hurst-Campbell company. Anco Industries was formed the following year, later becoming Hurst Performance Products, Inc., Hurst-Campbell's sales division. By 1965, Hurst-Campbell was bringing in more than $20 million annually, triggering the construction of bigger, better digs in Warminster, Pennsylvania. The Hurst Research Center, directed by Jack "Doc" Watson, also opened about the same time outside Detroit in Madison Heights. And Hurst-Campbell also bought out clutch-maker Schiefer Manufacturing and the Airheart brake company.

Hurst Performance's big break came in 1961 when Bunkie Knudsen and Pete Estes asked George Hurst in for a meeting at Pontiac. Estes had read *Hot Rod's* appraisal and had a proposition. A deal was then inked and Pontiac began offering Hurst shifters as a parts-counter option. And when the GTO debuted in October 1963, it featured a Hurst stick as standard equipment.

As Jim Wangers later explained in *Automobile Quarterly*, "We quickly learned that one of the first things a new customer would do after purchasing a high-performance stick-shift car was to take it down to the local hot rod shop and install a Hurst. I was finally able to convince both Estes and DeLorean that it meant more to Pontiac to be able to advertise the fact that our cars came equipped with a Hurst right from the factory than it meant to Hurst to say they were original equipment on a Pontiac. This was the first time GM had ever allowed a component supplier's name to be used in advertising."

Hurst's multi-faceted firm also was the aftermarket home to various modified factory muscle machines, a group led most prominently by the long-running Hurst/Olds line, first offered in 1968. Hurst got involved that year too with Chrysler Corporation, helping both Dodge and Plymouth wedge 426 Hemi V-8s into a limited run of Dart and Barracuda super-stock drag cars. Two years later, Hurst did the 300H, a 440-powered 1970 Chrysler that briefly brought back memories of the famed letter-series models of 1955–65.

Hurst teamed up with American Motors in 1969 to produce the SC/Rambler and the strip-ready AMX S/S, followed by the Rebel Machine in 1970. Appearing in 1970 as well was Pontiac's Grand Prix SSJ, a Hurst conversion that could've been equipped with a 455 V-8 and American Racing mags. A second-edition SSJ appeared in 1971 and a few more were sold in 1972.

George Hurst was no longer in the picture by then. Hurst-Campbell had gone public in 1968, instantly attracting the Sunbeam Corporation, which acquired controlling interest by buying out Bill Campbell's stock in 1970. Campbell's partner then left soon afterward to pursue other business ventures. Sunbeam itself was bought out in November 1981 by Allegheny International, which sold Hurst to Richard Chrysler, of Cars and Concepts in Detroit. Chrysler had started out in 1966 as a menial "floor-sweeper" at Hurst, eventually rising to management before leaving to found Cars and Concepts. Hurst was sold again early in 1986, this time to Mr. Gasket's Joe Hrudka.

Fifty-nine-year-old George Hurst died that same year on May 15.

Another "letter car" came from Chrysler in 1970, but this time the "H" was short for "Hurst." Special Hurst paint, a hood scoop, and rear spoiler were part of the 300H package.

Spokesmodel Linda Vaughn represented Hurst prominently during the 1960s and 1970s and still turns heads at automotive events today. Known better for her bikinis, a more formal "Miss Hurst Golden Shifter" here upstages the Hurst-created SSJ Grand Prix, offered from 1970 to '72.

BUICK

A restyled Skylark body made big news this year, and most everything rolled over beneath the GS-400's softly sculpted skin, save for the automatic transmission choice: Buick's Super Turbine 400 was traded for GM's nearly identical Turbo Hydra-matic 400. Still identified as a Super Turbine 400 by some factory sources this year, the TH-400 was limited to GS-400 applications. Body style availability too changed for 1968 as the big-block Gran Sport was only offered in hardtop and convertible forms.

The small-block GS came only as a hardtop, while the GS California—now marketed nationwide—was again only available as a vinyl-roofed sedan. New for the GS-400's little brothers was a 350-cid V-8 that necessitated another name change as GS-350 predictably superseded 1967's GS-340. Output for the GS-350's bigger small-block was 280 horsepower. Once again a three-speed manual was standard for both the GS-350 and GS-400 but in the former's case was available with either a floor shifter or mundane column shift—all previous manual-trans Gran Sports featured floor-mounted sticks. While a four-speed was again optional (now Hurst-stirred) behind both blocks, small or big, the 350's optional automatic was the carryover two-speed Super Turbine 300.

Barely noticed in 1968 was the new Stage 1 Special Package, a dealer option that on paper pumped the 400 V-8 up another 5 horses thanks mostly to a more aggressive cam and a boost to 11:1 compression. Anyone who took a Stage 1 GS to the strip knew that published 345-horsepower rating was a joke, which *Car Life* proved by scorching the quarter-mile in 14.4 seconds in an automatic transmission example. With headers and slicks, the elapsed time was cut to 13.50 clicks.

HOT OFF THE PRESS: 1968 BUICK GS

"The GS-400 is the kind of car you can drive and drive and not get tired of. For a while there may be a few machines that put the GS down at the track, but on the way to the track, that's a horse of a different color."

Eric Dahlquist, Hot Rod, *January 1968*

Skylark GS-400s were available in hardtop and convertible forms in 1968, while the small-block GS-350 was limited to the hardtop body style.

Left: Marketed in California only in 1967, the aptly named GS California vinyl-roofed sedan was sold nationwide the following year and again was fitted only with an automatic-backed small-block, Buick's new 350-cid V-8 in this case.

OLDSMOBILE

Another restyled Cutlass body appeared at the same time the 4-4-2 was promoted up to individual-model status. A 400 Rocket (again rated at 350 horsepower) remained standard for 1968's 4-4-2, but this was a "new" V-8 (see page 24) derived from Oldsmobile's 455-cid big-block, also introduced this year for the front-driven Toronado and full-size models. A 325-horsepower Rocket was used when the optional Turbo Hydra-matic was ordered, and the 360-horsepower W-30 option carried over. Still listed too was the Turnpike Cruiser package, now featuring a 290-horse 400.

Another W-machine debuted this year to help fool those damned insurance agents, who were rapidly making it all but impossible for Average Joe to cover his big-block muscle car. The "Ram Rod 350" Olds featured a 350-cid W-31 V-8 force-fed by the same ram-air ductwork used by the W-30 big-block. Running separately from the high-profile 4-4-2, Oldsmobile's 325-horsepower W-31 models (Cutlass and F-85) were quietly offered up through 1970.

Not so tough to miss were the special-edition machines manufactured in the spring of 1968 at Demmer Engineering in Lansing, Michigan. Earlier that year, Hurst's Doc Watson approached Olds chief engineer John Beltz with a simple proposition: why not let Hurst produce a limited run of 455-powered 4-4-2s for Oldsmobile? Marketing men claimed the idea would never fly, but Beltz pushed his Hurst/Olds through anyway.

Watson's friend, industrialist John Demmer, opened his small plant specifically to produce the Hurst/Olds. Legend has it that Oldsmobile delivered garden-variety 4-4-2s to Demmer Engineering minus engines, leaving the taboo 455 installations to the Hurst crew. In truth the cars all came complete off the Olds line in Lansing with their 390-horsepower 455s already clandestinely bolted in, an easy enough trick considering this really big big-block was essentially identical at a glance to the '68 4-4-2's standard 400.

All but the first (and maybe the second) Hurst/Olds built featured Turbo Hydra-matics controlled by Hurst Dual Gate shifters. Two Cutlass body styles were offered, Holiday hardtop and Holiday post-coupe, and all were painted the same: Peruvian Silver, a Toronado color, complemented by a decklid done in black.

New for Oldsmobile's 4-4-2 in 1968 was a "long-stroke" V-8 that displaced the same number of cubic inches, 400, as the "short-stroke" engine it replaced. Also new was the W-36 Rally stripe which ran vertically on each front fender behind the wheels. This stripe was standard with the W-30, optional on other models.

HOT OFF THE PRESS: 1968 OLDSMOBILE 4-4-2

"In action, there was no question that the 4-4-2 Holiday coupe looked every bit as quick and strong as it really is—a true high-performance car, and the best handling of today's Supercars."

Car Life, *June 1968*

Oldsmobile pioneered (in mass-production terms) completely shiftless driving in America with its Hydra-Matic automatic transmission, introduced in 1940. Unlike GM's "semi-auto" Automatic Safety Transmission (a 1937–39 Olds and 1938 Buick option), which still incorporated a conventional friction clutch for stopping and starting, Hydra-Matic Drive relied on a fluid coupling mated to a hydraulically controlled planetary gearbox to shift effortlessly through four forward speeds with no need to involve your left foot. Cadillac began offering Hydra-Matic in 1941, Pontiac in 1948.

Buick and Chevrolet officials, however, opted for their own torque-converter designs, with the former's Dynaflow debuting in 1948. Two years later, Chevy's Powerglide became the first optional automatic in Detroit's low-priced field. Though renowned for its sluggish nature, the two-speed Powerglide was so darned durable, hence its long career. But it never did fit well behind big, powerful V-8s, not like GM's modern, ultra-strong three-speed automatics—Cadillac's Turbo Hydra-matic and Buick's Super Turbine—that debuted in 1964.

While Chevrolet began offering the Turbo Hydra-matic 400 in 1965, it was limited initially to the full-size line's lo-po 396 Turbo Jet, leaving Powerglide to soldier on as the main automatic choice. The big-block-only TH 400 didn't become an SS 396 option until 1967 and wasn't mated to the top-dog L78 396 until 1969, the same year Chevy rolled out its new Turbo Hydra-matic 350, a three-speed automatic intended for six-cylinder and small-block V-8 applications. Though they shared names, the Turbo 400 and Turbo 350 auto boxes had little in common and were manufactured separately within the GM empire. And unlike its venerable two-speed forerunner, the TH 350 could handle most anything thrown at it, leaving the Powerglide this time to roll off into the sunset, finally retiring in 1973.

Buick's Super Turbine was identical to Chevy's Turbo Hydra-matic in 1964 but was updated the following year with Flint's proven variable-pitch stator, which increased torque multiplication on demand. Two versions were offered: the three-speed Super Turbine 400 and its two-speed Super Turbine 300 little brother. Big-block Gran Sports switched to the TH-400 in 1968, and the Super Turbine 300 was superseded by the TH-350 the following year. "Jetaway" was the name Oldsmobile used for the Super Turbine automatic offered as a 4-4-2 option in 1965 and '66.

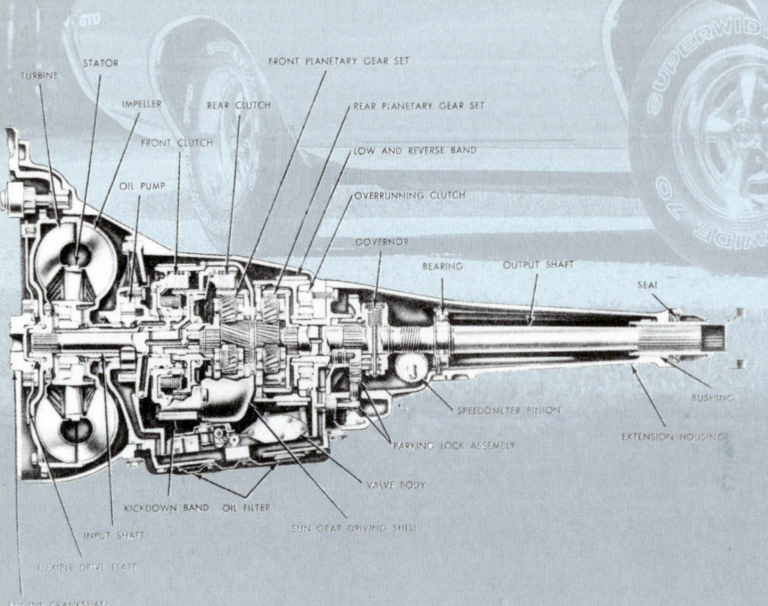

Chrysler got the upper hand on the competition (as far as high-performance automatic transmission development was concerned) in 1956, introducing its three-speed Torqueflite for its top-shelf Imperial and 300B models. Fitted with an aluminum case, the heavy-duty A-727 Torqueflite (shown here) appeared in 1962.

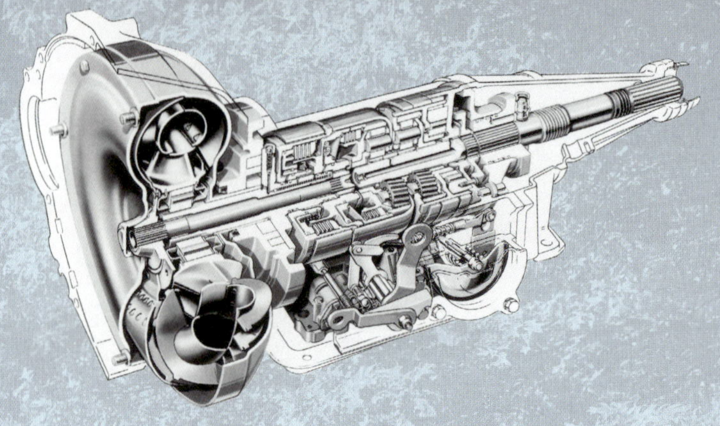

Ford's first "in-house" automatic (earlier units were developed with Borg-Warner's assistance), the C4 Cruise-O-Matic (shown here), appeared in 1964 for six-cylinders and light-duty V-8s. The beefier C6 then followed for high-perf applications two years later.

Automatically speaking, Dearborn's weapons of choice were the C4 and C6 Cruise-O-Matics, lightweight yet tough three-speed transmissions. The first auto box developed completely in-house by Ford, the C4 debuted in 1964 for smaller engines, while the heavy-duty C6 followed two years later for more powerful applications.

The Fairlane GT's "Sport Shift" C6 was highly touted in 1966 for its split-personality controls. "This unique concept in automatic transmission permits the driver to manually shift through the three gears, yet can provide fully automatic operation, the same as the conventional Cruise-O-Matic," claimed Ford ads. "Performance enthusiasts will welcome the capabilities of this new transmission, as it enables the driver to shift independently of the engine or car speed on both upshifts or downshifts, with the additional benefit of fully automatic operation if desired." The name was changed to "SelectShift" in 1967.

Last but by no means least, Chrysler Corporation's Torqueflite, introduced in iron-case A-488 form in 1956 (for Imperial and 300B), also was no stranger when it came to collecting kudos. "The three-speed Torqueflite is undoubtedly the best [auto] unit offered by any American manufacturer today when it comes to being punished by high horsepower," bragged *Hot Rod's* Ray Brock in 1960. "Since its first appearance, this transmission has become the standard, in terms of performance, for others to see," added *Car Life* six years later. "So far, no one has come close to it for responsiveness."

The seriously heavy-duty A-727 Torqueflite debuted in 1962 with an aluminum case, and a smaller, less beefy A-904 version (introduced in 1960, first for six-cylinder applications) began finding its way behind LA small-blocks in 1964. Pushbutton controls, mounted on the dash, were the norm up through 1964 (and for some early '65s) before conventional shift linkages appeared. And both versions, 727 and 904, began showing up in American Motors models in 1972 wearing the "Torque Command" label.

All Hurst/Olds models built for 1968 were painted silver with black accents. The deck lid also was done in black.

HOT OFF THE PRESS: 1968 HURST/OLDS

"Mix in talent (Olds), a dash of ideas (Hurst), and blend thoroughly with endless strings of enthusiasm. Result: HURST-OLDS."
Steve Kelly, Hot Rod, *July 1968*

The Hurst/Olds V-8 featured W-30 heads and fresh-air ductwork, but it wasn't a W-30. A Toronado 455 short-block was used, as was a milder cam and standard cast-iron intake manifold. W-30 heads reportedly weren't installed when optional air conditioning was ordered, though at least one such combination is known. Another W-30 trademark—red plastic inner fenderwells—also was included in all cases, thanks to John Beltz.

FORD

New Mustang options for 1968 included a restyled styled-steel wheel accented by a center cap and trim ring. That cap was adorned with appropriate lettering when included as part of the GT package. Paperwork also announced a W-code 427 four-barrel option, but apparently none were installed before the king of the FEs was discontinued in December 1967. Definitely dropped in was the 390 GT big-block, bumped up 5 horsepower. Both 289 and 302 Windsor small-blocks were offered, with the former fitted only with a two-barrel, the latter with both two- and four-barrels. GT buyers could choose between the 230-horsepower 302 four-barrel or 325-horsepower 390 and also had to pay extra for front disc brakes, as was the case in 1965. Priced at $64.77, front discs were mandated when the 390 was installed.

Another FE, the 428 Cobra Jet, became available in April 1968, thanks to Rhode Island Ford dealer Robert F. Tasca, who was more than disappointed when Ford's first big-block Mustangs began rolling onto his lot the previous year. As Tasca Ford's high-performance department manager Dean Gregson told *Hot Rod* magazine late in 1967, "we found the car so non-competitive, we began to feel we were cheating the customer. So we did something about it."

Using existing 390, 427, and 428 parts, Tasca Ford people created a "stock" pony car capable of roasting the quarter-mile in about 13 seconds. Bob Tasca carried a lot of weight around Dearborn, and when he proposed that Ford offer a regular-production counterpart people listened.

"Bob likes to say he was the father of the Cobra Jet, and he's right," explained engineer Bill Barr. "When Tasca came to town, he was always immediately given

Introduced in April 1968 in fastback, coupe, and convertible forms, Ford's Cobra Jet Mustang featured a long list of standard performance pieces, including power front discs, braced shock towers, a beefy 9-inch rear end, staggered rear shocks (on four-speed models), and a black-striped ram-air hood. An 8,000-rpm tach was standard with the four-speed, optional when a C6 automatic was chosen. Part of the deal, too, was the GT equipment group consisting of a heavy-duty suspension, F70 tires on styled-steel wheels, fog lamps, chromed quad exhaust tips, and "GT" identification. *Mike Mueller*

1968 FORD MUSTANG 428 COBRA JET

CONSTRUCTION: unitized body/frame w/lower shock tower bracing in front
MODEL AVAILABILITY: coupe, fastback & convertible (all w/GT Equipment Group)
PRICE: $3,600 (approximate)
WHEELBASE: 108 inches
WEIGHT: 3,623 pounds
SUSPENSION: heavy-duty; coils springs & 0.84-inch stabilizer bar, front; solid axle w/lead springs, rear; staggered shock absorbers in back w/4-speed trans
STEERING: manual (25.3:1) recirculating ball
WHEELS: 14x6 styled-steel
TIRES: F70 Wide Oval
BRAKES: power-assisted 11.3-inch front discs, 10-inch rear drums
ENGINE: 428-cid Cobra Jet FE-series V-8 w/Holley 4-barrel carburetor
TRANSMISSION: 4-speed manual or heavy-duty C6 Cruise-O-Matic automatic
AXLE RATIO: 3.50:1 in heavy-duty 9-inch differential; 3.91:1 and 4.30:1, optional

HOT OFF THE PRESS: 1968 FORD MUSTANG COBRA JET

"The CJ will be the utter delight of every Ford lover and the bane of all the rest because, quite frankly, it is probably the fastest regular-production sedan ever built."
Eric Dahlquist, Hot Rod, *March 1968*

HOT OFF THE PRESS: 1968 FORD TORINO GT 428 COBRA JET

"Everything considered, the Torino GT 428 is a real luxury wat to get performance—lots of it."
Dan Roulston, Car Craft, *March 1968*

an audience, and this time he flogged the company for what he wanted." Barr's team was then instructed to grant Tasca's wish.

Following Tasca's lead, they started with a 428 passenger-car block as a base, then added 427 low-riser heads and a big 735-cfm Holley four-barrel. Advertised output was a token 335 horsepower. As for the name, no one is really sure who actually dreamt it up, though it's obvious where the snake theme originated. According to Bob Tasca, Lee Iacocca had paid a high price for the rights to Carroll Shelby's established Cobra image and wasn't about to see all that cash go to waste.

"We already had the snake idea in our heads," added Bill Barr. "And we didn't do this like we normally did. We didn't just roll out the product with everyone standing around it scratching their asses trying to name it. Some artist in Styling had already created a drawing of the Cobra emblem—the snake with the wheels and exhausts coming out of its tail. We had the drawing, then the name came from there."

On the street, Ford's CJ Mustang left challengers sucking smoke. "Once you went down on the loud pedal, this baby could really fly," Barr claimed. "For stop-light Grand Prixs the 428 Cobra Jet was the bee's knees because nothing could stay with it." "The Cobra Jet [Mustang] began the era of Ford's supremacy in performance," echoed Tasca. "It was the fastest, in my opinion, the fastest production car built in the world at that point."

Along with Mustang, the 428 CJ also was made available midyear for Ranchero, Mercury's Cougar and all FoMoCo intermediates, which were restyled for 1968 and offered in two new forms, "formal" roof and fastback. Ford's Fairlane lineup furthermore was treated to a new flagship, Torino, fitted with extra trim and interior flash.

At the tip-top in 1968 was Torino GT, which like its Mustang cousin came standard with styled-steel wheels and Wide Oval rubber. Apparently bucket seats and a console were included in the GT deal early on then moved to the options list. A two-barrel 289 was the base engine and initial underhood options numbered three before the Cobra Jet came along: the four-barrel 302, a 265-horsepower two-barrel 390 and its four-barrel FE brother.

SHELBY MUSTANG

Ford officials renamed their Michigan-built Shelby Mustangs in 1968, the year a convertible was officially offered for public consumption. Changes to the "Shelby Cobra GT350/500" were minor, with the most noticeable involving the addition of safety-conscious side marker lights and the substitution of larger Thunderbird sequential taillights. A 250-hp 302 was standard for the GT350, a 360-horsepower 428 (now topped by a single Holley four-barrel) for the GT500. The new 428 Cobra Jet debuted midyear for a third model, GT500KR. Those last two letters stood for "King of the Road."

MERCURY

Cougar's GT package carried over from 1967 and this year could be combined with the 428 Cobra Jet. Before the CJ arrived, the hottest Cougar was the GT-E, fitted with the four-barrel 427 V-8 rated at 390 horsepower. Additional standard

According to promotional paperwork, Ford's notably updated Torino offered "sports flair styling" in 1968. Available in fastback and formal-roof forms, Torino GT came standard with bucket seats and styled-steel wheels adorned with trim rings and appropriate "GT" center caps. The fastback shown here is fitted with 1968's sensational midyear option: Dearborn's 428 Cobra Jet V-8. *Mike Mueller*

GT-E stuff included a C6 automatic trans, heavy-duty suspension, power-assisted steering and front discs, and FR70 radial rubber. CJ-equipped GT-E Cougars were built too, after Ford discontinued its famed 427 FE.

Offering more pizzazz than performance, 1968's Cougar XR7-G came standard with a 302 two-barrel, although both the 390 GT V-8 and 428 CJ were optional. Among XR7-G features were hood pins, racing mirrors, road lamps, a vinyl roof, and the GT-E's non-functional hood.

Mercury's midsize Cyclone lost its Comet affiliation in 1968, an appropriate move considering the latter nameplate was on its way out—it appeared only on a two-door coupe that year and again in 1969 before finally retiring. Offered in formal-roof hardtop and fastback forms, 1968's Cyclone/Cyclone GT came standard with a 210-horsepower 302 two-barrel small-block. Engine options mimicked Torino GT's, with the rare 427 phased out early and replaced in April by the 428 CJ Bucket seats, special handling equipment, F70 tires and turbine-style wheel covers were standard for Cyclone GT. Simulated wire covers or Ford's styled-steel rims were optional.

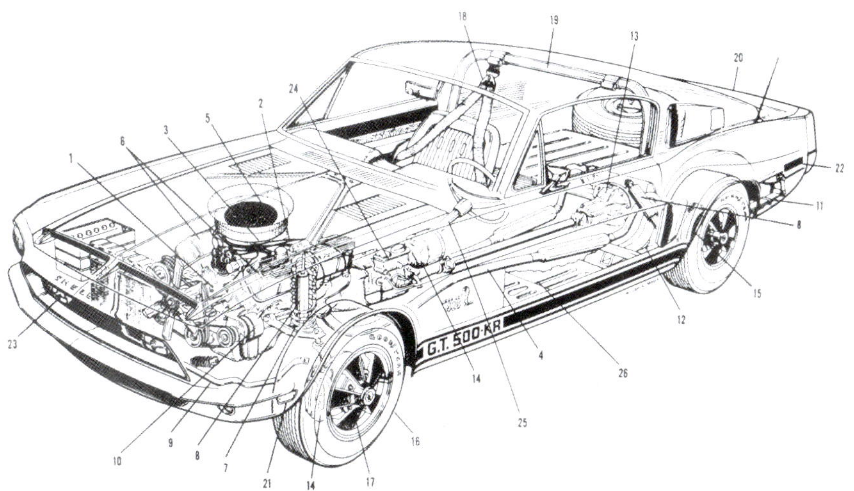

Now produced in Livonia, Michigan, Ford's Shelby Mustang was offered in three forms in 1968 beginning with the familiar GT350 powered by a 250-horsepower 302 Windsor small-block. The second-edition GT500 featured a 360-horsepower Police Interceptor 428 big-block. At the top was the new GT500KR (exposed here), fitted with a335-horsepower 428 Cobra Jet. "KR" stood for "King of the Road."

1968 FORD TORINO GT

CONSTRUCTION: unitized body/frame
MODEL AVAILABILITY: formal-roof hardtop, fastback & convertible (all w/bucket seats)
PRICE: $2,769, hardtop; $2,772, fasback; $3,001, convertible
WHEELBASE: 116 inches
WEIGHT: 3,760 pounds
SUSPENSION: coil springs & 0.65-inch stabilizer bar, front; solid axle w/leaf springs, rear; heavy-duty GT Handling Suspension, optional
STEERING: manual (29.4:1) recirculating ball, std; 21.6:1 power assist, optional
WHEELS: 14x6 styled-steel w/"GT" center caps
TIRES: F70 Wide Oval, std; FR70 Wide Oval radial std w/427 V-8, optional in other cases
BRAKES: 10-inch drums, front & rear; power-assisted 11.3-inch front discs, optional
ENGINE: 210-hp 302-cid V-8 w/two-barrel carburetor; std; 390-, 427- & 428-cid V-8s, optional
TRANSMISSION: column-shifted 3-speed, std; column-shifted Cruise-O-Matic automatic & 4-spd manual, optional; floor shift & console optional w/auto trans; Cruise-O-Matic included w/optional 427 V-8
AXLE RATIO: 3.00, std; 3.25:1 included w/4-speed; 2.79:1 included w/auto; 3.50:1 included w/427 V-8; 3.25:1 included with 390 GT V-8

Mercury introduced its 7.0 Litre GT-E package for Cougar (base model and XR-7) midyear in 1968. Early models featured 427 V-8s; beginning in May the new 428 Cobra Jet became the weapon of choice. Unique two-tone paint, a special grille, a "power-dome" hood with simulated intakes, and styled-steel wheels were included among the GT-E's long list of standard features.

1968 MERCURY COUGAR GT-E

CONSTRUCTION: unitized body/frame w/twin-scoop "Power-Dome" hood
MODEL AVAILABILITY: base hardtop & XR7 hardtop (both w/unique two-tone paint)
PRICE: $4,244.42, hardtop; $4,542.91, XR7 (GT-E package alone cost $1,311)
WHEELBASE: 111 inches
WEIGHT: 3,662 pounds
SUSPENSION: heavy-duty Super Competition Handling Package; coil springs & 0.95-inch stabilizer bar, front; solid axle w/leaf springs, rear; adjustable Gabriel shock absorbers
STEERING: power-assisted (20.3:1) recirculating ball
WHEELS: 14x6 styled-steel
TIRES: FR70 radial (either Firestone Super Sports Wide Oval or Goodyear Speedway Wide Tread) white-sidewall (red line versions reportedly were also available but no installations are known)
BRAKES: power-assisted 11.3-inch front discs, 10-inch rear drums
ENGINE: 390-hp 427-cid 4V V-8 or 428 Cobra Jet V-8 w/ram-air
TRANSMISSION: Select-Shift Merc-O-Matic automatic; 4-speed top-loader, optional
AXLE RATIO: 3.25:1, 3.50:1 & 3.90:1; Detroit Locker differential, available

Like its Torino cousin, Mercury's restyled 1968 Cyclone also appeared in fastback and formal-roof forms. A 210-horsepower 302 small-block was standard for both Cyclone and Cyclone GT (shown here in fastback garb); optional engines mimicked the midsize Ford's. A 427 big-block was offered early in the year before being replaced by the 428 Cobra Jet. Bucket seats and a beefed suspension were standard for 1968's GT.

AMERICAN MOTORS

Like Ford prior to 1960, American Motors stuck with 1957's AMA "racing ban" like glue, first under the ultra-conservative direction of future Michigan governor George Romney (father of presidential wannabe Mitt), who moved aside in February 1962, allowing fellow traditionalist Roy Abernethy to step up. Not quite as staid as his predecessor, Abernethy at least signed off on some serious futures investment (see "The American Way," page 105) to hopefully stem a river of red ink, resulting in, among other things, the new 290-cid Typhoon V-8, offered in small numbers midway into 1966. According to *Motor Trend's* Donald MacDonald, the 290's introduction "has led to speculation that AMC is about to deep-six its anti-racing philosophy and turn to competitive events as a means of knocking down its avidly gathered reputation for economy."

Abernethy was forced into early retirement in January 1967 by a stockholders' board avidly out for new blood. Labeled a scapegoat, board chairman Richard Cross had been sacked the previous year in favor of AMC's largest shareholder, Richard Evans, who in turn gave Roy Chapin Jr. his initial promotion on the way toward eventually filling Abernethy's shoes. Like Evans and American Motors' styling head Richard Teague, Chapin recognized the value of a sporty image, especially considering how young the market was growing at the time. AMC's Typhoon V-8 itself grew that year, to 343 cubic inches and 280 horsepower in top four-barrel form, fanning speculative flames even further.

"Is American Motors about to junk the auto industry's anti-racing resolution to which it has strictly adhered for 10 years?" asked an August 1967 *Motor Trend* report. "Until recently, AMC under George Romney and Ray Abernethy observed the letter and spirit of the AMA resolution. Now, however things are changing under Roy Chapin, with the help of Robert Evans."

Additional grist for the rumor mill had been supplied throughout 1966 by Teague's various "Project IV" dream cars, three of them wearing the same name: "AMX." Big hits on the show circuit, these flights of fancy inspired Evans to push for development of a regular-production rendition, a truly sporty two-place compact that was green-lighted in September 1966. Approval for a more conventional model, fitted with a back seat, had been given five months before. That latter

1968 CHEVROLET NOVA SS 396

CONSTRUCTION: unitized body/frame
MODEL AVAILABILITY: coupe
PRICE: Super Sport package cost $210.65
WHEELBASE: 111 inches
WEIGHT: 3,509 pounds
SUSPENSION: heavy-duty; coil springs & 0.6870-inch stabilizer bar, front; solid axle w/leaf springs, rear; staggered shock absorbers in back
STEERING: manual (28.3:1) recirculating ball, std; 20.7:1 power-assist, optional
WHEELS: 14x6 stamped-steel; Rally rims, optional
TIRES: E70 Uniroyal Tiger Paw
BRAKES: 9.5-inch drums, front & rear; 11-inch front discs, optional
ENGINE: 350-hp 396 Turbo Jet or 375-hp 396 Turbo Jet V-8s
TRANSMISSION: 3-speed manual, std; 4-speed & Turbo Hydra-matic 400 automatic, optional
AXLE RATIO: 3.55:1

1968 MERCURY CYCLONE GT

CONSTRUCTION: unitized body/frame
MODEL AVAILABILITY: hardtop & fastback (both w/bucket seats)
PRICE: $2,768 (for base Cyclone)
WHEELBASE: 116 inches
WEIGHT: 3,740 pounds (fastback w/optional 428 Cobra Jet V-8)
SUSPENSION: heavy duty; coil springs & stabilizer bar, front; solid-axle w/leaf springs, rear
STEERING: manual recirculating ball; power-assist, optional
WHEELS: 14x5.5 stamped-steel w/turbine-style wheel covers, std; styled-steel rims, optional
TIRES: F70 Wide Oval
BRAKES: 10-inch drums, front & rear; power-assisted 11.3-inch front discs, optional
ENGINE: 210-hp 302-cid V-8 w/two-barrel carburetor; std; 390-, 427- & 428-cid V-8s, optional
TRANSMISSION: 3-speed manual, std; 4-speed & Select-Shift Merc-O-Matic, optional
AXLE RATIO: 3.00:1, std

FAMILY TIES: AMERICAN MOTORS V-8s

Like Pontiac's long-running V-8, AMC's original Typhoon featured ample room for growth, hitting its zenith (401 cubic inches) in 1971. *Tom Shaw*

Studebaker was this country's first independent automaker to offer a modern OHV V-8 in 1951, followed by Packard four years down the road. Late in 1954, Packard agreed to supply this new engine to American Motors, with the deal calling for Packard to "consider" purchasing parts from Kenosha in return. AMC's Nash and Hudson lines both offered Packard's 320-cid V-8 in 1955, as well as a larger 352-cube version in 1956. But after Packard turned down AMC's reciprocal offers, a miffed George Romney ordered his engineers to produce their own in-house engine, which debuted, at 250 cubic inches, in the spring of 1956. An enlarged 327-cid rendition appeared the following year, and a high-perf rendition of this V-8 powered 1957's rambunctious Rambler Rebel. AMC's original Rambler V-8 remained in production up through 1966, when it was joined midyear by its thoroughly modern "Typhoon" replacement, a much lighter engine created by Dave Potter's engineering team using trendy thinwall-casting techniques. Weighing no more than 550 pounds, this second-generation V-8 featured an alloy foundation incorporating considerable nickel content, making it one of the most durable engines on the market. Its burly block also offered ample room for growth, with the original 290 Typhoon upstaged by a 343 version in 1967, followed in 1968 by the "AMX 390," a performance-oriented mill fitted with forged-steel crank and rods. That block was recast in 1970 with a taller deck height to allow longer strokes, in turn opening the door for the 290 and 343 to move on up to 304 and 360 cubic inches, respectively. The 390 was then stroked to 401 inches in 1971. Both the 1968–70 390 and 1971–74 401 were topped by four-barrel carbs only. All AMC V-8s built after 1969 also featured race-bred cylinder heads incorporating "dogleg" exhaust ports that reportedly breathed 50 percent better than earlier rectangular-port heads.

YEAR	CID	BORE & STROKE	CR	HORSEPOWER	TORQUE	CARBURETOR	VALVE SIZES
1966	290	3.750 x 3.280	9.0:1	200 @ 4,600	285 @ 2,800	Holley 2-barrel	1.787 x 1.406
1967	343	4.080 x 3.280	10.2:1	280 @ 4,800	365 @ 3,000	Carter AFB 4-barrel	2.02 x 1.625
1968	390	4.165 x 3.574	10.2:1	315 @ 4,600	425 @ 3,200	Carter AFB 4-barrel	2.02 x 1.625
1970	304	3.750 x 3.440	9.0:1	210 @ 4,400	305 @ 2,800	Motorcraft 2-barrel	1.787 x 1.406
1970	360	4.080 x 3.440	9.0:1	245 @ 4,400	365 @ 2,600	AMC 2-barrel	2.02 x 1.625
1971	401	4.170 x 3.680	9.5:1	330 @ 5,000	430 @ 3,400	Motorcraft 4-barrel	2.02 x 1.68

NOTE: CID is cubic-inch displacement; CR is compression ratio; bore/stroke & valve sizes in inches (intake x exhaust).

HOT OFF THE PRESS: 1968 AMC AMX

"If AMC had done something as bright as the AMX five years ago, they'd be in a lot better shape today."
Car and Driver, *March 1968*

1968 AMC AMX

CONSTRUCTION: unitized body/frame
MODEL AVAILABILITY: hardtop
PRICE: $3,245
WHEELBASE: 97 inches
WEIGHT: 3,410 pounds
SUSPENSION: heavy-duty; coil springs & stabilizer bar, front; solid axle w/leaf springs & torque struts, rear
STEERING: manual (24.1:1) recirculating ball, std; 19.3:1 "Quick Ratio" & 18.1:1 power-assist, optional
WHEELS: 14x5.5 stamped-steel
TIRES: E70 Goodyear
BRAKES: 10-inch drums, front & rear; 11.2-inch front discs & power-assist, optional
ENGINE: 225-hp 290-cid V-8 w/Carter four-barrel carburetor; 343- and 390-cid V-8s, optional
TRANSMISSION: floor-shifted Borg-Warner T10 4-speed, std; Shift-Command automatic (Warner Gear M11), optional
AXLE RATIO: 3.54:1, std; 3.15:1 included w/290 V-8 & auto trans (3.15:1 std w/manual trans 343 & 390 V-8s; 2.87:1 included w/auto trans 343 & 390 V-8s); 3.15:1 std w/Go Packages; 3.73:1, 3.91:1, 4.10:1 & 4.44:1 available as dealer options; Twin-Grip differential, optional

A second two-seat American sporting machine joined Chevrolet's Corvette in 1968 courtesy of staid, stoic (until now) American Motors, based in Kenosha, Wisconsin. Rolling on a truly tidy 97-inch wheelbase, AMC's new AMX was created by sectioning a foot from the equally new Javelin's floorpan, eliminating the back seat in the process. While Javelin featured a standard six-cylinder, it was V-8s only for the hot, little AMX.

machine, Javelin, AMC's new pony car, debuted on September 16, 1967. Created by sectioning 12 inches from Javelin's mid-section, America's "other" two-seater, predictably named AMX, was unveiled in February 1968. Both turned heads with ease, on the street and track, substantiating any and all rumors in bold fashion. AMC clearly was now in the race.

As handsome as they came at the time, Javelin followed in Mustang's hoofprints, being offered in both frugal six-cylinder and exciting V-8 forms. Two 290s, two- and four-barrel, were available, as was the 280-horsepower 343. Javelins also could be morphed into the plush SST, which featured a faux-wood steering wheel and reclining bucket seats. Maxing out performance was left to the available "Go Package," listed for both base Javelin and SST. This excellent option included the 343 four-barrel, power front discs, E70 redline tires on 14x5.5 wheels, a handling suspension, and body-side rally stripes.

Called "a hairy little brother to the Javelin" by Teague, AMX rolled on a wheelbase measuring 97 inches, 1 less than Corvette's stretch in 1968. The four-barrel 290 was standard, backed by a floor-shifted Borg-Warner four-speed. Optional V-8s numbered two: the 280-horsepower 343 and AMC's new 390, rated at 315 horsepower. Both the 343 and 390 could be ordered in AMX Go Packages, and the latter V-8 also became available for Javelin after the two-seater's February 1968 introduction. AMX's "Go" option also included a Twin-Grip differential, a heavy-duty radiator, a seven-blade flex fan with shroud, and rally stripes that ran up and over the body—just like a race car.

Appropriate, huh?

FAMILY TIES: AMC GROUP 19 PARTS

All rumors about American Motors plans to be born again as a muscle builder were proven true in September 1967 when the Wisconsin company put former racer Carl Chakmakian in charge of a then-modest Performance Activities department. In February 1968, Chakmakian issued a memo to AMC/Rambler dealers explaining in plain English that his bosses intended to try their hands at racing, and to do this required a whole host of hot parts to go along with the hot cars then in the works. In company parlance, these go-fast goodies became known as "Group 19" components, a reference to the catalog section devoted to high-perf hardware. Reportedly Group 19 equipment could only be acquired via dealer networks; none of it could be special ordered on a Javelin, AMX, or such direct from Kenosha. Group 19 pages featured everything from three-barrel Holley carbs, to Edelbrock cross-ram intakes, to four-wheel disc brake packages, to fiberglass body spoilers, to all the right engine stuff—cams, connecting rods, valvetrain gear, distributors, you name it. Pretty much everything AMC tested at the track turned up in the Group 19 listings, but then disappeared essentially overnight as the last of this country's great independents refocused on practicality after 1974. At least it was big fun while it lasted.

HOT OFF THE PRESS: 1968 SHELBY GT500KR

"It's big and strong and very highly tuned. At 6000 rpm, the Cobra Jet will pull a semi-trailer up Pikes Peak."

Car Life, *October 1968*

MOTOR OF THE YEAR: 1968 FORD 428 COBRA JET

Type	OHV FE-series V-8 w/ram-air hood
Displacement	428 cubic inches
Bore	4.13 inches
Stroke	3.98 inches
Horsepower	335 at 5,600 rpm (some sources claim 5,400 rpm)
Torque	445 at 3,400 rpm
Compression	10.6:1 (early Ford paperwork claimed 10.7:1)
Fuel delivery	735-cfm Holley 4-barrel carburetor on cast-iron version of Police Interceptor aluminum intake
Air cleaner	single-snorkel w/rubber "doughnut" that sealed to the ram-air hood's underside
Ignition	single-point, vacuum-advance distributor
Cooling	7-blade fan w/clutch
Cylinder block	high-nodularity cast-iron Police Interceptor w/reinforcing ribs, thickened main bearing bulkheads & two-bolt main bearing caps; high-capacity oil pump & oil pan windage tray
Crankshaft	"nodular-controlled" cast-iron w/2.7484-2.7492-inch main journals
Connecting rods	forged-steel Police Interceptor with 13/32-inch bolts (early) Ford paperwork mentioned 11/32-inch bolts
Pistons	cast-aluminum dished w/full-floating wrist pin
Cam	hydraulic 390 GT w/270 degrees duration on intake, 290 on exhaust, 46 degrees of overlap
Rocker ratio	1.73:1
Cylinder heads	cast-iron 427 low-riser w/smaller "as-cast" combustion chambers (72.8–75.8cc volume—volume for the 427 V-8's machined chambers was 88-91cc) & valve springs w/inner dampers
Valve sizes	2.097-inch intakes, 1.660-inch exhausts
Valve lift	0.481 inch, intake; 0.490 inch, exhaust
Exhaust system	cast-iron header-style manifolds, 2.25-inch pipes

CHAPTER 6

1969 A NEW KING IS CROWNED

SS 396 OUTSELLS GTO

Ordering an SS 396 Chevelle in 1969 meant checking off RPO Z25, basically the same midsize Super Sport package offered (in individual model form) from 1966 to '68, with a couple nice additions thrown in: power front disc brakes and five-spoke SS wheels. Those stoppers consisted of 11-inch rotors and single-piston calipers, while the new rollers were 14x7 units adorned with trim rings and small "SS" center caps. *Mike Mueller*

On the street or off the lot, few automobiles from Detroit's original muscle car era moved like Chevrolet's Super Sport Chevelle. Sheer numbers said it all. Counting the small-block models added back into the mix in 1971 and '72, total SS production for the years 1966 through 1972 was 390,981. Only Pontiac's GTO sold better—395,127 cars—during that span. But in this hot market segment's zenith years, 1969–71, SS Chevelles topped GTOs by 37 percent, 167,972 to 122,968. And in 1969, Chevy's midsize Super Sport finally brought down the king, unseating GTO for the annual high-performance sales lead, a position it held until its last appearance four years later.

So what made the SS A-body so super? For starters, it was a Chevelle, always a top-selling model during the 1960s. "Chevelle was 'America's Midsize Car,' " said Mecum Auctions consignment director John Kraman, a man who knows his way around collectible automobiles. "It was crisp, rugged, mechanically straight-forward. Chevelle was really the car that baby-boomers lusted after; they either had one or wanted one." And, according to National Chevelle Owners Association co-founder Mark Meekins, that little two-letter badge alone was in itself a great start towards a high-profile presence. In his opinion, adding a superlative to a popular 1950s connotation of "coolness" virtually guaranteed snazzy impressions for any model Chevrolet's idea guys opted to transform into a Super Sport, and that eventually included practically everything from Chevy II to Chevy trucks.

At its height, the entrenched SS 396 image was so highly revered by Chevy label-makers they didn't dare juggle the numbers after engineers late in 1969 bored out the Turbo Jet big-block to 402 cubes. "Ess-Ess-four-oh-two?" No way, it was "Ess-Ess-three-ninety-six" or nothing else. Even in the beginning, when that image represented not much more than a carrot hanging on a stick, most witnesses knew GM's low-priced leader had a winner. "No doubt a long line will form for these cars at Chevrolet dealerships," concluded *Car Life's* test crew after driving a rare Z16 Malibu in 1965.

Three years later, buff books were all paying homage to SS 396 as the up-and-coming heir to the supercar throne. "A five-minute stay in any drive-in any part of the country will be sufficient testament to the car's popularity," claimed *Super Stock's* Jim McCraw in 1968. A five-minute stay in any high school parking lot even as late as 1980 supported the SS 396's claim to all-time fame, as do auctioneers' hammers today.

SS 396 Chevelles rapidly gained prominence after 1965 mostly because they represented one of Detroit's biggest bangs for the buck. But at the same time, they were still practical transports; everyday rides that were by no means dull. As *Car Life* described it in 1970, "the best-selling Supercar isn't the quickest, but it looks tough. And it's kind to women and children. Adults can ride in the rear seat, as they should be able to in a car this size. With the handling package, brakes, etc., the SS 396 makes a fine family car."

SS 396 didn't become the segment leader by appealing only to teenage lead-foots, nor did it rise to the top by being the baddest mother in the valley—at least not in standard trim. Chevrolet managed this bloodless coup by offering a nicely balanced performer to a greater group of customers, most of them intent on using their Chevelles much more than one quarter-mile at a time. And, yes, many of those drivers planned to have the wife and kids along for the ride.

That balanced basic package grew even more desirable as the 1960s rocked and rolled on, with front disc brakes and attractive five-spoke sport wheels becoming standard equipment in 1969, followed by Chevy's F41 underpinnings in 1970. At its pinnacle that year, Chevelle SS arguably represented Detroit's finest combination of trick looks, big-block brute force, GT handling, and state-of-the-art stopping power—and all of this without one extra dollar spent on options.

"You cannot buy the hottest engine without also buying the suspension, tires and brakes that Chevrolet engineers have learned work best," reported *Road Test* in 1970. "Some manufacturers sell super cars with minimal suspension and

COUNTERPOINT: GTO VS. CHEVELLE SS

After establishing a division record for first-year new-model production, GTO really got rolling in 1965, surpassing 75,000 in sales. Another 96,946 followed in 1966, firmly demonstrating what horsepower hounds already knew: GTO was America's number one muscle car. Although Chevy's SS 396 did finally take over the top yearly performance sales spot to stay in 1969—86,307, to 72,287—Pontiac's powerful progenitor remained the big bully to beat on the street. As *Motor Trend* explained, the "GTO is the leader of super cars. It trails Chevy's SS 396 in sales, but it is the others who are trying harder. In image, performance, and class, the 'Tiger' is the car to equal." All told, GTO was the best-selling performance machine of the entire muscle car era. Counting the rebodied 1973 variety and downsized Ventura-based 1974 version, Pontiac sold 514,793 Goats. Even though Chevrolet did build 577,600 SS Chevelles between 1964 and 1973, more than one-sixth of that total consisted of the lower-performance small-block V-8 and frugal six-cylinder models built in 1964–65 and the 350-equipped cars of 1971–73. No matter how you looked at it, in its heyday GTO was Detroit's most popular muscle car.

1969 CHEVROLET CHEVELLE SS 396

CONSTRUCTION: body on perimeter-rail frame
MODEL AVAILABILITY: Malibu hardtop/cvt., 300 Deluxe sedan/hardtop
PRICE: RPO Z25 cost $347.60
WHEELBASE: 112 inches
WEIGHT: 3,895 pounds
SUSPENSION: heavy-duty; coil springs & 0.937-inch stabilizer bar, front; coil springs, rear
STEERING: manual (24:1) recirculating ball, std; 17.5:1 power-assist, optional
WHEELS: 14x7 five-spoke
TIRES: F70x14 Wide Oval
BRAKES: power-assisted 11-inch discs, front; 9.5-inch drums, rear
ENGINE: L35 396-cid Turbo Jet V-8 w/Rochester 4-barrel carburetor, std; L34 (350-hp) & L78 (375-hp) 396 Turbo Jets, optional
TRANSMISSION: 3-speed manual, std; Muncie 4-speed manual & TH-400 automatic, optional
AXLE RATIO: 3.31:1

brakes, assuming customers plan to go drag racing where such items matter little or will be altered." The Bow-Tie boys, on the other hand, chose to concentrate on Regular Joe. Not to mention his ol' lady.

That's not to say, however, that weekend warriors were overlooked. Sure, GM killjoys had put the squelch on their divisions' racing projects in January 1963, but that didn't stop Chevrolet engineers from keeping up the pace on the street. While Ford pumped tens of millions of dollars into an international competition program at the cost of disappointing street performance credentials, Chevy's movers and shakers were busy giving stoplight challengers what they wanted most—the chance to pick and chose a level of Super Sport performance that best suited their particular need for speed, as well as their wallet's capacity to support said need.

"Although [the SS 396] is not the fastest machine right off the showroom floor, it does possess much more potential than any other car in its field," wrote *Popular Hot Rodding*'s Lee Kelley in 1968. "With a minimum cash outlay and a lot of elbow grease, this car can be [a] street eliminator any night of the week. Chevy may not be in racing, but its cars sure are!"

And let's not overlook that unforgettable image. "As the politician-peddler says, it isn't what you are, it's what projects," began a *Car Life* commentary in 1970. "The Chevelle Super Sport 396 projects. While Ford rules NASCAR and Plymouth concentrates on the drags, Chevelle moves out of showrooms everywhere."

And wasn't that the whole idea?

CHEVROLET

Chevrolet changed the way it packaged its SS 396 Chevelle in 1969. A buyer this year had to check off RPO Z25, offered for Malibu sport coupe, convertible, and El Camino, plus two models in the low-priced, minimally trimmed 300 series; 300 Deluxe sport coupe and 300 Deluxe sedan. Z25 was basically the same SS 396 package offered from 1966 to '68, with two nice additions: the aforementioned power front discs and SS wheels. New on the options list were weight-saving aluminum cylinder heads (for the L78 396 only), loud chambered exhausts, and Chevy's F41 sport suspension.

Chevrolet's pony car was treated to a major facelift this year, and the SS Camaro appeared even hotter when topped off in front with the new ZL2 cowl-induction hood. Debuting as well was an optional body-colored Endura front bumper. The aluminum-head L89/L78 combo was again a rarely seen installation (only 311 built), and even fewer and farther between was the JL8 power-assisted four-wheel disc option. Only 206 JL8 Camaros are known for 1969.

Nearly all standard Z28 features carried over unchanged, and the Rally Sport package was again available, now featuring prominently styled headlight doors. Notable upgrades included a more durable 302 cylinder block (refitted with four-bolt mains), a thicker front stabilizer bar, and wider 15x7 wheels, although some early models apparently used 1968's 15x6 rims. Various changes were made to the Z28 equipment group during the year as more than one individual component came and went.

Simulated fender louvers were new for the latest Nova SS, now listed under RPO Z26. Front disc brakes were included in this package but didn't necessarily

Continued on page 130

300 + 396 = 1 RARE CHEVELLE

Along with El Camino, Chevrolet offered two distinct A-body model lines in 1964, base 300 and Malibu, with trim typically setting the two notably apart—the latter had a lot of bright stuff, the former not so much. Mundane, low-priced 300 models were limited to sedan and station wagon bodies, while the upscale Malibu group was led by a sport coupe and convertible, which in turn could be dressed up further in SS garb. A dressier 300 Deluxe series did arrive in 1965, but those ho-hum body style choices remained the same, at least until 1968, when a 300 Deluxe sport coupe was introduced. Then came the decision to offer RPO Z25, Chevy's repackaged SS 396 deal, for all 1969 Chevelles, making this the only year a midsize Super Sport came with window "posts"—and without Malibu accoutrements. The Z25 deal was available for both the 300 Deluxe sedan and 300 Deluxe hardtop. No breakdowns are available, but suffice it say that 1969's 300 Deluxe SS 396 represented a truly rare bird. Transforming a 300 Deluxe into an SS 396 required various unique touches. First, roof rail drip gutters, larger taillight bezels, and upper body accent stripes were added, as were the upper and lower rear cove moldings required to delineate the Super Sport's blacked-out tail panel. The Deluxe's rocker moldings were deleted, and the "300 Deluxe" fender script was, of course, traded for 1969's new "SS 396" badge. Inside, the dash and steering wheel both got the SS identification, but the 300 sedan door panels didn't—this because the 300's doors had vent windows and the Malibu hardtops didn't, meaning a different panel was required by the former. And because only Malibu models featured hideaway windshield wipers, the wiper arms on the 300 Deluxe SS 396 didn't retract beneath the cowl edge of the twin-bulge Super Sport hood. From there, however, everything else was basic Z25, right down to the sport wheels at the corners and bright exhaust extensions in back. The 300 Deluxe post-sedan shown here features the aluminum-head (L89) L78 396 Turbo Jet, a combination that truly qualified as few-and-far-between in 1969.

Both Chevrolet's A-body 300 Deluxe sport coupe and 300 Deluxe sedan were transformed into SS 396s in 1969, the only year a midsize Super Sport could be anything other than a top-of-the-line Malibu or Custom El Camino. The Hugger Orange paint seen here was one of two radioactive Camaro colors (the other was Daytona Yellow) offered to Chevelle SS customers at extra cost ($42.15) in 1969. *Mike Mueller*

A fully documented run of Indy 500 pace car replica SS Camaros appeared in 1969, this time officially listed under RPO Z11. All were SS/RS convertibles done in Dover White paint with Hugger Orange stripes and orange houndstooth interiors. Rally wheels and cowl-induction hoods were included in all cases, too. A similarly adorned pace car replica coupe also appeared with many of the same features, including both SS and RS equipment. A promotional package created for Chevrolet's Southwestern Branch Zone Office, this option was tabbed Z10. Estimates claim as many as 200 or 300 Z10 coupes were released during the spring of 1969. *Mike Mueller*

Chevrolet's nicely restyled 1969 Camaro body suited the Z28 to a T, even more so when topped off by the functional ZL-2 hood with its rear-facing scoop, introduced on November 25, 1968. Nearly all standard features carried over unchanged, and the Rally Sport package was again available, now featuring prominently styled headlight doors. New too was a more precise, definitely preferred, Hurst shifter in place of the clunky Muncie stick used in 1967 and '68. *Mike Mueller*

Pennsylvania-based Yenko Chevrolet created its first Camaro Super Car the hard way by swapping in a Corvette-sourced L72 427 V-8 and adding various hot hardware. A second 427 S/C Camaro followed in 1968, this time converted with a bit less fuss/muss thanks to a little-known paperwork loophole.

In GM parlance, this process was known as "COPO," short for "Central Office Production Order." Meant primarily for volume customers like trucking firms and police departments, COPOs represented a relatively easy way around corporate red tape while fulfilling special equipment orders. In most cases, a thumbs-up from Engineering was all that was needed to transform such requests into reality. Of course, if this process worked so well for power company trucks, it also could be applied to high-performance automobiles.

Making a COPO happen, however, was by no means a simple task. "There was considerable engineering work put into all COPO requests," said Pontiac Historical Services' Jim Mattison, who was working in Chevrolet's Fleet and Special Services department during the 1960s when Vince Piggins began using this paper trail to build some seriously hot Chevys. "Every COPO option had a material sheet that listed every part added and deleted to make the package work. It was very intricate and precise work. The only 'relatively easy' COPOs were the special paint vehicles that we did for fleet users, as well as individual [orders]."

Digging up COPO roots is not easy; not even Mattison can say when this practice originated. According to archivist Christo Datini at the GM Heritage Center, no internal records detailing COPO history have surfaced to date. "But I spoke to [former GM engineer and author] Ken Kayser about this, as he has seen a lot of Chevrolet paperwork over the years. He told me a story about one of his research trips to Chevrolet when he was given access to a parts drawing file. He was researching 1956–57 Corvettes and came across a binder labeled 'COPO.'"

"The binder simply listed numbers in order that were pulled and assigned as a COPO and the dates they were 'reserved for COPO,'" explained Kayser. "There was not a single word as to what the number was for. It was just so the numbers would not be used by the draftsmen and engineers."

"This would indicate that the COPO process was around at least as early as this," added Datini in February 2014. "Ken believes [COPOs] may have begun sometime after World War II."

COPO paperwork proved just the ticket to help make Yenko's transformations less troublesome in 1968. COPO #9737, identified as the "Sports Car Conversion," added heavy-duty cooling, upgraded brakes and suspension, and a 140-miles per hour speedometer to a special production run of 396-equipped Camaros, which Yenko then used as bases for its 427 S/C models. As in 1967, out went the stock engine, in went an L72.

But that was just the beginning. Reportedly Yenko people began meeting with GM officials in the summer of 1968 to discuss ways to make their S/C conversion even easier, with the goal being to do away with engine transplants altogether. While ordering 427-equipped Camaros direct from Chevrolet through typical RPO channels was of course impossible, end-running around corporate roadblocks using the COPO route appeared perfectly doable. Chevrolet general manager Pete Estes agreed, giving the go-ahead to Piggins' group to develop a special run of Corvette-powered pony cars.

COPO Camaros, whether fitted with the iron-block L72 or all-aluminum ZL–1 V-8s, were indistinguishable at first glance. Shown here is one of the 69 ZL–1 models built for 1969. *Mike Mueller*

Two COPO-coded Camaros appeared in 1969: #9561 and #9560. The COPO 9561 F-body was created for Yenko and featured the cast-iron L72 427. COPO 9560 was done for Gibb Chevrolet in Illinois. Like Don Yenko, Fred Gibb and his righthand man, racer Dick Harrell, also approached Vince Piggins in the summer of 1968 with a COPO request to build 427-powered Camaros, but not just L72s. They also wanted the exotic all-aluminum ZL1, which was installed in only two Corvettes in 1969.

To meet NHRA homologation rules, Gibb ordered 50 COPO 9560 Camaros for his lot in LaHarpe, Illinois, with the first two arriving on December 31, 1968. Another 19 went to various dealers across the country who also found out how tough it was to market this high-strung, high-priced pony.

Base price for a typical V-8 Camaro in 1969 was $2,272. COPO 9560 tacked on another $4,160.15. An official price was still in the works when Gibb placed his order; he guessed that $4,900 would be tops. Nearly all the cars had arrived in Illinois before GM billed him in March. More than a bit overwhelmed, he somehow managed to send 20 ZL1s back to the Norwood, Ohio, plant for reluctant redistribution.

1969 COPO V-8s

TYPE	OHV MK IV L72 BIG-BLOCK	OHV MK IV ZL1 BIG-BLOCK
Availability	Camaro, Chevelle*	Camaro, Corvette
Displacement	427 cid	427 cid
Horsepower	425 at 5,600 rpm	430 at 5,200 rpm
Torque	460 at 4,000 rpm	450 at 4,400 rpm
Compression	11:1	12:1
Fuel delivery	780-cfm Holley 4-barrel	850-cfm Holley double-pumper 4-barrel
Air cleaner	sealed to ZL2 ducted hood	sealed to ZL2 ducted hood
Intake manifold	aluminum, closed-divider	aluminum, open-divider
Ignition	single-point distributor	transistorized
Cooling	heavy-duty Harrison radiator	heavy-duty Harrison radiator
Cylinder block	cast-iron	aluminum w/cast-iron cylinder sleeves
Crankshaft	forged 1053 steel w/4-bolt mains	forged 5410 steel w/4-bolt mains
Connecting rods	forged steel, 3/8-inch bolts	forged steel, 7/16-inch bolts
Pistons	aluminum	aluminum
Cam	mechanical	mechanical
Cylinder heads	cast-iron closed-chamber	aluminum open-chamber
Valve sizes (inches)	2.19 intake; 1.72 exhaust	2.19 intake; 1.88 exhaust
Valve lift	0.519 inch	0.580 inch
Duration (degrees)	316, intake; 302, exhaust	357, intake; 364, exhaust

NOTE: *Bore and stroke for 427-cid V-8 was 4.251 inches x 3.76 inches.*

** L72 V-8 was introduced as an option for Corvette and full-size models in 1966.*

Rated at a laughable 430 horsepower, Chevrolet's ZL-1 427 V-8 featured all-aluminum construction. Included, too, was the paradoxical A.I.R. emissions equipment. *Mike Mueller*

A 427-powered COPO Chevelle, coded #9562, also appeared in 1969 and, like its 9561 Camaro cousin, was created initially for Yenko Chevrolet. But that sharp focus dissipated once the word got around. According to Mattison, he first let the cat out of the bag to Stan Emeritt (of Stan Emeritt Chevrolet in Detroit), who immediately asked the obvious question: why couldn't he take delivery of COPO models, too? Various other dealers also were soon calling with the same query, including Berger Chevrolet in Michigan. In the end, anyone with a little inside knowledge could've joined in on the fun. An August 1969 assembly manual addendum helped make that at least partially clear, explaining that "contrary to the implication in the COPO option name shown, [9737] is also applicable to other Chevrolet dealers' orders as well as 'Yenko Sports Cars, Inc.'"

Yenko Chevrolet did the most ordering by far in 1969, with the first 100 COPO 9561 Camaros built going to Canonsburg, followed by nearly 100 more later on, all to be decked out in "Yenko S/C" striping. Reportedly Berger also scored 50 COPO Camaros, plus a lesser number of COPO Chevelles. As for the total 1969 count, that remains a mystery. It is known that GM's Tonawanda engine plant turned out 1,015 L72 427s (193 automatics, 822 four-speeds) for F-body installations that year, but how many of those actually went into Camaros sold to the public is undocumented.

Tonawanda plant records also showed 277 L72s were produced for MQ-code manual-trans COPO 9562 applications, while another 96 MP-code L72s were intended for use with Turbo Hydra-matics. But this combined total, 373, represents engines manufactured, not cars built. Estimates claim as many as 323 COPO Chevelles were released, with 99 of those known to have gone from the Baltimore assembly plant to Yenko Chevrolet.

1969 COPO CHEVROLETS

	#9560	**#9561**	**#9562**
Model	Camaro	Camaro	Chevelle
Wheelbase	108 inches	108 inches	112 inches
Suspension	H-D coil/leaf	H-D coil/leaf	H-D coils, f/r
Wheels	14x7	14x7	15x6
Tires	F70x14	F70x14	F70x15
Brakes	power-assisted front discs, rear drums in all three cases		
Engine	ZL1 427 V-8	L72 427 V-8	L72 427 V-8
Transmission	4-speed manual or TH-400 auto in all three cases		
Axle ratio	4.10:1 Positraction*	4.10:1 Positraction*	4.10:1 Positraction*

** Special heavy-duty differential in 12-bolt housing*

Chevrolet's little-known COPO Chevelle was created in 1969 to allow Yenko Chevrolet to add an A-body Super Car to its 427-powered Camaro S/C, on the market since 1967. Various equipment combinations (four-speed/automatic, 14- or 15-inch wheels, etc.) are known for this rare machine. Estimates claim less than 350 were built. *Mike Mueller*

Simulated fender louvers appeared on 1969's Nova SS, offered now as an options package, RPO Z26. The engine lineup carried over from 1968, but the 300-horsepower 350 now could be backed up by Chevrolet's new TH-350 automatic. A TH-400 auto also was available behind the 350-horsepower 396, and a specially equipped version of this transmission was listed for the 375-horsepower L78. *Mike Mueller*

Continued from page 126

guarantee installation of Rally wheels as in the past. Joining those Rallys on 1969's options list were the Chevelle/Camaro Super Sport's 14x7 five-spoke wheels. And new too were available Turbo Hydra-matic automatic transmissions: the TH-350 for the 350 small-block, the TH-400 for the 396.

PONTIAC

Standard power carried over from 1968 for GTO, as did the no-cost economizing L65 V-8. The optional 400 HO was dropped in favor of the L74 Ram Air III, and another new choice, the impressive 370-horsepower Ram Air IV 40 (L67) also appeared. Mandatory L67 equipment included a heavy-duty radiator and a limited-slip differential containing either 3.90:1 or 4.33:1 gears. See page 72 for more on Pontiac's Ram Air V-8 legacy.

Also new for 1969 was the GTO Judge, announced in December 1968. That name spoofed the then-popular gag line, "Here comes da' Judge," borrowed from Rowan and Martin's hit television show *Laugh In*. Radioactive Carousel Red paint (on early cars; other shades became available later), splashy striping and decals, a blacked-out grille, and a high-flying wing on the decklid made sure this machine wasn't missed in a crowd. Additional standard stuff included the Ram Air III 400, trimless Rally rims shod in G70 rubber, and a Hurst shifter, in this case fitted with a unique T-handle.

1969 PONTIAC GTO JUDGE

CONSTRUCTION: body on perimeter-rail frame
MODEL AVAILABILITY: hardtop & convertible
PRICE: Judge package cost $337
WHEELBASE: 112 inches
WEIGHT: 3,735 pounds (hardtop)
SUSPENSION: heavy-duty; coil springs & 1.0-inch stabilizer bar, front; coils springs, rear
STEERING: manual recirculating ball, std; 22:1 power-assist, optional
WHEELS: 14x6 Rally II w/o trim rings
TIRES: G70 Goodyear Polyglas
BRAKES: 9.5-inch drums, front & rear, std; power-assisted 11.12-inch front discs, optional
ENGINE: 400-cid Ram Air III V-8 w/Quadra-jet 4-barrel carburetor, std; Ram Air IV V-8, optional (n/a w/air conditioning)
TRANSMISSION: Hurst-shifted 3-speed manual, std; 4-speed & TH-400 automatic, optional
AXLE RATIO: 3.55:1, std; 3.23:1 included w/optional air conditioning (3.90:1 included w/Ram Air IV V-8)

Pontiac's cost-conscious product planners initially envisioned a rather bare-bones machine when the GTO Judge project began. Early discussions mentioned a 350 HO small-block, one exterior paint choice on perhaps a bargain-basement pillared coupe, and even rubber floor mats in place of carpet. But in the end, the Judge emerged with standard Ram Air III power wrapped up in either hardtop or convertible bodies. About the only visible cost concession involved the Rally rims included in the deal—they appeared sans trim rings. *Mike Mueller*

Far and away the hottest Firebird 400 offered for 1969 was the Ram Air IV rendition with its conservatively rated 345 horses. A rare Ram Air IV convertible appears here. *Mike Mueller*

Echoing advancements made for GTO, Pontiac's restyled pony car for 1969 wore a new monochromatic Lexan nose. The 330-horsepower W66 V-8 remained standard for the Firebird 400, while the optional Ram Air III and Ram Air IV 400s were rated at 335 and 345 horsepower, respectively, in F-body applications, which now included the new Trans Am. Like its Z28 corporate cousin—and as its name implied—Trans Am was created to hopefully make Firebird a force in SCCA road racing. But this limited-edition model ended up lost in the shadows on the Trans-Am circuit, primarily because PMD engineers couldn't conjure up an SCCA-legal powerplant, one displacing no more than five liters.

Pontiac's "Trans Am Performance and Appearance" package (option code WS4) cost about $1,100 in 1969 depending on transmission and body style choices. Both coupes and convertibles were built, all done in Cameo White paint adorned with blue accents. Among the long list of WS4 features were fender-mounted air extractors, a fully functional twin-scooped hood, and a 60-inch-wide rear spoiler that, according to engineer Herb Adams, created 100 pounds of downforce at 100 miles per hour. Ram Air III power was standard, the Ram Air IV was optional.

Pontiac's original Trans Am made its public debut at the Chicago Auto Show on March 8, 1969. Beneath its beauteous skin was a beefed suspension that included a 1-inch sway bar, heavier front coils and rear leafs, stiffer shocks, and a limited-slip Safe-T-Track differential with 3.55:1 gears. Brakes were power front discs, and variable-ratio power steering was standard, too. The base engine was Pontiac's 335-horsepower L74 Ram Air III. *Mike Mueller*

1969 HURST/OLDS

CONSTRUCTION: body on perimeter-rail frame
MODEL AVAILABILITY: hardtop & convertible
PRICE: $4,376
WHEELBASE: 112 inches
WEIGHT: 3,716 pounds
SUSPENSION: heavy-duty; coil springs & 0.937-inch stabilizer bar, front; coil springs w/0.875-inch stabilizer bar, rear
STEERING: manual recirculating ball, std; 17.5:1 power-assist, optional
WHEELS: 15x7 Super Stock II
TIRES: F60 Goodyear Polyglas GT
BRAKES: power-assisted 11-inch discs, front; 9.5-inch drums, rear
ENGINE: 455-cid Rocket V-8 w/Quadra-jet 4-barrel carburetor
TRANSMISSION: Turbo Hydra-matic automatic w/Hurst Dual Gate shifter
AXLE RATIO: 3.42:1 w/G80 limited-slip differential; 3.23:1 included w/air conditioning; 3.90:1, optional (n/a w/air conditioning)

1969 BUICK GS-400 STAGE 1

CONSTRUCTION: body on perimeter-rail frame
MODEL AVAILABILITY: hardtop & convertible
PRICE: Stage 1 package cost $199.95
WHEELBASE: 112 inches
WEIGHT: 3,550 pounds
SUSPENSION: heavy-duty; coil springs & 0.970-inch stabilizer bar, front; live axle w/coil springs, rear (0.875-inch rear stabilizer bar, optional w/ride & handling package)
STEERING: Saginaw manual recirculating ball; 20.9:1 power-assist optional
WHEELS: 14x6
TIRES: 7.75x14, std; F70, optional
BRAKES: 9.5-inch drums, front & rear; power-assisted 11-inch front discs, optional
ENGINE: 400-cid Stage 1 V-8 w/Quadra-jet 4-barrel carburetor
TRANSMISSION: 3-speed manual, std; 4-speed & heavy-duty TH-400 automatic, optional
AXLE RATIO: 3.64:1, std (3.42:1 included w/optional air conditioning)

FLOWER POWER

The Mod Top's floral roof could've been ordered alone or with matching interior upholstery in 1969. A groovy rear-quarter window decal also helped announce a Mod Top Barracuda's arrival in 1969. *Mike Mueller*

Hip chicks were the target market in 1969 when Plymouth concocted its groovy Mod Top option—made up of way-out floral-patterned vinyl on the roof and inside—for Barracuda notchbacks and Satellites. "We've been designing cars with women in mind for years," began an advertisement that introduced "the car you wear." "Maybe that's why we have the biggest selection of interiors we've ever had. More colors…more fabrics and vinyls…more choices in seat designs."

Barracuda's mostly yellow Mod Top material was supplied by the Stauffer Plastics Division, known more for its shower curtains and tablecloths. Apparently another firm produced equally wild blue/green and green/gold flower arrangements offered that year for Satellites and Dodges, respectively, with the latter versions labeled "Floral Tops." "Redecorate your garage," was the ad pitch for 1969's blue-green Satellite Mod Top.

Yellow and blue Mod Top treatments appeared again for Barracudas and 'Cudas in 1970, and at least one Hemi E-body done in yellow flower power is known. Apparently Dodge considered offering the green/gold Floral Top package for Challenger and Dart in 1970 then backed off. Variations on the theme also were available, with the most common incorporating paisley vinyl inside and out. Mod Tops without floral interiors are known, too, as are floral interiors with standard vinyl roofs. Reportedly Barracuda convertibles could have been treated to floral inserts inside, but none were produced. After all, the name was Mod Top.

"Mod Top was something that came out of my office," said Plymouth product planning manager Jack Smith before a crowd of Mopar enthusiasts in 2000. "At the time, psychedelic clothing and the whole spirit of Carnaby Street prevailed in the youth market. We tried to steal into that general emotional atmosphere, creating a paisley pattern that we used as a vinyl roof on a car with paint colors that complemented it. It sounds a little strange by today's standards, but at the time, it struck a chord. We were trying to tell the kids, 'Hey, we understand. We want to give you something to drive.'"

On a new kind of trip perhaps?

MOD TOP MOPAR PRODUCTION

	MODEL	NO. BUILT
1969 PLYMOUTH		
	Satellite	1,637
	Barracuda	937
	total	**2,574**
1969 DODGE[1]		
	Dart Swinger hardtop	48
	Dart Swinger 340	50
	Dart Custom	25
	Dart GT hardtop	14
	Dart GTS hardtop	16
	Super Bee coupe	8
	Super Bee hardtop	18
	Coronet 440 hardtop	39
	total	**218**
1970 PLYMOUTH		
	Barracuda (blue)	26
	'Cuda (blue)	17
	Barracuda (yellow)	26
	'Cuda (yellow)	15[2]
	total	**84**
Grand Total		**2,876**[2]

1. Dodge paperwork referenced a "Floral Top" option

2. estimated (hence the grand total isn't exact, either)

Psychedelic times begat psychedelic measures. Hip chicks were the target market in 1969 when Plymouth designers concocted the Mod Top option. A similar floral-style vinyl roof (done in blue) also were offered that year for Plymouth's Satellite, and Dodge put Mod Tops on Darts, Coronets, and Super Bees. *Mike Mueller*

Freshened F-85 styling at both ends appeared for Oldsmobile's 4-4-2 in 1969. Dual exhausts again tucked nicely into the rear bumper. The Holiday hardtop rendition (demonstrated here) once again represented the most popular 4-4-2 model.

OLDSMOBILE

Dr. Oldsmobile, the mythical ruler of the Olds performance realm, unleashed a detuned version of the W-30 for 1969, undoubtedly as another sacrifice to the gods of insurance surcharges. Still fed by those two air intakes mounted beneath the front bumper, the W-32 used a less-aggressive cam and was rated 10 ponies less (350 horsepower) than the W-30. Standard 4-4-2 output again amounted to 350 or 325 horsepower depending on transmission choice.

A much more distinctive Hurst/Olds appeared for 1969 wearing a fiberglass wing on the decklid, twin "mailbox" hood scoops, and new paint: gold-accented Cameo White. At least two convertibles were built, one going to Hurst *figure* head Linda Vaughn, while the remaining 912 models were all Holiday hardtops. No post-sedan bodies were used this time around, nor did any four-speed manuals sneak into the mix. All cars, air conditioned or not, featured 455 Toronado V-8s wearing W-30 heads. A little detuning lowered advertised output to 380 horsepower.

Oldsmobile's small-block muscle car, the W-31 F-85/Cutlass, encored for 1969, again featuring the 325-horsepower Ram Rod 350 V-8. Shown here is a 1969 W-31 Cutlass Supreme hardtop.

1969 PLYMOUTH 440 'CUDA

CONSTRUCTION: unitized body/frame
MODEL AVAILABILITY: hardtop & fastback
PRICE: A13 440 Engine Conversion Package cost $344.75
WHEELBASE: 108 inches
WEIGHT: 3,740 pounds
SUSPENSION: heavy-duty; torsion bars & 0.94-inch stabilizer bar, front; solid axle w/leaf springs, rear
STEERING: manual (29:1) recirculating ball
WHEELS: 14x5.5 stamped-steel
TIRES: E70 Red Streak
BRAKES: 10-inch drums, front & rear
ENGINE: 440-cid Super Commando V-8 w/Carter 4-barrel carburetor
TRANSMISSION: Torqueflite automatic
AXLE RATIO: 3.44:1 or 3.91:1 in Sure-Grip differential

A new color scheme, Cameo White with gold accents, appeared for the second-edition Hurst/Olds in 1969. A rear wing was new this year, as were 15x7 Super Stock II wheels in place of the 14x6 rims used in 1968. *Mike Mueller*

A dealer-offered "Special Package" in 1968, Buick's famed Stage 1 big-block V-8 became an official factory option the following year. Both hardtop and convertible Stage 1 Gran Sports were built that year. *courtesy Mecum Auctions*

BUICK

A new hood announced the 1969 Gran Sport's arrival, and its centrally mounted scoop was functional for both GS-400 and GS-350. Breathing in the cooler outside air in both cases were the same V-8s used in 1968 still backed by a three-speed manual in base form. A floor shifter was standard for the GS-400 hardtop and convertible, a column shift for the GS-350 hardtop. A Hurst-shifted four-speed was available in all applications. New on the GS-350 options list was the Turbo Hydra-matic 350, the only transmission available for the last of the vinyl-roofed GS California sedans. The TH-400 remained optional for the GS-400.

The Stage 1 package was now an official factory option for GS-400 hardtops and convertibles. The Stage 1 400 was again token rated at 345 horsepower, and adding the available Stage 2 cam reportedly bumped that rating up another 5 horsepower, yet another questionable tally. Those who drove one of these bodacious Buicks knew better. "If [a Stage 2 GS] had a GTO sheet metal wrapper on it, you couldn't build enough of them," wrote *Hot Rod's* Steve Kelly.

PLYMOUTH

A convertible Road Runner appeared in 1969, just in time to help Detroit's second-best selling high-performance model claim *Motor Trend's* "Car of the Year" trophy. Minor exterior updates included a revised grille and recessed taillights, and the beep-beep horn beneath the hood was now adorned with a decal announcing it was "The Voice of the Road Runner." Sporty bucket seats debuted on the extra-cost list, and new for both of Plymouth's muscular B-bodies (GTX, too) was optional Air Grabber induction, which added comical "Coyote Duster" artwork to the air cleaner beneath a Road Runner's now-functional hood.

1969 DODGE CHARGER 500

CONSTRUCTION: unitized body/frame
MODEL AVAILABILITY: hardtop w/flush-mounted grille & rear window
PRICE: $3,843
WHEELBASE: 117 inches
WEIGHT: 3,740
SUSPENSION: heavy-duty; torsion bars w/ 0.94-inch stabilizer bar, front; solid axle w/leaf springs, rear
STEERING: manual recirculating ball, std; 18.8:1 power-assist, optional
WHEELS: 14x5.5 stamped steel, std; 15-inch rims included w/Hemi V-8
TIRES: F7x14 Red Streak Wide Tread, std; F70x15 included w/Hemi V-8
BRAKES: heavy-duty 11-inch drums, front & rear
ENGINE: 440-cid Magnum V-8 w/Carter 4-barrel carburetor, std; 426 Hemi, optional
TRANSMISSION: 4-speed manual or Torqueflite automatic
AXLE RATIO: 3.23:1

1969 DODGE DART SWINGER 340

CONSTRUCTION: unitized body/frame
MODEL AVAILABILITY: hardtop
PRICE: $2,857
WHEELBASE: 111 inches
WEIGHT: 3,310 pounds
SUSPENSION: heavy-duty; torsion bars & stabilizer bar, front; solid axle w/leaf springs, rear
STEERING: manual recirculating ball
WHEELS: 14x5.5 stamped-steel
TIRES: D70 Red Streak Wide Tread
BRAKES: drums, front & rear
ENGINE: 340-cid V-8 w/Carter 4-barrel carburetor
TRANSMISSION: Hurst-shifted 4-speed manual
AXLE RATIO: 3.23:1

Minor exterior updates for 1969's Road Runner included a revised grille, recessed taillights, and hood vents that faced upward instead of outward. A convertible model debuted, as did Plymouth's new Air Grabber option, which made those vents fully functional. Plainly done in black in 1968, the "beep-beep" horn beneath the hood was repainted in a light purple shade for 1969 and adorned further with a decal announcing it was "The Voice of the Road Runner." *Mike Mueller*

MOPAR AXLE PACKAGES

Mopar muscle buyers were treated to a whole host of B-body rear end options in 1969, beginning with the A36 Performance Axle Package, which featured a 3.55:1 Sure Grip differential, Hemi suspension, a high-capacity 26-inch-wide radiator with shroud, and a seven-blade "Slip Drive" (viscous) fan. This deal was limited to automatic transmission installations when the 440 or 426 Hemi V-8s were involved but could work in concert with a four-speed or Torqueflite behind the 383 four-barrel. Prices were $102.15 with the 383, $92.25 with the 440, and $64.40 with the Hemi. Next came the A31 High Performance Axle Package, also priced at $102.15, with its 3.91 Sure Grip gears and all the same A36 stuff. A31 was offered with the 383 four-barrel only (manual or automatic) and couldn't be combined with available air conditioning. Three other equipment groups—the A32 Super Performance Axle Package, A33 Track Pack, and A34 Super Track Pack—started out by trading the A36/A31's 8.75-inch heavy-duty axle for a brutal 9.75-inch Dana 60 unit. Limited to 440- and Hemi-equipped models, this trio also shared the Hemi suspension and heavy-duty cooling and couldn't coexist with air conditioning, either. Power front disc brakes and 4.10:1 Sure Grip gears were included in the A32 and A34 packages, while the A33 Track Pack featured 3.54:1 cogs and no discs. The Torqueflite was mandated with A32, a four-speed with A33 and A34. A32 prices were $271.50 with the 440, $242.15 with the Hemi. The Super Track Pack cost $256.45 regardless of engine choice, the Track Pack $142.85. The A32 and A34 options were offered for one more time in 1970, while A31 and A36 carried on into 1971 before retiring. A36 availability expanded that last year to include Dodge and Plymouth's 340 small-block. The A33 Track Pack made its encore, with the 440 only, in 1972.

1969 FORD MUSTANG MACH 1

CONSTRUCTION: unitized body-frame
MODEL AVAILABILITY: SportsRoof fastback
PRICE: $3,122
WHEELBASE: 108 inches
WEIGHT: 3,185 pounds (w/standard 351 V-8 & 3-speed transmission)
SUSPENSION: GT Handling package; coil springs & 0.95-inch stabilizer bar, front; solid axle w/leaf springs, rear
STEERING: manual (25.4:1) recirculating ball, std; 20.5:1 power-assist, optional
WHEELS: 14x5 styled steel, std; 14x6 mandatory w/428 Cobra Jet V-8
TIRES: E70 Wide Oval
BRAKES: 10-inch drums, front & rear; power-assisted 11-inch front discs, optional
ENGINE: 250-hp 351-cid Windsor V-8 w/Motorcraft 2-barrel carburetor
TRANSMISSION: 3-speed manual, std; 4-speed & SelectShift automatic, optional
AXLE RATIO: 2.75:1, std

1969 FORD FAIRLANE COBRA

CONSTRUCTION: unitized body-frame
MODEL AVAILABILITY: formal-roof and SportsRoof fastback
PRICE: $3,208, formal-roof; $3,183, SportsRoof
WHEELBASE: 116 inches
WEIGHT: 3,633 pounds, formal-roof; 3,689 pounds, SportsRoof
SUSPENSION: heavy-duty; coil springs & 0.85-inch stabilizer bar, front; solid axle w/leaf springs & staggered shock absorbers, rear
STEERING: manual (29.4:1) recirculating ball, std; 21.6:1 power-assist, optional
WHEELS: 14x6 stamped-steel
TIRES: F70 Wide Oval
BRAKES: 10-inch drums, front & rear; power-assisted 11.3-inch front discs, optional
ENGINE: 428-cid Cobra Jet V-8 w/Holley 4-barrel carburetor
TRANSMISSION: 4-speed manual, std; SelectShift automatic, optional
AXLE RATIO: 3.25:1; Traction-Lok differential, optional

1969 FORD TALLADEGA

CONSTRUCTION: unitized body-frame
MODEL AVAILABILITY: SportsRoof fastback
PRICE: $3,620
WHEELBASE: 116 inches
WEIGHT: 3,775 pounds
SUSPENSION: heavy-duty Competition package; coil springs & 0.85-inch stabilizer bar, front; solid axle w/leaf springs & staggered shock absorbers, rear
STEERING: manual (29.4:1) recirculating ball, std; 21.6:1 power-assist, optional
WHEELS: 14x6 argent-finish styled-steel w/bright trim rings & center caps
TIRES: F70 Wide Oval
BRAKES: power-assisted 11.3-inch discs, front; 10-inch drums, rear
ENGINE: 428-cid Cobra Jet w/Holley 4-barrel carburetor
TRANSMISSION: SelectShift C6 automatic
AXLE RATIO: 3.25:1

1969 MERCURY COUGAR ELIMINATOR

CONSTRUCTION: unitized body/frame
Model availability: hardtop
PRICE: Eliminator Equipment Package cost $129.60
Wheelbase: 111 inches
WEIGHT: 3,780 pounds
SUSPENSION: heavy-duty Performance Handling Package; coil springs & stabilizer bar, front; solid axle w/leaf springs, rear
STEERING: manual (25.3:1) recirculating ball; power-assist, optional
WHEELS: 14x6 argent-painted styled-steel w/bright trim rings & center caps
TIRES: F70 Goodyear Polyglas
BRAKES: 10-inch drums, front & rear; power-assisted11.3-inch front discs, optional
ENGINE: 351-cid Windsor V-8 w/Motorcraft 2-barrel carburetor, std; 351-4V, 390 GT, Boss 302 & 428 Cobra Jet V-8s, optional
TRANSMISSION: floor-shifted 3-speed manual, std (n/a w/Boss 302 & 428 CJ V-8s); 4-speed and Select-Shift automatic, optional (Boss 302 V-8 available w/4-speed only)
AXLE RATIO: 3.25:1, std; 3.00:1 included w/optional air conditioning; Traction-Lok differential, optional

Plymouth's Air Grabber hood of course also became a GTX option in 1969 and was automatically installed when the available Hemi was chosen over the still-standard 375-horse 440 Super Commando. All other standard features, inside and out, remained familiar. *Mike Mueller*

FORD BOSS 429 V-8

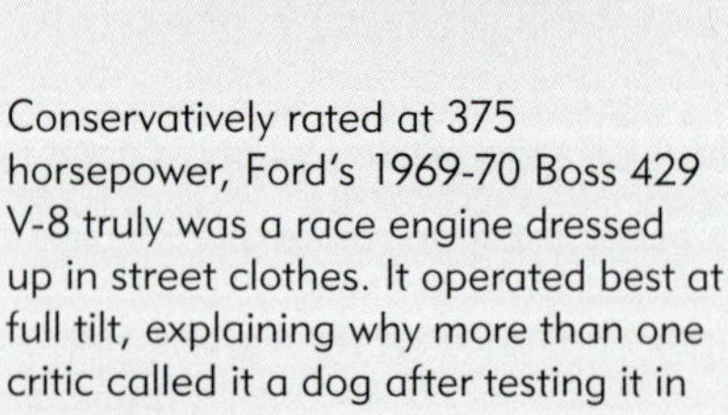

Conservatively rated at 375 horsepower, Ford's 1969-70 Boss 429 V-8 truly was a race engine dressed up in street clothes. It operated best at full tilt, explaining why more than one critic called it a dog after testing it in everyday traffic.

Boss 429 roots run back to 1968 when Ford introduced its 385-series "thinwall" big-block family for its luxury lines. Competition implications were explored immediately, leading engineers to cast a reinforced iron block with four-bolts holding down the bearing caps on four of the five mains. Huge, heavy cylinder heads with sewer-sized ports, massive inclined valves, and hemispherical combustion chambers were also cast in iron, but were recast in weight-saving aluminum once production was confirmed. Combustion chambers too were revised, leaving a shape that wasn't quite hemispherical, thus the commonly heard "semi-hemi" designation. Ford people preferred the "Blue Crescent" moniker, while racers made the "Shotgun motor" nickname popular. Three semi-hemi V-8 variations appeared during the Boss 429 run. The first 279 models off the Kar Kraft line were fitted with "S-code" engines. These NASCAR-style big-blocks featured beefy connecting rods that clamped to a cross-drilled forged-steel crank using large 1/2-inch bolts. Remaining Boss 429s for 1969 and most for 1970 got the "T-code" engine, which traded those heavy, rev-limiting rods for lighter pieces with 3/8-inch bolts. The first T engines featured the S-code's hydraulic cam and magnesium valve covers. But early in the T run, those magnesium covers were replaced with aluminum units and a slightly more aggressive solid-lifter cam superseded the hydraulic stick. The third Boss 429 rendition, found in very few 1970 models, was the "A-code" engine, which was basically a T motor with revised smog controls. All Boss 429 V-8s regardless of code were topped by a 735-cfm Holley four-barrel on a dual-plane aluminum intake. All also included a Drag Pack–style oil cooler. Advertised output was a 375 horsepower, a token number for sure. For more specs, see page 191.

Plymouth's Formula S package once more appeared for all three Barracuda body styles, with either the 340 small-block or 383 big-block, in 1969. But product planners opted to discriminate a bit more finely, promoting the Formula S as a "gentleman's hot rod," if you will. For the less refined, Plymouth introduced the bolder 'Cuda, also offered with the 340 (depicted here) or 383 V-8s. 'Cuda was limited to two bodies—no convertibles were built.

Power choices beneath that bonnet again consisted only of the base 383 and available Hemi, at least early in the model run. A third engine, a triple-carb 440, appeared in the spring of 1969 and was included in Chrysler's A12-code "Engine Conversion Package," available for both Road Runner and Dodge's Super Bee. For more on Plymouth's 1969 440 Six Barrel story, see page 138.

GTX updates included a wide flat-black paint band in place of the bright rocker moldings seen in 1968. Trimming out that band was a thin bright strip that was accented with a pinstripe done in red (on cars equipped with redline tires) or white (on cars with optional whitewalls). New optional touches included parallel black paint bands that ran over the hood and fender tops from the grille to the windshield. Now facing upward instead of out, 1969's twin hood vents were painted red for contrast whenever these bands were applied.

In A-body ranks, Barracuda's Formula S package remained available in all three body styles and once more could feature the 340 small-block or 383 big-block. New were bolder 'Cuda models, also fitted with either the 340 or 383, along with a four-speed stick and beefy Rallye suspension. Simulated hood scoops and black body accents helped set the 'Cuda 340 and 383 apart from their more polite Formula siblings. 'Cudas were limited to notchback and fastback applications; no convertibles were offered.

A third 'Cuda, featuring Chrysler's 440 big-block, appeared in April 1969, this after the guys at Mr. Norm's Grand-Spaulding Dodge in Chicago had marketed their 440-equipped "GSS" Dart the year before. Well aware of Grand-Spaulding's work, Chrysler officials opted to replicate it in the form of another Engine Conversion Package (this one coded A13 and featuring the 375-horsepower 440 four-barrel), offered in 1969 for both A-bodies, Barracuda and Dodge's Dart.

Slightly larger than its 383 cousin, the 440 RB represented a tight squeeze between pony car flanks. A unique driver's side exhaust manifold was required, and power steering and brakes were out of the question, as was optional air conditioning. Missing too was an available manual trans, because engineers didn't trust the car's driveline to handle those hefty torque jolts. The Torqueflite was the only transmission offered, and additional standard pieces included a Sure-Grip Dana rear end containing either 3.55:1 or 3.91:1 gears.

1969 MERCURY CYCLONE CJ

CONSTRUCTION: unitized body/frame
MODEL AVAILABILITY: fastback
PRICE: $3,224
WHEELBASE: 116 inches
WEIGHT: 3,860 pounds
SUSPENSION: heavy-duty Competition Handling; coil springs & stabilizer bar, front; solid axle w/leaf springs, rear
STEERING: manual recirculating ball, std; power-assist, optional
WHEELS: 14x6
TIRES: F70 Goodyear Polyglas
BRAKES: 10-inch drums, front & rear; power-assisted 11.3-inch front discs, optional Engine: 428-cid Cobra Jet V-8 w/Holley 4-barrel carburetor
TRANSMISSION: 4-speed manual, std; Select-Shift automatic, optional
AXLE RATIO: 3.50:1; Traction-Lok differential, optional

The most savage Barracuda for 1969 was created by checking off option code "A13," which specified the installation of a 440 RB big-block between A-body fenders. Both coupe and fastback versions were built, all fitted with Torqueflite automatic transmissions. *Mike Mueller*

Dodge's Charger R/T rolled into 1969 and again offered the 375-horsepower 440 Magnum as standard equipment. Deleting those bumblebee stripes in back was possible for all Scat Pack models, as demonstrated here. This 1969 Charger R/T also is equipped with Dodge's Special Edition package, a new option. *Mike Mueller*

DODGE

New for 1969's Charger was the upscale Special Edition package, which added leather/vinyl bucket seats, a sport steering wheel, and a simulated wood-grain instrument panel. Hood-mounted turn signals and deep-dish wheel covers went on outside. Combining SE prestige with R/T performance resulted in Dodge's hardest-charging B-body yet.

Another new variation, Charger 500, debuted in the fall of 1968 to hopefully help improve performance on –stock car tracks. The work of Detroit's Creative Industries, this purposeful B-body featured a flush nose fashioned by mounting a '68 Coronet grille—complete with fixed headlights—into the recessed cavity common to garden-variety Chargers. In back, the Creative fellows fabricated a steel plug to fill in the "tunneled" rear window. The end result was a more aerodynamic body capable of running 5 miles per hour faster on top end.

Created to make Dodge's B-body more competitive on NASCAR tracks, 1969's Charger 500 was equipped with either a Hemi or 375-horse 440, either one backed by a Hurst-shifted four-speed or A727 Torqueflite automatic. Just so you know, the latter's chrome shift knob was a leftover from the 1968 Charger's parts bin—other automatic-trans 1969 Chargers used a wood-grain knob. Additional unique items included filler pieces for the headlight bezels and a Coronet headlight switch. While those headlights were fixed, a vacuum tank remained in place beneath a Charger 500's hood as the hoses that would've activated the standard model's hideaway lamps were simply cut. *Mike Mueller*

SIX TO GO

Dodge and Plymouth didn't offer the 440 big-block for Super Bee and Road Runner when they debuted, but that changed in 1969. New that summer were two special models, the 440 Six Pack Super Bee and its 440 Six Barrel Road Runner running mate, both outfitted identically to go right from a dealer's lot to the strip. Included in each deal was a new 390-horsepower 440 created most notably by replacing the 375-horsepower RB's single Carter four-barrel with three Holley two-barrels mounted on an aluminum Edelbrock intake. Flow for the 375-horsepower 440's one Carter was 650 cfm. Those three Holleys equaled 990 cfm, with the center one flowing 250, the two ends 370. Vacuum, as opposed to mechanical linkage, decided when all six throats would sing together. Externally, the only other addition was a dual-point distributor.

Internally, the triple-carb and four-barrel 440 V-8s were essentially the same as far as compression and cam timing were concerned, but the 390-horsepower version was equipped for higher revolutions thanks to various items taken off the high-performance parts shelf. Stiff Hemi valve springs, beefed-up rocker arms and connecting rods, molybdenum-filled piston rings, and flash-chromed valves were used, while cam lobes and lifter surfaces were specially machined to equalize wear typically realized when high-tension valve springs were slamming the valves back shut. Mopar engineers had discovered earlier the damage Hemi valve springs could do to an unsuspecting cam; in some

Wheel covers or hood hinges weren't included in Plymouth's 440 Six Barrel Road Runner package in 1969. The fiberglass bonnet simply lifted off by hand after four pins were pulled.

Also introduced midyear in 1969, Dodge's 440 Six Pack Super Bee shared its makeup with its 390-horsepower Road Runner cousin. Both coupe and hardtop versions were built in each case. *Mike Mueller*

cases owners were flattening lobes after only 10,000 miles. As the cam lobes actuated the lifters inside the 390-horsepower 440 engine, the lifters would rotate, distributing wear more evenly over friction surfaces.

Race-ready extras included heavy-duty cooling, the fully beefed Hemi suspension, and "naked" 15-inch rims. No wheel covers were included: those black-painted wheels were simply adorned with chrome lug nuts, nothing else.

Hood hinges also were left off. Standard was a fiberglass lid that simply lifted away by hand (two pairs, that is) once four chrome-plated locking pins were released. "All very racy, but we're sure the novelty of the two-man hood would wear off quickly," observed *Car Life's* critics. That lift-off hood also incorporated a large, wide-open scoop that directed cooler outside air into those six throats below. Again in *Car Life's* words, that scoop "gapes wide open, seemingly ready to ingest all that gets near it including water, dirt, or birds." Special drain tubes in the air cleaner took care of the water; birds were on their own.

Priced considerably less than their Hemi-powered counterparts, the two triple-carb siblings were every bit as quick, if not quicker than their vaunted Hemi running mates. Being a bigger bang for the buck surely was a fair claim. As *Hot Rod's* Steve Kelly explained, "if the price and temperament of a hemi-head engine haven't been enough to thoroughly discourage street-driving performance-car buyers from ordering the 426 in their new Dodge (or Plymouth), then the new 390-horsepower Mopar Six-Pack option will deal the final blow."

Those three Holley two-barrel carburetors more than doubled the flow compared to the 375-horsepower 440's single Carter four-barrel. *Mike Mueller*

1969-½ MOPAR 440-6 B-BODY

CONSTRUCTION: unitized w/front subframe bolted to body structure
MODEL AVAILABILITY: Dodge Super Bee coupe/hardtop & Plymouth Road Runner coupe/hardtop
PRICE: A12 Engine Conversion Package cost $470
WHEELBASE: 117 inches, Dodge; 116 inches, Plymouth
WEIGHT: 3,585 pounds, Super Bee hardtop
SUSPENSION: independent A-arms w/heavy-duty torsion bars & 0.94-inch sway bar, front; solid axle w/heavy-duty leaf springs, rear
STEERING: recirculating ball
WHEELS: 15x6JJ stamped-steel w/chrome lugnuts (no wheel covers were included)
TIRES: G70x15 Goodyear Polyglas Red Steak
BRAKES: heavy-duty 11-inch drums, front & rear
ENGINE: 440-cid RB-series V-8 w/3 Holley 2-barrel CARBURETORS
TRANSMISSION: Hurst-shifted A833 Hemi 4-speed manual or Torqueflite automatic
AXLE RATIO: 4.10:1 Sure-Grip gears in a 9.75-inch Dana 60 rear end

DODGE/PLYMOUTH 440 SIX PACK/SIX BARREL V-8

Type	OHV RB-series V-8
Displacement	440 cubic inches
Bore	4.320 inches
Stroke	3.750 inches
Horsepower	390 at 4700 rpm
Torque	490 at 3200 rpm
Compression	10.1:1
Fuel delivery	3 Holley 2-barrel carburetors on Edelbrock aluminum intake
Air cleaner	open-element oval unit sealed to hood's underside by foam "doughnut"
Ignition	dual-point distributor
Cooling	26-inch heavy-duty radiator & 7-blade torque-drive fan
Cylinder block	cast-iron deep-skirt
Crankshaft	forged-steel
Connecting rods	forged-steel (beefier "Six Pack rods" were installed in 1970)
Pistons	aluminum alloy
Cam	hydraulic w/268 degrees duration on intake, 284 degrees on exhaust, 46 degrees of overlap
Rocker ratio	1.5:1
Cylinder heads	cast-iron open-chamber
Valve sizes	2.08-inch intakes, 1.74-inch exhausts
Valve lift	0.450 inch, intake; 0.465 inch, exhaust
Exhaust system	free-flowing cast-iron manifolds w/dual 2.5-inch main pipes, 2.25-inch tailpipes

Next to nothing changed mechanically as far as Dodge's standard Super Bee was concerned in 1969. A "pillarless" hardtop model debuted this year and outsold its established coupe running mate by a wide margin—must've been those easier-to-use roll-up rear-quarter windows. New on the options list (for Coronet R/T, too) was the Ramcharger fresh-air hood, which replaced the standard ornamental bulge that carried over from 1968 with twin functional scoops. The Ramcharger lid was included as part of the deal when a Super Bee buyer forked over the ample green required to install a 426 Hemi.

The three digits in this aero-conscious car's name referred to NASCAR homologation standards, which stated that at least 500 production examples of any given model had to be built to make that machine legal for stock car competition. But Creative Industries actually fell a bit short of this minimum requirement, rolling out an estimated (an actual count isn't available) 392 Charger 500s for 1969. NASCAR gave Dodge the green light, nonetheless. On the street, Charger 500s were powered by the 375-horsepower 440 or 426 Hemi, either one backed by a Hurst-shifted four-speed or durable A727 Torqueflite.

Like 1969's Charger R/T, Coronet R/T also carried over from 1968 in nearly identical fashion, as did the basic Coronet body, which typically featured updates

TIME SLIPS: 1969

MODEL	¼-MILE PERFORMANCE	SOURCE
Yenko Camaro 427 S/C	12.59 seconds at 108.2 mph	*SSDI*, July 1969
Plymouth Road Runner 440 6 Bl	12.91 seconds at 111.8 mph	*SSDI*, June 1969
Chevrolet Camaro SS 396 L89	13.0 seconds at 108.6 mph	*1969 Supercar Annual**
Chevrolet COPO Camaro ZL1	13.16 seconds at 110 mph	*Hi-Performance Cars*, August 1969
Yenko Chevelle 427 S/C	13.31 seconds at 108.0 mph	*SSDI*, August 1969
Plymouth Road Runner Hemi	13.32 seconds at 107.7 mph	*Rodder & Super/Stock*, May 1969
Dodge Charger 500 Hemi	13.35 seconds at 104 mph	*Hi-Performance Cars*, April 1969
Dodge 440 Six Pack Super Bee	13.56 seconds at 105.8 mph	*Hot Rod*, August 1969
Plymouth GTX (440 V-8)	13.56 seconds at 104.9 mph	*Rodder & Super/Stock*, May 1969
Ford Mustang Mach 1 428 CJ	13.69 seconds at 103.4 mph	*Popular Hot Rodding*, January 1969
Dodge Charger R/T (440 V-8)	13.83 seconds at 102.2 mph	*SSDI*, April 1969
Mercury Cyclone (428 SCJ)	13.86 seconds at 101.7 mph	*Motor Trend*, January 1969
Shelby GT500 Mustang	13.87 seconds at 104.5 mph	*SSDI*, September 1969
Pontiac GTO Judge (RA III)	13.88 seconds at 102.6 mph	*Speed & Supercars*, April 1969
Plymouth 440 'Cuda	13.89 seconds at 103.2 mph	*SSDI*, August 1969
Ford Mustang Mach 1 (428 CJ)	13.90 seconds at 103.2 mph	*Car Life*, March 1969
Pontiac Trans Am (RA III)	13.90 seconds at 102.5 mph	*Drag Strip*, April 1969
Mercury Cougar (428 SCJ)	13.90 seconds at 101.2 mph	*1969 Supercar Annual**
Ford Fairlane Cobra (428 SCJ)	13.94 seconds at 101.7 mph	*1969 Supercar Annual**
Oldsmobile 4-4-2 W-30	13.94 seconds at 100.1 mph	*1969 Supercar Annual**
Pontiac GTO (RA IV)	13.99 seconds at 107.0 mph	*1969 Supercar Annual**
Dodge Super Bee (383 V-8)	14.04 seconds at 99.5 mph	*Car and Driver*, January 1969
Ford Boss 429 Mustang	14.09 seconds at 102.85 mph	*Car Life*, July 1969
Plymouth 'Cuda 383	14.12 seconds at 97 mph	*1969 Supercar Annual**
AMC Hurst SC/Rambler	14.14 seconds at 100.9 mph	*Road Test*, May 1969
Pontiac Firebird 400 (RA IV)	14.21 seconds at 103.0 mph	*1969 Supercar Annual**
Plymouth 'Cuda 340	14.22 seconds at 99.1 mph	*Motor Trend*, October 1968
AMC Javelin (390 V-8)	14.32 seconds at 95 mph	*1969 Supercar Annual**
Chevrolet Camaro Z28	14.34 seconds at 101.4 mph	*Hot Rod*, January 1969
AMC AMX (390 V-8)	14.40 seconds at 91 mph	*1969 Supercar Annual**
Chevrolet Chevelle SS 396	14.41 seconds at 101.4 mph	*Car and Driver*, January 1969
Dodge Dart Swinger 340	14.46 seconds at 100.6 mph	*SSDI*, June 1969
Ford Boss 302 Mustang	14.57 seconds at 97.6 mph	*Car and Driver*, June 1969
Buick Gran Sport Stage 1	14.89 seconds at 103 mph	*1969 Supercar Annual**
Oldsmobile Cutlass W-31	14.90 seconds at 96.0 mph	*Car Life*, March 1969
Chevrolet Nova SS 396 (L78)	15.20 seconds at 92 mph	*Car Craft*, September 1968

NOTE: *SSDI is* Super Stock & Drag Illustrated *magazine*

* Hi-Performance Cars *magazine*

UNDER THE HOOD: 1969'S HOTTEST V-8s*

MODEL	CID	BORE & STROKE	CR	HORSEPOWER	TORQUE
Dodge/Plymouth Hemi	426	4.250 x 3.750	10.25:1	425 @ 5,000	490 @ 4,000
Dodge/Plymouth (3x2)	440	4.320 x 3.750	10.1:1	390 @ 4,700	490 @ 3,200
Dodge/Plymouth	440	4.320 x 3.750	10.1:1	375 @ 4,600	480 @ 3,200
Dodge/Plymouth	383	4.250 x 3.380	10:1	335 @ 5,000	425 @ 3,400
Dodge/Plymouth	340	4.040 x 3.310	10.5:1	275 @ 5,000	340 @ 3,200
Chevrolet SS 396 (L78)	396	4.094 x 3.76	11:1	375 @ 5,600	415 @ 3,600
Chevrolet L72[1]	427	4.25 x 3.76	11:1	425 @ 5,600	460 @ 4,000
Chevrolet ZL1[1]	427	4.25 x 3.76	12:1	430 @ 5,200	450 @ 4,400
Chevrolet Camaro Z28	302	4.00 x 3.00	11:1	290 @ 5,800	290 @ 4,200
Pontiac GTO (RA III)	400	4.120 x 3.75	10.75:1	366 @ 5,400	445 @ 3,600
Pontiac GTO (RA IV)	400	4.120 x 3.75	10.75:1	370 @ 5,500	445 @ 3,900
Pontiac Firebird (RA III)	400	4.120 x 3.75	10.75:	335 @ 5,000	430 @ 3,600
Pontiac Firebird (RA IV)	400	4.120 x 3.75	10.75:	345 @ 5,400	430 @ 3,700
Hurst/Olds	455	4.125 x 4.250	10.5:1	380 @ 5,000	500 @ 3,200
Olds 4-4-2 W-30	400	3.87 x 4.25	10.5:1	360 @ 5,400	440 @ 3,600
Olds W-31	350	4.057 x 3.385	10.5:1	325 @ 5,400	360 @ 3,600
Buick Stage 1	400	4.040 x 3.90	10.25:1	345 @ 5,800	440 @ 3,200
Ford/Mercury 428 CJ	428	4.13 x 3.98	10.6:1	335 @ 5,200	440 @ 3,400
Ford/Mercury (Cleveland)	351	4.00 x 3.50	10.7:1	290 @ 4,800	385 @ 3,200
Ford Boss 302	302	4.00 x 3.00	10.5:1	290 @ 5,800	290 @ 4,300
Ford Boss 429	429	4.36 x 3.59	10.5:1	375 @ 5,200	450 @ 3,400
AMC AMX	390	4.165 x 3.574	10.2:1	315 @ 4,600	425 @ 3,200

NOTE: *CID is cubic-inch displacement; CR is compression ratio; bore/stroke in inches*

NOTE: *Chevrolet Turbo Jet V-8 was bored out from 396 cubic inches to 402 late in 1969*

1. COPO V-8s for Camaro (L72 & ZL1) & Chevelle (L72).

**Discounting factory super-stocks, full-size models & Corvette*

at both ends. Taillights varied: base models (and Super Bee) featured a pair of long, thin lamps reminiscent of Charger's, while the R/T was adorned with what looked like three lenses running across the tail. In truth, the middle unit actually was a reflector patterned after the working taillights located to each side.

New options for 1969 included simulated air ducts (for the rear quarter panels) and the Ramcharger hood, identified by the two scoops added in place of a base R/T's totally non-functional "power bulge." Like Plymouth's Air Grabber, the Ramcharger lid featured a fiberglass plenum underneath that sealed to a special oval air cleaner housing, allowing those twin scoops to direct outside air into the carb(s) below. R/T engine choices again consisted of the four-barrel 440 Magnum or dual-Carter Hemi.

The Ramcharger option also fit 1969's Super Bee nicely, as did those extra-cost rear-quarter scoops. Engine availability mirrored Road Runner's, with the A12 440 Six Pack (again, see page 138) appearing midway into the run. A new "pillar-less" hardtop also joined the existing Super Bee coupe this year, and both were adorned with a new die-cast "Rumble Bee" character up front in the grille.

Dodge's A-body was again offered in GT and GTS forms for 1969, with either the 340 or 383 once more available in the latter's case. Another performance choice, Dart Swinger 340, also appeared this year as a cost-conscious alternative to the GTS in Dodge's Scat Pack pecking order. By cutting

Continued on page 145

Like Plymouth's GTX, Dodge's Coronet R/T carried over with only minor changes for 1969. Exterior identification was updated slightly as 1968's front fender badges disappeared in favor of incorporating the name within the bumblebee stripe in back. If Scat Pack striping was deleted, appropriate badges were added to the quarter panels. New optional simulated air scoops also could be added to those panels just behind the doors. *Mike Mueller*

BY THE NUMBERS: 1969 PRODUCTION

CHEVROLET SS 396

RPO Z25	**86,307**	(includes Malibu hardtop/convertible, 300 hardtop/sedan & El Camino)

CHEVROLET CAMARO SS

L48 (350 V-8)	20,962	
L34 (396 V-8)	2,018	
L35 (396 V-8)	6,752	
L78 (396 V-8)	4,889	
L89 (396 V-8)	311	(added aluminum heads to L78 V-8)
total	**34,932**	(includes hardtops & convertibles;

also includes 3,675 Indy Pace Car convertible replicas)

CHEVROLET CAMARO Z28

	20,302	(all hardtops)

CHEVROLET NOVA SS

L48 (350 V-8)	10,355	
L34 (396 V-8)	1,947	
L78 (396 V-8)	5,262	(includes 311 w/L89 aluminum-head option)
total	**17,654**	(all sedans)

PONTIAC GTO

hardtop, std V-8	54,776	(22,032 w/manual trans, 32,744 w/auto)
hardtop, 400 2-bl	1,246	(all w/automatic trans)
hdtp, Ram Air III	8,129	(6,143 w/manual, 1,986 w/auto)
hdtp, Ram Air IV	700	(549 w/manual trans, 151 w/auto)
hdtp subtotal	64,851	
cvt., std V-8	6,800	(2,415 w/manual trans, 4,385 w/auto)
cvt., 400 2-barrel	215	(all w/automatic trans)
cvt., Ram Air III	362	(249 w/manual trans, 113 w/auto)
cvt, Ram Air IV	59	(45 w/manual trans, 14 w/auto)
cvt. subtotal	7,436	
grand total	**72,287**[1]	

[1]GTO Judge production (included in above totals)

hardtop	6,725	
convertible	108	
total	**6,833**	(includes standard RA III & optional RA IV V-8s)

PONTIAC FIREBIRD 400

	11,522[1]	(includes hardtops & convertibles; 4,601 w/manual trans, 6,921 w/auto)

[1]Ram Air production (included in above totals)

HO/RA III hdtp	723	(480 w/manual trans, 243 w/auto)
HO/RA III cvt.	144	(87 w/manual trans, 57 w/auto)
Ram Air IV hdtp	85	(12 w/manual trans, 5 w/auto)
Ram Air IV cvt.	17	(12 w/manual trans, 5 w/auto)
total	**969**	

PONTIAC TRANS AM

hardtop (RA III)	634	(520 w/manual trans, 114 w/auto)
hardtop (RA IV)	55	(46 w/manual trans, 9 w/auto)
cvt. (RA III)	8	(4 w/manual trans, 4 w/auto)
total	**697**	(L74 Ram Air III V-8 also known as "400 HO")

OLDSMOBILE 4-4-2

sports coupe	2,475
Holiday hardtop	19,587
convertible	4,296
total	**26,358**

HURST/OLDS

hardtop	912	
convertible	2	
total	**914**	(some sources claim 906 or 912)

BUICK GRAN SPORT

GS-350 sedan	3,574	(California Special, all w/automatic trans)
GS-350 hardtop	6,305	(58 w/column-shifted 3-spd, 175 w/floor-shifted 3-spd, 632 w/4-spd, 5,440 w/auto)
GS-400 hardtop	6,346	(117 w/floor-shifted 3-spd, 785 w/4-spd, 5,444 w/auto)
GS-400 cvt.	1,564	(48 w/floor-shifted 3-spd, 213 w/4-spd, 1,303 w/auto)
Stage 1 hardtop	1,256	(9 w/floor-shifted 3-sped, 415 w/4-spd, 832 w/auto)
Stage 1 cvt.	212	(4 w/floor-shifted 3-spd, 77 w/4-spd, 131 w/auto)
total	**19,257**	

FORD MUSTANG GT

	5,396	(includes coupes, fastbacks & convertibles)

FORD MUSTANG MACH 1

	72,458	(all SportsRoofs w/351-, 390- or 428-cid V-8s)

FORD MUSTANG BOSS 302

	1,628	(all SportsRoofs)

FORD MUSTANG BOSS 429

	857	(all SportsRoofs)

FORD MUSTANG 428 COBRA JET

coupe	243
SportsRoof	12,896
convertible	122
total	**13,261***

FORD TORINO GT

formal-roof	17,951	(includes 5,068 w/bucket seats)
SportsRoof	61,314	(includes 20,440 w/bucket seats)
convertible	2,552	(includes 928 w/bucket seats)
total	**81,817**	

FORD COBRA

formal-roof	3,786
SportsRoof	11,099
total	**14,885**

FORD TALLADEGA

	745

SHELBY MUSTANG

GT350 fastback	673	
GT350 Hertz	151	
GT350 cvt.	139	
GT500 fastback	1,157	
GT500 cvt.	244	
GT500 cvt. Hertz	1	
total	**2,361**	(includes 6 pilot/pre-production models)

MERCURY COUGAR ELIMINATOR

2,250 (all hardtops)

MERCURY CYCLONE

5,882 (all fastbacks)

MERCURY CYCLONE CJ

3,261 (all fastbacks)

MERCURY CYCLONE SPOILER II

353 (known)

PLYMOUTH ROAD RUNNER

cp. w/383 V-8	31,397	(18,191 w/4-speed, 13,206 w/auto)
cp. w/Hemi	356	(194 w/4-speed, 162 w/auto)
hdtp w/383 V-8	45,629	(21,278 w/4-speed, 24,351 w/auto)
hdtp w/Hemi	421	(234 w/4-speed, 187 w/auto)
cvt. w/383 V-8	1,880	(769 w/4-speed, 1,111 w/auto)
cvt. w/Hemi	10	(4 w/4-speed, 6 w/auto)
total	**79,693**	(includes US deliveries only; total including deliveries outside US was 84,420—this figure also includes 440 Six Barrel models)

PLYMOUTH 440 SIX BARREL ROAD RUNNER

coupe	615	(388 w/4-speed, 227 w/auto)
hardtop	797	(422 w/4-speed, 375 w/auto)
total	**1,412**	(included in above total Road Runner count)

PLYMOUTH GTX

hdtp w/440 V-8	13,866	(4,004 w/4-speed, 9,862 w/auto)
hdtp w/Hemi	197	(complete breakdown n/a)
cvt. w/440 V-8	540	(178 w/4-speed, 362 w/auto)
cvt. w/Hemi	11	(5 w/4-speed, 6 w/auto)
total	**14,614**	(includes US deliveries only; total including deliveries outside US was 15,602)

PLYMOUTH BARRACUDA FORMULA S

hdtp w/340 V-8	325	(complete breakdown n/a)
hdtp w/383 V-8	98	(53 w/4-speed, 45 w/auto)
fstbk w/340 V-8	1,431	(complete breakdown n/a)
fstbk w/383 V-8	603	(331 w/4-speed, 272 w/auto)
cvt. w/340 V-8	83	(complete breakdown n/a)
cvt. w/383 V-8	17	(7 w/4-speed, 10 w/auto)
total	**2,557**	

PLYMOUTH 'CUDA 340

hardtop	98	(68 w/4-speed, 30 w/auto)
fastback	568	(402 w/4-speed, 166 w/auto)
total	**666**	

PLYMOUTH 'CUDA 383

hardtop	83	(complete breakdown n/a)
fastback	378	(130 w/4-speed, 248 w/auto)
total	**461**	

PLYMOUTH 440 'CUDA

(A13) **340** (includes hardtops & fastbacks, all w/auto trans)

DODGE CHARGER R/T

hdtp w/440 V-8	18,344	(3,605 w/4-speed, 14,739 w/auto)
hdtp w/Hemi	432	(207 w/4-speed, 225 w/auto)
total	**18,776**	(includes US deliveries only; total including deliveries outside US was 20,057—RT/SE total was 4,243)

DODGE CHARGER 500

392

DODGE CHARGER DAYTONA

503

DODGE CORONET R/T

hdtp w/440 V-8	6,351	(1,541 w/4-speed, 4,810 w/auto)
hdtp w/Hemi	97	(58 w/4-speed, 39 w/auto)
cvt. w/440 V-8	416	(99 w/4-speed, 317 w/auto)
cvt. w/Hemi	10	(4 w/4-speed, 6 w/auto)
total	**6,874**	(includes US deliveries only; total including deliveries outside US was 7,238)

DODGE SUPER BEE

coupe w/383 V-8	7,122	(3,427 w/4-speed, 3,695 w/auto)
coupe w/ Hemi	91	(38 w/4-speed, 53 w/auto)
hdtp w/383 V-8	16,709	(7,363 w/4-speed, 9,346 w/auto)
hdtp w/Hemi	165	(92 w/4-speed, 73 w/auto)
total	**24,087**	(includes US deliveries only; total including deliveries outside US was 27,846—this figure also includes Six Pack Super Bee models)

DODGE 440 SIX PACK SUPER BEE

coupe	420	(267 w/4-speed, 153 w/auto)
hardtop	1,487	(826 w/4-speed, 661 w/auto)
total	**1,907**	(included in above total Super Bee count)

DODGE DART SWINGER 340

16,637 (8,834 w/4-speed, 7,803 w/auto)

DODGE DART GTS

hdtp w/340 V-8	3,645	(1,022 w/4-speed, 2,623 w/auto)
hdtp w/383 V-8	1,272	(784 w/4-speed, 488 w/auto)
hdtp w/440 V-8	640	(A13 conversion, all w/auto trans)
cvt. w/340 V-8	272	(58 w/4-speed, 214 w/auto trans)
cvt. w/383 V-8	73	(34 w/4-speed, 39 w/auto trans)
total	**5,902**	(includes US deliveries only; total including deliveries outside US was 6,702)

AMERICAN MOTORS AMX

w/290 V-8	918	(619 w/4-speed, 299 w/auto)
w/343 V-8	1,572	(843 w/4-speed, 729 w/auto)
w/390 V-8	5,803	(3,620 w/4-speed, 2,183 w/auto)
total	**8,293**	(all hardtops)

AMC HURST SC/RAMBLER

1,502 (1,002 w/Type A paint; 500 w/Type B)

** These statistics are copyrighted Ford Motor Company and Marti Auto Works material; Marti Auto Works has the entire production database of all Ford vehicles from 1967 to the present—visit www.martiauto.com for more details.*

NOTE: *Production data was supplied by various sources, including Christo Datini at the GM Heritage Center, Galen Govier (Mopar material) at Galen's Tag Service (www.galengovier.com, the Shelby American Automobile Club (www.saac.com), and American Motors enthusiast Eddie Stakes at www.planethoustonamx.com.*

IN WITH THE GOOD AIR

When it comes to making maximum power, relatively cool intake air is preferred because it is inherently denser. But wouldn't you know it? Really warm stuff is all you get under a hood. The only way to deliver cooler atmosphere into an engine is to import it from outside, a fact not lost on all muscle builders during the 1960s—witness the various "ram-air" systems that were proliferating by 1970.

Who did it first? Chevrolet arguably deserves credit for pioneering modern ram-air development by creating the "airbox" option for its new fuel-injected Corvette in 1957. That box—a long plenum mounted just inside the driver's fender—allowed external airflow entering just beside the radiator to make its way directly into the Ramjet fuel injection's metering equipment.

Chevy engineers tried out a different design a few years later. Found atop both the Z11 427 drag-car engine and the fabled "Mystery Motor" V-8 in 1963 was an air cleaner housing that extended rearward to the firewall, where it drew in its breath from the high-pressure area that naturally develops at the base of a car's windshield at speed. Long used by NASCAR racers, this design was first offered by Chevrolet, as a dealer-installed option, for early Chevelles. Chevy's first Z/28 Camaro also could be fitted with an optional cowl-induction air cleaner, delivered in the trunk when ordered.

Cowl Induction became a full-fledged factory option (RPO ZL2) for the Super Sport Chevelle in 1970. Featuring a vacuum-operated flap at the rear of a bulge stacked up on the already bulging SS hood, the ZL2 lid featured ductwork below that sealed down against a special air cleaner. A different ZL2 hood appeared as a Camaro option in 1969. Though it didn't have the flap, it also took advantage of that high-pressure buildup at a windshield's base.

Optional cowl-induction ductwork was delivered inside a new Z28's trunk in 1967. Chevrolet engineers developed this design five or so years earlier for NASCAR racing applications. It also was available from dealers for early Chevelles. *Mike Mueller*

Arguably the coolest ram-air equipment in 1969 was Ford's "Shaker," a black scoop that protruded up through hood and vibrated along with the engine whenever the hammer went down. Dodge and Plymouth's own Shaker scoop followed in 1970. *Mike Mueller*

Oldsmobile's W-30 package debuted for 1966 with its twin flexible hoses running from the L69 V-8's chrome air cleaner down to plastic ducts protruding through the front bumper below the headlights. These hoses, resembling something found behind your dryer at home, remained part of the W-30 deal up through 1969. In 1970 the W-30 started sucking in the good air through a new fiberglass hood that featured two larger scoops at its leading edge.

Buick's Stage 1 V-8 also was treated to two scoops when it was enlarged to 455 cubes in 1970. Like the W25 hood featured atop the W-30 4-4-2 that year, Buick's functional hood sealed down to yet another special air cleaner using a large foam-rubber "doughnut."

A functional hood scoop became available by way of Pontiac dealers for GTO midway in 1965 then became a factory option the following year. Ram-air equipment was offered too for the new Firebird in 1967 and came standard with the first Trans Am two years later. Pontiac's second-edition Trans Am featured a trademark rear-facing hood scoop that poked right through a hole in the hood to shake to and fro whenever the go-pedal was floored.

"Shaker" scoops also appeared from Ford and Chrysler. First protruding through a Mustang's hood in similar fashion in 1969, Ford's faced forward and was made available for both big- and small-block V-8s. Plymouth people claimed their Shaker, first seen as an option for the E-body Barracuda in 1970, was good for an 0.15- or 0.20-second improvement in a quarter-mile run. Arguably the highest profile piece of ram-air equipment ever offered, the Mopar Shaker was standard in the 1970 Hemi 'Cuda's case, optional atop other performance V-8s. Officially known as the Air Grabber option, it also was available for Dodge's Challenger.

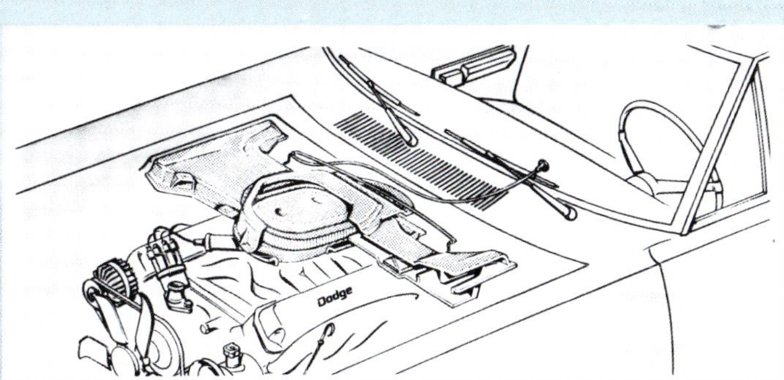

Dodge's Ramcharger option, introduced for 1969, added two functional scoops to the hood of a Super Bee or Coronet R/T. A cable-controlled flap allowed cooler, denser ambient atmosphere a direct path into the air cleaner below. Plymouth's version of this ram-air system was called Air Grabber.

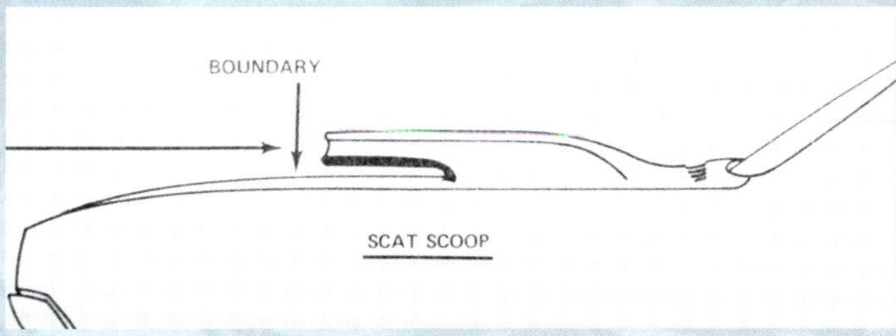

Dodge engineers moved the 1970 Challenger T/A's "snorkel" scoop up away from the aerodynamic boundary layer of slow-moving air that impedes intake flow at speed.

Air Grabber equipment first appeared in 1969 for Dodge and Plymouth's B-body muscle cars. In the case of Dodge's Coronet R/T and Super Bee, standard hoods were adorned with a single scoop that did nothing but look a little cool. Adding the Air Grabber option traded that hood for another with two fully functional scoops. In 1970, Plymouth's Air Grabber was redesigned and instead of traditional scoops featured a central flap that showed off a toothy snarl whenever it opened for business.

A fiberglass hood incorporating a wide-open scoop was used in 1969 atop the triple-carb 440 V-8 introduced midyear for Plymouth's Road Runner and Dodge's Super Bee. Those three Holley two-barrels below had no problem sucking in the atmosphere through that huge scoop. Fiberglass hoods also were fashioned for Dodge and Plymouth's AAR 'Cuda and T/A Challenger, with former's hood featuring a basic NACA-style opening, the latter's a snorkel-type incorporating openings located up above the boundary layer of air that inhibits flow into flush scoops at speed.

Raised up even higher was the opening in the boxy scoop seen atop the hood of AMC's 1969 S/C Rambler. Another angular scoop was standard for AMC's 1970 Rebel Machine, this one incorporating a tachometer in its left rear corner.

Hood scoops remained plentiful as the 1970s rolled on, but few actually did any scooping. With horsepower becoming harder to come by, it was no loss that form took precedence over function.

Ads referred to 1969's Dart Swinger 340 as "6,000 rpm for less than $3,000." A heavy-duty suspension was standard along with Dodge's 275-horsepower 340 LA small-block, as were Scat Pack stripes, a Hurst-shifted four-speed (with a bench seat), and D70 tires. *Mike Mueller*

Continued from page 141

back here and there, product planners managed to put the Swinger 340's bottom line at about $2,850. Ads referred to it as "6,000 rpm for less than $3,000." *Car Life* called it 1969's "Best Compact." Dodge's supreme compact that year featured the A13 440 Engine Conversion, an installation that required modifying the K-member below, fabricating a motor mount for the driver's side, and using the 383 A-body's special left-hand exhaust manifold.

FORD

Available Mustang engines hit an all-time high in 1969 as two extreme Boss motors, displacing 302 and 429 cubic inches, joined the lineup. New too was a "SportsRoof" body (formally known as a fastback) that included simulated rear-quarter air intakes and a ducktail spoiler in back. This was the last year for Mustang GT, which featured a 250-horsepower 351 Windsor two-barrel in base form. Missing were the GT badges found on earlier fenders; only the gas cap and styled-steel wheels' center caps carried this identification in 1969.

Dodge and Hurst people again put their heads together in 1969, this time resulting in the 440-powered GTS Dart. All of these beastly A-bodies were hardtops fitted with Torqueflite automatics. Bucket seats and a console were included inside. *Mike Mueller*

Ford's Mach 1 Mustang debuted in SportsRoof-only form in 1969. Styled-steel wheels were standard, as was a heavy-duty suspension and plenty of exterior pizzazz. Various V-8s were available, including the 335-horsepower 428 Cobra Jet, with or without Dearborn's optional ram-air "Shaker" hood scoop. *Mike Mueller*

HOT OFF THE PRESS: 1969 CHEVROLET MALIBU SS 396

"As a first car for someone who doesn't want to spend the extra money for top performance or the more exotic machinery, a Chevelle 396 SS without all the luxury options makes a good choice."
Bill Sanders, Motor Trend, *January 1969*

HOT OFF THE PRESS: 1969 PONTIAC GTO JUDGE

"The Judge is at its best on the highway, where the engine runs fast enough to be happy, and the suspension needn't do things it doesn't like to do."
Car Life, *March 1969*

HOT OFF THE PRESS: 1969 HURST/OLDS

"The Hurst/Olds is intended to be a kind of American Grand Touring machine and it succeeds admirably. It accelerates like a rocket-sled, stops and corners better than many of its European peers and it uncannily smooth on the road."
Eric Dahlquist, Motor Trend, *June 1969*

Neither the GT package nor ram-air equipment were required this year when a pony car buyer opted for the 428 Cobra Jet, still rated at 335 horsepower with or without that induction option. Included in 1969's ram-air deal was Ford's too-cool "Shaker" hood scoop, which protruded right through the hood and vibrated side to side along with the CJ below under torque load, hence its name.

Customers in 1969 also could convert a Cobra Jet into a Super Cobra Jet by checking off the Drag Pack axle option, which consisted of either a 3.91:1 or 4.30:1 strip-ready ratio in a Traction-Lok limited-slip differential. Recognizing that these gears were best suited for on-track action, engineers beefed up the SCJ by adding forged-aluminum pistons (in place of the CJ's cast slugs), formidable LeMans rods, and an external oil cooler, mounted on the front of the radiator core support on the driver's side.

Available for any Mustang in any body style, the 428 Cobra Jet was best showcased in the all-new Mach 1, available only as a SportsRoof. A posh interior and GT Handling suspension were standard, as were dual exhausts and the GT's two-barrel 351 small-block. Along with the 428 CJ (with or without the Shaker), power options included a 290-horsepower 351 and 320-horsepower 390. Among visual attractions were dual color-keyed racing mirrors, tape stripes, a pop-open gas cap, and a blacked-out hood with a non-functional scoop and competition-style hood pins. Meant mostly as a sporty class act, Mach 1 was truly ready to fly with the CJ installation, making it, according to *Car Life,* "the quickest standard passenger car though the quarter-mile we've ever tested."

Every bit as impressive were the aforementioned Boss Mustangs, two horses of notably different colors. Developed in prototype form by Kar Kraft Engineering in Brighton, Michigan, Boss 302 was refined at Ford Engineering, where Matt Donner was responsible for its superb chassis, made up of "mostly adjustments" in his words. Power came from a 290-horsepower 302 V-8 based on a modified Windsor block featuring four-bolt mains. On top of that went new free-breathing canted-valve cylinder heads then being readied for the upcoming 351 Cleveland V-8. Topping things off was an unforgettable image done by designer Larry Shinoda, who, like his boss, Bunkie Knudsen, had defected to Ford from General Motors. Shinoda supplied the stripes, the spoilers, and the window

In 1969, Ford finally produced a direct response to Chevrolet's Z28 Camaro, Boss 302 Mustang, fitted with an exclusive small-block V-8, a superb chassis, and flashy exterior graphics. That latter treatment was supplied by Larry Shinoda, a former GM designer who had previously contributed to the Trans-Am-ready Camaro's image.

slats, and he also suggested the groovy name. His superiors didn't like the idea at first, but what did those squares know?

While the nimble Boss 302 was born to do battle with Chevy's Z28 on SCCA road courses, the brutal Boss 429 was created to legalize its "Blue Crescent" V-8 for stock car competition. As mentioned, NASCAR rules at the time involved a 500-unit-production minimum, but nowhere was it specified that any model and engine in question be built together. Once legalized, the Boss 429 big-block went to work on NASCAR tracks behind the extended snouts of the Fairlane-based Talladega, detailed here on the next page. Clearly loopholes were made to be driven through.

Boss 429 development also occurred at Kar Kraft, but in this case so too did full production, with the first completed car rolling off the Brighton line in January 1969, nearly three months before Ford finished its first Boss 302. The bigger Boss motor didn't drop easily into the pony car platform, hence the need for a special assembly line. Able to operate at a slower, steadier pace, the Kar Kraft crew had to perform various time-consuming modifications, including widening the engine compartment by 2 inches. They also added specially reinforced shock towers to increase underhood clearance. Upper A-arm location points in turn were moved outward an inch and lowered another inch. A reshaped power brake booster was used to avoid a conflict on the driver's side with that huge valve cover, and the battery was relocated to the trunk.

On the outside went a huge functional hood scoop and flared front fenders, needed to supply clearance for the same wheel/tire combo used by Boss 302. Beneath that scoop was the star of the show, the 375-horse Boss 429 V-8 with its "semi-hemi" aluminum cylinder heads. According once more to *Car Life*, the sum of these parts equaled "the best enthusiast car Ford has ever produced."

Ford enthusiasts also were treated to more midsize muscle in 1969 as the continuing Torino GT was joined by the Fairlane-based Cobra, available in

HOT OFF THE PRESS: 1969 BUICK GS-400 STAGE 1

"It takes a day or two to figure out a few things on the car, but no time at all for a fast ride through the quarter."

Steve Kelly, Hot Rod, *June 1969*

HOT OFF THE PRESS: 1969 PLYMOUTH GTX

"Watching a '69 GTX in the rearview mirror, it looks like a mean, hungry animal, and we could imagine how it would feel to be slip-streamed by Richard Petty at Daytona or Charlotte."

Bill Sanders, Motor Trend, *January 1969*

HOT OFF THE PRESS: 1969 PLYMOUTH 440 'CUDA

"[Engineers] have the 440 tucked neatly in the 'Cuda; it looks fine there. The difficulty is that there is no room left for anything else."

Car Life, *June 1969*

Ford's small-block Boss 302 was joined in 1969 by the big-block Boss 429, created to legalize its "semi-hemi" V-8 for NASCAR competition. Beneath that functional hood scoop—the largest ever planted atop a Mustang hood—were 375 horses supplied by a race engine that didn't get along with everyday operation in the least. A chin spoiler was standard, as were 15-inch Magnum 500 rims.

HOT OFF THE PRESS: 1969 DODGE CHARGER 500

"You don't have to wear a driving suit, crash helmet, or goggles in this Dodge à la NASCAR stocker—but if it makes you feel better, go ahead."

Steve Kelly, Hot Rod, *February 1969*

HOT OFF THE PRESS: 1969 DODGE CHARGER DAYTONA

"Daytona Charger wasn't designed for the street but it has got to be the ultimate boulevard mind-boggler of all times!"

Hi-Performance Cars, *November 1969*

HOT OFF THE PRESS: 1969 DODGE SUPER BEE 440 SIX PACK

"Triple carburetors and the 440 engine make the Super Bee the terror of Grudge night."

Car Life, *July 1969*

After paying dearly for Carroll Shelby's Cobra image, Ford's movers and shakers wasted little time sticking that revered snake label on almost everything that moved. Make that *really* moved. After 1968's 428 Cobra Jet V-8 came 1969's Fairlane-based Cobra, a midsize muscle machine fitted exclusively with that 335-horsepower CJ big-block. Cobras were offered in formal-roof and fastback forms for 1969. *Mike Mueller*

SportsRoof and "notchback" coupe forms. Standard Cobra equipment included the 428 CJ backed by a four-speed, F70 Wide Oval rubber, and a competition suspension package featuring staggered rear shocks. While early models apparently wore external decals (according to initial promotional artwork), more familiar were the cast coiled-snake emblems located on the Cobra's fenders and decklid.

A second muscular midsizer appeared in response to Dodge's efforts to give its B-body an aerodynamic advantage on NASCAR tracks. Immediately following the Charger 500's debut late in 1968 in Charlotte, North Carolina, Ford racing chief Jacque Passino headed across town to Holman-Moody, Dearborn's "competition wing," where Ralph Moody already had built a similar machine based on the fastback Fairlane. Using longer Mercury Cyclone fenders, Moody had fashioned an extended nose that could slice through the wind with ease. Hot on the idea, Passino took Moody's prototype back to Michigan for Bunkie Knudsen's approval, which was surely a given. Ford's NASCAR coordinator, Charlie Gray, then suggested that the new model be named after the superspeedway then being built in Alabama near the town of Talladega.

Officials at Ford's Atlanta plant dedicated most of the January 1969 assembly schedule to the new Talladega, based on the Fairlane SportsRoof. Modifications included special fenders with stamped-steel extensions welded on, a flush-mounted Cobra grille, and a unique downward-sloping header panel that filled the space between grille and hood. Rocker panels also were cut and re-rolled 1 inch higher than stock sheetmetal, an expensive trick that allowed race teams to lower Talladega bodies that extra inch over their racing frames while still maintaining NASCAR's rigidly enforced minimum ground clearance. At the track, Talladegas were fitted with 427s and Boss 429s to help them bust the 190-miles per hour barrier. Back on the street, all models featured 428 Cobra Jets backed by C6 automatics.

Standard in 1969 for Ford's NASCAR-ready Talladega was a 428 Cobra Jet backed by a C6 automatic trans. Paint choices numbered three: Wimbledon White, Royal Maroon, and Presidential Blue. *Mike Mueller*

Scoops abounded on 1969's restyled Shelby Mustang, again offered in GT350 or GT500 forms. Hardtop and convertible versions continued, too, with both body styles incorporating roll bars. The KR model didn't return this year as all GT500s now featured the 428 Cobra Jet V-8. *Mike Mueller*

SHELBY MUSTANG

The KR reference was dropped in 1969 as all GT500s were now Cobra Jets, and the GT350 again got a new standard V-8, a 351 Windsor small-block rated at 290 horsepower. New was a restyled fiberglass nose that featured various NACA ducts: two up front to supply cooling air into the engine compartment, two in back to let the hot air escape, and one in the middle for the engine's ram-air equipment. The fiberglass fenders incorporated brake-cooling ducts ahead of the front wheels, and another set of scoops allowed rear brake cooling. Rear scoops varied by body style: fastback scoops were inset up high, convertible scoops protruded and were lower to avoid a conflict with the top mechanism.

Rear styling remained familiar, save for revised aluminum exhaust outlets located side by side in the center of the valance panel. Although a five-spoke wheel was now standard, some early 1969 Shelby Mustangs apparently were fitted with Magnum 500s after defects showed up in the new rims.

MERCURY

Ford's bitchin' Boss 302 Mustang made such an impression, Lincoln-Mercury officials decided they'd try a similar tack with Cougar. Taking its name from the dragstrip, a prototype "Eliminator" was prepared for an October 1968 debut at the Los Angeles Auto Show. Spoilers front and rear fit like gloves and reportedly worked; they weren't simply for looks. Positive public response convinced L-M execs to rush this Boss knock-off to market as a midyear 1969 model. Regular-production examples were introduced in March that year.

Standard Cougar Eliminator equipment included F70 Goodyear Polyglas tires and the Competition Handling Suspension. And like that flaming orange prototype, all ready-for-sale Eliminators turned heads with ease thanks to eye-popping Competition paint choices. The base engine beneath that big hood scoop was a 351 four-barrel Windsor V-8.

HOT OFF THE PRESS: 1969 DODGE DART SWINGER 340

"The 340 is another of those 'naturals' like the small-block Chevy that breathes and revs well. Most of its power is spread over the upper rpm ranges. This keeps traction-busting torque from overpowering the chassis and blowing a drag run or landing the driver in trouble in a curve."

Car Life, *September 1969*

HOT OFF THE PRESS: 1969 FORD MUSTANG BOSS 302

"Without a doubt the Boss 302 is the best-handling Ford ever to come out of Dearborn and may just be the new standard by which everything from Detroit must be judged,"

Car and Driver, *June 1969*

HOT OFF THE PRESS: 1969 FORD MUSTANG BOSS 429

"When you see this horse pawing 1320 feet of asphalt for the first time, you'll have to agree that as a descriptive term, 'pony' just won't get the job done on the 429 Mustang."

John Thawley, Hot Rod, *February 1969*

Unlike Ford's Boss Mustang—which relied solely on the Boss 302 V-8—Mercury's running mate, Cougar Eliminator, was offered in 1969 with various power sources along with that Cleveland-head small-block. Larry Shinoda also was responsible for the Eliminator's exterior image. *Mike Mueller*

Mercury's Cyclone Spoiler appeared midyear for 1969 to honor two legendary race drivers: Cale Yarborough and Dan Gurney. Special two-tone paint schemes were applied to this Montego-based fastback: blue-on-white for the "Dan Gurney Special," red-on-white for its "Cale Yarborough Special" sibling.

HOT OFF THE PRESS: 1969 FORD MUSTANG MACH 1 CJ

"Are you ready for the first great Mustang? One with performance to match its looks, handling to send imported-car fans home mumbling to themselves, and an interior as elegant, and livable, as a gentleman's club?"

Car Life, *March 1969*

HOT OFF THE PRESS: 1969 FORD FAIRLANE COBRA

"The Cobra's performance was surprisingly good, the price is within reason, the fastback roof is the best looking around."

Car Life, *January 1969*

Mercury also showcased the 428 Cobra Jet V-8 in a special midsize model for 1969: Cyclone CJ. Available only as a fastback, Cyclone CJ came standard with a four-speed stick, Competition Handling package, and F70 tires. The ram-air hood (with racing-style lock pins) and styled-steel wheels seen here were optional. *courtesy National Automotive History Collection, Detroit Public Library*

Mercury's counterpart to Ford's "long-nose" Talladega was the Cyclone Sports Special, or "Spoiler II." Though this NASCAR-targeted Merc looked a lot like its Talladega cousin, differences were many because Montego and Fairlane bodies were nowhere near identical. Dressed up just like Cyclone Spoiler (in Dan Gurney Special and Cale Yarborough Special forms), Spoiler II also came standard with a 351 small-block V-8 in place of the 428 CJ installed in all Talladegas. *Mike Mueller*

Optional engines included a 320-horsepower 390 FE big-block, the Mustang's Boss 302 small-block, and the crowd-pleasing 428 CJ. Ordering the Cobra Jet added an even stronger suspension with higher rate springs, a thicker front stabilizer, and staggered rear shocks. A functional ram-air hood also was available for the 335-horsepower CJ, and the bone-jarring Cobra Jet suspension was included as well with the 290-horsepower Boss 302. Boss 429 V-8s were stuffed into a pair of 1969 Eliminators for drag duty, too, and this duo was later modified with 1970 front bodywork.

Almost forgotten amidst all this flash was the Cougar Sports Special, much more show than go compared to the Eliminator. Various Sports Special options packages were offered, all featuring unique rocker moldings, turbine-type wheel covers, body-side stripes, and a driver's side racing mirror. An interior Decor Group and/or Performance Handling suspension was included, too, in some of these packages. All Cougar V-8s (save for the Boss 302) were available along with the Sports Special deal. A 1969 Cyclone Sports Special, with a bench seat instead of buckets, also was offered.

As in 1968, Mercury's latest Cyclone was a member of the Montego family but this year was only offered in fastback form—no more formal-roof hardtop version. Cyclone GT also didn't return, at least not as a complete model. While a GT appearance group was available for the 1969 Cyclone, it only added bucket seats, a rim-blow steering wheel, a driver's side racing mirror, turbine wheel covers, white-sidewall tires, and an appropriate trunk emblem.

In place of the GT came the Cyclone CJ, fitted predictably with the 428 Cobra Jet V-8, backed by a four-speed manual trans. A Competition Handling package was included in the deal, as were low-restriction dual exhausts and a blacked-out grille. Adding optional ram-air also meant racing-style hood pins appeared up front.

A second Cyclone variation, Spoiler, appeared midyear with a standard rear wing, hence the name. Only two Spoiler paint schemes—honoring legendary NASCAR drivers—were offered: two-tone red-on-white for the "Cale Yarborough Special," blue-on-white for its "Dan Gurney Special" running mate. Contrary to garden-variety 1969 Cyclones, which came standard with a 220-horsepower 302 topped by a two-barrel carb, the Spoiler duo featured only four-barrel V-8s, either the 351 Windsor, 390 FE or 428 CJ.

FLAG WAVER

One of the best performance buys of the 1960s, 1969's SC/Rambler could damn near break into the 13-second bracket on the quarter-mile right off the lot—this after the customer plunked down a few bucks less than three grand. *Mike Mueller*

Hurst SC/Ramblers were offered in two paint schemes. Type A finishes featured red body sides, while Type B cars were mostly white with lower body sides done in blue with a red-stripe accent. *Mike Mueller*

Based on American Motors' Rogue hardtop, 1969's Hurst SC/Rambler certainly could hold its own when it came to turning heads. "[This] is the ideal vehicle for the motorist who wants better than average performance and also a car that is uniquely different from 70 million others on the streets today," said AMC marketing services veep R. William McNealy Jr. in February 1969. Public introduction came the following month during the Chicago Auto Show.

In keeping with a newly established AMC tradition, this little screamer was done up in a patriotic finish that *Super Stock & Drag Illustrated* magazine called "the wildest stock paint in captivity." Wheel centers were blue, as was a big arrow on the hood that directed ambient atmosphere into a boxy "cold-air" scoop. Red-painted body sides accented the white finish on 1,012 of the 1,512 examples modified under Hurst's direction on the Kenosha line, resulting in what are known as "Type A" models. The remaining 500 "Type B" cars featured mostly white wrappers sans both the red body treatment and blue hood arrow. Gone too in Type B applications was the wide blue striping that continued rearward over the Type A's roof and decklid.

Beneath the SC/Rambler's fully-functional, boxy hood scoop was a 390-cid V-8 topped by a Carter four-barrel carb. Output was 315 horsepower. *Mike Mueller*

Sources have long claimed that these two varieties were fully segregated during production; the first 500 built were A's, the next 500 were Bs, the final 512 were again As. But this apparently wasn't the case; some early-production SC/Ramblers are known with the Type B scheme. Red-sided or not, all exteriors were further dressed up with dual "teardrop" racing mirrors, hood pins, a blacked-out grille and tail panel, and appropriate Hurst badges. Fender lips also were folded in to allow clearance for the car's standard Goodyear Polyglas Wide-Tread tires.

Additional standard equipment included power front discs, a suitably beefed suspension with rear axle torque links, a Hurst-shifted (duh!) Borg-Warner T-10 close-ratio four-speed, and a Twin-Grip differential containing 3.54:1 gears. A sport steering wheel, bucket seats, and a Sun tachometer strapped to the steering column were added inside. Beneath that vacuum-controlled hood scoop—which drew guffaws from some critics—was a 315-horsepower 390 V-8 fitted with heavy-duty cooling and twin "Special-Tone" mufflers.

As affordable as it was eye-popping, SC/Rambler was stickered at a tad short of $3,000—and for that humble price a customer was promised quarter-mile trips in 14.3 seconds. Can you say "biggest bang for the buck?"

1969 AMC 390

Type	OHV V-8 w/cold-air induction
Displacement	390 cubic inches
Bore	4.17 inches
Stroke	3.57 inches
Horsepower	315 at 4600 rpm
Torque	425 at 3200 rpm
Compression	10.2:1
Fuel delivery	Carter AFB 4-barrel carburetor
Air cleaner	single-snorkel housing w/open-element lid sealed to hood scoop by foam "doughnut"
Ignition	Delco-Remy single-point distributor
Cooling	heavy-duty radiator w/Power-Flex fan & shroud
Cylinder block	cast-iron w/2-bolt main bearing caps
Crankshaft	forged steel w/2.2481-inch rod journals
Connecting rods	forged steel
Pistons	cast aluminum
Cam	hydraulic w/0.425-inch lift, 265-degrees duration
Rocker ratio	1.6:1
Cylinder heads	cast-iron w/rectangular ports & 51cc combustion chambers
Valve sizes	2.025-inch intakes, 1.625-inch exhausts
Exhaust system	dual Special-Tone mufflers (supplied by Thrush)

1969 AMC HURST SC/RAMBLER

CONSTRUCTION: unitized body/frame w/subframe connectors
MODEL AVAILABILITY: Rogue hardtop
PRICE: $2,998
WHEELBASE: 106 inches
WEIGHT: 3,160 pounds
SUSPENSION: heavy-duty coil springs and sway bar, front; solid axle w/heavy-duty leaf springs and torque links, rear; heavy-duty shock absorbers (staggered in back)
STEERING RATIO: 20:1 (manual)
WHEELS: 14x6 Magnum 500 w/blue-painted centers, bright trim rings, & "American Motors" center caps
TIRES: E70 Goodyear Polyglass Wide-Tread redline
BRAKES: 11.2-inch front discs w/power assist; 10-inch rear drums
ENGINE: 390-cid V-8 w/Carter 4-barrel carburetor & vacuum-controlled cold-air induction
TRANSMISSION: Hurst-shifted Borg-Warner T-10 close-ratio 4-speed manual w/10.5-inch Borg & Beck clutch
AXLE RATIO: 3.54:1 in Twin-Grip differential

HOT OFF THE PRESS: 1969 SHELBY GT500

"Shelby's fifth generation of performance cars emerges as the most tastefully done Mustangs on the road."

Motor Trend, *February 1969*

New for American Motor's 1969 Javelin were three high-profile paint options: Big Bad Blue, Big Bad Orange, and Big Bad Green. Also introduced this year (for Javelin only) was the "Mod Package," which added a small spoiler to the roof's trailing edge. This deal also included reverse C-stripes and rocker trim that mimicked side exhausts. *Mike Mueller*

MOTOR OF THE YEAR: 1969 BUICK STAGE 1

Type	OHV V-8 w/chrome dress-up & "cool dual" induction hood
Displacement	400 cubic inches
Bore	4.040 inches
Stroke	3.900 inches
Horsepower	345 at 5,800 rpm
Torque	440 at 3,200 rpm
Compression	10.25:1
Fuel delivery	re-jetted Rochester Quadra-jet 4-barrel carburetor & high-capacity fuel pump
Air cleaner	dual-snorkel w/foam-sealed air-induction inlets
Ignition	re-curved distributor
Cooling	heavy-duty radiator, heavy-duty water pump, 7-blade fan w/clutch
Cylinder block	cast-iron w/heavy-duty oil pump
Crankshaft	cast-nodular-iron w/3.250-inch main journals
Connecting rods	forged-steel
Pistons	cast-aluminum
Cam	hydraulic w/316 degrees duration on intake, 340 on exhaust, 115 degrees of overlap
Rocker ratio	1.59:1
Cylinder heads	cast-iron w/tubular pushrods &heavy-duty valve springs w/dampers
Valve sizes	2.125-inch intakes, 1.75-inch exhausts
Valve lift	0.407-inch intake; 0.454 inch, exhaust
Exhaust system	cast-iron manifolds w/2.25-inch main pipes, reverse-flow mufflers & 2.00-inch tailpipes

Optional leather seats became available inside 1969's AMX, as did an available Hurst shifter. Big Bad colors also were offered this year for AMC's two-seater. *courtesy National Automotive History Collection, Detroit Public Library*

A third Cyclone, the Spoiler Sports Special or "Spoiler II," was released to go NASCAR racing like Ford's Talladega. Looking quite similar with its long, dropped snout and rolled rockers, the Spoiler II in fact differed much in detail, only because Montego and Fairlane bodies themselves weren't identical. Mercury's aero-racer also came standard with a 351 small-block instead of the 428 Cobra Jet. On the outside, Spoiler IIs featured the conventional Spoiler's rear wing and the same two-tone paint choices, Yarborough red or Gurney blue.

AMC

Relocated badges, revised stripes and an updated grille announced the arrival of American Motors' second-edition Javelin, a still-handsome pony that again could be dressed up in upscale SST garb. Notable updates included the midyear switch from a Ford-sourced four-speed shifter to a Hurst stick and inclusion of twin hood scoops (non-functional plastic units finished in satin black) when an optional Go Package was installed. Engine choices carried over from 1968, with the 343 and 390 four-barrel V-8s again offered in the Go deal, available once more for both Javelin and AMX.

Promotional paperwork, also appearing midway into the model run, asked "Who's afraid of the Big Bad Colors?" Consisting of Big Bad Blue, Big Bad Orange, and Big Bad Green, these radiant shades could be sprayed onto any Javelin/AMX with any engine, including the base six-cylinder. Body-colored bumpers were included, too, and available for Big Bad Javelins (not AMXs) was the new "Mod Package," which added a lip spoiler to the roof's trailing edge, a reverse C-stripe (colored red, white or black), and rocker panels that mimicked side-exhaust heat shields. A Mod Pack AMX was not possible because the two-seater's different-shaped roofline did not accept the Javelin-friendly spoiler.

This year's AMX was treated to more simulated wood-grain touches inside, and optional leather seats appeared for the first time. AMC's 225-*c* 290 four-barrel V-8 remained standard beneath the hood, which was reinforced with a stiffened inner panel after cracks showed up in 1968 lids.

HOT OFF THE PRESS: 1969 MERCURY COUGAR ELIMINATOR

"Eliminator is exactly what it is designed to be; a performance car, competition oriented whether that competition be on the drag strip, the oval or the road racing circuit."

Road Test, *September 1969*

HOT OFF THE PRESS: 1969 MERCURY CYCLONE CJ

"The Cyclone CJ can best be described as a gentleman's muscle car. Its competition-oriented external appearance is certainly in keeping with its wide-open throttle performance."

Car and Driver, *January 1969*

HOT OFF THE PRESS: 1969 AMC HURST SC/RAMBLER

"While some may laugh and others scratch their heads, this quite honest attempt by [American Motors] to provide a budget performance car that handles well and runs quick in pure-stock form will be a force to be reckoned with both on and off the strip."

A. B. Shuman, Car Craft, *April 1969*

CHAPTER 7

1970 NO SUBSTITUTE FOR CUBIC INCHES

MUSCLE CAR MANIA HITS ITS ZENITH

At 450 horsepower, Chevrolet 454-cid LS6 V-8 was the highest-rated engine produced during Detroit's original muscle car era. An option for Chevelle SS 454 only in 1970, the LS6 returned (in low-compression 425-horsepower form) for Corvette only in 1971. *Mike Mueller*

Prior to 1970, the leader in Detroit's cubic-count sweepstakes was the Mopar 440, known on the street as Plymouth's Super Commando and Dodge's Magnum. But overnight this big RB found itself back in the pack after General Motors officials finally opted to lift the lid off their high-perf intermediates and pony cars. Already pushed a couple clicks beyond GM's now-invalid 400-cid limit even before 1969's model run ended, Chevrolet's Mk IV Turbo Jet ballooned to 454 cubes for 1970—and still didn't take the muscle car market's displacement cake. Bigger by 1 little inch were Buick, Olds and Pontiac's hulking V-8s, two of which threw around their newfound weight better than the other.

Like its identically displaced, yet unrelated counterpart from Olds, Pontiac's 455 was handicapped to some degree by its lengthy stroke, a reality that helped churn out tons of torque but at the same time inhibited high-revving capabilities.

Left: Chrysler's 440-cid RB V-8 was *the* big bully on the muscle car block prior to 1970. Introduced in 1966, this brute was transformed into a high-performance mill (tagged Super Commando in Plymouth nomenclature, Magnum in Dodge terms) the following year, then was treated to triple-carb induction in 1969. Shown here is Dodge's 1970 440 Six Pack, rated at 390 horsepower. *Mike Mueller*

Its 360-horsepower tag notwithstanding, this L75 V-8 especially proved that size doesn't always matter.

"For street-prowling youths whose social standing depends upon having the meanest tire burner on The Avenue, the GTO may have lost its luster," claimed *Car and Driver* after testing the new 455 Goat. Sure, its LS1 Super Duty successor would be making muscle car history three years down the road (see chapter 10), but 1970's L75 was probably best suited to hauling truly young passengers around in Safari wagons. Fortunately the L67 Ram Air IV 400 was still around—for both GTO and Firebird—to roast the weenies with the best of 'em.

Oldsmobile's 455, introduced for Toronado and full-sizers in 1968, was even more undersquare than Pontiac's and featured an even longer stroke, yet it had no trouble keeping up with 1970's hottest muscle machines as the 4-4-2's new heart and soul. Adding the W-30 option with its ram-air induction equipment added only 5 more horses to the base 455's rating, at least on paper. Most witnesses knew actual power at the pedal surely went beyond that published 370 figure.

"With a .125-inch longer stroke than bore dimension, the [Olds] 455 is not going to be the '70 rev king," announced *Motor Trend* in reference to that year's 4-4-2. "But the 500 lbs. of torque gets the car launched like a Saturn V." "The W-30 455 reflects a fairly conservative way to get high torque and horsepower," added a *Road Test* review. "The payoff from this plant should be high reliability, low maintenance and good life expectancy before overhaul." Could it get any better?

Flint's fine-car builders thought so. Any Buick fan will tell you that their favorite engines always "ran better than they had a right to" back in the 1950s and 1960s, but cheese-and-rice, what the hell was going on in 1970? Dropping another 55 cubes into the proven Stage 1 mix simply wasn't fair, and Buick engineers didn't help matters by laughingly rating this oversquare monster at a mere 360 horsepower, equaling "some kind of understatement record," according to *Motor Trend's* Bill Sanders.

"Performance verges on a precipitous mechanical hysteria," wrote Sanders after watching a 455 Stage 1 Gran Sport smoke the quarter-mile in an alarming 13.38

Above: All members of Buick's modern big-block family (introduced in 1967) shared the same stroke: 3.90 inches. Increasing the bore to 4.3125 inches in 1970 resulted in 455 cubic inches, which served the Stage 1 legacy well. Output for 1970's 455 Stage 1 was 360 horsepower. *Mike Mueller*

Initially installed in full-size models and Toronado in 1968, Oldsmobile's 455 V-8 became the 4-4-2's heart two years later. Optional W-30 treatment carried over for this really big big-block. *Mike Mueller*

seconds. "The first time you put your foot to the boards, a premonition of impending whiplash emanates from the base of the Achilles tendon." On top of that, this drag king was a Buick, a classy car capable of living comfortably in the everyday world. "It's not temperamental," he added. "You can drive through city traffic, then run at the strip and get those fantastic ET's, then head right back to the old slow grind with no protest."

Undersquare like Buick's Stage 1, Chevy's biggest big-block yet was created by stroking the 427 from 3.76 inches to 4.00. Not all at Chevrolet, however, felt this was a good idea. "Increasing stroke without enlarging the bore doesn't necessarily translate into a real increase in power," said engine development man Tom Langdon, who had worked on the all-aluminum ZL1 in 1969. "Some of that extra power is eaten up by increased friction. A good [L88] 427 would put out about 600 horsepower. The 454 pulled more torque [on the dyno], but power was just about the same as the L88."

Langdon also wasn't sure about the 454's stamina under stress. "The L88 already had demonstrated substantial durability problems," he continued. "Increasing the stroke to go from 427 cubic inches to 454 only aggravated [things.] We hadn't even solved the 427's problems yet and we were making [them] worse."

Maybe so, but that didn't stop Chevrolet from keeping up with GM's other divisions. Two 454s were offered for 1970's Super Sport Chevelle, a rather tame 360-horsepower LS5 and the almighty LS6, which *Car Life* called "the best supercar engine ever released by General Motors." Affixed to the LS6's air cleaner was an output tag announcing the highest (by far) output rating seen during the original muscle car era: 450 horsepower.

What that figure translated into on the street was downright scary. "Driving a 450-horsepower Chevelle is like being the guy who's in charge of triggering atom bomb tests," explained a *Super Stock* report. "You have the power, you know you have the power, and you know if you use the power, bad things may happen. Things like arrest, prosecution, loss of license, broken pieces, shredded tires, etc." "That's LS as in Land Speed Record," added *Motor Trend's* A. B. Shuman.

Chrysler's Hemi also continued setting speed records in 1970, especially when delivered in Dodge/Plymouth's new E-body pony cars, resulting in the ultimate 425-horse Mopar. Right behind was the aforementioned 440, topped in supreme form by three Holley two-barrels. In Dearborn, Ford's brutal Boss 429 was joined in intermediate ranks by a new Cobra Jet V-8, this one also displacing 429 cubes. Clearly GM's new big-inch V-8s faced ample, not to mention able, competition.

Calling this the peak year for the great American muscle car was like saying a bear is public polluter—in the woods, no less.

1970 CHEVROLET CHEVELLE SS 454 LS6

CONSTRUCTION: body on perimeter-rail frame
MODEL AVAILABILITY: hardtop & convertible
PRICE (w/four-speed): $3,723.36, Malibu coupe; $3,976.36, Malibu convertible; $3,854.36, El Camino*
** Includes model base price plus RPO Z15 ($514.35), LS6 V-8 ($269), M22 transmission ($221.80) & T60 heavy-duty battery ($15.80)*
PRICE (w/automatic): $3,791.95, Malibu coupe; $4,044.95, Malibu convertible; $3,922.95, El Camino*
** Includes model base price plus RPO Z15 ($514.35), LS6 V-8 ($269), M40 transmission ($290.40) & T60 heavy-duty battery ($15.80)*
WHEELBASE: 112 inches
WEIGHT: 3,759 pounds
SUSPENSION: heavy-duty; coil springs & 1.25-inch stabilizer bar, front; solid axle w/coil springs & 0.875-inch stabilizer bar, rear
STEERING: Saginaw manual (24:1) recirculating ball; power-assist, optional
WHEELS: 14x7 five-spoke w/"SS" center cap
TIRES: F70x14
BRAKES: power-assisted 11-inch discs, front; 9.5-inch drums, rear
ENGINE: LS6 454-cid 454 Turbo Jet V-8 w/Holley 4-barrel carburetor
TRANSMISSION: Muncie M22 "Rock Crusher" 4-speed manual or Turbo Hydra-matic automatic
AXLE RATIO: 3.31:1

FAMILY TIES: CHEVROLET MK IV V-8s

Chevrolet engineers wasted little time restoring the Mystery Motor's (see page 43) bore after introducing their Mk IV big-block V-8 in the spring of 1965. Per GM's A-body displacement limit, Super Sport Chevelles rolled on into 1966 with the 396 Turbo Jet. But new for Corvette and full-size models were 427 cubes worth of Mk IV muscle. Two 427 Turbo Jets were offered that first year, the 390-horse L36 and 425-horsepower L72, with that latter beast showing up three years later beneath the hoods of a handful of Chevelles and Camaros via the clandestine COPO (see page 129) pipeline. While big Chevy's were limited to the L36 from 1967 to 1969, Sting Ray buyers were treated to various meaner, nastier 427s, including 1967's L71, which used three Holley two-barrel carbs to help produce a ceiling-shattering 435 horses. New too that year was the race-ready L88 with its aluminum heads and totally uncivilized makeup. An aluminum-head option (RPO L89) also appeared in 1967 for the L71, but few noticed—only 16 sets were installed. All three 427 deals—L71, L88, and L89—remained available up through 1969, when they were joined by the exotic all-aluminum ZL1, installed in only two Corvettes, along with 69 COPO Camaros. Back in the real world, a tiny bore boost performed late in 1969 pushed the 427's little brother up to 402 cubic inches for the midsize muscle car that continued wearing "SS 396" badges. Muddying the waters further was the "Turbo Jet 400" label Chevy officials stuck on this slightly bigger big-block—a tag that surely confused some customers considering 1970's release of the company's biggest small-block to date, the LF6 400 Turbo Fire V-8. Introduced as well in 1970 was the supreme Mk IV, the 454 Turbo Jet, available between fiberglass fenders and beneath A-body Super Sport hoods. The 402-cid LS3 Turbo Jet was last offered as a Chevelle option in 1972; its 454-cube LS4 running mate retired after 1975.

YEAR	CID	RPO	BORE & STROKE	CR	HORSEPOWER	TORQUE	CARBURETOR	VALVE SIZES
1965	396	L35	4.094 x 3.76	10.25:1	325 @ 4,800	410 @ 3,200	Quadra-jet 4-barrel	2.06 x 1.72
1966	427	L72	4.250 x 3.76	11:1	425 @ 5,600	460 @ 4,000	Holley 4-barrel	2.19 x 1.72
1967	427	L88	4.250 x 3.76	12.5:1	430 @ 5,200	450 @ 4,400	Holley 4-barrel	2.19 x 1.88
1969	427	ZL1	4.250 x 3.76	12:1	430 @ 5,200	450 @ 4,400	Holley 4-barrel	2.19 x 1.88
1970	402	L34	4.1260 x 3.76	10.25:1	350 @ 4,200	415 @ 3,400	Quadra-jet 4-barrel	2.06 x 1.72
1970	454	LS5	4.250 x 4.00	10.25:1	360 @ 5,400	500 @ 3,200	Quadra-jet 4-barrel	2.06 x 1.72
1971	454	LS6	4.250 x 4.00	9:1	425 @ 5,600	475 @ 4,000	Holley 4-barrel	2.19 x 1.88

NOTE: *CID is cubic-inch displacement; RPO is Regular Production Option; CR is compression ratio; bore/stroke & valve sizes in inches (intake x exhaust).*

NOTE: *1970 LS5 V-8 listed here is Chevelle version; Corvette LS5 produced 390 hp that year.*

NOTE: *LS6 V-8 was only available for Corvette in 1971; it was a Chevelle-only option in 1970.*

Chevrolet's biggest Mk IV big-block, the 454 Turbo Jet, arrived in 1970. That year's Corvette was treated to a 390-horse LS5 (shown here), while 1970's SS 454 Chevelle's LS5 was rated at 360 horsepower.

Late in 1969, Chevrolet's 396 Turbo Jet was bored out slightly to 402 cubic inches. While the name remain unchanged in 1970, this Mk IV big-block was adorned with "Turbo Jet 400" decals the following year.

HEAVY METAL

Quite a bit of jargon is bandied about whenever engineers speak of the various processes used to put the "heavy" in heavy-duty parts. To detail a few examples:

SHOT PEENING is an age-old "cold-working" process that hardens a metal's surface by blasting it with tiny round shot (metallic, glass, or ceramic), with each shot performing like a miniscule ball-peen hammer, hence the name. Peening spreads a metallic surface plastically, improving its mechanical properties by inducing comprehensive stresses, which resist metal fatigue and some forms of corrosion. In certain situations, shot-peening reportedly can increase fatigue life by up to 1,000 percent.

MAGNAFLUXING uses strong magnetic fields to test a metal's structural integrity. Metallic flaws disrupt these magnetic fields, and said disruptions will show themselves under a black light when the material being tested is coated with certain substances, most often iron oxide. This process can be done wet or dry using either fine iron oxide powder or a comparable liquid solution.

TUFTRIDING is one of various "case-hardening" procedures; others include flame or induction hardening, carburizing, carbonitriding, nitriding, and nitrocarburising. Case hardening is pretty much what it sounds like: the surface of a metal object, or the "case," is hardened (by infusing carbon, mostly) while its interior remains relatively "soft." Like nitriding, tuftriding involves subjecting an object to certain gases at certain heat levels (high in the latter's case, not so much in the former's) to form nitrides, which help enhance resistance to wear, metal fatigue, and corrosion.

Also commonly heard are four-digit "codes" used in reference to different grades of steel. These are SAE International standards, which define the various percentages of various metals in various alloys. The first digit indicates the main alloying element(s), the second signifies the secondary alloying element(s), and the last two spell out the amount of carbon present in hundredths of a percent by weight. The basic "families" look like this:

SAE CODE PREFIXES	ALLOY TYPE
1xxx	Carbon steels
2xxx	Nickel steels
3xxx	Nickel chromium steels
4xxx	Molybdenum steels
5xxx	Chromium steels
6xxx	Chromium-vandium steels
7xxx	Tungsten steels
8xxx	Nickel-chromium-molybdenum steels
9xxx	Silicon-manganese steels

For example, the SAE 5140 stock used to forge the crank in Chevrolet's LS6 454 V-8 was a "chrome-moly" alloy consisting of about 0.40 percent carbon by weight.

And speaking of forging (or impact extruding), this centuries-old process involves shaping metals with localized compressive forces—say, between an anvil and a hammer. While forging costs considerably more than casting, it produces greater metallic consistencies and strength, primarily by forming a continuous internal "grain" that work just like wood grains to enhance rigidity. Casting—pouring liquid metal into a mold—often leads to inconsistencies, perhaps even tiny air bubbles in the piece.

1970 CHEVROLET CAMARO Z28

CONSTRUCTION: unitized body/frame
MODEL AVAILABILITY: hardtop
PRICE: $3,794
WHEELBASE: 108 inches
WEIGHT: 3,580 pounds
SUSPENSION: heavy-duty; coil springs & 1.00-inch stabilizer bar, front; solid axle w/leaf springs & 0.625-inch stabilizer bar, rear
STEERING: manual (24:1) recirculating ball, std; variable-ratio power-assist, optional
WHEELS: 15x7 five-spoke
TIRES: F60x15 Goodyear Polyglas
BRAKES: power-assisted 11-inch discs, front; 9.5-inch drums, rear
ENGINE: LT1 350-cid Turbo Fire V-8 w/Holley 4-barrel carburetor
TRANSMISSION: 4-speed manual or Turbo Hydra-matic automatic
AXLE RATIO: 3.73:1 in Positraction differential (4.10:1, optional)

1970 PONTIAC FIREBIRD FORMULA

CONSTRUCTION: unitized body/frame
MODEL AVAILABILITY: hardtop with twin-scooped hood
PRICE: $3,370
WHEELBASE: 108.1 inches
WEIGHT: 3,815 pounds
SUSPENSION: heavy-duty; coil springs w/1.125-inch stabilizer bar, front; solid axle w/leaf springs & 0.625-inch stabilizer bar, rear
STEERING: manual recirculating ball, std; variable-ratio power-assist, optional
WHEELS: 14x7 stamped-steel
TIRES: F70x14
BRAKES: power-assisted 11-inch discs, front; 9.5-inch drums, rear
ENGINE: L78 400-cid V-8 w/Quadra-jet 4-barrel carburetor
TRANSMISSION: Hurst-shifted 3-speed manual, std; 4-speed & TH-400 automatic, optional
AXLE RATIO: 3.07:1

Even though they predictably cost considerably more, LS6 Chevelles (demonstrated here) outsold their less impressive LS5 counterparts in 1970. Chevy's 450-horsepower SS 454 was offered in both hardtop and convertible forms this year. *Mike Mueller*

CHEVROLET

Chevy's Z25 package for 1970 once again was offered only for Custom El Caminos and Malibu hardtops and convertibles. Now included in the deal was exclusive instrumentation copped from the new Monte Carlo and the F41 sport suspension. Z25 buyers this year also could choose between a four-gear or automatic—no three-speed, heavy-duty or otherwise, was available. New on the options was the ZL2 Cowl Induction hood.

Standard SS 396 power now came from the 350-horsepower L34 as the L35 didn't return. The L78 carried over one last time, and optional L89 aluminum heads returned, too, but were cancelled early in the year—only 18 pairs were installed before the axe fell. Creating an SS 454 Chevelle required checking off RPO Z15.

Camaro received a new face for 1970, but various glitches delayed its unveiling. When Chevrolet's new models debuted in September 1969, F-body buyers initially were told to take leftovers and like it. Execs meanwhile continued teasing the pony car public. "We will give an entirely new direction to this market," claimed general manager John DeLorean in a January 1970 *Motor Trend* interview. Chevy's upcoming new Camaro, in his words, would be "so sensational that I think we will more than make up for lost ground."

Indeed, almost all was forgiven when the next-gen Camaro finally did emerge in February 1970. Updates beneath its sleek, sexy skin included an improved chassis, better insulation, and standard front discs. Though a convertible version wasn't offered, Super Sport and Rally Sport renditions were. Less prominent without its hideaway headlights, the Z22 Rally Sport group was identified by two small front bumpers in place of Camaro's standard full-width unit.

New for the "1970-½" Z28 was the Corvette's LT-1 small-block, a 350 V-8 rated at 360 horsepower in F-body applications. With a much wider, more usable powerband compared to its 302 predecessor, the LT-1 was much more responsive—to both full-throttle bursts and slow-speed operation. And such relatively civilized compatibility allowed engineers to offer an automatic (albeit a beefed-up Turbo Hydra-matic with a high-stall torque converter) as a Z28 option for the first time. Now at the corners were 15x7 sport wheels and F60 Wide Ovals.

Chevrolet's latest Z28 fit into the redesigned 1970-½ Camaro shell like Raquel Welch in the furs she donned for the 1966 flick *One Million Years B.C.* "It's quiet, quick, beautiful and all the parts look and act as though they belong together," claimed *Sports Car Graphic*'s Paul Van Valkenburgh—in reference to the car, not the sex kitten. Behind that pointed prow was a new power source, the Corvette's LT-1 350 V-8, rated at 370 horsepower beneath fiberglass hoods. As the new heart of the Z28, the LT-1 small-block was tabbed at 360 horses. *Mike Mueller*

Revised taillights and a new grille graced 1970's Nova. Chevrolet's 300-horsepower L48 350 small-block remained the base engine for this year's Nova SS, and optional big-blocks also rolled over from 1969.

Nova SS rolled on nearly unchanged into 1970 with the L48 350 standard, the L34 and L78 396 Turbo Jets optional. This was the last year for the SS 396 Nova.

Truly new on the scene was the aforementioned Monte Carlo, more or less a stretched Chevelle. General manager Pete Estes, who had replaced Bunkie Knudsen in July 1965, put his head together with chief designer David Holls to create this luxury cruiser, which was then introduced in September 1969 by Estes' successor, John DeLorean. Monte Carlo was inspired by Pontiac's Grand Prix, itself a lengthened version of Pontiac's A-body (redefined as a G-car) first seen in 1969. A 350 V-8 was standard.

Adding RPO Z20 traded that small-block for the LS5 454, resulting in what *Car Life* called a "gentleman's bomb," the SS454. Front discs were standard for all Monte Carlos, and the TH-400 automatic was a mandatory SS454 addition. Some four-speed sticks may have been installed by special order.

1970 PONTIAC TRANS AM

CONSTRUCTION: unitized body/frame
MODEL AVAILABILITY: hardtop w/ram-air hood scoop & various aerodynamic cladding additions
PRICE: $4,305
WHEELBASE: 108.1 inches
WEIGHT: 3,782
SUSPENSION: heavy-duty; coil springs w/1.25-inch stabilizer bar, front; solid axle w/leaf springs & 0.88-inch stabilizer bar, rear
STEERING: variable-ratio power-assisted recirculating ball
WHEELS: 15x7 Rally II
TIRES: F60x15 white-letter
BRAKES: power-assisted 11-inch discs, front; 9.5-inch finned drums, rear
ENGINE: L74 400-cid Ram Air III V-8 w/Quadra-jet 4-barrel carburetor, std; 400-cid Ram Air IV V-8, optional
TRANSMISSION: Hurst-shifted M20 wide-ratio 4-speed, std; M21 close-ratio 4-speed and TH-400 automatic, both no-cost options
AXLE RATIO: 3.55:1 or 3.73:1 w/manual trans; 3.55:1 w/automatic

Basically a stretched, more prestigious A-body, Chevrolet's Monte Carlo was inspired by Pontiac's repackaged 1969 Grand Prix, itself based on a modified midsize foundation. Adding the optional SS454 package (RPO Z20) transformed the upscale Monte Carlo into what *Car Life* called a "gentleman's bomb." A heavy-duty suspension and Chevy's 360-horsepower LS5 Mk IV big-block was included in the Z20 deal. A vinyl roof was optional. *Mike Mueller*

Called "The Humbler" by ads, 1970's GTO featured a restyled Endura-clad facade that couldn't be fitted with optional hideaway headlights as in 1968 and 1969. New options included Pontiac's L75 455-cid V-8, rated at 360 horsepower. GTO Judge returned for 1970 and like base models remained available in hardtop and convertible forms.

1970 BUICK GSX

CONSTRUCTION: body on perimeter-rail frame
MODEL AVAILABILITY: hardtop
PRICE: $4,479
WHEELBASE: 112 inches
WEIGHT: 3,875 pounds
SUSPENSION: heavy-duty; coil springs & 1.00-inch stabilizer bar, front; coil springs & 0.875-inch stabilizer bar, rear
STEERING: manual recirculating ball; power-assist, optional
WHEELS: 15x7 five-spoke
TIRES: G60 Goodyear Polyglas GT
BRAKES: power-assisted 11-inch discs, front; 9.5-inch finned drums, rear
ENGINE: 350-hp 455-cid V-8 w/Quadra-jet 4-barrel carburetor, std; Stage 1 V-8, optional
TRANSMISSION: 4-speed manual or TH-400 automatic
AXLE RATIO: 3.42:1 in limited-slip differential, std; 3.64:1 included w/Stage 1

PONTIAC

A minor LeMans restyle this year did away with GTO's hidden headlight possibility, and new mechanicals included a thicker front stabilizer bar, a standard rear stabilizer, and optional variable-ratio power steering. "Here come da' Judge" again this year, now with a standard front chin spoiler in most cases.

Gone was 1969's two-barrel 400, replaced by the L75 455, which included ram-air induction. The base 400, Ram Air III, and L75 all were backed by a three-speed manual out of the box, while a four-speed and TH-400 automatic again were the only choices behind the L67 Ram Air IV.

Like its Camaro counterpart, Pontiac's midyear 1970 Firebird was big hit, with *Car and Driver* calling it "functional styling at its best." PMD's F-body lineup was revised this year as the base Firebird (six or V-8) was followed by the V-8-only Esprit. In place of Firebird 400 was the new Formula 400, and at the top was the flagship Trans Am.

Standard Formula 400 equipment included a unique fiberglass hood with two rather dramatic (though non-functional) scoops up front. Standard power came from the newly named L78 400, rated at 330 horsepower. The L74 Ram Air III and road-hugging Trans Am suspension were optional. Installing the L74 typically put those twin scoops to work sucking in ambient atmosphere.

Also offered only in full-roofed form, 1970's standard Trans Am now included Rally II wheels (without trim rings) and a snazzy engine-turned aluminum

GM's all-new F-body shape also suited 1970's Firebird just fine. Replacing the Firebird 400 this year was the equally new Formula, which came standard with two aggressive-looking (yet non-functional) hood scoops. Ram-air equipment was optional.

1970 PLYMOUTH HEMI 'CUDA

CONSTRUCTION: unitized body/frame w/special heavy-duty K-frame up front
MODEL AVAILABILITY: sport coupe
PRICE: Hemi V-8 alone cost $871.45
WHEELBASE: 108 inches
WEIGHT: 3,880 pounds
SUSPENSION: heavy-duty; torsion bars & 0.94-inch stabilizer bar, front; solid axle w/leaf springs, rear (Hemi/440 leaf springs incorporated 5.5 leafs, compared to 4.5 in other applications)
STEERING: manual recirculating ball
WHEELS: 15x7
TIRES: F60
BRAKES: heavy-duty 11-inch drums, std front & rear; power-assisted 10.97-inch front discs, optional
ENGINE: 426-cid Hemi V-8 w/2 Carter 4-barrel carburetors
TRANSMISSION: A833 4-speed manual w/Hurst shifter or Torqueflite automatic
AXLE RATIO: 3.23:1 in Dana 60 rear end w/9.75-inch ring gear

Polar White replaced Cameo White for Pontiac's second-edition Trans Am, which, like its Z28 cousin, showed up late in February 1970 due to various delays encountered while bringing GM's next-generation F-body to market. The 1970 Trans Am also could be ordered in a second color: Lucerne Blue. Standard striping returned but was redone in one bold center line accented with black edging. The stripe color inside that black border was white on blue cars, blue on white ones.

FAMILY TIES: FORD CLEVELAND V-8s

Lightweight, relatively efficient and—most importantly—emissions legal, Ford's 351 Cleveland V-8 was a perfect candidate for performance applications in the smog-conscious early Seventies. It was still capable of 285 horsepower in maximum 4V form in 1971. *Mike Mueller*

"Man, you've got to have a mind like a data processor to keep track of which engine is today's 'hot one,'" wrote *Sports Car Graphic's* Paul Van Valkenburgh concerning Ford's 1970 V-8 lineup. "Call up E&F (Ford's Engine and Foundry) to ask how many different designs they've built recently and they'll say, 'You mean right now, or by quitting time?'" Along with two big-block families, Dearborn also offered two distinctly different 351-cid small-blocks that year, as the existing version, built in Windsor, Ontario, was joined by a thoroughly modernized 335-series running mate manufactured in Cleveland, Ohio, hence its name. The new 351 Cleveland was the product of Ford's plan to create lighter, cleaner-running, more efficient V-8s for a future where higher fuel economy and lower emissions would be key requirements. But the Cleveland small-block's free-breathing canted-valve heads also promised ample performance potential, demonstrated by the Boss 351 and Cobra Jet renditions, introduced in 1971, and the 351 HO, offered in 1972. These three hot 351C V-8s (along with 1970's four-barrel version) featured four-bolt main bearing caps, while all two-barrel examples (and 1971–74's 4V editions) were held together on the bottom end by two-bolt caps. Heads also differed between 2V and 4V applications, with two-barrel units relying on "open" combustion chambers. Four-barrel heads were of compression-conscious closed-chamber design and were treated to larger (2.19/1.71 inches) valves. The Cleveland cylinder block also was recast in 1971 with a 1-inch taller deck to allow for a lengthened stroke, resulting in the perfectly square 400C V-8, a mild-mannered mill never meant to feed anyone's appetite for speed. Main bearings were enlarged, too, to 3.00 inches, same as the Windsor's, meaning the 351W's crank would work in the 400C block. This combo clicked in 1975 (the year after the 351C retired), resulting in the 351M (for "Modified") small-block, another less-than-tasty V-8 that left Ford fans wondering "where's the beef?"

YEAR	CID	BORE & STROKE	CR	HORSEPOWER	TORQUE	CARBURETOR	VALVE SIZES
1970	351	4.00 x 3.50	9.5:1	250 @ 4,800	355 @ 2,600	Motorcraft 2-barrel	2.05 x 1.65
1971	400	4.00 x 4.00	9:1	260 @ 4,400	400 @ 2,200	Motorcraft 2-barrel	2.05 x 1.65
1975	351*	4.00 x 3.50	8:1	148 @ 3,800	243 @ 2,400	Motorcraft 2-barrel	2.05 x 1.65

NOTE: CID is cubic-inch displacement; CR is compression ratio; bore/stroke & valve sizes in inches (intake x exhaust).

* 351M V-8, created by installing a 351W crank into a 400C block

Left: A totally new Skylark body appeared for Buick's 1970 Gran Sport, still offered in small- and big-block forms as hardtops or convertibles. While the GS-350 remained, its big brother was now the GS-455.

Above: Along with one of the muscle car era's highest profile exteriors, Buick's first GSX also came standard with an impressive suspension, power front discs, and 15x7 sport wheels wearing fat G60 Goodyear tires. Black was the only available shade inside, where bucket seats, a "consolette," a Rallye steering wheel, gauges, and a Rallye clock were all standard. Summed up, the A9 GSX package added roughly $1,100 to a Gran Sport's bottom line in 1970. *Mike Mueller*

instrument panel insert. A Hurst-shifted four-speed went behind the base Ram Air III; a close-ratio four-gear and TH-400 automatic were no-cost options. Pontiac's 370-horsepower Ram Air IV, tagged LS1 in F-body applications, was available at extra cost.

More notable, however, was the new T/A body, which featured restyled front fender air extractors, a front air dam, wheel-opening "spats," an integral rear deck spoiler, and a rear-facing shaker-style hood scoop—a Trans Am trademark that remained in place for 10 years. Yet another familiar feature—later nicknamed the "screaming chicken" logo—debuted in 1970 in decal form at the Trans Am's Endura nose. Remaining rather humble early on, this decal would eventually grow to cover the hood, making it the only hokey aspect of this purposeful machine.

BUICK

Two engines were available for 1970's GS 455: a 350-horse base big-block and the Stage 1. Now simply labeled "GS," Buick's small-block Gran Sport featured a 315-horsepower 350 V-8 backed by a column-shifted three-speed in base form.

Showcasing the new 455 was the gonzo GSX hardtop, introduced on February 9, 1970. Spoilers were standard front and rear, joined by black body-side accent stripes, color-coordinated headlight bezels (typical GS units were chromed), and a hood tach. Only two paint choices were offered: Apollo White or Saturn Yellow. The Stage 1 V-8 was a $113 GSX option; it cost $199 when ordered for the GS-455. Unlike the GS Stage 1, its 360-horse GSX sibling carried no exterior identification, meaning most stoplight challengers never knew what hit them.

1970 PLYMOUTH DUSTER 340

CONSTRUCTION: unitized body/frame
MODEL AVAILABILITY: sport coupe
PRICE: $2,547
WHEELBASE: 108 inches
WEIGHT: 3,110 pounds
SUSPENSION: heavy-duty; torsion bars & 0.88-inch stabilizer bar, front; solid axle w/leaf springs, rear
STEERING: manual (28.7:1) recirculating ball, std; power-assist, optional
WHEELS: 14x5.5 stamped-steel; 14-inch Rallye rims, optional
TIRES: E70
BRAKES: power-assisted 10.79-inch discs, front; 10-inch drums, rear
ENGINE: 340-cid V-8 w/Carter 4-barrel carburetor
TRANSMISSION: 3-speed manual, std; Hurst-shifted 4-speed & Torqueflite automatic, optional
AXLE RATIO: 3.23:1

Right: All 4-4-2 models—hardtop, coupe, and convertible—were fitted with Oldsmobile's 455 V-8 in 1970, and the topless rendition was chosen to pace the Indianapolis 500 in May 1970. A pace car replica package, option code Y-74, was offered this year for both Cutlass and 4-4-2 droptops.

1970 FORD BOSS 302 MUSTANG

CONSTRUCTION: unitized body/frame
MODEL AVAILABILITY: SportsRoof w/front chin spoiler (rear spoiler & rear window "slats," optional)
PRICE: $3,720
WHEELBASE: 108 inches
WEIGHT: 3,260 pounds
SUSPENSION: heavy-duty; coil springs & 0.85-inch stabilizer bar, front; solid axle w/leaf springs & 0.50-inch stabilizer bar, rear; Gabriel shock absorbers, staggered in back
STEERING: quick-ratio (16:1) manual recirculating ball, std; 16:1 power-assist, optional
WHEELS: 15x7 stamped-steel w/stainless hub cap & trim ring; std; 15x7 Magnum 500 five spoke, optional
TIRES: F60x15 fiberglass-belted black-sidewall
BRAKES: power-assisted 11.3-inch discs, front; 10-inch drums, rear
ENGINE: Boss 302 V-8 w/Holley 4-barrel carburetor; ram-air Shaker hood scoop, optional
TRANSMISSION: Hurst-shifted 4-speed manual only
AXLE RATIO: 3.50:1; 3.91:1, 4.30:1 & Traction-Lok differential, optional

1970 DODGE CHALLENGER T/A 340 SIX PACK

CONSTRUCTION: unitized body/frame
MODEL AVAILABILITY: sport coupe
PRICE: T/A package cost $865.70
WHEELBASE: 110 inches
WEIGHT: 3,600 pounds
SUSPENSION: heavy-duty; torsion bars & 0.95-inch stabilizer bar, front; solid axle w/leaf springs & 0.75-inch stabilizer bar, rear
STEERING: manual (24:1) recirculating ball; 15.7:1 power-assist, optional
WHEELS: 15x7 stamped-steel; 15-inch Rallye rims, optional
TIRES: E60, front; G60, rear
BRAKES: power-assisted 10.7-inch discs, front; 10-inch drums, rear
ENGINE: 340-cid V-8 w/three Holley 2-barrel carburetors
TRANSMISSION: A833 4-speed w/Hurst shifter or Torqueflite automatic
AXLE RATIO: 3.55:1 in 8.75-inch Sure-Grip differential

OLDSMOBILE

In 1970, Oldsmobile's W-25 fiberglass hood—featuring two gaping scoops at its nose—replaced all the ductwork previously found in the W-30 package. Included as well in the W-31 deal, the W-25 lid was a $158 option on other 4-4-2s. An optional fiberglass rear wing also debuted this year, as did power brakes and air conditioning in W-30 applications.

A 4-4-2 convertible paced the Indianapolis 500 in 1970, resulting in a requisite run of Y-74 pace car replicas. Both Cutlass and 4-4-2 Y-74 convertibles were built, with the latter coming only with the 365-horse 455. Some Cutlass pace car replicas featured 350 small-blocks.

PLYMOUTH

Cliff Voss' Advanced Styling Studio began work on another next-gen Barracuda in February 1967, with the goal being to develop a fresh facade that featured more room beneath for as much motor as possible. To that end, Plymouth's all-new E-body was some 5 inches wider than its A-body forerunner, allowing the installation of any big-block with little fuss or muss, a trick made possible by incorporating the bigger B-body's wide cowl structure.

On top went some groovy sheet metal—credited primarily to stylist John Herlitz—that was shaped into two body styles: coupe and convertible. Models included base Barracuda, the more prestigious Gran Coupe, and the reborn 'Cuda, a member of Plymouth's new Rapid Transit System, introduced late in 1969. 'Cuda engine choices included the 275-horsepower 340 small-block, 335-horsepower 383 big-block, 375-horsepower 440 RB, 390-horsepower 440 Six Barrel, and 426 Hemi.

External identification boldly read "Hemi 'Cuda" in the latter's case even though this 425-horsepower E-body wasn't officially classed as an individual model. Plymouth's new Shaker hood scoop was standard and was painted red on Rallye Red cars, black in other cases. By year's end buyers also could chose a blue Shaker for Blue Fire Metallic cars, and argent units became available, too.

Another tri-carb V-8, this one a small-block, also appeared in 1970 beneath E-body hoods, with the goal this time to go SCCA racing in what Plymouth called its AAR 'Cuda, named for Dan Gurney's All American Racers team. Powering this Trans-Am pony car was a hopped-up 340 topped by three Holley two-barrels and backed by either an A833 close-ratio four-speed or

Don Yenko began swapping L72 427 V-8s into Novas in 1969 but found the combination much too mean for the street. He then used the COPO pipeline the next year to take delivery of Corvette-powered Novas, these fitted with LT-1 350 small-blocks. These COPO Novas were then converted into "Yenko Deuce" models. *Steve Statham*

SUPER NOVAS

Early in the summer of 1968, Illinois Chevrolet dealer Fred Gibb noticed that drag racing's auto-trans super-stock classes were strangely devoid of capable Chevys, thanks in part to the absence of an automatic option for the new 375-horse Nova SS. He then contacted Vince Piggins, who concocted COPO #9738, which added Chevrolet's Turbo Hydra-matic 400 into the L78 Nova mix.

All 50 COPO 9738 Novas built came to life during the first two weeks of July 1968, and all featured the same equipment: L78 396, TH-400 trans, heavy-duty radiator, 4.10:1 Posi differential, painted 14x6 steel wheels, power-assisted drum brakes, bucket seats, and floor shifter with console. The radio was deleted and two interior colors were specified, black or blue. Exterior finishes were Fathom Blue, Grecian Green, Matador Red, and Tripoli Turquoise. Gibb kept one COPO Nova to race himself and sold the rest—the price on his LaHarpe lot was $3,592.12.

The plot thickened further after some 20 or so COPO 9738 cars ended up in the hands of Gibbs' comrade, drag racer Dick Harrell, who operated his own dealership network based out of Kansas City, Missouri. Harrell traded out the L78s in his COPO Novas for 450-horsepower 427s backed by competition-prepped automatics. Additional equipment varied, with some featuring Jardine headers, Rally wheels, M&H slicks, traction bars, and fiberglass hoods with Corvette-style "stingers." Cragar mags also appeared. The typical price for a Harrell Nova was about $4,400.

Yenko, Nickey, and Baldwin/Motion Performance all offered 427 Nova conversions, too, with Baldwin/Motion later making truly wild 454 swaps as well. Unlike Yenko's A- and F-body Super Cars, which began life in 1969 as 427-equipped COPO models, its S/C Nova that year was a swap job performed in the Pennsylvania dealership's shop.

Yenko Chevrolet planted only a few dozen 427s into SS 396 Nova bodies in 1969, basically because the combo was just too nasty for public consumption. Stuffing 450 horses beneath those compact hoods translated into some seriously surreal performance, like rest to 60 mph in something like four seconds. Even Yenko himself later called his 427 Nova "a real beast." "It was almost lethal," he added. "In retrospect, this probably wasn't the safest car in the world."

So Yenko Chevrolet came back in 1970 with a less-explosive Nova. Soaring insurance rates had transformed his S/C Chevelle/Camaro from a tough sell into a nearly impossible transaction, leaving him little choice but to send these two mean machines into the archives. In their place came the small-block Yenko Deuce, a 350-equipped Nova created through yet another COPO, this one coded #9010.

A COPO was required because the 350 V-8 in this case wasn't offered for the 1970 Nova. Standard that year for the revamped Z28, optional for Corvette, was Chevy's hottest small-block yet, the solid-lifter LT-1, rated at 370 horsepower for the latter, 360 for the former. The COPO 9010 deal transplanted the 360-horse 350 into brown-paper-wrapper Novas, not Super Sports, but Yenko made up for the missing imagery by adding his own trademark graphics. Additional standard features included an M21 four-speed and 4.10 Posi gears. A Hurst shifter, power front discs, five-spoke SS wheels, and a hood-mounted tach were listed as "standard options." The TH-400 automatic also was available.

A typical Yenko Deuce started at $4,395, not a bad price considering how little it cost to operate in dangerous daily traffic. As Yenko later explained, "insurance companies wouldn't insure a 427 Camaro, but a 350 Nova was a normal family car. All the customer had to tell his agent was that the car was a 350 Nova. It was none of the agent's concern that the 350 was the solid-lifter LT-1 Corvette motor. We built 200 of these cars and never heard a peep from the insurance companies."

In truth the actual count was a bit lower. Apparently Chevrolet released 178 COPO 9101 Novas in 1970, with 176 going to Yenko Chevrolet. The other two were delivered to Central Chevrolet, in London, Ontario, thanks to salesman Dave Mathers, who originally ordered 10 of these rather plain looking muscle machines. The pair he did receive remains safe and sound in collectors' hands today.

Both Dodge and Plymouth introduced Trans-Am-ready pony cars in 1970: Dodge's being the Challenger T/A, Plymouth's the AAR 'Cuda. Each was powered by a triple-carb 340 small-block rated at 290 horsepower. "AAR" referred to Dan Gurney's All American Racers team. Hood pins, blackout treatments for the grille and functional fiberglass hood, a competition-type fuel filler, and a rear ducktail spoiler were all part of the deal. *Mike Mueller*

Plymouth's all-new E-body pony car was offered in three forms for 1970: base Barracuda, upscale Gran Coupe, and sporty 'Cuda. Standard for the latter model were foglamps, twin hood scoops (simulated), and "hockey stick" body-side stripes. Here those stripes announce the presence of 1970's ultimate E-body, the Hemi 'Cuda. A fully functional Shaker scoop superseded those faux inlets up front on the Hemi 'Cuda. *Mike Mueller*

1970 BOSS 429 MUSTANG

CONSTRUCTION: unitized body/frame w/ram-air hood & trunk-mounted battery
MODEL AVAILABILITY: SportsRoof w/front chin spoiler
PRICE: $4,900
WHEELBASE: 108 inches
WEIGHT: 3,716 pounds
SUSPENSION: heavy-duty w/front geometry modified to make room for Boss 429 V-8; coil springs & 0.94-inch stabilizer bar, front; solid axle w/leaf springs & 0.62-inch stabilizer bar, rear; Gabriel shock absorbers, staggered in back
STEERING: power-assisted (16:1) recirculating ball w/fluid cooler
WHEELS: 15x7 Magnum 500 five-spoke
TIRES: F60x15 Wide Oval white-letter
BRAKES: power-assisted 11.3-inch discs, front; 10-inch drums, rear
ENGINE: 429-cid Boss 429 V-8 w/Holley 4-barrel carburetor & aluminum heads
TRANSMISSION: Hurst-shifted 4-speed manual only
AXLE RATIO: 3.91:1 in Traction-Lok differential, std; 3.50:1 and 4.30:1, optional

727 Torqueflite automatic. A fiberglass hood crowned by a large, gaping scoop was standard, as were fat Goodyears, E60s in front, G60s in back, resulting in a pronounced forward rake. Common today, that big/small tire combo was a Detroit first in 1970.

Another Rapid Transit System member was the new Duster 340, based on Plymouth's plebian A-body Valiant, available only with four doors in 1970. Like the original Barracuda, Duster was hastily created by more or less mating a swoopy two-door coupe body to a Valiant nose. The end result was a car that bought like a compact but impressed like few other low-priced rides Detroit then had to offer. And when fitted with the hot 340 small-block, Duster was instantly transformed into what *Car and Driver* called "a pocket Road Runner." According to *Hot Rod's* Steve Kelly, the Duster 340 "qualifies as one of the best, if not the best, dollar buy in a performance car."

Duster 340's base price was an easy $2,547, making it the cheapest RTS member. Included was a decent collection of high-perf hardware, beginning with a beefed chassis and free-flowing dual exhausts. Duster 340 also was the only RTS constituent featuring standard front discs.

Remaining RTS members were Road Runner, GTX, and the full-size Fury GT. A nicely restyled B-body shell served as the base for 1970's Road Runner and GTX, which again shared hoods. Road Runner's base price dropped slightly as a heavy-duty three-speed superseded the four-speed in the standard package. The 440 Six Barrel joined the Hemi on the options list, and reportedly one 440

FAMILY TIES: FORD 385-SERIES V-8s

Called "Ford's new clean machine" by *Motor Trend*, the 385-series V-8 was a product of Washington's increasing demands to reduce emissions. "Racing and research not only improve the breed, they also clean the air," wrote *MT's* Dennis Shattuck about this milestone mill, which debuted in 1968 at 429 cubic inches for Thunderbird, a whopping 460 for Lincoln. Along with being Detroit's first engine designed from the ground up with environmental protection in mind, the 385 family also combined two proven technologies to maximize the attraction. Its comparatively compact (for such a big big-block) foundation was created using the same thinwall casting practices that helped make Ford's Windsor V-8 a lightweight sensation in 1962. And atop that skirtless block went big-port cylinder heads fitted with canted valves that mimicked the "porcupine" arrangement introduced to rave reviews by Chevrolet's Mk IV Turbo Jet V-8 in 1965. Hot rodders initially may have been disappointed by the 429's two-bolt main bearing caps, but they couldn't deny the performance potential presented by those free-flowing heads. As it was, reinforcing four-bolt mains were added in 1970 when engineers transformed the so-called "Thunder Jet" into the 429 Super Cobra Jet, a 375-horsepower update to the 370-horsepower Cobra Jet introduced as well that year. The 385-series big-block also served as a base for 1969's Boss 429 V-8, though very little carried over in the transition from luxury liner to on-track terror. The CJ/SCJ duo made the scene only through 1971, while garden-variety 429s remained on the Ford/Mercury options list until 1974. Ford began offering the 460 in 1972, Mercury in 1973, and this behemoth continued powering cars, trucks, and vans until 1996.

A gentle giant when introduced for Ford's luxury liners in 1968, the 429-cid 385-series big-block was transformed into one of America's greatest muscle car mills in 1970. Output for the resulting 429 Cobra Jet was 370 horsepower, a figure that didn't change when the optional Shaker hood scoop was installed.

YEAR	CID	BORE & STROKE	CR	HORSEPOWER	TORQUE	CARBURETOR	VALVE SIZES
1968	429	4.36 x 3.59	10.5:1	360 @ 4,600	480 @ 2,800	Motorcraft 4-barrel	2.08 x 1.66
1968	460	4.36 x 3.85	10.5:1	365 @ 4,600	500 @ 2,800	Motorcraft 4-barrel	2.08 x 1.66

NOTE: *CID is cubic-inch displacement; CR is compression ratio; bore/stroke & valve sizes in inches (intake x exhaust).*

Left: The most affordable member of Plymouth's Rapid Transit Authority in 1970, the Valiant-based Duster 340, was described as "the little car that could" by ads. Chrysler's new Rallye wheels were standard for this "Super Compact," as was the 275-horsepower 340 LA V-8.

Above: Plymouth's GTX was offered only as a hardtop beginning in 1970. Attractive Rallye wheels joined the options list this year and were offered in 14- and 15-inch diameters. Big, fat F60 tires were available on those 15-inch Rallye rims. *Mike Mueller*

four-barrel 1970 Road Runner hardtop, fitted with an automatic transmission, is known. Standard for Hemi models was a redesigned Air Grabber hood featuring a pop-up flap adorned with a snarling, toothy grin reminiscent of World War II fighter plane nose art.

A topless GTX didn't return for 1970, but the standard 375-horsepower 440 did, along with the optional Hemi, joined by the 440 Six Barrel. All optional axle packages rolled over from 1969.

Plymouth's restyled B-body pleased most Road Runner fans in 1970. Body style choices (hardtop, coupe, and convertible) repeated and were joined by a third engine choice, the 390-horsepower 440 Six Barrel, which had debuted midyear in 1969 beneath the lift-off hoods of those special-edition race-ready Road Runner and Super Bee models. *Mike Mueller*

1970 FORD TORINO COBRA

CONSTRUCTION: unitized body/frame
MODEL AVAILABILITY: SportsRoof
PRICE: $3,270
WHEELBASE: 117 inches
WEIGHT: 4,185 pounds
SUSPENSION: heavy-duty Competition Handling package; coil springs & 0.95-inch stabilizer bar, front; solid axle w/leaf springs, rear; Gabriel shock absorbers (staggered in back w/manual trans)
STEERING: manual (29.4:1) recirculating ball; 21.6:1 power-assist, optional
WHEELS: 14x7 stamped-steel, std; 15x7 Magnum 500 five-spoke, optional
TIRES: F70x14 Goodyear Polyglas, std; F60x15 Wide Oval, optional
BRAKES: 10-inch drums, std front & rear; power-assisted 11.3-inch discs, optional
ENGINE: 360-hp 429-cid Thunderjet V-8 w/ Motorcraft 4-barrel carburetor, std; 370-hp 429 Cobra Jet & 375-hp 429 Super Cobra Jet (both with or without ram-air), optional
TRANSMISSION: Hurst-shifted 4-speed, std; Cruise-O-Matic automatic, optional
AXLE RATIO: 3.25:1

Dodge's Challenger T/A shared nearly all of its makeup with its AAR 'Cuda running mate with one noticeable exception: its fiberglass hood incorporated a "snorkel" scoop with twin inlets in place of the flat "NACA duct" design used by Plymouth. New SCCA rules for the 1970 Trans-Am season allowed manufacturers to de-stroke production engines to meet its 305-cid limit, explaining why Chrysler was able to offer its two race-ready pony cars with the 340-cube small-block.

DODGE

Harry Cheeseborough, senior v.p. of Styling and Product Planning, was charged with developing a Dodge pony car in the fall of 1966, and he turned to Bill Brownlie's studio to fashion the form. While the original plan included sharing Plymouth's E-body platform, the machine Cheeseborough and crew had in mind took shape as a longer, larger little horse meant to compete with Mercury's upscale Cougar. Initial specifications included a 111-inch wheelbase, same as the A-body Dart's. But in the end it was a 110-inch stretch—still 2 inches longer than the E-body Plymouth's—that was approved. As for the name, Brownlie preferred Challenger as a suitable complement to the existing Charger nameplate.

While the two E-bodies shared front/rear tracks, ample engine bays, and all glass, that was about it as far as carryovers were concerned. Four headlights appeared up front instead of two, and a markedly different taillight treatment also made sure that even casual witnesses couldn't mistake Challenger for Barracuda.

Challenger's 1970 lineup began with a base six-cylinder model offered in three forms: hardtop, convertible, or "Special Edition" sports hardtop. The definitely

HOT OFF THE PRESS: 1970 CHEVROLET MALIBU SS 396

"The Chevelle SS 396 has been a very fine seller and it is not difficult to see why. It has strong youth appeal but Chevrolet management feels that it is beginning to be noticed by a much older segment of the buying public. It is a car that can put a little excitement into the life of a jaded motorist without making him look like a total hot rodder."

Road Test, *1970*

HOT OFF THE PRESS: 1970 CHEVROLET CAMARO Z28

"The Z28 is as close to a mild-mannered racing car as the industry has come."

Car Life, *May 1970*

HOT OFF THE PRESS: 1970 PONTIAC GTO

"The[455] GTO is a driver's car but this is not to say that you have to be an enthusiast to appreciate it."

Car and Driver, *January 1970*

1970 MERCURY CYCLONE SPOILER

CONSTRUCTION: unitized body/frame w/ram-air hood & front/rear spoilers
PRICE: $3,759
WHEELBASE: 117 inches
WEIGHT: 3,773
SUSPENSION: heavy-duty Competition Handling package; coil springs & 0.95-inch stabilizer bar, front; solid axle w/leaf springs, rear
STEERING: manual (29.4:1) recirculating ball; 21.6:1 power-assist, optional
WHEELS: 14x7 stamped-steel
TIRES: G70 x14
BRAKES: 10-inch drums, std front & rear; 11.3-inch power-assisted front discs, optional
ENGINE: 370-hp 429-cid Cobra Jet V-8 w/Quadra-jet 4-barrel carburetor w/ram-air; 375-hp 429 Super Cobra Jet, optional
TRANSMISSION: Hurst-shifted 4-speed, std; Select-Shift C6 automatic, optional
AXLE RATIO: 3.50:1 in Traction-Lok differential

dressy SE had leather bucket seats, an upscale vinyl roof with a smaller, "opera"-type rear window, and an overhead console

Next up the pricing pecking order was the V-8 Challenger, offered with the 318-cid small-block in the same three body styles. Optional V-8s included the 340 small-block and two 383 big-blocks: a two-barrel version and its four-barrel big brother. The 340 was offered as part of a package that included 15x7 Rallye wheels wearing E60 tires. Later in the model run the Shaker hood also became an option for 340-powered Challengers.

At the top was Challenger R/T, standard with a 383 Magnum V-8. The 375-horsepower 440, 390-horsepower 440 Six Pack and Hemi were optional and limited to the R/T. Other popular options included Rallye wheels and the Shaker, which only was seen early on atop the 440 Six Pack and 426 Hemi. It became available with any of Challenger's four-barrel-fed V-8s midway in 1970.

Challenger T/A, Dodge's counterpart to Plymouth's AAR 'Cuda, appeared in March 1970, also with a triple-carb 340, a Six Pack in this case. The rest of the T/A package expectedly mimicked the AAR's, save most noticeably for the hood, which in the Challenger's case featured a snorkel-type scoop. Increasing the camber of the heavy-duty rear leaf springs was again required to both supply ample ground clearance for those circuitous exhausts and allow a suitable fit for the mismatched rear rubber.

1970 AMC REBEL MACHINE

CONSTRUCTION: unitized body/frame
MODEL AVAILABILITY: hardtop
PRICE: $3,475
WHEELBASE: 114 inches
WEIGHT: 3,731 pounds
SUSPENSION: heavy-duty; coil springs & 0.94-inch stabilizer bar, front; solid axle w/coil springs & 0.95-inch stabilizer bar, rear
STEERING: Saginaw manual (32.6:1) recirculating ball, std; variable-ratio power assist, optional
WHEELS: 15x7 "Machine" rims
TIRES: E60 Goodyear Polyglas
BRAKES: power-assisted 11.14-inch discs, front; 10-inch drums, rear
ENGINE: 390-cid V-8 w/Holley 4-barrel carburetor & ram-air hood
TRANSMISSION: Hurst-shifted Borg-Warner T10 4-speed or optional Shift-Command automatic
AXLE RATIO: 3.54:1 std w/either transmission; Twin-Grip differential, optional (3.91:1 gears optional w/manual trans, 3.15:1 w/automatic)

UNDER THE HOOD: 1970'S HOTTEST V-8s*

MODEL	CID	BORE & STROKE	CR	HORSEPOWER	TORQUE
Chevrolet SS 454 (LS6)	454	4.25 x 4.00	11.25:1	450 @ 5,600	500 @ 3,600
Chevrolet SS 396 (L78)	402	4.1260 x 3.76	11:1	375 @ 5,600	415 @ 3,600
Chevrolet Z28 (LT1)	350	4.00 x 3.48	11:1	360 @ 6,000	380 @ 4,000
Dodge/Plymouth Hemi	426	4.25 x 3.750	10.2:1	425 @ 5,000	490 @ 4,000
Dodge/Plymouth (3x2)	440	4.320 x 3.750	10.1:1	390 @ 4,700	490 @ 3,200
Dodge/Plymouth	440	4.320 x 3.750	10.1:1	375 @ 4,600	480 @ 3,200
Dodge/Plymouth	383	4.250 x 3.380	9.5:1	335 @ 5,200	425 @ 3,400
Dodge/Plymouth[1]	340	4.040 x 3.310	10.5:1	290 @ 5,000	345 @ 3,400
Dodge/Plymouth	340	4.040 x 3.310	10.5:1	275 @ 5,000	340 @ 3,200
Pontiac GTO (L75)	455	4.151 x 4.210	10:1	360 @ 4,300	500 @ 2,700
Pontiac (RA IV)	400	4.120 x 3.75	10.5:1	370 @ 5,500	445@ 3,900
Buick Stage 1	455	4.3125 x 3.90	10.5:1	360 @ 4,600	510 @ 2,800
Olds 4-4-2 W-30	455	4.125 x 4.250	10.5:1	370 @ 5,200	500 @ 3,600
Olds W-31	350	4.057 x 3.385	10.5:1	325 @ 5,400	360 @ 3,600
Ford/Mercury SCJ	429	4.36 x 3.59	11.3:1	375 @ 5,600	450 @ 3,400
Ford/Mercury CJ	428	4.13 x 3.98	10.6:1	335 @ 5,200	440 @ 3,400
Ford Boss 302	302	4.00 x 3.00	10.5:1	290 @ 5,800	290 @ 4,300
Ford Boss 429	429	4.36 x 3.59	10.5:1	375 @ 5,200	450 @ 3,400
Ford/Mercury (Cleveland)	351	4.00 x 3.50	11:1	300 @ 5,400	380 @ 3,400
AMC (The Machine)	390	4.165 x 3.574	10.2:1	340 @ 5,100	427 @ 3,600
AMC (Javelin/AMX)	390	4.165 x 3.574	10.2:1	325 @ 5,000	420 @ 3,200

NOTE: *CID is cubic-inch displacement; CR is compression ratio; bore/stroke in inches*

NOTE: *Chevrolet LS6 V-8 was Chevelle SS 454 option only; L78 was available for Chevelle, Camaro & Nova Super Sports.*

NOTE: *FoMoCo 429 CJ/SCJ was option for midsize Fords & Mercurys; 428 CJ/SCJ was option for Mustang & Cougar.*

**Discounting Corvette*

1. Exclusive V-8 for Plymouth AAR 'Cuda & Dodge Challenger T/A

CURIOUS YELLOW

Creating a Rallye 350 Olds in 1970 was a matter of ordering the W-45 Appearance Package, available that year for F-85 club coupes, Cutlass pillared coupes (shown here), and Cutlass Holiday hardtops. A monochromatic yellow exterior was the norm in all cases. *Mike Mueller*

The good Doctor Oldsmobile tried his hand at small-block performance again in 1970, this time in far-from-quiet fashion. For starters, the new Rallye 350 came in only one screaming shade: Sebring Yellow. Its Super Stock II wheels too were done in yellow, as were the bumpers thanks to a urethane coating that helped resist minor bruising.

"Tests give this new finish an extremely high rating in its resistance to weather and road damage," explained division manager John Beltz while introducing the Rallye 350 (available by way of option code W-45) in February 1970. "It has been found to be much more durable than chrome or paint. And there's another advantage. Nicks and gouges in the bumper are easily repairable with a urethane lacquer spray repair kit."

Maybe so, but the attraction still didn't work for everyone. Apparently more than one dealer retrofitted conventional chrome bumpers for conservative customers who simply couldn't handle that monochromatic look. Some press critics also weren't entirely amused. "It's Wurlitzer heavy," was a description used by *Car Life's* editors, who also took shots at the car's optional rear spoiler, calling it a "popsicle-stick like affair that droops over on the ends."

But not all press was bad. "Beneath that gaudy paint and wing lurk bargains in performance and handling," continued that *Car Life* report on the upswing. Along with contrasting black striping, dual sport mirrors, and a black-out grille, the W-45 package included Oldsmobile's FE2 Rallye-Sport suspension, N-10 dual exhausts, W-25 "force-air" fiberglass hood, and L74 350 V-8, rated at 310 horsepower.

"Its 350 V-8, combined with a specially designed suspension system, provides a fine combination of effortless performance and smooth handling for a beautiful driving experience," added John Beltz. "In addition, it is competitively priced in the industry's intermediate market."

Cost was key. Oldsmobile people were not only proud of a tidy bottom line—nearly $70 less than a comparably equipped Road Runner—they also were quick to point out additional savings. According to a sales promotion brochure, Rallye 350 "provides unquestioned performance at a level that may offer substantial insurance rate benefits to the buyer." In *Motor Trend's* words, it was best at "bridging the insurance gap."

While still other critics noted that installing the W-31 small-block surely would have enhanced the appeal, most witnesses recognized that such an application would defeat the main purpose—keeping Allstate, State Farm, and the rest at bay.

Simulated air scoops on the quarter-panels became standard for Dodge's final Coronet R/T, still offered as a hardtop or convertible in 1970. New on the options list (for both Coronet R/T and Super Bee) was the 440 Six Pack.

HOT OFF THE PRESS: 1970 PONTIAC FIREBIRD

"It's exciting in a way that Detroit could never master before. As an option you can reach for a small, black padded [steering wheel] that is surely fresh from a Formula One car. The tachometer has been turned so that the red line is straight up, and a small clock fits into the right side of the dial, strongly suggesting the instrumentation on a high-revving Japanese motorcycle."

Car and Driver, *March, 1970*

Yet another revised grille appeared for Charger in 1970, as did the Charger 500, not to be confused with 1969's NASCAR-ready aero racer. For only $150, a Charger 500 buyer this time was treated to vinyl bucket seats, a clock, wheel lip moldings, and appropriate badges. Another $161.85 could add the Special Edition package, which according to factory paperwork couldn't be combined with the optional Hemi. Nonetheless, 13 such combos were built—9 with automatic transmissions, 4 with four-speeds. As in 1969, the SE option was available for Charger R/T, which now included dummy scoops on the doors. Engine choices carried over, too. Among new midyear options were a rear spoiler and reflective hood tape that spelled out "440" or "Hemi."

A notably freshened body was new for 1970's Coronet R/T and Super Bee, which again shared a bulging hood incorporating non-functional openings. In the former's case, an "R/T" badge appeared between the updated B-body's split grilles, another graced the center of a blacked-out rear panel, and body-side emblems were located in simulated scoops that were now standard. Familiar Scat Pack bumblebee striping again brought up the rear, as did new taillights segmented into three sections on each side. The Super Bee taillight for 1970 once more was less ornate to help denote its lower place in the Coronet pecking order.

The optional Ramcharger hood carried over into 1970 for both R/T and Super Bee and again traded the standard power bulge for two fully functional scoops. Still included with the Hemi, the Ramcharger option cost $73 when fitted atop the R/T's base 440, the Super Bee's standard 383, or the available 440 Six Pack. A

Left: In 1970 the Dodge boys milked one more year out of the Charger body introduced for 1968, mildly updating 1969's grille and taillights to differentiate it from its predecessor. A customer in 1970 could still combine the R/T and SE packages, but reportedly the latter group could not be ordered along with the optional Hemi. Even so, 13 Hemi-powered Special Edition Chargers (9 with automatics, four with 4-speeds) were built that year, including the example shown here. *Mike Mueller*

floor-shifted three-speed was included this year as part of the base Super Bee deal to back down the bottom line. "Naturally, last year's four-speed job costs more, but don't you think the whole idea of the new Super Bee is getting less," went Dodge's sale pitch. "We think you just might buy the idea."

Dart Swinger 340 became more affordable this year, too, also thanks to the inclusion of a three-speed stick into the standard mix. At least the second-edition Swinger 340 was the only member of 1970's Scat Pack to offer standard front disc brakes. Up front was a new hood incorporating non-functional scoops copped from the B-body Ramcharger lid.

Dart GT/GTS didn't carry over into 1970, nor did any optional big-blocks, by way of Hurst or otherwise. Forget the 440, even the more palatable 383 was no longer a viable A-body choice considering what insurance companies were now charging, by the pound, to cover such high-powered, lightweight muscle machines.

Above: Dodge's hardtop Super Bee outnumbered its less expensive coupe running mate by nearly a 3-1 margin in 1970. New options included an alternative tape stripe treatment. Instead of wrapping around the tail bumblebee-style, these reverse "C-stripes" were offered in five body-contrasting colors: black, white, red, green, and blue.

TIME SLIPS: 1970

MODEL	¼-MILE PERFORMANCE	SOURCE
Plymouth Hemi 'Cuda	13.10 seconds at 107.1 mph	*Car Craft*, November 1969
Chevrolet Malibu SS 454 (LS6)	13.12 seconds at 107 mph	*Car Craft*, November 1969
Plymouth Road Runner Hemi	13.34 seconds at 107.5 mph	*SSDI*, December 1969
Buick GS 455 Stage 1	13.38 seconds at 105.5 mph	*Motor Trend*, January 1970
Pontiac GTO (RA IV)	13.60 seconds at 104.5 mph	*SSDI*, June 1970
Dodge Challenger R/T Six Pack	13.62 seconds at 104.3mph	*Car Craft*, November 1969
Ford Torino Cobra 429 SCJ	13.63 seconds at 105.9 mph	*SSDI*, March 1970
Buick GSX Stage 1	13.66 seconds at 100.2 mph	*Car Craft*, July 1970
Dodge Super Bee Six Pack	13.80 seconds at 102.0 mph	*Hi-Performance Cars*, January 1970
Plymouth GTX Hemi	13.85 seconds at 104.0 mph	*Rodder & Super/Stock*, September 1970
Oldsmobile 4-4-2 W-30	13.89 seconds at 101.1 mph	*Popular Hot Rodding*, April 1970
Pontiac Trans Am (RA III)	13.90 seconds at 102.0 mph	*Hot Rod*, February 1970
Dodge Charger R/T Six Pack	13.95 seconds at 101.0 mph	*Hi-Performance Cars*, February 1970
Mercury Cyclone 429 CJ	13.97 seconds at 100.0 mph	*SSDI*, February 1970
Dodge Challenger T/A	13.99 seconds at 100.0 mph	*Hi-Performance Cars*, August 1970
Dodge Challenger R/T Hemi	14.00 seconds at 104.0 mph	*Road & Track*, June 1970
Ford Boss 302 Mustang	14.03 seconds at 100.6 mph	*SSDI*, January 1970
Plymouth Duster 340	14.09 seconds at 99.8 mph	*SSDI*, March 1970
Chevrolet Camaro Z28	14.10 seconds at 99.8 mph	*Popular Hot Rodding*, August 1970
Ford Mustang Mach 1 428 CJ	14.11 seconds at 101.1 mph	*SSDI*, November 1969
Chevrolet Nova SS 396	14.15 seconds at 98.2 mph	*SSDI*, June 1970
Plymouth Superbird (440 V-8)	14.26 seconds at 103.7 mph	*Road & Track*, April 1970
AMC Rebel Machine	14.40 seconds at 100.6 mph	*SSDI*, January 1970
Plymouth 'Cuda AAR	14.40 seconds at 98.4 mph	*Sports Car Graphic*, June 1970
Mercury Cougar Eliminator*	14.40 seconds at 98.0 mph	*Hi-Performance Cars*, March 1970
Pontiac GTO Judge (RA III)	14.45 seconds at 100.0 mph	*Hi-Performance Cars*, July 1970
AMC AMX	14.46 seconds at 95.6 mph	*SSDI*, September 1970
Chevrolet Monte Carlo SS454	14.90 seconds at 92 mph	*Motor Trend*, November 1969
Oldsmobile Rallye 350	15.27 seconds at 94.33 mph	*Car Life*, May 1970

NOTE: *SSDI is* Super Stock & Drag Illustrated *magazine*

** w/Boss 302 V-8*

BY THE NUMBERS: 1970 PRODUCTION

CHEVROLET CHEVELLE SS

SS 396	53,599	(RPO Z25 for Malibu coupe/ convertible & El Camino
SS 454	8,773	(RPO Z15 for Malibu coupe/ convertible & El Camino
total	**62,372**	

CHEVROLET MONTE CARLO

SS454	**3,823**	(all hardtops)

CHEVROLET CAMARO SS

L48 (350 V-8)	10,012	
L34 (396 V-8)	1,864	
L78 (396 V-8)	600	
total	**12,476**	(includes hardtops & convertibles)

CHEVROLET CAMARO Z28

	8,773	(all hardtops)

CHEVROLET NOVA SS

	19,588	(all sedans; includes 1,802 w/L34 396 V-8 & 3,765 w/L78 396 V-8)

PONTIAC GTO

hardtop, std V-8	27,496	(9,348 w/manual trans, 18,148 w/auto)
hardtop, 455 V-8	3,747	(1,761 w/manual trans, 1,986 w/auto)
hdtp, Ram Air III	4,356	(3,054 w/manual trans, 1,302 w/auto)
hdtp, Ram Air IV	767	(627 w/manual trans, 140 w/auto)
hdtp subtotal	36,366	
cvt., std V-8	3,060	(887 w/manual trans, 2,173 w/auto)
cvt., 455 V-8	399	(158 w/manual trans, 241 w/auto)
cvt., Ram Air III	288	(174 w/manual trans, 114 w/auto)
cvt, Ram Air IV	37	(13 w/manual trans, 24 w/auto)
cvt. subtotal	3,784	
grand total	**40,150**[1]	

[1]GTO Judge production (included in above totals)

hardtop	3,629	
convertible	168	
total	**3,797**	(includes standard RA III & optional RA IV V-8s; 455 V-8 also became special-order Judge option late in model year)

PONTIAC FIREBIRD FORMULA

w/L78 400 V-8	7,019	(2,381 w/manual trans, 4,638 w/auto)
w/RA III (L74)	689	(396 with manual trans, 293 w/auto)
total	**7,708**	(all hardtops)

PONTIAC TRANS AM

w/RA III (L74)	3,108	(1,769 w/manual trans,1,339 w/auto)
w/RA IV (LS1)	88	(29 w/manual trans, 59 w/auto)
total	**3,196**	(all hardtops)

OLDSMOBILE 4-4-2

sports coupe	1,688	
Holiday hdtp	14,709	
convertible	2,933	
total	**19,330**	

OLDSMOBILE RALLYE 350

Cutlass coupe	160	
F-85 club cpe	1,020	
Holiday hrdtp	2,367	
total	**3,547**	

BUICK GRAN SPORT

GS-350 hdtp	9,948	(48 w/column-shifted 3-spd, 176 w/floor-shifted 3-spd, 884 w/4-spd, 8,840 w/auto)
GS-455 hdtp	5,589	(66 w/floor-shifted 3-spd, 510 w/4-spd, 5,013 w/auto)
Stage 1 hdtp	2,465	(16 w/floor-shifted 3-spd, 664 w/4-spd, 1,785 w/auto)
GSX hdtp	278	(81 w/4-spd, 197 w/auto)
GSX Stage 1	400	(118 w/4-spd, 282 w/auto)
GS-455 cvt.	1,184	(18 w/floor-shifted 3-spd, 126 w/4-spd, 1,040 w/auto)
Stage 1 cvt.	232	(1 w/floor-shifted 3-spd, 67 w/4-speed, 164 w/auto)
total	**20,096**	

FORD MUSTANG MACH 1

	40,970	(all SportsRoofs w/351- or 428-cid V-8s)

FORD MUSTANG 428 COBRA JET

coupe	70	
SportsRoof	3,372	
convertible	47	
total	**3,489***	

FORD MUSTANG BOSS 302

	7,013	(all SportsRoofs)

FORD MUSTANG BOSS 429

	499	(all SportsRoofs)

FORD TORINO COBRA

	7,675	(all SportsRoofs)

FORD TORINO GT

SportsRoof	56,819	
convertible	3,939	
total	**60,758**	(w/302-, 351- & 429-cid V-8s)

FORD FALCON 429 CJ/SCJ

w/CJ	14	(6 w/manual trans, 8 w/auto)
w/CJ Ram Air	10	(4 w/manual trans, 6 w/auto)
w/SCJ	55	(36 w/manual trans, 19 w/auto
w/SCJ Ram Air	80	(48 w/manual trans, 32 w/auto)
4-door	2	(1 SCJ w/auto trans, 1 CJ Ram Air w/auto trans)
total	**161***	(all sedans)

SHELBY MUSTANG

GT350 fstbk	261	
GT350 cvt.	57	
GT500 fstbk	380	
GT500 cvt.	90	
total	**788**	

MERCURY COUGAR ELIMINATOR

	2,267	(all hardtops)

MERCURY CYCLONE

base fastback	1,695	
GT	10,170	
Spoiler	1,631	
total	**13,496**	

PLYMOUTH ROAD RUNNER

cpe w/383 V-8	14,057	(1,330 w/3-speed, 5,839 w/4-speed, 6,888 w/auto)
cpe w/440-6	651	(429 w/4-speed, 222 w/auto)
cpe w/Hemi	74	(44 w/4-speed, 30 w/auto)
hdtp w/383	20,216	(584 w/3-speed, 7,933 w/4-speed, 11,639 w/auto)

hdtp w/440-6	1,130	(697 w/4-speed, 433 w/auto)
hdtp w/Hemi	75	(59 w/4-speed, 16 w/auto)
cvt. w/383 V-8	621	(13 w/3-speed, 179 w/4-speed, 429 w/auto)
cvt. w/440-6	34	(20 w/4-speed, 14 w/auto)
cvt. w/Hemi	3	(1 w/4-speed, 2 w/auto)
total	**36,861**	(includes US deliveries only; total including deliveries outside US plus Superbird was 41,318)

PLYMOUTH SUPERBIRD

hdtp w/440 V-8	1,084	(458 w/4-speed, 626 w/auto)
hdtp w440-6	716	(308 w/4-speed, 408 w/auto)
hdtp w/Hemi	135	(58 w/4-speed, 77 w/auto)
total	**1,935**	

PLYMOUTH GTX

hdtp w/440 V-8	6,398	(1,471 w/4-speed, 4,927 w/auto)
hdtp w/440-6	678	(350 w/4-speed, 328 w/auto)
hdtp w/Hemi	71	(43 w/4-speed, 39 w/auto)
total	**7,147**	(includes US deliveries only; total including deliveries outside US was 7,748)

PLYMOUTH DUSTER 340

w/3-spd	3,401	
w/4-speed	7,390	
w/auto trans	11,008	
total	**21,799**	(all sport coupes; includes US deliveries only; total including deliveries outside US was 22,117)

PLYMOUTH 'CUDA

hdtp w/340 V-8	6,032	(1,872 w/3-speed, 2,372 w/4-speed, 1,788 w/auto)
hdtp w/383 V-8	4,595	(150 w/3-speed, 1,905 w/4-speed, 2,540 w/auto)
hdtp w/440 V-8	952	(334 w/4-speed, 618 w/auto)
hdtp w/440-6	1,755	(902 w/4-speed, 853 w/auto)
hdtp w/Hemi	652	(284 w/4-speed, 368 w/auto)
cvt. w/340 V-8	262	(19 w/3-speed, 88 w/4-speed, 155 w/auto)
cvt. w/383 V-8	209	(9 w/3-speed, 68 w/4-speed, 132 w/auto)
cvt. w/440 V-8	34	(6 w/4-speed, 28 w/auto)
cvt. w/440-6	29	(17 w/4-speed, 12 w/auto)
cvt. w/Hemi	14	(5 w/4-speed, 9 w/auto)
total	**14,534**	(includes US deliveries only; total including deliveries outside US plus AAR 'Cuda was 19,515)

PLYMOUTH AAR 'CUDA

	2,724	(all hardtops; 1,120 w/4-speed, 1,604 w/auto)

DODGE CHARGER R/T

hdtp w/440V-8	8,574	(1,443 w/4-speed, 7,131 w/auto)
hdtp w/440-6	684	(347 w/4-speed, 337 w/auto)
hdtop w/Hemi	112	(56 w/4-speed, 56 w/auto)
total	**9,370**	(includes US deliveries only; total including deliveries outside US was 10,337)

Includes 1,452 R/T SE models

DODGE CORONET R/T

hdtp w/440 V-8	1,948	(405 w/4-speed, 1,543 w/auto)
hdtp w/440-6	194	(97 w/4-speed, 97 w/auto)
hdtp w/Hemi	13	(4 w/4-speed, 9 w/auto)
cvt. w/440 V-8	219	(16 w/4-speed, 203 w/auto)
cvt. w/440-6	16	(7 w/4-speed, 9 w/auto)
cvt. w/Hemi	1	(w/4-speed)
total	**2,391**	(includes US deliveries only; total including deliveries outside US was 2,615)

DODGE SUPER BEE

coupe w/383 V-8	3,431	(385 w/3-speed, 1,336 w/4-speed, 1,710 w/auto)
coupe w/440-6	196	(109 w/4-speed, 87 w/auto)
coupe w/Hemi	4	(all w/4-speed)
hdtp w/383 V-8	9,404	(284 w/3-speed, 3,383 w/4-speed, 5,737 w/auto)
hdtp w/440-6	1,072	(599 w/4-speed, 473 w/auto)
hdtp w/Hemi	32	(21 w/4-speed, 11 w/auto)
total	**14,139**	(includes US deliveries only; total including deliveries outside US was 15,506)

DODGE CHALLENGER R/T

hdtp w/383	8,939	(355 w/3-speed, 2,570 w/4-speed, 6,014 w/auto)
hdtp w/440	2,802	(916 w/4-speed, 1,886 w/auto)
hdtp w/440-6	1,640	(847 w/4-speed, 793 w/auto)
hdtp w/Hemi	287	(137 w/4-speed, 150 w/auto)
SE hdtp w/383	2,506	(30 w/3-speed, 400 w/4-speed, 2,076 w/auto)
SE hdtp w/440	875	(142 w/4-speed, 733 w/auto)
SE hdtp w/440-6	296	(135 w/4-speed, 161 w/auto)
SE hdtp w/Hemi	59	(22 w/4-speed, 37 w/auto)
cvt. w/383	684	(19 w/3-speed, 149 w/4-speed, 516 w/auto)
cvt. w/440	163	(34 w/4-speed, 129 w/auto)
cvt. w/440-6	99	(61 w-4-speed, 38 w/auto)
cvt. w/Hemi	9	(5 w/4-speed, 4 w/auto)
total	**18,359**	(includes US deliveries only; total including deliveries outside US was 19,938)

DODGE CHALLENGER T/A

	2,400	(all hardtops; 989 w/4-speed, 1,411 w/auto)

DODGE DART SWINGER 340

w/3-spd manual	955	
w/4-speed	4,423	
w/auto trans	5,004	
total	**10,382**	(all hardtops; includes US deliveries only; total including deliveries outside US was 13,781)

AMERICAN MOTORS AMX

w/360 V-8	1,583	(836 w/4-speed, 747 w/auto)
w/390 V-8	2,533	(1,632 w/4-speed, 901 w/auto)
total	**4,116**	(all hardtops)

AMERICAN MOTORS REBEL MACHINE

	1,936	(some sources claim 2,306)

** These statistics are copyrighted Ford Motor Company and Marti Auto Works material; Marti Auto Works has the entire production database of all Ford vehicles from 1967 to the present—visit www.martiauto.com for more details.*

NOTE: *Production data was supplied by various sources, including Christo Datini at the GM Heritage Center, Galen Govier (Mopar material) at Galen's Tag Service (www.galengovier.com, the Shelby American Automobile Club (www.saac.com), and American Motors enthusiast Eddie Stakes at www.planethoustonamx.com.*

HOT OFF THE PRESS: 1970 PONTIAC TRANS AM

"Somehow, a small subversive element within Pontiac wriggled out from under the tedious, nay-saying, government-fearing, corporate thumb long enough to bolt together the Trans Am—a hard-muscled, lightning-reflexed commando of a car, the likes of which doesn't exist anywhere in the world, even for twice the price."

Car and Driver, *June 1970*

Right: The quad headlights that graced 1969's Mustang were traded for dual units the following year and the Boss 302/Boss 429 duo returned for an encore. While Magnum 500 wheels were standard for the big-block Boss, they were extra-cost items for its small-block little brother. All Boss 302 mechanicals carried over into 1970, joined by a new Hurst shifter inside.

Like Boss 302, Ford's Boss 429 was treated to more paint choices and a standard Hurst shifter in 1970. Nearly all other mechanicals also rolled over from 1969. *Mike Mueller*

Ford's midsize Cobra returned for 1970 but this time only as a Torino SportsRoof. In place of 1969's 428 Cobra Jet was Ford's 385-series 429 Thunderjet V-8, rated at 360 horsepower. On the options list was the 370-horsepower 429 Cobra Jet and its 375-horsepower Super Cobra Jet brother, both offered with or without that ram-air Shaker hood scoop. *Mike Mueller*

FORD

Mustang's expansive 1969 engine lineup carried over and was joined by a new small-block, the 351 Cleveland (see page 162). Both 351s, Windsor and Cleveland, were briefly listed together, creating more than a little confusion. The 428 Cobra Jet also returned, and a notable SCJ change in 1970 involved the addition of the Detroit Locker differential, which became part of the Drag Pack option along with the 4.30:1 axle. The Traction-Lok remained for 3.91 gears. Mach 1 was treated to a rear stabilizer bar this year, dual exhausts again were included behind four-barrel engines, and the Shaker scoop was available for all V-8s, not just CJs.

Mechanically 1970's Boss 302 was nearly identical save for the addition of 1969's planned rear sway bar. Color choices increased to 13, including Grabber Blue, Grabber Green, and Grabber Orange. A Shaker was a new option for the last of Ford's Trans-Am pony cars.

Kar Kraft shipped out its final Boss 429 Mustang on January 6, 1970. Like its small-block running mate, the second-edition big-block Boss was treated to more color choices. Nearly all other cosmetics carried over, with the one notable exception involving that big hood scoop, which this time was painted low-gloss black. Other upgrades included the addition of a Hurst shifter and the relocation of the rear sway bar from below the axle to above.

A restyled SportsRoof body appeared in 1970 for Torino Cobra, now powered by Ford's 429 Thunder Jet big-block in standard form. Optional was the new 385-series Cobra Jet, the 370-horsepower 429 V-8. Like its FE cousin, the 429 CJ could be ordered with or without ram-air equipment, which again mattered not at all to the guys in charge of advertised output. The same was true when a Shaker scoop was planted atop the 429 Super Cobra Jet, included in the Cobra's Drag Pack option. SCJ 429s were rated at 375 horsepower, ram-air or not. All CJ Cobras, Super or otherwise, were fitted with the Competition Suspension package, which added higher rate springs, a stiffer front stabilizer bar, and heavy-duty Gabriel shocks. Rear Gabriels were staggered on four-speed cars.

SHELBY MUSTANG

Carroll Shelby contacted Ford vice president John Naughton in the fall of 1969, asking him to finally discontinue the GT350/500. Naughton complied, but there still remained cars left in the pipeline. These leftovers were updated with 1970 serial numbers and also repackaged with chin spoilers and black hood stripes. And when they sold, that was that.

Feature editor Joe Scalzo broke the bad news in *Car Life's* October 1969 issue. "The Shelby, most enthusiasts agreed, had been dead, or close to death, for years. Each year since its 1965 inception [it] had become more of a compromised car: and even by Shelby's own admission it had lost its identity as a Supercar. As the stylists heaped on more chrome, they at the same time removed more and more of the car's performance features. As the time of its death it had entered a never-never land where it had neither the luxury of, say, the Mach 1, nor the performance and handling of the Boss Mustangs."

Case closed.

Still looking damn good in 1970, Ford's Torino GT could be equipped with all the hot hardware found on that year's Cobra, including the 429 Cobra Jet and Super Cobra Jet V-8s. A 220-horsepower 302 small-block was standard for 1970's GT, now offered only in SportsRoof and convertible forms—1969's formal-roof rendition did not return.

MERCURY

Cougar Eliminator for 1970 offered bolder graphics, more paint choices, and a new standard V-8 beneath that big black hood scoop: the Cleveland-built 351 four-barrel. The 351 Windsor and 390 FE were dropped from the options list, but the 428 CJ and Boss 302 remained, as did the Boss 429, at least on paper. No Shotgun-motored Eliminators were built this time.

Mercury's midsize Cyclone was no longer available in fastback form, but it still looked cool as hell based on a restyled Montego hardtop body. Among standard Cyclone stuff were G70 tires, a competition handling package, and a 360-horsepower 429. F70 rubber, a scooped hood, concealed headlights and Hi-back bucket seats were standard for 1970's Cyclone GT, which reverted to individual model status. Curiously the GT was fitted with a 351 Windsor two-barrel in base form.

A ram-air 429 Cobra Jet was the weapon of choice for the supreme 1970 Cyclone, Spoiler, a model built only for the street this time, not NASCAR tracks. As one might have guessed, front and rear spoilers were part of this package, as were the base Cyclone's exposed headlights and the GT's buckets. The 429 SCJ was optional.

Above: Leftover 1969 Shelby Mustangs were simply sold as 1970 models during the breed's final run. Ford's last GT350/GT500 duo was updated with a chin spoiler and black hood stripes. *Mike Mueller*

Left: Bolder graphics (including a blacked-out hood scoop), more paint choices, and a new standard V-8 appeared for 1970's Cougar Eliminator. That engine was Ford's 351 Cleveland small-block, rated at 300 horsepower. The Boss 302 and 428 Cobra Jet remained available at extra cost. *Mike Mueller*

HOT OFF THE PRESS: 1970 PLYMOUTH DUSTER 340

"We believe that Duster 340 will offer more performance per dollar than any other car in Detroit—or the world for that matter."

Car and Driver, *September 1969*

HOT OFF THE PRESS: 1970 PLYMOUTH SUPERBIRD

"The Superbird, in concept, is a vehicle for the raw competition of NASCAR tracks. But, in street versions, it is also a fun car when you get used to being stared at."

Road Test, *April 1970*

Now based on Mercury's Montego hardtop, 1970's Cyclone was offered in three flavors: base model, GT, and Spoiler, with the latter machine predictably fitted with aerodynamic body parts front and rear. A 360-horsepower 429 was standard for Cyclone, a 351 Windsor two-barrel for Cyclone GT, and the 370-horsepower 429 CJ for Spoiler.

American Motors rolled out 100 Trans Am Javelins for 1970, all done in red, white, and blue paint. The 390 Go Package was included, plus SST amenities, a decklid wing, and a chin spoiler. Some were sold without that latter feature.

AMERICAN MOTORS

A restyled Javelin wearing a slightly longer nose appeared for 1970, as did a notably improved front suspension incorporating double ball-joints in place of the previously used trunnion design. A prominent "power blister" hood was new for AMX and could be fitted with optional ram-air, a first for AMC's pony car. While a functional "Frigid-Air" hood scoop had been available for Javelin/AMX since 1968, that package was a dealer option supplied by an outside contractor, Trend Setter, the same company that manufactured those "Sidewinder" exhausts. Beginning in 1970, a ram-air hood was a true factory option and could be installed on Javelin, too, that is as long as a four-barrel V-8 rested beneath.

Ram-air was included in 1970's Go Package, which carried over in nearly identical fashion, save for striping, now an extra. Additional changes to the "Go" deal included switching (early in the year) from redline tires to raised-white-letter rubber and trading out the 343 for AMC's new 360, rated at 290 horsepower. Now putting out 325 horses, the 390 rolled over from 1969, as did those Big Bad Colors (complemented by chrome bumpers this time) and Mod Package options.

Two special-edition Javelins also appeared for 1970, both of them inspired by American Motors' SCCA racing successes. In the fall of 1969, AMC rolled out 100 Trans Am Javelins, all of them painted red, white, and blue and loaded down with every hot part on the shelf (ram-air 390, Go Package, etc.) plus SST amenities. A decklid wing and chin spoiler were included, too, although some models reportedly were sold without that front unit.

Javelin received a slightly longer nose in 1970, and new for this year's AMX was a "power blister" hood that could become functional by adding AMC's first factory-direct ram-air option. An available 290-horsepower 360 V-8 replaced 1969's 343 in the Javelin/AMX's optional Go Package. *Mike Mueller*

HOT OFF THE PRESS: 1970 BUICK GS 455 STAGE 1

"Buick, long known for sedate 'old people' cars, has altered its image [with trendy styling.] Now it shakes the very foundation of the 'Establishment' with the GS 455 Stage 1, a production car assault on the nation's drag strips."

Road Test, *March 1970*

WINGED WONDERS

Various liberal interpretations of "factory stock" had been keeping Bill France busy trying to stay one step ahead of crafty competitors every since he founded the National Association of Stock Car Auto Racing league in February 1948. By 1967, NASCAR's main homologation standard was simple: sell 500 examples to Average Joe and any manufacturer could take any model racing on stock car tracks.

Faced with this minimum requirement, Detroit's automakers were soon building some of the wildest machines ever let loose on the streets. Easily the most extreme were Dodge's Charger Daytona and Plymouth's Superbird, released in 1969 and '70, respectively. Unlike many muscle cars that only looked the part, Superbird and Daytona bodies were truly aerodynamic, this because designers had finally discovered that brute horsepower wasn't the only key to speed.

Physical laws being relatively constant, at least in most states other than Texas, 500 or more horses could only do so much any way with a stock body possessing all the aerodynamics of a parachute. A "wall" apparently existed at about 175 miles per hour as all that muscle simple couldn't punch its way through the wind. Ford Motor Company racers breached that barrier first when its sleek Fairlane and Mercury Cyclone fastback bodies appeared in 1968. Left in the dust, the Dodge boys found that their new Charger shell only appeared sleek. In reality, its recessed grille and tunneled rear window created considerable drag at high speeds, leaving it easy prey for Ford/Mercury's more slippery rivals.

Dodge's first response to the FoMoCo challenge was Charger 500,

Competitive pressures (coming from NASCAR tracks) resulted in the production of Dodge's Charger Daytona (foreground) and Plymouth's Superbird, both offered for one year only: the former for 1969, the latter for 1970. The extra downforce created by those wedge-shaped noses and tall, "towel-rack" spoilers helped these two reach 200 miles per hour with ease on superspeedway. Their aluminum rear wings differed considerably. The Superbird's was taller and sweeped backward at a sharper angle. Its pedestal bases also were wider. Daytona wings used three-piece tape stripes done in three contrasting colors; red, white, or black. Superbird wings were always body-colored. *Mike Mueller*

The metal noses differed in various ways. Superbird's front cap (background) swept upward slightly and also carried a continuation of the hood's center crease, which the Daytona's snout didn't. Air inlets also were located differently. The chin spoilers below, however, were identical. *Mike Mueller*

named after France's production rule. While it initially looked promising, the Charger 500's early announcement, made before the 1968 season ended, only helped inspire a quick reply from the competition for 1969: Ford's Fairlane-based Talladega and Mercury's Cyclone Spoiler II, cars that reached the 190 miles per hour plateau. Dodge then replied back in April 1969 with an even more aggressive aero-racer, Charger Daytona, a product of some serious wind-tunnel testing.

Hand-crafted at Creative Industries in Detroit, Daytona featured a pointed steel beak with a chin spoiler, a fully functional modification that stretched the car by about a foot and a half. In back went a cast-aluminum "towel rack" wing towering over the rear deck. And like Charger 500, Daytona was fitted with a leaded-in steel plug to allow the installation of a flush rear window. Reportedly the new nose could produce nearly 200 pounds of downforce; that huge rear wing, 650 pounds. In racing trim, the Daytona was the first NASCAR competitor to surpass the 200 miles per hour barrier.

Not long afterward, Plymouth designers kicked off their own aero-car project. Born in June 1969 then temporarily canceled in August, Superbird was rapidly readied for NASCAR's 1970 season. Though it looked a lot like Daytona, it was very much of a different feather. For starters, the Road Runner front clip wouldn't accept that nose graft as easily as the Charger's did. Thus, a hood and front fenders were copped from the Coronet line for this application. Various other measurements differed, including the rear wing, which was taller, wider, and raked back more than Daytona's. Yet another difference came on top, where Superbird's roof was covered in vinyl to hide the seams around the flush rear windows' mounting plug.

Hand leading those seams was ditched to save time and money. Cost-conservation became an issue when NASCAR rulesmakers adjusted their homologation standards for the 1970 season. Now a manufacturer had to build either 1,000 street versions or a number equal to half of that company's dealers, whichever was higher. Plymouth officials were then faced with the task of creating nearly four times as many Superbirds as Dodge did Daytonas.

With Ford racing interest dwindling, the two winged Mopars took command on NASCAR tracks in 1970. Superbirds won eight races, Daytonas four, and another victory was scored by a Charger 500. The tally at Ford was four wins each for the Talladega and Cyclone Spoiler II, these recorded before Henry Ford II finally decided to cancel his corporation's competition programs late in the year. Bill France did the rest, instituting a carburetor restrictor plate rule for the high-flying Hemi-powered Mopars to help keep speeds (and the cars themselves) down to earth. This restriction then helped convince Chrysler officials to give up on Superbird. Like Daytona, it was a one-hit wonder. But damn, to have either one today.

Ford's Falcon broke Detroit's record for new-model sales in 1960 by doing exactly what a compact does best. It was comparatively small (109.5-inch wheelbase), light (less than 2,300 pounds), affordable (about $1,900), and its 144-cube six was easy on gas, to the tune of about 27 miles per gallon. But proving they just couldn't leave well enough alone, Dearborn product planners also began adding sportiness into the mix, first in the form of the bucket-seated Falcon Futura in 1961, followed by the V-8-powered Sprint midyear in 1963. A crisper restyle arrived the next year, then Falcon was reinvented for 1966 on a shortened Fairlane platform riding on a 110.9-inch wheelbase.

No longer so tidy, not nearly as frugal, this third-gen rendition quickly lost face and was on the way out even before Ford introduced its next new small car, Maverick, in April 1969. Sagging sales, coupled with the fact that Falcon, in its existing fashion, couldn't keep up with tightening federal auto safety standards, convinced the Blue Oval gang to close the book on their original compact in December that year. In January 1970, the name was transferred to the lowest-level Fairlane 500 models for a brief run before both legacies, Fairlane and Falcon, were killed off forever at year's end. Ford built only 26,071 Fairlane-based two-door Falcon sedans for 1970.

Unlike its Comet cousin from Mercury—itself more or less a lengthened Falcon until 1966—Ford's pioneering compact was never morphed into a muscle car, at least not in the States. A few Hi-Po

The oil lines running up above the windshield washer fluid reservoir (upper right) identify this FE big-block as a Super Cobra Jet—part of the SCJ package was an external oil cooler, mounted to the driver's side of the radiator. With or without optional ram-air, the 429 SCJ was rated at 375 horsepower. *Tom Shaw*

If not for an optional Shaker scoop, a Cobra Jet Falcon was certainly capable of sneaking up on all comers in 1970. In its last year, Ford's Falcon nameplate briefly appeared on midsize models, meaning any V-8 available for Fairlane (also not long for the world) and Torino also could be installed in Dearborn's bare-bones budget buggy. *Tom Shaw*

Falcons were marketed in Canada during the 1960s, but that was it as far as flying truly high was concerned. Until 1970, that is.

Now an intermediate, Ford's "1970-½" Falcon could be fitted with any V-8 in that year's Fairlane/Torino arsenal, right up to the 429 Cobra Jet, available in 370-horsepower base form or 375-horsepower Super Cobra Jet mode. Installing the optional ram-air Shaker was possible, too, and once again didn't affect advertised output in either case, CJ or SCJ. As was the case with its 428-cid forerunner, a 429 CJ was transformed into an SCJ by checking off the Drag Pack option, which included either a 3.91:1 Traction-Lok or 4.30:1 Detroit Locker rear axle. Various engine mods (four-bolt block, more cam, bigger carb) also came along in the Drag Pack deal, as did an external oil cooler.

The Falcon CJ/SCJ's supporting cast was the same as that year's Cobra. The heavy-duty Competition Suspension was included and featured staggered rear shocks in manual-trans applications. A four-speed (with Hurst shifter) was a mandatory option; Ford's C6 Cruise-O-Matic automatic was optional. Standard wheels were 14x7 units shod in F70 Wide Oval white-sidewall (WSW) rubber. Raised-white-letter (RWL) F70 tires were available at extra cost, as were G70 (WSW or RWL) Wide Ovals and 15x7 rims (either standard stamped-steel or Magnum 500 five-spokers) wearing super-fat F60 RWL Wide Ovals.

Summed up, a CJ Falcon buyer got a certified "sleeper," a less costly "Cobra sedan" that left more than one stoplight challenger scratching his noggin in 1970 wondering what those disappearing taillights were attached to.

1970 FORD 429 COBRA JET/SUPER COBRA JET

Type	OHV 385-series V-8 w/cast-aluminum finned valve covers
Displacement	429 cubic inches
Bore	4.36 inches
Stroke	3.59 inches
Horsepower	370 at 5,400 rpm, CJ; 375 at 5,600 rpm, SCJ
Torque	450 at 3,400 rpm, CJ & SCJ
Compression	11.3:1, CJ & SCJ
Induction	700-cfm Rochester Quadra-Jet 4-barrel on a cast-iron intake, CJ; 780-cfm Holley 4-barrel on similar intake modified to mount Holley carb, SCJ; ram-air Shaker hood scoop, optional for both CJ & SCJ
Air cleaner	single-snorkel unit (various sizes used depending on ram-air installation and CJ/SCJ choice; snorkel angle also varied)
Ignition	single-point Autolite distributor w/automatic trans; dual-point w/4-speed (Autolite rev-limiter included with 4-speed)
Cooling	7-blade fan w/shroud (oil cooler included w/SCJ)
Cylinder block	cast-iron w/beefed main bearing webs & 2-bolt main bearing caps, CJ; SCJ used 4-bolt mains
Crankshaft	cast-iron w/3.00-inch main journals
Connecting rods	forged-steel with 3/8-inch bolts
Pistons	cast-aluminum in right- & left-hand valve relief configurations, CJ; forged-aluminum, SCJ (429 Thunderjet pistons were interchangeable from one cylinder bank to the other)
Cam	hydraulic w/hardened pushrods & guide plates, CJ; mechanical, SCJ
Duration	282 degrees on intake, 296 degrees on exhaust, 58 degrees of overlap, CJ: 300 degree on intake/exhaust, 72 degrees of overlap, SCJ
Rocker ratio	1.73:1 stamped-steel units on screw-in studs, adjustable on early CJs and all SCJs (CJ V-8s built after November 1, 1969, used non-adjustable rockers on positive-stop studs)
Cylinder heads	cast-iron w/14mm spark plugs (429 Thunderjet featured 18mm plugs), canted valves, round ports & 71.5cc-75.5cc combustion chambers
Valve sizes	2.242-inch intakes, 1.722-inch exhausts
Valve lift	0.506-inch intake/exhaust, CJ; 0.509-inch intake/exhaust, SCJ
Exhaust	streamlined cast-iron manifolds

Like its SC/Rambler forerunner of 1969, American Motors' Rebel Machine initially was offered in 1970 with a patriotic red, white and blue exterior. Later versions were done in any Rebel color. Standard stuff included a blacked-out grille, a functional hood scoop incorporating a lighted 8,000-rpm tach, and 15x7 sport wheels shod in E60 Goodyear white-letter rubber. *Mike Mueller*

HOT OFF THE PRESS: 1970 OLDSMOBILE 4-4-2 W-30

"Unconfirmed reports have it that a formal protest against Oldsmobile has been lodged by Superman. W-machines are the cause."

Steve Kelly, Hot Rod, *May 1970*

HOT OFF THE PRESS: 1970 OLDSMOBILE RALLYE 350

The Rallye 350 is a new kind of car aimed at the younger driver who has trouble getting insurance, especially if the car of his choice weighs less than 10 pounds per horsepower. With 310 bhp and 3500+ pounds, the Rallye 350 is in the clear with your insurance agent."

Karl Ludvigsen, Motor Trend, *February 1970*

Racer Mark Donahue worked closely with American Motors engineers to help give him every advantage at the track at the wheel of AMC pony cars, and one result was the large ducktail spoiler that showed up in 1970 for the aptly named (and autographed) Mark Donahue Javelin. Apparently the original plan called for this special-edition machine to be based on SST models only, but standard Javelin versions also were sold.

Large ducktail bodywork highlighted 1970's other specialty, the Mark Donahue Javelin, named for AMC's ace Trans-Am driver. Donahue's signature even appeared on that race-ready rear spoiler, appropriately so because he designed it. All examples apparently were supposed to be SST Javelins, but some were not. Ram-air too was promised but failed to show in some cases. A 360 four-barrel was standard, the 390 optional.

New for 1970, too, was the Rebel Machine, a midsize muscle car equipped with a 390 V-8 pumped up to 340 horsepower. Finding those 15 extra ponies was simply a matter of improving intake and exhaust flow, with the former aided by a vacuum-controlled ram-air hood scoop that simply couldn't be missed. Heavy-duty cooling also was standard, as were power front discs, E60 Goodyears on 15x7 rally rims, and a beefed suspension that relied on stiff station wagon springs in back—which, according to ads, gave the Machine "a raked, just mowed the lawn look."

The Machine's image was typically patriotic, at least early on. All at first were done in Frost White paint complemented by Electric Blue accents and red striping Once this initial supply ran out, customers began finding Machines done in any 1970 Rebel color contrasted with silver striping and a blacked-out hood.

AMC designers also had proposed a decal for this car that depicted a "hip-type cat" riding a gear like a unicycle and holding a protest sign announcing "Up with the Rebel Machine." Kenosha killjoys, however, shot this "anti-establishment" idea down, resulting in the less controversial labels found on the fenders and glove box that simply read "The Machine."

HOT OFF THE PRESS: 1970 PLYMOUTH AAR 'CUDA

"If you look at the AAR 'Cuda as a ready-made street rod, what you see begins to make sense."

Car and Driver, *July 1970*

HOT OFF THE PRESS: 1970 FORD TORINO COBRA

"The fastback Cobra version of Ford's new Torino chassis makes little pretense at being anything but a single-minded car, just as the optional Cobra Jet engine with Drag Pack leaves little doubt as to what it's all about."

Car and Driver, *December 1969*

HOT OFF THE PRESS: 1970 MERCURY CYCLONE SPOILER

"The Spoiler is fat for both show and go. [It] has a deck-mounted foil and valance-mounted spoiler. Additional exterior trim sets [it] off and earmarks it as a supercar for certain."

Terry Cook, Car Craft, *September 1969*

MOTOR OF THE YEAR: 1970 CHEVROLET 454 TURBO JET LS6

Type	OHV Mk IV big-block w/chrome dress-up
Displacement	454 cubic inches
Bore	4.25 inches
Stroke	4.00 inches
Horsepower	450 at 5,600 rpm
Torque	500 at 3,600 rpm
Compression	11.25:1
Fuel delivery	780-cfm Holley 4-barrel carburetor on low-rise aluminum intake
Air cleaner	3 available: open-element, dual-snorkel w/chrome-plated lid, Cowl Induction type w/ZL2 hood option
Ignition	Delco-Remy single-point distributor w/heavy-duty points, springs & weights
Cooling	heavy-duty radiator w/2.70-inch thick core (1.26-inch core on L34 and LS5 radiators)
Cylinder block	heavy-duty cast-iron w/4-bolt main bearing caps & provision for external oiling system
Crankshaft	Tuftrided cross-drilled forged SAE 5140 chrome-moly steel
Connecting rods	Magnafluxed forged-steel with 7/16-inch bolts
Pistons	TRW forged-aluminum
Cam	mechanical w/316 degrees duration on intake, 302 degrees on exhaust
Rocker ratio	1.70:1
Cylinder heads	cast-iron closed-chamber w/rectangular ports
Valve sizes	2.19-inch intakes, 1.72-inch exhausts (w/dual valve springs)
Valve lift	0.512 inch
Exhaust system	cast-iron rectangular-port manifolds

HOT OFF THE PRESS: 1970 AMC REBEL MACHINE

"The Rebel Machine...has to be a put-on of the put-ons. But don't be fooled. The put-on is only skin deep. For $3,300 to $3,400 you can get a machine that's pure guts. The Machine performs like a champ, both in straight-out acceleration and excellent handling."

Bill Sanders, Motor Trend, *November 1969*

HOT OFF THE PRESS: 1970 DODGE CHALLENGER R/T

"Hey fella, you want to buy a body that'll upstage your 42-D girlfriend in a see-through? Could you use a street-stock, smooth-idling mill that'll pull the hide off a rhinoceros? How would you like a two-door outdoor living room that pampers you like an anxious stewardess?"

Sports Car Graphic, *November 1969*

CHAPTER 8

1971 THE SQUEEZE IS OFF

COMPRESSION CUTS REIN IN HORSEPOWER

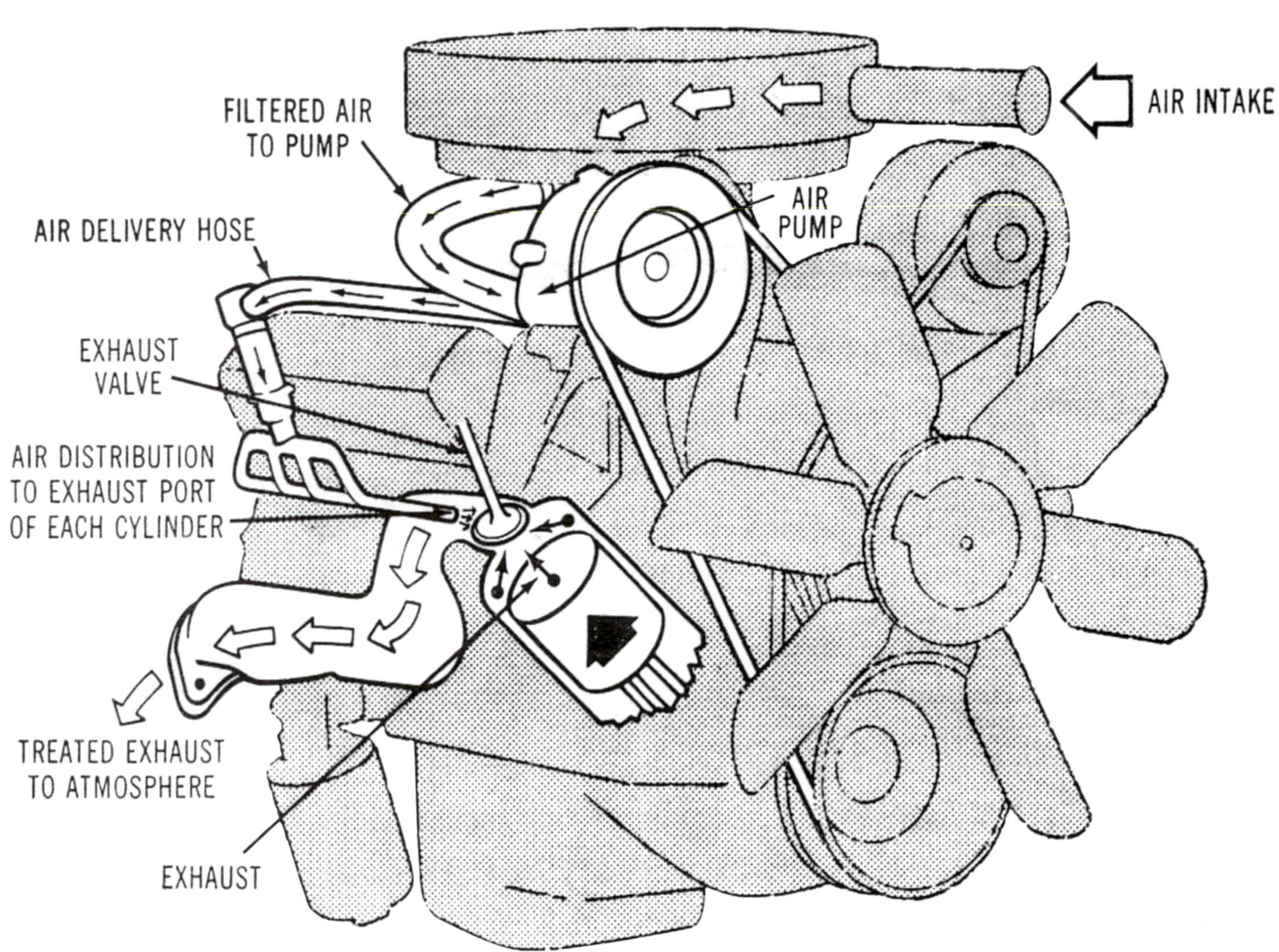

Like Ford's Thermactor, General Motors Air Injection Reactor (A.I.R., shown here) pumped ambient atmosphere into the exhaust flow to help further burn escaping hydrocarbons. A.I.R. pumps debuted on California-marketed models in 1966; they were optional that year on cars sold in other states.

What the internal combustion process spits out has never been good for any living thing, breathing or otherwise, especially so when these spent gases accumulate in massive concentrations in massive metropolitan areas. Like Los Angeles. Pacific Coasters had become well aware of the problems presented by too many cars in too small an area by the early 1950s. Crop damage in Southern California due to "smog" had been detected as early as 1944, and within 15 years state leaders were loudly calling for ways to cure this growing plague, the product of automotive hydrocarbon emissions plus prolonged sunlight exposure.

Detroit's earliest response was the positive crankcase ventilation system, developed by General Motors' AC Division in September 1961. After that date, all cars sold in California were equipped with PCV valves, which rerouted internal engine fumes back into the carburetor to be burned, as opposed to wafting

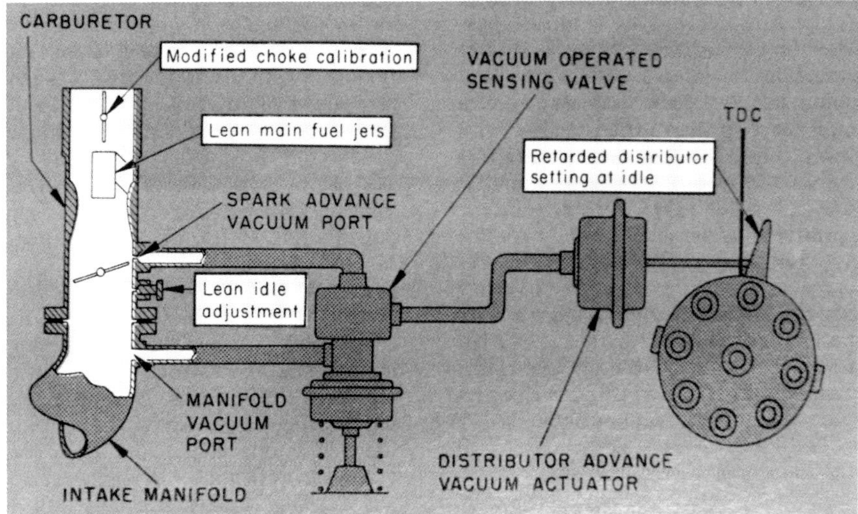

Left: Chrysler's early attempts to curb emissions worked from the intake side, not the exhaust like rival air pumps. While cheaper to manufacture, this "Cleaner Air Package" was criticized by some because it required more maintenance compared to Ford, GM, and AMC designs.

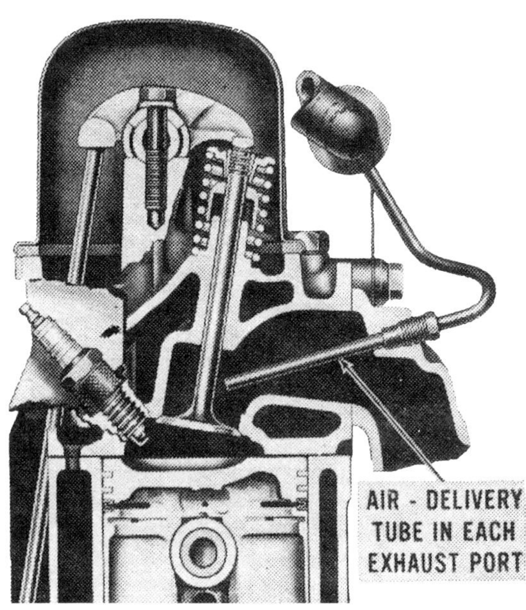

Above: American Motors' early emissions control system was called "Air-Guard" and worked much like Ford and GM's air pumps.

directly into the atmosphere via those obsolete road-draft tubes. PCV valves then became the norm on all American cars two years later.

California lawmakers at the same time began focusing in on the real root of the smog dilemma, resulting in this country's first limits on tailpipe emissions, applicable to all cars sold in their state beginning with the 1966 model year. Initial goals involved cutting said emissions by roughly half.

To meet these standards, Ford created its Thermactor system, an air-pump design that injected ambient atmosphere (and thus extra oxygen) into the exhaust flow directly outside the port to aid the additional burning of escaping hydrocarbons. GM also chose this route, using an Air Injector Reactor (A.I.R.), as did American Motors, calling its unit "Air-Guard." In all three cases, the pump featured an articulating-vane arrangement originally developed by GM's Saginaw Steering Gear Division.

Less costly but reportedly more maintenance-intensive was Chrysler's Cleaner Air Package (CAP), which reduced emissions by maximizing the burn inside the cylinders. CAP consisted of a leaner-jetted carburetor and a special distributor that automatically advanced the spark on deceleration to better handle the wasteful flood of fuel entering the combustion chamber upon throttle-down. The state's Motor Vehicle Pollution Control Board certified it for use in California early in 1965, followed by the three rival air-pumps in July.

While this equipment did help California cars meet those 1966 standards, it brought along a few downsides. Warm-up operation became more of a hassle, fuel economy fell off, and throttle response suffered. According to *Car Life*, there was "something amiss in Thermactor-equipped models," which tended "to 'run out of breath' some 1,000-1,500 rpm before they should." "It would seem [Ford's] adoption of the [this] system may have been done in too great a rush," continued that report. "As usual, the customer gets the ultimately frayed end of the stick—this time in a loss of performance." Car buyers out west were the first to feel that loss, but they weren't alone for long.

Addressing emissions issues at the federal level dated back to Washington's Air Pollution Control Act of 1955, which simply provided for research to

1971 CHEVROLET CHEVELLE SS

CONSTRUCTION: body on perimeter-rail frame
MODEL AVAILABILITY: hardtop & convertible
PRICE: RPO Z15 cost $357
WHEELBASE: 112 inches
WEIGHT: 3,670 pounds (small-block hardtop)
SUSPENSION: heavy-duty F41; coil springs & 1.125-inch stabilizer bar, front; coil springs & 0.875-inch stabilizer bar, rear
STEERING: manual (24:1) recirculating ball, std; power-assist, optional
WHEELS: 15x7 five-spoke (Camaro type)
TIRES: F60x15
BRAKES: power-assisted 11-inch discs, front; 9.5-inch drums, rear
ENGINE: L65 245-hp 350-cid Turbo Fire V-8 w/Rochester 2-barrel carburetor, L48 270-hp 350-cid Turbo Fire V-8 w/Rochester 4-barrel carburetor, LS3 402-cid Turbo Jet 400 V-8, or LS 5 454-cid Turbo Jet V-8
TRANSMISSION: 3-speed manual, std; 4-speed & Turbo Hydra-matic, optional (LS5 V-8 only available w/either M22 4-speed & TH-400 automatic)
AXLE RATIO: 3.31:1

BLACK FLAGGED

Major proof that Ford was preparing to quit the performance game came on November 20, 1970, when sales group V.P. Mathew McLaughlin announced his corporation's pull-out from all motorsport activities, save for some limited support of drag racing and off-road activities. "The greatest peacetime non-governmental competitive effort to occur in this century has quietly drawn to a close—the victim of progress," lamented *Motor Trend's* Jim Brokaw.

Henry Ford II, the same man who had denounced the AMA racing ban in 1962 then poured tens of millions of dollars into his own personal vendetta with Enzo Ferrari on tracks around the world, almost overnight rededicated himself, at all costs, to environmental concerns. "In 1969, Henry II pledged the assets of the company to help whip the pollution problem," continued Brokaw. "He wasn't fooling. Shortly after his speech, Ford announced the allocation of $18 million for the installation of anti-smoke equipment on the factories' smoke stacks. Two months later, [1970's] racing budget was drastically reduced by about 75 percent."

"Ford also said performance advertising is now going to be scanned to ensure it's not offensive to lawmakers and safety experts," added Charles Malone in *Car Life's* March 1970 issue. "It's clear management has concluded that sales produced by racing probably will not be worth the bad publicity and aggravation building up against musclecars and street racing."

More big news followed in September 1969 after Henry II fired his prized president, Bunkie Knudsen, whose career had always seemed tied by an umbilical to the great American muscle car. "Knudsen likes performance and dabbles in it, some say, more than he should," said California Ford dealer Chuck Foulger not long after the former GM exec defected to Dearborn in February 1968. "But he knows what the market wants and he knows how to accomplish his goals. I think Bunkie's dynamic thinking is just what Ford needs." Then, yes. Not so much a year later.

The main man behind Ford's Total Performance campaign in 1963, Lee Iacocca had changed his mind as well by 1969. During the late-1950s, when his company was falling behind high-powered GM rivals, Iacocca openly supported keeping racing parts available despite the AMA ban. "[He] knew what sold cars to young people in those days," added Jim Brokaw. "And he knew, as did anyone who bothered to note birth statistics from 1946 on, who was shortly going to engulf the market, a veritable army of young, aggressive customers."

A decade later, however, those buyers had grown older and wiser, and market-minded Iacocca was paying close attention to changing attitudes. In his reversed opinion, not only did racing generate bad press, it now also represented a bad investment. "It's no secret that Iacocca questions the value returned for each racing dollar [spent]," explained a January 1971 *Motor Trend* report. "It is also no secret that deposed former president Knudsen was a staunch supporter of racing, and anything that was in to Bunkie is currently out."

Out too was Special Vehicles Division director Jacque Passino, who resigned the day before Thanksgiving in 1970. The SVD remained, but was reduced and refocused toward safety/emissions research and development. Kar Kraft, home to the Boss 429 Mustang, quietly went away after the last Shotgun-motor pony car rolled off its line in January 1970, and the parts pipeline to the Holman-Moody race shop down in North Carolina was shut off as well.

Un, deux, trois...

That's how Autolite-equipped Fords finished in the 24-hour race at Le Mans, France: 1, 2, 3.

The famous French long-distance race had an American accent this year. A U.S. car not only won the 24-hour race for the first time, but two more finished second and third. All three were Autolite-equipped Ford GT-40 Mark II sports racers. Sacre bleu! You could almost hear traditions shattering. But at Autolite we make a habit of helping shatter old ideas, of breaking new trails. So it's not surprising that the winning Le Mans Fords used complete Autolite ignition systems—including Autolite spark plugs, wire and cable, batteries, and alternators. We helped pioneer the successful rear engine racing car at Indianapolis. (We also introduced spark plugs with the exclusive Power Tips that clean themselves while you drive. And vibration-guarded batteries with sta•ful reservoirs to minimize damage through water loss.) We like riding with winners, something Autolite products have been doing a lot lately. Why don't you go Autolite, too? You're always right with Autolite.

✦AUTOLITE

Ford

MOTOR TREND / NOVEMBER 1966 85

Ford Motor Company literally was on top of the world in 1966 after a trio of 427-powered GT40s finished 1-2-3 at Le Mans that summer. Within four years, however, the Dearborn gang was all but done with racing.

In for 1971 were Ford's latest low-buck compacts, which according to some Dearborn officials weren't meant only for cash-challenged customers. "I would not be at all surprised to see the Maverick-type car, the Pinto with a lot of goodies on it become the hot things at the dragstrip," said Ford general manager John Naughton during a *Motor Trend* interview late in 1970. A hot Pinto? Clearly Naughton was playing with a different deck—and he wasn't through dealing it.

"A lot of people think the demise of the muscle car is at hand. I don't believe that because I don't think the American male will all of a sudden turn off his love for performance. There may be a complete redefinition by size, by category, by weight, by horsepower, by type car, but kids are going to continue to tinker with cars." As long as they had something to tinker with, that is.

Others weren't so optimistic about the future of Blue Oval brand playtoys. "This is probably the last chance you'll have to buy a machine of this kind," explained a *Sports Car Graphic* review of Ford's last great muscle Mustang, 1971's Boss 351. "Ford is now diverting racing dollars into solving safety and pollution problems and [satisfying] government mandates. We have heard that all ['72] Fords will be detuned to run on regular fuel. That means lower compression. The current exhaust-popping 11:1 [ratios] will probably be lowered 15 to 20 percent, and the only way to regain the lost power is through expensive modifications—which will probably become illegal. Perhaps we'll just learn to live with the situation, like war and taxes. But we have a few years left. We might as well live it up while we can."

For Ford fans, 1971 represented the end of the road.

"consider" the situation. America's initial Clean Air Act followed in 1963 and began defining air-quality standards. Amending that edict, 1965's Motor Vehicle Air Pollution Control Act then established the first nation-wide smog-reduction deadline. By 1968, all of Detroit's products would start curbing emissions or else. Standard that year for models sold in all 50 states were the pollution controls formerly mandated only on "California-equipped" cars.

More than one critic felt this new coast-to-coast directive was demanding too much too soon. "Technology is not yet up to [controlling emissions] without considerable expense, reduced performance, and lower gas mileage," claimed Joseph Callahan, *Automotive News'* engineering editor, in 1966.

Indeed, Detroit's automakers reportedly spent $500 million on the way to meeting that 1968 target date, and these costs were typically passed right on to the consumer, adding about $50 to the average car's bottom line that year. What buyers got for those fifty extra bucks was a reported 80 percent reduction in hydrocarbon emissions, another 70 percent in carbon monoxide. But that was just the beginning.

Federal lawmakers in 1968 also proposed that hydrocarbon emissions be reduced another 30 percent by 1970. And early in 1969, California legislators turned their attentions to oxides of nitrogen (NOx), with the goal being to add further controls for these emissions by 1971.

Also an unsavory ingredient in the smog recipe, NOx results when ambient atmosphere—consisting of 80 percent nitrogen, 20 percent oxygen—is subjected to the ultra high heats and pressures inside a combustion chamber. Reducing these emissions is more or less simply a matter of cutting chamber temps, and to that end car buyers were introduced to the Exhaust Gas Recirculation (EGR) valve in 1972. As its name implied, this unit delivered some burnt by-products back into those chambers, in effect diluting the fuel/air charge with non-combustible matter. This in turn gave spark plugs less material to ignite, meaning less heat was released. Presto—lower oxides of nitrogen emissions.

Even stricter standards (scheduled for 1975) were mandated by another revised Clean Air Act in 1970. And in December that year, President Richard Nixon signed an executive order establishing the Environmental Protection Agency, an office tasked with, among other things, actually enforcing and policing those standards. EPA certification testing began shortly thereafter; any engine that failed to make this grade was sent home with a note stating simply "not for public sale."

Additional EPA actions early on involved the eradication of leaded fuels, both to eliminate deadly by-products and pave the way for the next new wave of emissions controls, consisting of catalytic converters (see chapter 11). Leaded fuels fouled "cats," hence the need to switch to unleaded gas, which in those days was primarily available in low-octane flavors. Those diminished octane ratings and high compression ratios of course didn't mix, either, meaning Detroit had no choice but to drastically cut combustion-chamber squeezes across the board.

In 1970, GM announced that 90 percent of its early 1971 models would be able to run on 91-octane low-lead gasoline; 100 percent by the end of the year. Chrysler reported 93 percent of its 1971 products would do the same, with that remaining 7

1971 PONTIAC GTO

CONSTRUCTION: body on perimeter-rail frame
MODEL AVAILABILITY: hardtop & convertible
PRICE: $3,446, hardtop; $3,676, convertible
WHEELBASE: 112 inches
WEIGHT: 3,619 pounds (hardtop)
SUSPENSION: heavy-duty with coil springs & 1.125-inch stabilizer bar, front; solid axle w/coil spring & 0.875-inch stabilizer bar, rear
STEERING: manual recirculating ball, std; power-assist, optional
WHEELS: 14x6 stamped-steel
TIRES: G70 fiberglass-belted
BRAKES: 9.5-inch drums, front & rear; power-assisted 10.94-inch front discs, optional
ENGINE: 300-hp L78 400-cid V-8 w/Quadra-jet 4-barrel carburetor, std; 325-hp L75 455 and 455 HO V-8s, optional
TRANSMISSION: Hurst-shifted 3-speed, std; 4-speed & TH-400 automatic, optional
AXLE RATIO: 3.55:1, std (3.23:1included w/air conditioning)

1971 OLDSMOBILE 4-4-2

CONSTRUCTION: body on perimeter-rail frame
MODEL AVAILABILITY: hardtop & convertible (W-25 air-induction hood, optional)
PRICE: 3,835 pounds (hardtop)
WHEELBASE: 112 inches
WEIGHT: $3,551, hardtop, $3,742, convertible
SUSPENSION: heavy-duty Rallye; coil springs & 0.937-inch stabilizer bar, front; coil springs & 0.875-inch stabilizer bar, rear
STEERING: manual recirculating ball, std; variable-ratio power-assist, optional
WHEELS: 14x7 stamped-steel; Super Stock rims, optional
TIRES: G70x14 Wide Oval
BRAKES: 9.5-inch drums, front & rear; 11-inch front discs, optional (std w/W-30)
ENGINE: 270-hp 455-cid Rocket V-8 w/Quadra-jet 4-barrel carburetor; 455-cid W-30 V-8, optional (W-25 hood included w/W-30)
TRANSMISSION: Hurst-shifted heavy-duty 3-speed manual, std; 4-speed & TH-400 automatic, optional
AXLE RATIO: 3.23:1, std

FAMILY TIES:
OLDS W-30 AIR INDUCTION

Apparently the good Doctor Oldsmobile couldn't bear the thought of cutting a hole in the hood of his beloved 4-4-2 in 1966. When it came time to put the "outside" in the W-30 Outside Air Induction package, he pooh-poohed a typical scooped bonnet, opting instead to rob his wife's laundry room back home. Or so it seemed. Two flexible hoses that looked an awful lot like dryer ducting ran from a chrome-plated air cleaner (called a shroud) down to openings in the front bumper normally reserved for turn signals, which were moved inboard. In those lamps' original locations went a pair of black plastic scoops that protruded slightly outward, inspiring more than one wise-crack about resemblances to Hoover vacuum cleaners. The joke, however, was on the competition once the L69 400's three Rochester two-barrels began sucking in cooler, denser ambient atmosphere. Triple-carburetion didn't carry over for 1967's W-30 (it was superseded by a single Rochester Quadra-jet), but that dryer ductwork did. And an updated Cutlass facade (now featuring "blinkers" mounted between the dual headlamps, not below) mandated new inlets, split scoops that featured two openings each, one on top of the turn signal, the other underneath. While flexible hoses continued directing outside air into W-30 V-8s (as well as their W-31 and W-32 siblings) in 1968 and 1969, the plastic inlets were moved below the front bumper, putting them in harm's way should a jaywalking varmint dash in front or an immovable curb stand too high. Finally, in 1970, Doc O introduced his W-25 hood with conventional ram-air ducting that sealed to a foam "doughnut" atop the 455 V-8's air cleaner. This twin-scooped fiberglass lid became a standard W-30 feature; it was optional on other 4-4-2s built up through 1972. By the way, Dr. Oldsmobile didn't actually make the scene until 1969—please forgive the poetic license practiced here.

W-30 air intakes were located in the F-85's front bumper where turn signals normally resided in 1966. Those lamps were moved inboard to make room for the plastic ducts. *Mike Mueller*

New W-30 intakes appeared in 1967, this due to styling changes that required the use of a "split" scoop located between revised dual headlamps. Featuring two openings each—one above the turn signal, one below—these smaller scoops did not stand out in a crowd as much as the 1966 design. *Mike Mueller*

W-30 intake ducts (at top above dual-snorkel air cleaner) were relocated below the bumpers of 1968's 4-4-2, just where you wouldn't want them when parking against large curbs. Also appearing here is the W-30's high-perf cam, aluminum six-blade clutch fan, heat-treaded valve springs with dampers, and those ever-present "dryer hose" ram-air tubes. *Mike Mueller*

All that ductwork was no longer needed in 1970 thanks to the addition of Oldsmobile's fiberglass W-25 hood, which featured two large scoops. The W-30 air cleaner now sealed to this hood's underside, allowing a more direct route for outside air to find its way into the Rochester Quadra-jet below. *Mike Mueller*

percent made up of Dodges and Plymouths equipped with the 426 Hemi and tri-cab 440 V-8s, two of Detroit's few remaining high-compression survivors.

Lower compression in turn limited horsepower, leaving America's muscle-builders no choice but to start axing high-perf equipment. Early victims included Chevrolet's LS6 Chevelle, initially planned for 1971 in low-compression 425-horsepower form then quietly cancelled before John Q. Public could get his hands on one. Another hot A-body, Oldsmobile's W-31 Cutlass, also was road-tested by journalists late in 1970 then rubbed out before 1971 production began. This giant-killing small-block may have fooled the insurance man but couldn't evade the exhaust-pipe sniffer.

Following his LS6 test in the spring of 1970, *Hot Rod's* Steve Kelly came away suitably thrilled—as anyone would be after riding herd over 450 horses. But he also recognized the obvious. "This could be the last [supercar] because strict legislation concerning emission output will render this type of car worthless. Nonleaded gasoline will be mandatory in California late in 1971, and one year later the entire United States will follow. Unless some other way of using this kind of fuel is found, compression ratios of 8.5 to 9.0:1 will be the order of engine operation. We savored every moment of this car, for the memory may have to last a long time."

Too true.

1971 DODGE CHARGER R/T

CONSTRUCTION: unitized body/frame
MODEL AVAILABILITY: hardtop
PRICE: $3,777
WHEELBASE: 115 inches
WEIGHT: 3,685 pounds
SUSPENSION: heavy-duty; 0.92-inch torsion bars & 0.88-inch stabilizer bar, front; solid axle w/leaf springs, rear
STEERING: manual (24:1) recirculating ball; 18.7:1 power-assist, optional (required w/Hemi)
WHEELS: 14x6; 15x7, optional
TIRES: G70x14; G60x15, optional
BRAKES: heavy-duty 11-inch drums, front & rear; power-assisted 10.97-inch front discs, optional
ENGINE: 440-cid Magnum V-8 w/Carter 4-barrel, std; 440 Six Pack & 426 Hemi, optional
TRANSMISSION: 4-speed manual or Torqueflite automatic
AXLE RATIO: 3.23:1

1971 DODGE CHARGER SUPER BEE

CONSTRUCTION: unitized body/frame
MODEL AVAILABILITY: hardtop
PRICE: $3,245
WHEELBASE: 115 inches
WEIGHT: 3,700 pounds
SUSPENSION: heavy-duty; torsion bars & 0.88-inch stabilizer bar, front; solid axle w/leaf springs, rear
STEERING: manual (24:1) recirculating ball; 18.7:1 power-assist, optional (required w/Hemi)
WHEELS: 14x6, std; 15x7 optional
TIRES: F70x14
BRAKES: 10-inch drums, front & rear; power-assisted 10.97-inch front discs, optional
ENGINE: 300-hp 383-cid V-8 w/Carter 4-barrel carburetor; 340-cid V-8, 440-cid V-8, 440 Six Pack & 426 Hemi, optional
TRANSMISSION: 3-speed manual, std; 4-speed & Torqueflite automatic, optional
AXLE RATIO: 3.23:1

1971 DODGE DEMON 340

CONSTRUCTION: unitized body/frame
MODEL AVAILABILITY: sport coupe
PRICE: $2,721
WHEELBASE: 108 inches
WEIGHT: 3,165 pounds
SUSPENSION: heavy-duty; torson bars & 0.88-inch stabilizer bar, front; solid axle w/leaf springs, rear
STEERING: manual (28.7:1) recirculating ball, std; power-assist, optional
WHEELS: 14x5.5
TIRES: E70x14
BRAKES: 10-inch drums, front & rear; power-assisted 10.79-inch front discs, optional
ENGINE: 340-cid V-8 w/Carter 4-barrel carburetor
TRANSMISSION: 3-speed manual, std; 4-speed & Torqueflite automatic, optional
AXLE RATIO: 3.23:1

Only one SS equipment group, RPO Z15, was listed for 1971's Chevelle, which now featured single headlamps up front. New standard Super Sport stuff included 15x7 five-spoke Camaro sport wheels wearing F60 rubber. Four engines were available this year, two 350 small-blocks and two Mk IV big-blocks, including the LS5 454. All models simply wore "SS" fender badges save for the LS5 renditions, which kept their "SS 454" identification.

HOT OFF THE PRESS: 1971 CHEVROLET CAMARO SS 396

"It took a lot of work to keep the SS396 Camaro alive for 1971, and figuring how far down in power it dropped, the result is surprising."
Steve Kelly, Hot Rod, *July 1971*

HOT OFF THE PRESS: 1971 CHEVROLET CHEVELLE SS 350

"[The] biggest selling image car of them all, the SS in basic form combines family usefulness and above average performance."
Road Test, *June 1971*

CHEVROLET

Only one SS equipment group, RPO Z15, was listed for 1971's Chevelle and could be paired with small-block power for the first time in six years. New standard features included 15x7 five-spoke Camaro sport wheels wearing F60 rubber, but gone were those revered "SS 396" badges. Simple "SS" identification was applied in small- or big-block applications, unless the LS5 was installed. "SS 454" tags remained for Chevrolet's biggest big-block.

Rated at 245 horsepower, the entry-level L65 350 featured 8.5:1 compression, as well as two items Chevelle SS buyers also hadn't seen since 1965: a two-barrel carburetor and single exhaust. The 270-horsepower L48 350 relied on 8.5:1 compression and a single tailpipe, too, but traded the L65's two-barrel for a four-holer. At the top of the list was the aforementioned LS5 454, now rated at 365 horsepower, and the 300-horsepower Turbo Jet 400, which actually displaced 402 cubic inches.

Only minor updates appeared for 1971's Camaro, and the Super Sport and Rally Sport versions continued on essentially unchanged. A compression cut to 9:1 dropped output down to 330 horsepower for 1971's Z28, which came standard with front and rear spoilers.

An SS454 Monte Carlo encored for 1971, and Nova SS also continued, this time with only one available engine, the L48 small-block. Basically the same 350-powered SS Nova rolled over into 1972, an available six-cylinder returned to the Z26 package in 1973, and the last of the breed came and went rather meekly three years later.

Left: A mildly revised nose and new hood (with more dramatic scoops moved up toward its leading edge) appeared for 1971's GTO. This was the last year for both a convertible GTO and the Judge. New on 1971's options list were Honeycomb wheels, available in both 14x7 and 15x7 sizes. Both versions returned in 1972 but with different center caps. Pontiac's optional Rally II wheel also was offered in two sizes for 1971, in this case 14x6 and 15x7.

PONTIAC

Featuring humble 8.2:1 compression, GTO's base L78 400 was advertised at 300 horsepower in 1971. In place of 1970's Ram Air III and IV options was the 325-horsepower L75 455, available only with the TH-400 automatic. The top option was the LS5 455 HO, which was installed in all 1971 Judges. Rated at 335 horsepower, the HO featured round-port heads and free-flowing exhaust manifolds similar to those used by the Ram Air IV. An aluminum intake was included, too, and ram-air induction was optional. New on the options list were snazzy Honeycomb wheels, which featured molded urethane centers backed by a conventional steel structure.

All Firebirds (except Trans Am) received fake fender vents this year, and Formula could've been dressed up further by adding the T/A's rear spoiler at extra cost. The base Formula V-8 was now the 255-horsepower L30 350. The L78 400 was available, as were the L75 and the LS5 455s. Optional was the Y96 Handling Package, which featured the Trans Am's springs, stabilizer bars, and F60 raised-white-letter tires on 15-inch honeycomb wheels.

Polycast Honeycomb wheels were now standard for 1971's Trans Am, again available only in Polar White and Lucerne Blue. Familiar Rally II wheels remained on the options list, and high-back Vega buckets appeared inside in place of the low-back seats seen previously. The only available engine was the 455 HO, backed by either a Hurst-shifted close-ratio four-speed or TH-400 automatic.

Above: Pontiac's 350-cid V-8, rated at 255 horsepower, became the Formula's base engine in 1971.

HOT OFF THE PRESS: 1971 OLDSMOBILE 4-4-2

"Anyone who supposes that the '71 442 has significantly less actual power and performance than the '70 model because the 455 engine has been de-rated is in for a large surprise. From a standstill through about 60 mph, this car has to rank as one of the liveliest automatic equipped production vehicles we've driven in several years."

Road Test, *May 1971*

Left: Both Pontiac's familiar Rally II wheels and the new Honeycomb rims were available for 1971's Trans Am. The only available engine this year was the 455 HO, rated at 335 horsepower.

HOT OFF THE PRESS: 1971 PLYMOUTH ROAD RUNNER

"They're going to be eating their livers, those other car company guys, when they see the new Road Runner. It has a look born of purpose and muscles where the others have flab."

Car and Driver, *October 1970*

1971 PLYMOUTH ROAD RUNNER

CONSTRUCTION: unitized body/frame
MODEL AVAILABILITY: hardtop
PRICE: $3,147
WHEELBASE: 115 inches
WEIGHT: 3,640
SUSPENSION: heavy-duty; torsion bars & 0.88-inch stabilizer bar, front; solid axle w/leaf springs, rear
STEERING: manual recirculating ball; power-assist, optional
WHEELS: 14x6
TIRES: F70x14
BRAKES: 10-inch drums, front & rear; power-assisted 10.79-inch front discs, optional
ENGINE: 300-hp 383-cid V-8 w/Carter 4-barrel carburetor, std; 340-cid V-8, 440+6 & 426 Hemi, optional
TRANSMISSION: 4-speed manual or Torqueflite automatic
AXLE RATIO: 3.23:1

HOT OFF THE PRESS: 1971 PLYMOUTH GTX

"In an era when the term 'Super Car' is being whispered rather than shouted through the halls of Detroit, Plymouth bucks the trend by proudly announcing the birth of its all-new GTX."

Car and Driver, *November 1970*

Oldsmobile's 4-4-2 stood tall as an individual model for one last time in 1971. Only two bodies were offered this year: Cutlass Holiday hardtop and Cutlass Supreme convertible. *Mike Mueller*

OLDSMOBILE

This was the last year for a stand-alone 4-4-2 model, and only two varieties were offered: a Holiday hardtop and Cutlass Supreme convertible. The W-30 remained, but those darned compression cuts helped drop output to 300 horsepower. The 4-4-2's standard 455 V-8 was rated at 270 horsepower this year.

FAMILY TIES: FORD "NASA" HOOD

Ford's ram-air Mustangs in 1971 were fitted with a new hood featuring two prominent scoops. Promotional people curiously called this a "NASA hood," undoubtedly because they figured many more Americans could identify with the National Aeronautics and Space Administration compared to its predecessor, the National Advisory Committee for Aeronautics, founded in March 1915 to promote and practice flight research. Among this pioneering organization's many innovations was the aptly named "NACA duct," an air inlet specially designed to maximize flow in high-speed situations—say, like flying at the speed of sound. Once discovered by race car builders in the 1960s, NACA ducts began showing up in all locations where brakes (and drivers) needed cooling and hoods needed scooping. Dissolved in October 1958, NACA was long forgotten by the time those two fully functional NACA-style openings were added to the second-generation Mach 1 hood. But practically every human on this planet (and certainly all those on the moon) at that time were well aware of NASA. Realizing this, Ford's label-makers morphed the NACA duct into the NASA scoop. All that aside, the twin NACA ducts on 1971's NASA hood funneled cooler air into a plastic housing on the hood's underside. This housing, in turn, was sealed to the air cleaner by a large rubber "doughnut" similar to the arrangement used atop the 1968's 428 Cobra Jet. Vacuum-controlled diaphragms inside the plastic ductwork opened up at full throttle to allow denser outside atmosphere to flow directly to the air cleaner, which again used a conventional snorkel to breathe in well-heated underhood air during normal operation. Whatever the name, the system sure sucked—in a good way.

FAMILY TIES: FORD BOSS V-8s, 1969–71

	1969-70 BOSS 302	**1969-70 BOSS 429**	**1971 BOSS 351**
Type	modified Windsor V-8	modified 385-series V-8	HO Cleveland V-8
Displacement	302 cid	429 cid	351 cid
Bore	4.00 inches	4.36 inches	4.00 inches
Stroke	3.00 inches	3.59 inches	3.50 inches
Horsepower	290 @ 5,800	375 @ 5,200	330 @ 5,400
Torque	290 @ 4,300	450 @ 3,400	370 @ 4,000
Compression	10.5:1	10.5:1	11:1
Fuel delivery	780-cfm Holley 4-barrel,	735-cfm Holley 4-barrel	750-cfm Autolite 4-barrel
Intake manifold	aluminum high-rise	aluminum high-rise	aluminum dual-plane
Ram-air	optional in 1970	standard	standard
Ignition	dual-point distributor, Autolite rev-limiter	dual-point distributor Autolite rev-limiter, 1970	dual-point distributor Autolite rev-limiter
Cooling	5-blade flex fan	7-blade fan, 1969 5-blade flex fan, 1970	heavy-duty w/flex fan
Oiling	high-capacity pump, baffled oil pan & windage tray	high-capacity pump, 8-quart oil pan & oil cooler	high-capacity pump
Cylinder block	cast-iron, 4-bolt mains	cast iron, 4 bolt mains	cast-iron, 4-bolt mains
Crankshaft	forged-steel, hardened & cross-drilled	forged-steel, balanced	high nodular cast-iron
Connecting rods	forged-steel, 3/8-inch bolts	forged-steel	forged-steel, 3/8-inch bolts, shot-peened & magnafluxed
Pistons	forged-aluminum TRW	forged-aluminum	forged aluminum pop-up
Cam	mechanical	hydraulic, "S" & early "T" mechanical, later "T"	mechanical
Duration, intake & exhaust	290 degrees	300 degrees	324 degrees
Overlap	58 degrees	72 degrees	92 degrees
Rocker ratio	1.73:1	1.53:1, intake; 1.71:1, exhaust	1.73:1
Cylinder heads	cast-iron Cleveland	aluminum "semi-hemi"	cast-iron w/canted valves
Valve sizes	2.23/1.71	2.27/1.89	2.195/1.714
Valve lift	0.477/0.477	0.458/0.509	0.491/0.491

NOTE: *Valve sizes & lift are in inches, intake/exhaust*

NOTE: *Boss 302 & Boss 351 valvetrains featured canted valves, hardened pushrods w/guide-plates, screw-in rocker studs, stamped-steel rockers & single valve springs w/dampers.*

NOTE: *Early "S" Boss 429 V-8s used short, beefier connecting rods w/0.50-inch bolts; "T" engines used longer, lighter rods w/0.375-inch bolts.*

NOTE: *Boss 302 V-8s used 4-bolt bearing caps on three inner mains only; Boss 429s featured 4-bolt caps on all but the rear main; Boss 351s included 4-bolt caps on all five mains.*

Totally new "fuselage styling" appeared for Plymouth's B-body in 1971, the year Road Runner was limited to one body style only: hardtop. An available small-block V-8, the 275-horsepower 340, appeared for the first time. Plymouth also offered a rear spoiler option, and this wing could be complemented with a two-part front spoiler available by way of dealer installation. Additional new options included rear window louvers, a partial "canopy" vinyl roof, black-out tape treatment for the rear valance, and a color-keyed elastomeric front bumper.

1971 FORD MUSTANG BOSS 351

CONSTRUCTION: unitized body/frame
MODEL AVAILABILITY: SportsRoof with "NASA" ram-air hood
PRICE: $4,420
WHEELBASE: 109 inches
WEIGHT: 3,560 pounds
SUSPENSION: heavy-duty Competition package; coil springs & stabilizer bar, front; solid-axle w/leaf springs & stabilizer bar, rear; Gabriel shock absorbers (staggered in back)
STEERING: variable-ratio recirculating ball
WHEELS: 15x7 stamped-steel w/bright center caps & trim rings; 15x7 Magnum 500, optional
TIRES: F60x15 Goodyear Wide Oval
BRAKES: power-assisted 11.3-inch discs, front; 10-inch drums rear
ENGINE: 351-cid High Output (HO) V-8 w/Motorcraft 4-barrel carburetor
TRANSMISSION: Hurst-shifted 4-speed manual
AXLE RATIO: 3.91:1 in Track-Lok differential

GTX's standard hood again featured parallel vents in 1971 that contained engine identification. Enlarged "GTX" badges returned in their same locations and bucket seats reappeared as part of the basic deal. The engine trio carried over with a few minor adjustments: the standard 440 was rated at 370 horsepower, while the renamed "440+6" dropped 5 horses, too, to 385. No one dared touch the venerable Hemi's 425-horsepower advertised tag. *Mike Mueller*

BUICK

While fender badges still included engine displacement, all Gran Sport Skylarks, small- or big-block, were plainly identified on paper as "GS" models in 1971. The standard GS engine was the 350 small-block, now rated at 260 horsepower. Revised advertised outputs for the optional 455 V-8 and its Stage 1 brother were 315 and 345 horses, respectively. The GSX hardtop returned in similar fashion but now was available with either engine, 350 or 455. A column-shifted three-speed manual was standard behind the 350, and no floor-shifted examples were produced. Small-block options again included a four-speed and TH-350 automatic.

PLYMOUTH

Fresh "fuselage styling" and a shortened 115-inch wheelbase appeared for Chrysler's B-bodies in 1971, and Plymouth's midsize models all became Satellites after the Belvedere badge was dropped. Both GTX and Road Runner were offered only as hardtops this year, and they again shared hoods. New options included spoilers at both ends, rear window louvers, and a color-keyed elastomeric front bumper. New for Road Runner was an available small-block, the 275-horsepower 340. The familiar 383 big-block remained standard but lost a few horses after compression was cut to 8.5:1. Renamed "440+6," the optional triple-carb RB also dropped 5 ponies, while the Hemi remained at 425 untouchable horses. In its last year as a stand-alone model, GTX once more came standard with the 440 Super Commando, now rated at 370 horsepower.

Buick officially announced six exterior colors for 1971's GSX hardtop: Stratomist Blue, Arctic White, Lime Mist, Platinum Mist, Cortez Gold, and Bittersweet Mist. Other special-order shades were possible, too, as this example attests. *Mike Mueller*

WHAT'S THE BUZZ?

American Motors finally retired its venerable Rambler nameplate in 1969, replacing it with a badge fabulously familiar in stock car racing circles 15 years before: "Hornet." Hudson's Hornet dominated NASCAR competition up until 1954—when its parent company merged with Nash to form AMC—then rolled on through 1957 before getting the axe. Both legacies, Hudson and Nash, were shut down that year as George Romney's team opted to concentrate on Rambler, which morphed into an entire model family for 1958. Rambler American, the runt of this litter, gained some notable size in 1964 and was still wearing much the same face five years later, hence the decision to revive the breed, to remake AMC's economy car ideal. And rename it.

Price, weight, and overall size remained almost unchanged, and wheelbase even went up 2 inches, yet 1970's Hornet still qualified as an affordable compact, certainly so in base six-cylinder form. A V-8 model was offered, too, in keeping with plans to compete with a varying range of rivals.

"In introducing Hornet, we're using all the experience we've developed in designing solid quality features for smaller cars," explained AMC chairman Roy Chapin Jr. in the summer of 1969. "But we're using it to approach the small car market on a broader basis than we've ever approached it before. With Hornet the buyer can choose the kind of small car he wants to express his personal feelings. If you want an economy [model], you can have it. If you want a performance version, you can have that, too."

Meeting that latter need was Hornet SC/360, introduced for 1971. "SC" stood for "Super Coupe," a bit of a reach as far as base renditions were concerned. Standard was a 360 two-barrel V-8 (with single exhaust) backed by a floor-shifted (without console) three-speed gearbox. Slotted rally-type wheels (sans trim rings), D70 Goodyear Polyglas tires, a custom steering wheel, individual reclining seats, exterior striping, and a reflective red rear body panel also were included in the deal, priced at a tidy $2,663.

It was left to one of AMC's trademark Go Packages to transform this Clark Kent compact into a bullet-besting caped crusader, first and foremost by trading that 245-horsepower base engine for a 285-hp four-barrel-fed 360 with dual exhausts. And a big blacked-out ram-air hood scoop. And Hurst-shifted four-speed. And special handling gear.

American Motors made one last stab at specialty super car production in 1971, this time using the compact Hornet, introduced the year before. A prominent ram-air hood was optional for the Hornet SC/360. That scoop was supplied by aviation manufacturer Rockwell. *Tom Shaw*

A 245-horse 360 two-barrel V-8 was standard for the Hornet SC/360; shown here is the optional 360 four-barrel, rated at 285 horsepower. *Tom Shaw*

And in-dash tach. "Beauty rings" (for the wheels) remained missing in action, but at least the D70 rubber included in this $199 option group was adorned with trendy white lettering.

Able to break into the 14-second quarter-mile club, a Go-equipped SC/360 was capable of some serious super-hero action with only a little tinkering. *Car Craft's* test crew bolted on better tires, headers and traction bars and managed 13.78 seconds at 101.92 miles per hour on the strip.

More than one witness, then and later, could only wonder what an SC/401 might've done, but that combo surely would've never gotten off the ground in 1971 considering how strong "anti-muscle" factions had grown by then. Instead, the Kenosha crowd chose to build "a sensible alternative to the money-squeezing, insurance-strangling muscle cars of America." Even then, Hornet SC/360 still ended up a tough sell, with less than 800 finding homes—this after AMC officials reportedly called for a 10,000-unit production run.

1971 AMC HORNET SC/360

CONSTRUCTION: unitized body/frame
MODEL AVAILABILITY: Hornet sedan
PRICE: $2,663
WHEELBASE: 108 inches
WEIGHT: 3,300 pounds
SUSPENSION: coil springs & sway bar, front; solid axle w/leaf springs, rear; heavy-duty springs/shocks, optional w/ Go Package
STEERING: Saginaw manual (24:1) recirculating ball; variable-ratio power assist, optional
WHEELS: 14x6 slot-style; 14x6 spoke-style, optional
TIRES: D70x14 Polyglas (Space Saver spare included)
BRAKES: 10-inch drums, front/rear; power front discs, optional
ENGINE: 360-cid V-8 w/Motorcraft 2-barrel carburetor (4-barrel V-8, optional)
TRANSMISSION: floor-shifted 3-speed manual w/11-inch heavy-duty clutch, std.; Hurst-shifted 4-speed manual & column-controlled Shift-Command automatic trans, optional
AXLE RATIO: 3.15:1, std w/3-speed (3.54:1, optional); 2.87:1, std w/optional automatic trans & base V-8 (3.15:1, optional); 3.54:1, std w/4-speed (3.15:1 & 3.91:1, optional); 3.15:1, std w/auto trans & 4-barrel V-8 (3.54:1, optional)

Right: Plymouth's 1971 E-body was quickly identified by its four headlights, two more than the 1970 models carried. Three body styles were offered this year: a bargain-basement coupe with a 198-cid slant-six, a Barracuda hardtop with a 225 six, and a sexy convertible in its last year. The three-tiered model line rolled over, with the base Barracuda (coupe or hardtop) followed by the classy Gran Coupe, and the performance-packed 'Cuda fitted with its twin-scooped hood. Hemi 'Cuda remained the Plymouth pony car king. *Mike Mueller*

Above: The most affordable member of Plymouth's Rapid Transit System returned for 1971 in nearly identical fashion save for some slight image enhancement on the outside and a Carter Thermo-Quad four-barrel in place of the AVS carburetor previously found under the hood. The 340 small-block was still rated at 275 horsepower despite a minor dip in compression, the addition of slightly more restrictive exhaust manifolds, and the inclusion of the evaporative control system seen before only on California-sold models. Most mechanicals carried from 1970 save for front disc brakes, which moved onto the options list.

Above: Front and rear spoilers were optional for 1971's restyled Charger R/T, as was a vinyl top and a power sunroof. *Mike Mueller*

HOT OFF THE PRESS: 1971 DODGE CHARGER

"The Dodge Boys' latest effort boasts [of] tasteful styling, excellent handling and ride characteristics plus as much performance as anyone could ask for."
Marty Schorr, Hi-Performance Cars, *January 1971*

Two more headlights were added to Plymouth's 1971 E-body, and the base Barracuda (bargain-basement coupe, hardtop, or convertible) again was offered along with the classy Gran Coupe and 'Cuda, with its twin-scooped hood. 'Cudas (hardtop or convertible) also were adorned with four small simulated louvers on each front fender, and the grille was painted to match the body whenever the optional color-keyed elastomeric bumper group was ordered. Available engines carried over from 1970, save for the 440 four-barrel.

No longer identified as a Valiant variant, Duster 340 returned for 1971 wearing a snazzy new grille and unmistakable body-side stripes. New options included a blacked-out hood featuring righteous "340 Wedge" graphics. Most mechanicals remained from 1970 save for front disc brakes, which moved to the options list.

DODGE

Charger's new curvaceous body for 1971 helped make it look hot even if it wasn't, and base coupes fitted with a slant-six or 318 V-8 clearly weren't. It was V-8 power only for the next step up, Charger 500, which featured standard bucket seats. At the top was Charger SE, dressed up with hideaway headlights and a vinyl landau roof. Optional for the SE but not the 500, Dodge's 440 Magnum remained standard for 1971's Charger R/T, which was *Hi-Performance Cars* magazine's "Top Performance Car of the Year."

With Coronet transformed into a luxury-conscious family car fitted with four doors only on a stretched 118-inch wheelbase, Dodge's Super Bee was left without a hive after 1970. But this hyperactive bug found a new home in 1971's Charger 500 lineup. A bulging, blacked-out hood was standard for the Charger Super Bee, as was a 300-horsepower 383 Magnum V-8. Front and rear spoilers were optional, along with trendy color-keyed bumpers. Engine choices included the 340 small-block, 440 Magnum, 440 Six Pack and 426 Hemi. Super Bee did not return for 1972.

Updated taillights and a revised split-grille were new for 1971's Challenger, and those grille inserts were painted silver on base models, black on R/Ts. Challenger R/T also was treated to restyled body-side stripes and simulated brake-cooling scoops in front of each rear wheel. The SE package didn't return, nor did an R/T convertible. Standard for 1971's R/T hardtop was the familiar 383 Magnum; optional engines were the same as 'Cuda's.

Although a handful of Swinger 340s were built for Canadian consumption in 1971, Dart's high-performance career effectively ended the previous year. But in its place came Demon 340, Dodge's variation on Plymouth's Duster 340 theme. The two shared the same fastback A-body shell with differing nose/tail treatments expectedly setting them apart. Mechanicals were essentially identical.

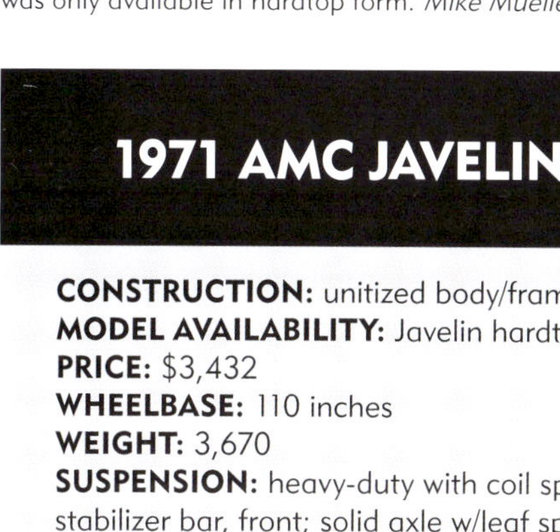

Slightly revised taillights appeared for 1971's Challenger, still offered with or without a roof. In its final year, Challenger R/T was only available in hardtop form. *Mike Mueller*

TIME SLIPS: 1971

MODEL	¼-MILE PERFORMANCE	SOURCE
Ford Torino Cobra 429 SCJ	13.30 seconds at 106.0 mph	*1971 Supercar Annual**
Ford Mustang Mach 1 429 SCJ	13.40 seconds at 105.0 mph	*1971 Supercar Annual**
Plymouth Road Runner Hemi	13.50 seconds at 106.5 mph	*1971 Supercar Annual**
Ford Mustang Boss 351	13.50 seconds at 103.0 mph	*1971 Supercar Annual**
Pontiac Trans Am	13.70 seconds at 104.0 mph	*1971 Supercar Annual**
Plymouth Road Runner 440+6	13.71 seconds at 101.2 mph	*Car Craft*, January 1971
Plymouth 'Cuda 440+6	13.72 seconds at 106.0 mph	*SSDI*, April 1971
Dodge Charger Super Bee Hemi	13.73 seconds at 104.0 mph	*Motor Trend*, December 1970
Dodge Challenger R/T 440-6	13.75 seconds at 104.0 mph	*1971 Supercar Annual**
Oldsmobile 4-4-2 W-30	13.90 seconds at 101.0 mph	*1971 Supercar Annual**
Plymouth Duster 340	13.90 seconds at 100.8 mph	*Speed & Supercars*, October 1971
AMC Javelin AMX (401 V-8)	14.30 seconds at 98.8 mph	*Sport Car Graphic*, April 1971
Pontiac GT-37 (400 V-8)	14.32 seconds at 98.8 mph	*Speed & Supercars*, October 1971
Chevrolet Chevelle SS 454	14.35 seconds at 97.1 mph	*Car Craft*, January 1971
Pontiac Firebird Formula 400	14.38 seconds at 98.0 mph	*1971 Supercar Annual**
Chevrolet Camaro Z28	14.40 seconds at 101.0 mph	*1971 Supercar Annual**
Plymouth GTX (440 V-8)	14.40 seconds at 98.7 mph	*Road & Track*, December 1970
Dodge Demon 340	14.49 seconds at 98.25 mph	*Motor Trend*, January 1971
Buick GS 455 Stage 1	14.50 seconds at 101.0 mph	*1971 Supercar Annual**
Mercury Cougar XR7 429 CJ	14.65 seconds at 98.0 mph	*1971 Supercar Annual**
Plymouth 'Cuda 340	14.67 seconds at 96.0 mph	*SSDI*, February 1971
Dodge Demon 340	14.80 seconds at 95.0 mph	*Hi-Performance Cars*, August 1971
AMC Hornet SC/360	14.80 seconds at 94.63 mph	*Hot Rod*, December 1970
Chevrolet Camaro SS 396	14.83 seconds at 96.3 mph	*Hot Rod*, July 1971
Pontiac GTO Judge (455 HO)	14.90 seconds at 95.0 mph	*Motor Trend*, October 1970
Dodge Charger R/T (440)	14.93 seconds at 96.4 mph	*Motor Trend*, December 1970
Chevrolet Nova SS 350	15.92 seconds at 87.63 mph	*Motor Trend*, January 1971

NOTE: *SSDI is Super Stock & Drag Illustrated magazine*

* Hi-Performance Cars *magazine*

1971 AMC JAVELIN AMX

CONSTRUCTION: unitized body/frame
MODEL AVAILABILITY: Javelin hardtop
PRICE: $3,432
WHEELBASE: 110 inches
WEIGHT: 3,670
SUSPENSION: heavy-duty with coil spring & stabilizer bar, front; solid axle w/leaf springs, rear
STEERING: manual recirculating ball, std; quick-ratio manual & variable-ratio power-assist, optional
WHEELS: 14x6 slotted, std; 14x6 spoke-style & 15x7 slotted, optional
TIRES: E70x14 Goodyear white-letter, std; E60x15 white-letter, optional
BRAKES: 10-inch drums, front & rear; 10.9-inch power-assisted front discs, optional
ENGINE: 245-hp 360-cid V-8 w/2-barrel carburetor, std; 360-cid 4-barrel & 401-cid V-8s, optional
TRANSMISSION: floor-shifted 3-speed manual, std; Hurst-shifted 4-speed & Shift-Command automatic, optional
AXLE RATIO: 3.15:1, std (2.87:1 included with auto trans); 3.54:1 & 3.91:1 (required available Twin-Grip differential), optional

HOT OFF THE PRESS: 1971 DODGE DEMON 340

"Demon is [a] repainted, striped Duster with a bit more styling flair and a lot more quality control. One bright light on the Dodge scene is that the 340 engine is included in the base price."
Jim Brokaw, Motor Trend, *January 1971*

A 285-horsepower 351 Cleveland small-block was standard in 1971 for the last of Ford's Torino Cobra SportsRoofs. A heavy-duty suspension remained, as did optional 429 Cobra Jet and Super Cobra Jet big-blocks.

FORD

Reviews among the automotive press were mixed concerning Ford's bigger, hopefully better pony car for 1971, which in some opinions looked considerably tail-heavy in SportsRoof form. In truth, most of the weight still rested on the front wheels, especially so when the optional 429 Cobra Jet was installed. Superseding its 428-cube forerunner, the 429 CJ also could be transformed into a Super Cobra Jet by ordering the Drag Pack option, and a ram-air hood remained available in both cases, with no change again made to advertised output. An external oil cooler once more was included as part of the SCJ deal, but apparently not all Super Cobra Jet Mustangs received this equipment in 1971.

Small-block fans that year could opt for the 351 Cleveland 4V, rated at 285 horsepower, or the 280-horsepower 351 Cobra Jet, introduced midyear. Unlike its Cleveland running mate, which featured two-bolt main bearing caps, the low-compression 351 CJ was based on a burly block incorporating four-bolt mains.

The sporty Mach 1 once more served as the most suitable home to any of Mustang's performance V-8s, even without a flashy hood. This year's standard lid was plain-Jane pony car—no scoops, no black-out treatment, no competition-style hood pins. And beneath that bonnet was a 210-horsepower 302 Windsor small-block, added into the equation this year, in Ford's words, "to broaden the Mach 1's potential market appeal."

BY THE NUMBERS: 1971 PRODUCTION

CHEVROLET SS & SS 454

	19,293	(RPO Z15 for Malibu hardtop/convertible & El Camino; includes all engines, small- & big-block)

CHEVROLET "HEAVY CHEVY"

	6,727	(all Chevelle hardtops)

CHEVROLET CAMARO SS

	8,377	(all hardtops; includes 1,533 w/LS3 396 V-8)

CHEVROLET CAMARO Z28

	4,862	(all hardtops)

CHEVROLET NOVA SS

	7,105	(all sedans)

CHEVROLET RALLY NOVA

	7,700	(all sedans)

PONTIAC GTO

hdtp, std V-8	8,432	(6,421 w/manual trans, 2,011 w/auto)
hdtp, 455	534	(all w/auto trans)
hdtp, 455 HO	888	(412 w/manual trans, 476 w/auto)
hdtp subtotal	9,854	
cvt., std V-8	587	(508 w/manual trans, 79 w/auto)
cvt., 455	43	(all w/auto trans)
cvt. w/455 HO	48	(27 w/manual trans, 21 w/auto)
cvt. subtotal	678	
grand total	**10,532***	

*GTO Judge production (included in above totals)

hardtop	357
convertible	17
total	**374**

PONTIAC FIREBIRD FORMULA

w/350 or 400	7,131	(1,694 w/manual trans, 5,437 w/auto)
L75 (455 V-8)	350	(all w/auto trans)
LS5 (455 HO)	321	(166 w/manual trans, 155 w/auto)
total	**7,802**	(all hardtops)

PONTIAC TRANS AM

w/manual	885	
w/auto trans	1,231	
total	**2,166**	(all hardtops w/455 HO V-8)

OLDSMOBILE 4-4-2

hardtop	6,285
convertible	1,304
total	**7,589**

BUICK GRAN SPORT

hdtp w/350 V-8	5,986	(25 w/column-shifted 3-spd, 358 w/4-spd, 5,603 w/auto)
hdtp w/455 V-8	1,481	(103 w/4-spd, 1,378 w/auto)
Stage 1 hdtp	801	(114 w/4-spd, 687 w/auto)
cvt. w/350 V-8	656	(6 w/column-shifted 3-spd, 51 w/4-spd, 599 w/auto)
cvt. w/455 V-8	165	(18 w/4-spd, 147 w/auto)
Stage 1 cvt.	81	(9 w/4-spd, 72 w/auto)
total	**9,170**	(includes 124 GSX hardtops w/350, 455 or 455 Stage 1 V-8s)

FORD MUSTANG MACH 1

	36,498	(all SportsRoofs w/302-, 351- or 429-cid V-8s)

FORD MUSTANG BOSS 351

	1,806	(all SportsRoofs)

FORD TORINO COBRA

	3,054	(all SportsRoofs)

FORD TORINO GT

SportsRoof	31,641	
convertible	1,613	
total	**33,254**	(w/302-, 351- & 429-cid V-8s; 390-cid FE-series V-8 also was Ford option early in year before being replaced by 400-cid Cleveland V-8)

MERCURY COUGAR GT

	787	(all hardtops)

MERCURY CYCLONE

base fastback	444
GT	2,287
Spoiler	353
total	**30,840**

PLYMOUTH ROAD RUNNER

hdtp w/340 V-8	1,681	(438 w/4-speed, 1,243 w/auto)
hdtp w/383	11,682	(3,730 w/4-speed, 7,952 w/auto)
hdtp w/440-6	246	(137 w/4-speed, 109 w/auto)
hdtp w/Hemi	55	(28 w/4-speed, 27 w/auto)
total	**13,644**	(includes US deliveries only; total including deliveries outside US was 14,218)

PLYMOUTH GTX

hdtp w/440 V-8	2,538	(327 w/4-speed, 2,211 w/auto)
hdtp w/440-6	135	(62 w/4-speed, 73 w/auto)
hdtp w/Hemi	30	(11 w/4-speed, 19 w/auto)
total	**2,703**	(includes US deliveries only; total including deliveries outside US was 2,942)

PLYMOUTH 'CUDA

hdtp w/340 V-8	3,300	(151 w/3-speed, 1,141 w/4-speed, 2,008 w/auto)
hdtp w/383 V-8	1,739	(70 w/3-speed, 501 w/4-speed, 1,168 w/auto)
hdtp w/440-6	237	(108 w/4-speed, 129 w/auto)
hdtp w/Hemi	107	(59 w/4-speed, 48 w/auto)
cvt. w/340 V-8	140	(8 w/3-speed, 30 w/4-speed, 102 w/auto)
cvt. w/383 V-8	128	(8 w/3-speed, 33 w/4-speed, 87 w/auto)
cvt. w/440-6	17	(5 w/4-speed, 12 w/auto)
cvt. w/Hemi	7	(2 w/4-speed, 5 w/auto)
total	**5,675**	(includes US deliveries only; total including deliveries outside US was 6,602)

PLYMOUTH DUSTER 340

w/manual trans	4,265	
w/auto trans	6,213	
total	**10,478**	(all sport coupes; includes US deliveries only; total including deliveries outside US was 12,886)

DODGE CHARGER R/T

hdtp w/440 V-8	2,504	(332 w/4-speed, 2,172 w/auto)
hdtp w/440-6	178	(80 w/4-speed, 98 w/auto)
hdtp w/Hemi	63	(30 w/4-speed, 33 w/auto)
total	**2,745**	(includes US deliveries only; total including deliveries outside US was 3,118)

DODGE CHARGER SUPER BEE

hdtp w/340 V-8	320	(complete breakdown n/a)
hdtp w/383	3,858	(203 w/3-speed, 766 w/4-speed, 2,889 w/auto)
hdtp w/440 V-8	26	(complete breakdown n/a)
hdtp w/440-6	99	(30 w/4-speed, 69 w/auto)
hdtp w/Hemi	22	(9 w/4-speed, 13 w/auto)
total	**4,325**	(includes US deliveries only; total including deliveries outside US was 5,054)

DODGE CHALLENGER R/T

hdtp w/340 V-8	1,078	(34 w/3-speed, 313 w/4-speed, 731 w/auto)
hdtp w/383 V-8	2,509	(59 w/3-speed, 465 w/4-speed, 1,985 w/auto)
hdtp w/440-6	246	(127 w/4-speed, 119 w/auto)
hdtp w/Hemi	70	(58 w/4-speed, 12 w/auto)
total	**3,903**	(includes US deliveries only; total including deliveries outside US was 4,630)

DODGE DEMON 340

w/3-spd	998	
w/4-speed	2,051	
w/auto trans	4,932	
total	**7,981**	(all sport coupes; includes US deliveries only; total including deliveries outside US was 10,089)

AMERICAN MOTORS JAVELIN/AMX

	2,054	(all hardtops; 1,309 w/360 V-8, 745 w/401V-8

AMC HORNET SC/360

360 2-barrel	206	(19 w/3-speed, 187 w/auto)
360 4-barrel	578	(23 w/3-speed, 306 w/4-speed, 249 w/auto)
total	**784**	(all sedans)

NOTE: *Production data was supplied by various sources, including Christo Datini at the GM Heritage Center, Ford Motor Company & Kevin Marti at Marti Auto Works (www.martiauto.com), Galen Govier (Mopar material) at Galen's Tag Service (www.galengovier.com), and American Motors enthusiast Eddie Stakes at www.planethoustonamx.com.*

Dodge copied Plymouth's Duster 340 in 1971 with its Demon 340, equipped all but identically to its corporate cousin.

With Coronet gone after 1970, Dodge's Super Bee migrated into the Charger lineup for one final appearance in 1971. Black striping was part of the package; Rallye rims or five-spoke sport wheels were optional. A 300-horsepower 383 Magnum V-8 was standard, too. *Mike Mueller*

A one-hit wonder, built for 1971 only, Ford's Boss 351 Mustang was fitted with the 351 High Output (HO) Cleveland V-8, an able small-block that could throw its weight around like most big-blocks. Rated at 330 horsepower, the HO featured superb free-flowing heads that were nearly identical to the canted-valve units used by the Boss 302 save for revised cooling passages. The coveted Mach 1 sports interior was optional inside, while full instrumentation and high-back bucket seats were standard. *Mike Mueller*

If enhancing sex appeal was desired, a standard 302 Mach 1 could be adorned with a non-functional "NASA" hood at no extra cost. Included in the deal when an optional 351 or 429 was installed, the NASA unit's twin scoops could be activated by adding the aforementioned Dual Ram Induction option. All Mach 1s also featured a heavy-duty Competition Suspension.

Joining Mach 1 in 1971 was Ford's Boss 351 Mustang, available as well only in SportsRoof wrappings. At the heart of this wild horse was the 351 High Output (HO) Cleveland V-8, rated at 330 horsepower. Supporting cast members included the Dual Ram Induction hood, a Hurst-shifted wide-ratio four-speed, Competition Suspension, and power front discs. According to *Car and Driver*, this one-hit wonder "offers dragstrip performance that most cars with 100 cubic inches more displacement will envy."

Ford's hottest intermediates, Torino GT and Cobra, rolled over one last time into 1971, with the latter machine featuring a little less standard cast-iron beneath its hood. Supplanting 1970's base 429 Thunder Jet was the 285-horsepower 351 Cleveland small-block, which like its big-block forerunner was backed by a Hurst-shifted four-speed in standard Cobra applications. The 429 Cobra Jet, Super or not, with or without ram-air, was again optional for Cobra and GT in 1971.

UNDER THE HOOD: 1971'S HOTTEST V-8s*

MODEL	CID	BORE & STROKE	CR	HORSEPOWER	TORQUE
Dodge/Plymouth Hemi	426	4.25 x 3.750	10.2:1	425 @ 5,000	490 @ 4,000
Dodge/Plymouth (3x2)	440	4.320 x 3.750	10.3:1	385 @ 4,700	490 @ 3,200
Dodge/Plymouth	440	4.320 x 3.750	9.5:1	370 @ 4,600	480 @ 3,200
Dodge/Plymouth	340	4.040 x 3.310	10.5:1	275 @ 5,000	340 @ 3,200
Pontiac HO	455	4.151 x 4.210	8.4:1	335 @ 4,800	480 @ 3,600
Chevrolet SS 454	454	4.25 x 4.00	8.5:1	365 @ 4,800	465 @ 3,200
Chevrolet SS	402	4.1260 x 3.76	8.5:1	300 @ 4,800	400 @ 3,200
Chevrolet Camaro Z28	350	4.00 x 3.48	9:1	330 @ 5,600	360 @ 4,000
Buick GS Stage 1	455	4.3125 x 3.90	8.5:1	345 @ 5,000	460 @ 3,000
Olds 4-4-2 W-30	455	4.125 x 4.250	8.5:1	350 @ 4,700	460 @ 3,200
Ford/Mercury SCJ	429	4.362 x 3.59	11.3:1	375 @ 5,600	450 @ 3,400
Ford Mustang (HO)	351	4.00 x 3.50	11:1	330 @ 5,400	370 @ 4,000
Ford/Mercury	351	4.00 x 3.50	10.7:1	285 @ 5,400	370 @ 3,400
American Motors	401	4.165 x 3.68	9.5:1	330 @ 5,000	430 @ 3,400

NOTE: *CID is cubic-inch displacement; CR is compression ratio; bore/stroke in inches.*

** Discounting Corvette*

Everything that made an SS 396 Chevelle so hot in 1966 and 1967 was available to El Camino buyers—save for all that Super Sport nomenclature. Note the mag-style "Z16" wheel covers on this 1967 El Camino, which is powered by a 396 Turbo Jet big-block. *Mike Mueller*

An individual model in 1968, El Camino SS became available (like its Chevelle running mate) in 1969 via RPO Z25. The Z15 SS 454 package then joined the Z25 SS 396 deal on the El Camino options list in 1970. An LS5-equipped 1970 SS 454 is shown here; a few LS6 models also were built that year. *Mike Mueller*

Look up "best of both worlds" in the dictionary and you'll likely find photos of Ford's Ranchero and Chevrolet's El Camino, rivals that packaged car-like convenience and class together with pickup-type practicality like nothing seen before. Ranchero came first in 1957, followed by El Camino in 1959. The Ford reappeared annually for 23 years, while its copycat competitor survived 27 model runs, but not consecutively. Temporarily shelved after 1960, El Camino reappeared in 1964 and rolled on up through early 1988. Dearborn closed the tailgate on its Ranchero in 1979.

Ranchero was reintroduced in 1960 as a variation on Ford's compact Falcon theme then moved on up into midsize Fairlane ranks in 1967, where it would stay through evolutions as a Torino-based model (until 1977) followed by an LTD II variation for its last three renditions. Reborn on Chevrolet's A-body platform in 1964, El Camino quickly soared in popularity, outselling its Blue Oval counterpart by at least a 2-1 margin almost every year.

When fully loaded down with options, both could stand on their own as certified status-mobiles complemented by all bells and whistles. Or even hot performance in some cases. In 1957 it was possible—albeit briefly—to equip Ranchero with either of Ford's two top Thunderbird 312 V-8s, one crowned with twin four-barrel carbs, the other force-fed by a McCulloch supercharger. Leading the way beneath the original El Camino's hood was an optional triple-carb 348 V-8.

More performance began filtering into Chevrolet's "car-truck" mix after its midsize makeover as all available Chevelle features carried over the fence into the El Camino realm—save for Super Sport imagery. At least one model was even test-fitted with the Corvette's 365 horsepower L76 327 V-8 in 1964 before this potent small-block was recalled from A-body options lists. Installing any of Chevy's Mk IV big-blocks became possible in 1966, and the breed's first SS 396 rendition followed two years later.

Chevrolet's promotion of the El Camino as a sporty plaything typically inspired a similar effort at Ford, which in 1967 began helping Ranchero customers forget all about those small-thinking Falcon years. Once an intermediate, Ford's hybrid began making flashier impressions, first with the Fairlane Ranchero 500 (with its added exterior brightwork), then the truly upscale Fairlane Ranchero 500 XL, fitted with a sporty bucket seat/console interior. An optional 390 FE big-block also appeared this year.

The Fairlane reference was dropped in 1968. And with Chevy's SS 396 El Camino running about, Dearborn also traded its topline XL model for a real sport truck, the Ranchero GT. GT imagery included appropriate badges, special striping, and styled-steel wheels.

By then it had become obvious that work had given way to play in the car-truck field. "El Camino and Ranchero have established a new trend in the fun car market, and people all over the country are getting on the bandwagon," claimed *Motorcade* magazine's Lee Kelley in a December 1967 report. Ford's efforts to keep up with Chevrolet in that market included adding the 335-horse 428 Cobra Jet V-8 to the Ranchero's options list early in 1968. The 429 Cobra Jet also was an available in 1970 and '71, as were the various renditions of Dearborn's 351 Cleveland small-block.

After the muscle car era's close, both Ford and Chevrolet traded power for prestige, with two-tone paint schemes and tape stripes taking over. While snazzy GT and Super Sport renditions were offered right up to the end of the road, little or no actual performance supported these images. Lesser known appearance options included El Camino's Conquista paint package, available from 1974 to '77, and the black-only Royal Knight, introduced in 1978 with a large, Trans Am–like hood decal. Ford's eye-catching promotions included the White Sales Special in 1971 and Explorer package in 1976. Dearborn also marked the end of the Ranchero line in 1979 with a Limited Production version, a truly dressy concoction that came complete with an exclusive exterior plate engraved with the owner's initials.

Ford's Ranchero first took on a true sporty air in 1968, the year a GT rendition debuted with standard bucket seats and argent-painted styled-steel wheels. And being a Fairlane-based model, Ranchero GT also could be fitted with the optional 428 Cobra Jet V-8, introduced in April that year. A 1969 Cobra Jet Ranchero GT appears here. *courtesy Mecum Auctions*

HOT OFF THE PRESS: 1971 FORD BOSS 351 MUSTANG

"The Boss 351 has but one purpose—it is the bare bones from which a Trans-Am racing sedan can be built (actually the stylist have made sure those bones aren't all that bare). But with Ford's withdrawal from racing it could be the last of its breed from Dearborn."
Car and Driver, *February 1971*

Small-block V-8s also became standard across the board for Mercury's midsize muscle cars in 1971. While a 351 two-barrel again was included in the Cyclone GT deal, a 351 four-barrel was the base engine for the base Cyclone and its Spoiler running mate.

Mercury's Eliminator failed to return for 1971, but a Cougar GT was offered. All Cougars, GT or not, could be fitted this year with the same optional V-8s familiar to Mustang buyers, including the 280-horsepower 351 Cobra Jet and its 429-cube big brother. This rare 1971 XR-7 features the ram-air 429 CJ. *Mike Mueller*

MERCURY

Making its enlarged Mustang cousin appear comparatively humble, Mercury's reborn Cougar simply no longer qualified as a pony car in 1971. It wasn't necessarily all that much bigger than its predecessors; the rub was that it now totally targeted prestige-conscious buyers right between their star-struck eyes. The sporty feel imparted by the short-lived Eliminator was gone, and not even a reborn GT rendition could convince customers otherwise. Priced at a tidy $130, 1971's GT package did offer a decent return on investment—heavy-duty suspension, performance cooling, dual racing mirrors, and instrumentation were part of the deal—and available V-8s did include the 280-horse 351 Cobra Jet and 370-horsepower 429 CJ. But this showboat was just too damned heavy, literally, and too heavily laden with status-seeking intentions. Although another GT followed in 1972, it didn't matter—Mercury had built its last truly muscular Cougar in 1970.

Like Ford's Cobra, Mercury's Montego-based muscle cars left their standard big-blocks behind after 1970, too. While a 351-2V was again included in 1971's Cyclone GT deal, the four-barrel Cleveland V-8 became the base engine for Cyclone and its Spoiler alter ego, which was treated to new body-side striping. A four-speed (with Hurst stick) also was the norm behind this 285-horsepower small-block in midsize Merc applications, while a Select-Shift automatic transmission was standard for 1971's GT in place of 1970's three-speed manual. Included beneath Cyclone and Spoiler was a "Cross Country" ride package instead of the competition handling equipment installed the previous year. Cross Country ride was a no-cost option for GT, and the 429 Cobra Jet was available at extra cost for all three Cyclone renditions.

HOT OFF THE PRESS: 1971 MERCURY CYCLONE

"While Mercury enjoys a strong trade in cars for the family man, they haven't abandoned the bachelor market. That's why they offer the Cyclone series."
Motor Trend, *January 1971*

AMC

A special "Machine Go" package returned in 1971 for American Motor's radically restyled Matador. But while this option offered much of the same punch felt in 1970, it just wasn't the same without all the patriotic striping, hood-scooping, and hoopla. "The Machine" identification did not carry over, nor did the 340-horsepower 390 V-8, although AMC's new 330-horsepower 401 certainly was no slouch. Next to no one noticed 1971's Machine; production claims run as low as 43, as "high" as 68.

Totally new as well this year was AMC's latest pony car, repackaged (with the help of Trans-Am driver Mark Donahue) on a slightly longer wheelbase. "We've made Javelin the hairiest looking sports car in American, even at the risk of scaring some people off," claimed ad copy. "We may lose a few librarians for customers, but we think we'll gain a few enthusiasts." Donahue was especially pleased with the bulging fenders, which promised ample room for racing rubber but served little purpose on the street other than to announce "look what we stole from Chevrolet's latest Corvette."

AMC stylists also mimicked the Sting Ray's T-top roof with faux panels sculptured into the overhead sheet metal. Customers could enhance this mirage by adding optional vinyl coverings to those "twin-canopy" recesses, resulting in what *Car and Driver* called "clearly a step backward from the smooth good taste that has shown itself in other [AMC] cars like Hornet." This creased roof (with or without the vinyl) returned for an encore in 1972 before being smoothed over the following year.

AMC continued offering a base Javelin and upscale SST in 1971, but the two-seat AMX did not return, despite Dick Teague's best-laid plans. Sagging sales simply didn't support this sporty breed's continuation. And besides, customers just wouldn't stop asking, "Why not a back seat?"

In response to these queries, Kenosha people simply transferred the AMX badge to their fully freshened four-place Javelin, creating a new flagship that simply refused to be lost in a crowd. At the nose was a wire screen flush-mounted in front of the grille; out back was Donahue's trademark ducktail spoiler. The AMX hood was a metal-framed fiberglass unit sporting a non-functional cowl-induction "scoop." Standard beneath that lid was a 245-horsepower 360 two-barrel V-8; optional was a 360 four-barrel or the 401. A chin spoiler could be added at extra cost up front, and that hood could be put to work force-feeding outside air into the engine by ordering either of the two familiar Go Packages, again centered around the AMX's available four-barrel V-8s.

Along with that ram-air equipment, 1971's 360/401 Go Package once more included power front discs, special handling suspension, heavy-duty cooling, Twin-Grip differential, and Space-Saver spare. Added into the "Go" mix this year were the 1970 Machine's 15x7 wheels wearing E60 white-letter tires, a hood T-stripe, a rear black-out panel, and Rally Pak instrumentation, with that latter group consisting of a 140 miles per hour speedometer, all gauges, and the so-called "tic-tak-toc" tachometer/clock combo. Available for all Javelins prior to 1971, AMC's pony car Go Packages were limited to the top-shelf AMX from here until the breed's 1974 swan song.

American Motors' pony car was radically restyled on a longer wheelbase for 1971. Both a base Javelin and SST version again were offered this year, but the two-seat AMX didn't return. A Javelin-based AMX (now featuring a back seat, of course) did, however, and remained on the scene right up until the end of the road for this attractive breed in 1974.

HOT OFF THE PRESS: 1971 AMC JAVELIN AMX

"The 2-passenger AMX is history now. One high [American Motors] official, without a trace of mirth explained the situation by saying, 'Most of our customers have asked, why not a rear seat?,' and went on to suggest that by tacking the AMC nameplate to a version of the Javelin the company was only responding to the wishes of its public."

Car and Driver, *October 1970*

HOT OFF THE PRESS: 1971 AMC HORNET SC/360

"What the folks in the red, white and blue jackets have wrought is a low-insurance mini-Road Runner. Over 4,000 rpm, the willing 360-incher comes on with a winding scream that'll raise goose bumps the size of tennis balls. Even the horn is distinctly beep, beep."

Ralph Guldahl Jr. Hot Rod, *December 1970*

MOTOR OF THE YEAR: 1971 OLDSMOBILE W-30

Type	OHV V-8 w/W25 ram-air hood
Displacement	455 cubic inches
Bore	4.125 inches
Stroke	4.250 inches
Horsepower	350 at 4,700 rpm
Torque	460 at 3,200 rpm
Compression	8.5:1
Fuel delivery	750-cfm Rochester Quadra-jet 4-barrel carburetor on aluminum intake
Air cleaner	single-snorkel w/foam "doughnut" that sealed to the W25 hood's ram-air ductwork
Ignition	single-point distributor
Cooling	19.5-inch 6-blade fan w/clutch
Cylinder block	cast-iron w/2-bolt main bearing caps
Crankshaft	nodular cast-iron w/2.9993-inch main journals
Connecting rods	forged-steel
Pistons	cast-aluminum
Cam*	hydraulic w/328 degrees duration (intake & exhaust), 108 degrees of overlap * w/air conditioning: 285 degrees duration on intake, 287 degrees on exhaust, 57 degrees of overlap
Rocker ratio	1.6:1
Cylinder heads	cast-iron, 69.75cc volume chamber
Valve sizes	2.077-inch intakes, 1.630-inch exhausts
Valve lift	0.475 inch, intake & exhaust (0.472 w/air conditioning)
Exhaust system	cast-iron manifolds w/2.25-inch main pipes, reverse-flow mufflers & 2.00-inch tailpipes

FULL-SIZE FLYERS

Pontiac's GTO may have rewritten the book on high-performance in 1964, but that didn't necessarily translate into an immediate end for the previous chapter. Detroit continued marketing full-size muscle cars throughout the decade, though in ever-decreasing numbers. Plymouth's Sport Fury GT, introduced as a Rapid Transit System member in 1970, arguably represented the last of this breed, showing up a year after Chevrolet's final example, Impala SS 427. Both Pontiac and Ford had stopped taking serious shots at this niche-market a couple years prior.

Without a doubt it was Chevy's full-size Super Sports that led the way in this segment during the 1960s. After debuting only with either of the two W-series V-8s, 348 or 409, in 1961, the SS trim option could be paired the following year with any Impala engine, be it six-cylinder or small-block V-8. With its scope now widened, Impala SS sales soared to 99,311 in 1962, followed by 153,271 in 1963 and 185,325 in 1964. Remaining constant each year was an optional 409, which maxed out at 425 horsepower in 1963.

Production peaked at 243,114 in 1965 then went downhill from there: 119,314 in 1966, 73,932 in 1967, and 38,210 in 1968. The 409 made one last RPO appearance in 1965 just as the new 396 Mk IV V-8 entered the race. Both the 396 and its 427 big brother were optional from 1966 to '68, but in 1969 Chevrolet product planners chose to offer only the SS 427 Impala, introduced two years before as a top-shelf running mate for the mass-marketed full-size SS.

In 1967, the new SS 427 package (RPO Z24) included the 385-horsepower L36 427 and a stiffened suspension. Customers snatched up 2,124 SS 427s, coupes and convertibles, that first year, followed by another 1,778 in 1968. Not only did Chevrolet roll out only the SS 427 in 1969, it did so with far less fanfare. The '67 SS 427 had its exclusive domed hood (with fake vents) and large "SS 427" cross-flag emblems. The '68 rendition had its unique fender "gills." The 1969 model, on the other hand, left most interested onlookers squinting to make out those small "427" badges hidden atop the side marker lights

Chevrolet's last full-size muscle machine, Impala SS 427, appeared in 1969. Standard beneath the hood was a 390-horsepower Mk IV big-block. *Mike Mueller*

on each front fender. Chevrolet sold 2,455 SS 427 Impalas in 1969 before ending its original full-size Super Sport legacy. Buyers in 1970 could install the 454-cid Mk IV beneath Impala or Caprice hoods, but it just wasn't the same.

Pontiac's big-car performer was the 2+2, first offered in 1964 as a $291 option package for 389-powered Catalina hardtops and convertibles. That price jumped to $418 in 1965 as a 421 V-8 (optional the previous year) was made standard 2+2 fare. Three different High Output 421s were offered, beginning with a 338-horsepower rendition fed by a four-barrel carb. Trading the four-barrel for Tri-Power resulted in the 356-horsepower HO, and another 20 horses were let loose by adding three open-element air cleaners, a hotter cam, special valvetrain gear, and low-restriction exhaust manifolds. As in 1964, the basic 2+2 package in 1965 also included a Hurst-shifted heavy-duty three-speed manual, bucket seats, and a typically beefed suspension. After showing up for 1966 as an individual model, Pontiac's 2+2 made one last appearance, again as an options package, in 1967.

Offered from 1964 to '67, Pontiac's 2+2 represented the division's last shot at full-size performance. Pontiac built 11,251 2+2 models for 1965, including this convertible, fitted with a 376-horsepower 421 Tri-Power V-8. *Mike Mueller*

Hot no matter how you looked at it during the 1960s was Ford's 427 Galaxie, introduced midyear in 1963. Two versions were offered up through 1967, one with the 410-horsepower four-barrel FE big-block, the other with its 425-horsepower dual-carb sibling. In either case, this Blue Oval brute represented a supercar for supermen. A knee-bending clutch backed by either a Borg-Warner T-10 (1963–64) or top-loader (1964–67) four-speed were the only drivetrain choices. Additional mandatory hardware included bigger brakes and wheels (15-inchers instead of 14s) and beefed-up axle shafts, U-joints, and driveshaft. According to a *Speed & Custom* road test, a 425-horse 1964 Galaxie could do the quarter-mile in 13.96 seconds.

More image-conscious was Ford's 7-Litre Galaxie, which ads called "either the quickest quiet car or the quietest quick car." Introduced for 1966, the 7-Litre came standard with bucket seats on the inside, mag-style wheel covers on the outside. Power front discs were included, too, as was a 345-horsepower 428 FE. Purely a showboat, this boulevard cruiser could be transformed into a real battleship by installing the optional 427, but few buyers even considered this expensive proposition. A 7-Litre returned in barely noticeable fashion in 1967.

Dearborn's Galaxie XL GT appeared for 1968 and '69, but it was a matter of nice try, no cigar. Even with the optional 429 V-8, the "Michigan Strong Boy," as ads called it, was simply a muscle car imposter, though certainly a sporty one. The same could be said for Mercury's X-100 Marauder fastback, a real head-turner (but major slug) offered for 1969 and '70. Another parting shot at full-size performance came from Oldsmobile from 1968 to '70 in the form of the intriguing Toronado GT, fitted with a 400-horsepower 455.

As for Plymouth's aforementioned Sport Fury GT, it came standard with a 350-horse 440 in 1970, the 370-horsepower Super Commando in 1971. The 390-horsepower 440 Six Barrel was an option that first year. Reportedly, total production was only 666 in 1970 (61 of those with the triple-carb 440) and 375 in 1971.

Ford offered its 7-Litre Galaxie with or without a roof in 1966. And while most featured the 428-cid big-block, a few were released with the supreme FE, the 427. *Tom Shaw*

The fifth member of Plymouth's new Rapid Transit System, 1970's Fury GT came standard with a 350-horse 440 RB big-block. The 370-horsepower Super Commando 440 was standard in 1971.

CHAPTER 9

1972 NUMBERS GAME

OUTPUT WANES

Revised trim that completely encompassed the Super Sport Chevelle's blacked-out grille and headlights appeared in 1972. Simple "SS" badges again adorned 350- and 402-powered models, while "SS 454" identification was used one last time for supreme Mk IV installations. *Mike Mueller*

Chevrolet's Mk IV big-block wasn't even a year old when engineers restored the Mystery Motor's original bore diameter (4.25 inches), transforming their 396 Turbo Jet into the 427 Turbo Jet. Superseding 1965's 425-horse L78 V-8, 1966's 427-cid L72 initially was listed at 450 horsepower but ended up also wearing a 425-horsepower tag by the time it was released into the wild. What was up?

According to *Motor Trend*, one elucidation "for this curious state of affairs is that, since [1965's] congressional safety inquisition (see page 59) there has been a gentlemen's agreement among parties concerned not to advertise more than 425 hp. No official explanations have been offered [for the last-second adjustment], and Chevrolet's sticking to the 425 hp figure in its latest literature."

Anyone who believed that number instantly changed their mind after dropping the hammer on a 1966 L72 Sting Ray. "Chevrolet insists that there are only

425 horses in there, and we'll just have to take their words for it," began a *Car and Driver* review of the hottest Vette yet. "Though we feel compelled to point out that these are 425 horses of a size and strength never before seen by man—horses as tall as houses, with hooves as big as bushel baskets."

Such was the roller coaster ride car buyers were taken on by Detroit's power publishers 50 to 60 years back. Over-rating engine outputs became the norm during the 1950s when automakers battled fiercely for the horsepower derby's top spot, and this spurious practice rolled over unabated into the 1960s. Did Ford's tide-turning 352-cid FE V-8 really make 360 horses in 1960? Highly doubtful.

Then along came that mythical 425-horsepower ceiling, which both Ford and Chevy reached in 1963 with their 427 FE and 409 V-8s, respectively. While the Corvette's triple-carb 427 did rise up to 435 horses in 1967, no supercars dared crash that glass roof during the 1960s. Regardless of how much muscle Detroit's monster engines were truly making, not one company came completely clean until Chevrolet finally did release a totally truthful "450 HP" decal for its LS6 454 Turbo Jet in 1970. Did Chrysler's 426 street Hemi only make 425 horses? Again doubtful.

Under-rating engines also began to occur during the 1960s after clever factory guys determined they could pull the wool over the eyes of stock class drag racing rules-moguls. Sanctioning officials at the strip have long paired regular-production racers together based on their power-to-weight ratios, hence low-balling that first variable could translate into a real advantage on the quarter-mile. A dominant Super/Stock force in 1968, did Ford's Cobra Jet Mustang really pound the ground with a mere 335 ponies? Get outta town! Fortunately pro drag racing people weren't the fools the Detroit guys figured—in most cases, they correctly "refactored" an engine deemed a little short on advertised output to keep the playing field level.

Fooling insurance agents became the name of the game, too, during the 1960s once premiums began to soar for high-horsepower models. Again, power-to-weight ratios came into play, leaving many buyers unable to afford coverage for any muscle car, but especially the compact kind. So when Mopar A-bodies began hitting the streets in 1968 with 340 small-blocks beneath their hoods, most in the know understood why that token 275-horsepower rating came along for the trip.

Of course actual outputs themselves began rolling south after 1971's industry-wide compression cuts. Chevrolet's L48 350, for example, dipped from 1970's 300 horsepower to 270. Disappointing, sure, but the worst lay ahead.

That same small-block was advertised at a measly 175 horses in 1972. Where did all those ponies go? Nowhere, actually; that precipitous drop occurred primarily on paper as Chevy promotional people, like all their rivals, ceased publishing "gross" ratings in favor of more honest "net" standards. All those gaudy "brake horsepower" (bhp) figures seen prior to 1972 resulted from independent engine tests run with no accessories in action, no "smog" equipment in place, nor full exhaust systems bolted up—none of the real-world realities that naturally reduce a horsepower count long before those ponies reach the rear wheels.

Beginning in 1972, these tests featured "complete" engines running on stands; that is, all belts were in place turning alternator pulleys, air pumps, etc., and spent gases were delivered all the way through stock mufflers. Output ratings were still

FAMILY TIES: REV READERS

Keeping tabs on shift points wasn't always that easy during Detroit's original muscle car era. First off, a tachometer was optional in nearly every case. But coming up with the cash to install one was the least of a street racer's worries.

Once in place, many factory tachs pushed the limits of "readability," either being too small or too far from a driver's field of view. Some went wide right, others left, a few down low, and a couple were even square instead of round. Pontiac, Buick, and AMC also tried hood-mounted units, which may have looked awfully cool but didn't always remedy visibility issues, certainly so during rainy ventures. But once the designers stopped playing around, rpm readouts found their proper home, directly ahead, within the steering wheel's circumference or just above.

Among the more questionable tachometer designs of the original muscle car era was the horizontal-scale unit available for Ford's Torino Cobra in 1970. Its small size and poor location (to the instrument panel's far left) made it all but useless. *Mike Mueller*

AMC's 1969 SC/Rambler came standard with an 8,000-rpm Sun Tach strapped to the steering column—an installation familiar to both street racers and drag-masters alike. *Mike Mueller*

Known as a "knee-knocker," the 1966 SS 396 Chevelle's optional tach was located down below the dashboard to the right of the steering column. *Mike Mueller*

Initially offered as a dealer option in 1967, GTO's hood-mounted tach became a factory-installed extra-cost item after April 1. Shown here is 1968's optional 8,000-rpm unit. Three different styles appeared that year, with the third created exclusively for the new Ram Air II V-8. *Mike Mueller*

BY THE NUMBERS: 1972 PRODUCTION

CHEVROLET SS & SS 454

	24,946	(RPO Z15 for Malibu hardtop/convertible & El Camino)

CHEVROLET "HEAVY CHEVY"

	9,508	(all Chevelle hardtops)

CHEVROLET CAMARO SS

	6,562	(all hardtops; includes 970 w/LS3 396 V-8)

CHEVROLET CAMARO Z28

	2,575	(all hardtops)

PONTIAC GTO

coupe (400)	119	(59 w/manual trans; 60 w/auto)
coupe (455)	5	(all w/automatic trans)
coupe (455 HO)	10	(3 w/manual trans; 7 w/auto)
cpe sub-total	134	
hardtop (400)	4,803	(1,519 w/manual trans; 3,284 w/auto)
hardtop (455)	235	(all w/automatic trans)
hardtop (455 HO)	635	(310 w/manual trans; 325 w/auto)
hdtp sub-total	5,673	
grand total	**5,807**	

PONTIAC FIREBIRD FORMULA

w/350 V-8	2,544	
w/400 V-8	2,429	
w/455 HO	276	
total	**5,249**	(all hardtops)

PONTIAC TRANS AM

w/manual trans	458	
w/auto	828	
total	**1,286**	(all hardtops w/455 HO V-8)

OLDSMOBILE 4-4-2

Cutlass hardtop	751	
Cutlass S coupe	123	
Cutlass S hdtp	7,800	
Cutlass Supreme	1,171	(convertible)
total	**9,845***	(includes 772 w/W-30 package)

* GM paperwork claims 9,843 total, including 770 W-30 cars.

HURST/OLDS

hardtop	499	(220 w/sunroof)
convertible	130	
total	**629**	

BUICK GRAN SPORT

hardtop (350)	5,896	(16 w/column-shifted 3-speed, 353 w/4-speed, 5,526 w/TH-350 auto, 1 w/TH-400)
hardtop (455)	1,099	(84 w/4-speed, 1,015 w/auto)
hardtop (Stage 1)	728	(101 w/4-speed, 627 w/auto)
convertible (350)	645	(5 w/column-shifted 3-speed, 39 w/4-speed, 601 w/auto)
convertible (455)	126	(12 w/4-speed, 114 w/auto)
convert. (Stage 1)	81	(15 w/4-speed, 66 w/auto)
total	**8,575***	

* GSX breakdown (these numbers included in above total)

GSX (350)	16	(all hardtops: 1 w/4-speed, 15 w/TH-350 auto)
GSX (455)	4	(all hardtops: 1 w/4-speed, 3 w/TH-400 auto)
GSX (Stage 1)	24	(all hardtops: 2 w/4-speed, 22 w/TH-400 auto)
total	**44**	

DODGE CHALLENGER RALLYE

	8,128	(all hardtops)

DODGE CHARGER RALLYE

coupe	460	
hardtop	3,431	
total	**3,791**	

DODGE DEMON 340

	10,222	(all sport coupes)

PLYMOUTH ROAD RUNNER

	7,628	(all hardtops; includes 672 GTX 440-cid V-8)

PLYMOUTH 'CUDA

	7,828	(all hardtops; 5,864 w/340-cid V-8)

PLYMOUTH DUSTER 340

	15,681	(all sport coupes)

FORD MUSTANG MACH 1

	27,675	(all SportsRoofs w/302- or 351-cid V-8s)

FORD GRAN TORINO SPORT

"formal" roof	31,239	
SportsRoof	60,794	
total	**92,033**	

MERCURY MONTEGO GT

	5,820	(all fastbacks)

MERCURY COUGAR GT

	300	(all hardtops)

AMERICAN MOTORS JAVELIN AMX

	3,220	(all hardtops; 565 w/304-cid V-8, 1,830 w/360-cid V-8, 825 w/401-cid V-8)

NOTE: *Production data was supplied by various sources, including Christo Datini at the GM Heritage Center, Ford Motor Company & Kevin Marti at Marti Auto Works (www.martiauto.com), Galen Govier (Mopar material) at Galen's Tag Service (www.galengovier.com), and American Motors enthusiast Eddie Stakes at www.planethoustonamx.com.*

A rear spoiler was no longer included in 1972's Z28 package, priced at $769.15, but could be added at extra cost. A beefed suspension, power brakes, Positraction differential, and a 255-horsepower 350 V-8 remained standard attractions. *courtesy Mecum Auctions*

calculated "at the flywheel," but now all underhood power-robbing variables were entered into the equation, hence the new net aspect.

Why Detroit switched from gross to net horsepower ratings was no mystery. Tricking customers was the main goal this time. Even tougher emissions standards ahead promised more radical power cuts, and hopefully these wouldn't appear so drastic once net advertising took root.

At least the roller coaster finally came to rest.

CHEVROLET

Save for restyled front marker lights and a new grille, 1972's Chevelle was a near perfect copy of its predecessor. Chevy's Z15 package rolled over almost identically, too, with the most notable change coming where it hurt as all A-body V-8s, including the truly meek Turbo Fire 307, became available for the latest SS. Net outputs were 130 horsepower for the 307 small-block, 165 for the L65 350, 175 for the L48 350, 240 for the LS3 big-block, and 270 for the LS5 454. An available Powerglide returned for the 307, which, like the L65, was backed in base form by a three-speed manual. Chevelle SS buyers in California could only order the two 350 V-8s in 1972.

Chevrolet's SS Camaro rolled out for one more year before succumbing to sagging popularity. In its place for 1973 was the new Type LT Camaro, offered with a V-8 only. Spoilers were no longer standard for 1972's Z28, which also experienced fading sales.

The GTO package was only offered for LeMans coupes and hardtops in 1972. The base V-8 again was the L78 400, net rated at 250 horsepower. A three-speed manual was standard behind the L78, while an automatic once more was the only choice with the optional L75 455. All transmissions were available behind the LS5 455 HO, demonstrated here. *Mike Mueller*

A restyled grille, echoing the Honeycomb wheel design introduced the previous year, identified a 1972 Trans Am at a glance up front. Honeycomb wheels were optional this year. Now net-rated at 300 horsepower, the LS5 455 HO again was the only engine offered. Available behind the HO was a Hurst-shifted four-speed or TH-400 automatic. *Mike Mueller*

Ordering a 4-4-2 in 1972 required checking of the same option code, W-29, previously used in 1967. A 350 two-barrel small-block was the base engine for the W-29 package, offered for four body styles: Cutlass hardtop, Cutlass S club coupe and hardtop, and Cutlass Supreme convertible.

PONTIAC

Now available by way of an option package for LeMans coupes and hardtops only, 1972's GTO again could be fitted with the same three V-8s: base L78 400, L75 455 or LS5 455 HO. Net output ratings were 250, 250, and 300 horsepower, respectively. Optional ram-air also was listed for the HO and 400. The familiar Endura nose returned, but standard bucket seats didn't. An optional ducktail spoiler was initially considered for 1972, but only a couple installations are known.

A 175-horsepower L30 350 was standard for this year's Firebird Formula; the L78 and LS5 were optional. A restyled grille, apparently inspired by the Honeycomb wheels introduced the year before, represented the easiest way to identify 1972's Trans Am. Those Honeycomb rims became options this year, while the Rally II wheels returned as standard equipment. Again the only engine choice was the LS5 455.

GM's decision to drop its 400-cube displacement limit for its intermediate models rendered the Hurst/Olds redundant in 1970, the year all 4-4-2 models were treated to 455-cid V-8s. But a Hurst/Olds returned for 1972, available in hardtop and convertible forms.

OLDSMOBILE

The 4-4-2 became available in 1972 by way of the W29 4-4-2 Appearance and Handling Package, available for the Cutlass and Cutlass Supreme. The L32 350 small-block, topped by a two-barrel, was now standard, net-rated at 160 horsepower. A 180-horsepower 350 (L34) was optional, as were the L75 455 and W-30 big-block, both rated the same as in 1971.

HURST/OLDS

The Hurst/Olds returned for 1972, just in time to serve as the official pace car for the 56th running of the Indianapolis 500. Cameo White was again the exclusive finish but this time was accented with highly reflective gold decals instead of paint. Standard power came from a 270-horsepower 455 Rocket V-8; the 300-horsepower W-30 was optional. The TH-400, with Dual Gate shifter and console, remained in place as the only transmission choice. The W-25 forced-air hood topped things off up front, and power front discs were again included, as was the heavy-duty Rallye

Buick's Skylark GS again was available in small- or big-block forms with or without a top in 1972.While most Gran Sports were fitted with either four-speed manuals or Turbo Hydra-matic automatics, 21 350-equipped models (16 hardtops, 5 convertibles) featured mundane column-shifted three-speeds. Go figure.

Suspension. Super Stock III wheels, done in Hurst Gold and downsized back to 14 inches, went on at the corners wearing Goodyear G60 rubber. Coupes came with vinyl tops and could be enhanced further with an optional electric sunroof. Reportedly 220 sunroof-equipped models were built for 1972.

BUICK

Net-rated output figures dropped published power further for the last of the Skylark-based Gran Sports in 1972. The standard 350 small-block now was tagged at 195 horsepower, the 455 at 225, and the Stage 1 at 270. Other mechanicals carried over from 1971, as did the GSX package for one last time. *Hi-Performance Cars* magazine awarded the GS-455 its "Top Performance Car of the Year" award for 1972.

UNDER THE HOOD: 1972's HOTTEST V-8s*

MODEL	CID	BORE & STROKE	CR	HORSEPOWER	TORQUE
Pontiac (HO)	455	4.151 x 4.210	8.4:1	300 @ 4,000	415 @ 3,200
Chevrolet SS 454	454	4.25 x 4.00	8.5:1	270 @ 4,000	390 @ 3,200
Chevrolet Z28	350	4.00 x 3.48	9.0:1	255 @ 4,600	280 @ 4,000
Buick GS (Stage 1)	455	4.3125 x 3.90	8.5:1	270 @ 4,400	390 @ 3,000
Olds 4-4-2 (W-30)	455	4.125 x 4.250	8.5:1	300 @ 4,700	410 @ 3,200
Ford/Mercury (HO)	351	4.00 x 3.50	8.8:1	275 @ 6,000	286 @ 3,800
Ford/Mercury (CJ)	351	4.00 x 3.50	9:1	266 @ 5,400	301 @ 3,600
Dodge/Plymouth	440	4.320 x 3.750	8.2:1	280 @ 4,800	375 @ 3,200
Dodge/Plymouth	340	4.040 x 3.31	8.5:1	240 @ 4,800	290 @ 3,600
AMC	401	4.165 x 3.68	8.5:1	255 @ 4,600	345 @ 3,300

NOTE: *CID is cubic-inch displacement; CR is compression ratio; bore/stroke in inches.*

** Discounting Corvette*

TAG TEAM

Chrysler's street Hemi had no chance whatsoever of surviving past 1971, but apparently Dodge and Plymouth officials planned on keeping the triple-carb 440 around at least for one more year. Or was that "hoped to?" Brochures listed the Six Pack RB option for 1972's Charger, and Plymouth paperwork also mentioned 440+6 availability for that year's Road Runner. Compression remained high (10.3:1) for this supercar survivor, which predictably was off-limits to California customers. But equally predictable were EPA certification test results for this brute—a big fat "F." Though completely emissions-illegal, a few six-throat 440 B-body installations (at least two Chargers and two Road Runners) did manage to escape into the wild early in the 1972 model run. Then that was that.

Featuring feasible compression (8.2:1), a four-barrel-fed 440 did earn its EPA diploma for 1972 and, at 280 horsepower, represented the highest rated V-8 available to B-body buyers that year. In Plymouth's case, installing this 440 in a Road Runner meant "GTX" identification was added to the fenders and decklid, creating a combo similar to Dodge's Charger Super Bee of 1971.

While 1972's GTX deal wasn't banned in California, the Road Runner's optional Air Grabber hood was. Both four-speeds and automatics were available behind Plymouth's 440 that year, but it was automatics only for the package in 1973 and '74. GTX identification wasn't seen again until Dodge used it in 2004 for a special run of high-profile pickup trucks painted in Hemi Orange, Sublime Green, Plum Crazy purple, or Banana Yellow.

Plymouth's GTX didn't return for 1972, but Road Runners equipped that year with the optional 440 big-block were treated to "GTX" fender identification. *courtesy Mecum Auctions*

Road Runner was still an impressive package in 1972, even without optional 440+6 or Hemi V-8s. A 255-horse 400-cid big-block was standard; a 240-horsepower 340 small-block or 280-horsepower 440 big-block were optional. Installing that latter RB V-8 added "GTX" external identification.

Single headlights returned for Plymouth's E-body pony car in 1972, available in base Barracuda or 'Cuda forms only. The Gran Coupe and convertible body did not roll over from 1971.

PLYMOUTH

Standard for 1972's Road Runner was a new 400 cubic-inch big-block, created by boring the old 383. Net output for this four-barrel-fed V-8 was 255 horsepower. Options included a 240-horsepower 340 small-block and 280-horsepower 440 four-barrel. Contributing to the 340's output drop was the substitution of the 360 two-barrel V-8's wimpy heads. While exhaust valve size remained the same (1.60 inches), the intake unit shrank from the 340's generous 2.02 inches to a tame 1.88. On a positive note, Chrysler's electronic ignition system became standard for the latest 340 V-8.

A rear sway bar joined the standard heavy-duty suspension package in 1972, and the Air Grabber hood remained an option for one last year. Two high-profile tape treatment options were offered for 1972, hopefully to distract customer's attentions away from what was going on beneath the skin.

A two-door hardtop was the only Barracuda body choice in 1972 after 1971's low-budget coupe was axed along with the short-lived E-body convertible and luxury-minded Gran Coupe. Single headlights returned for 1972, and two pairs of large, round taillights appeared in back. Manual front disc brakes were standard for both the base Barracuda and V-8-only 'Cuda, now fitted with a rear sway bar and a mundane 318-cid small-block in base form. The 340 was the only optional 'Cuda engine.

All 1972 E-body engines could be backed by the optional Torqueflite, but the available four-speed manual was saved for the 340. Like the Hemi and 440+6 big-blocks, that way-cool Shaker hood, the various spoilers, and big 15-inch wheels all failed to return. The only rear end option was the Performance Axle package, which included a heavy-duty 3.55:1 Sure-Grip differential, a fan shroud, and a 26-inch radiator. This extra-cost group (only offered with the 340 V-8) also included a power steering oil cooler when optional steering assist was added.

The bold body-side stripes added to 1971's Duster 340 were updated this year, with additional cartoon work somewhat reminiscent of Warner Brothers' Tasmanian Devil character added at their trailing ends. This was the easiest way to tell the two models apart at a glance.

Charger was also dressed up in Rallye garb in 1972 as Dodge's B-body R/T failed to return, too.

Right: A dust-trailing cartoon reminiscent of Warner Brothers' Tasmanian Devil was added to the Duster 340's body-side stripes in 1972. High-profile optional hood graphics carried over from 1971. *Mike Mueller*

Above: Superseding the R/T model for 1972 was Dodge's Challenger Rallye, quickly identified by its scooped hood and the strobe stripes running down its body sides.

DODGE

No more Challenger convertibles for 1972, either; all were now hardtops with roll-up rear-quarter glass. Exterior upgrades included yet another restyled grille and new round taillights, two to each side. The R/T also failed to return; same for all optional big-blocks. In place of the R/T was Challenger Rallye with its 318 small-block, performance hood, strobe side stripes, and heavy-duty suspension. The 340 was optional.

Charger R/T also was superseded in 1972 by a Rallye edition, available for base coupes and hardtops. Along with exclusive exterior treatments, the Rallye package included a heavy-duty suspension and F70 tires. The 150-horsepower 318 was standard, the 400 big-block was optional, along with the 340 and 280-horsepower 440. The former was only available with the Rallye option, while the latter was listed only for the Rallye and top-shelf SE. Base Charger buyers were out of luck as far as Dodge's hottest V-8s were concerned.

In A-body ranks, Dodge offered another Demon 340 in 1972 before deciding to drop the name, not the car. More than one uptight, right-thinking individual had complained about the use of such evil imagery, convincing promotional people to cave. The same basic model then returned for 1973 and 1974 bearing the name Dart Sport 340.

TIME SLIPS: 1972

MODEL	¼-MILE PERFORMANCE	SOURCE
Buick GS 455	14.10 seconds at 97.0 mph	*Motor Trend,* June 1972
Oldsmobile 4-4-2 (W-30)	14.37 seconds at 98 mph	*Hi-Performance Cars,* August 1972
Chevrolet Camaro Z28	14.5 seconds at 93.0 mph	*Motor Trend,* October 1971
Pontiac GTO (455 HO)	14.6 seconds at 95.2 mph	*Motor Trend,* October 1971
Chevrolet Chevelle SS 454	14.76 seconds at 97.6 mph	*SSDI,* June 1972
Ford Mustang (351 HO)	15.1 seconds at 95.6 mph	*Car and Driver,* March 1972
Dodge Demon 340	15.18 seconds at 92.8 mph	*SSDI,* June 1972
Chevrolet Camaro Z28	15.2 seconds at 86.6 mph	*Motor Trend,* August 1972
Hurst/Olds	15.30 seconds at 93.0 mph	*Hi-Performance Cars,* August 1972
Plymouth Barracuda (340)	15.5 seconds at 91.7 mph	*Car and Driver,* January 1972
Pontiac Firebird Formula 455	15.5 seconds at 89.5 mph	*Motor Trend,* October 1971
Ford Mustang (351 CJ)	15.55 seconds at 89.5 mph	*Motor Trend,* October 1971
Plymouth Duster 340	15.6 seconds at 89.5 mph	*Car and Driver,* September 1972
Ford Gran Torino Sport	17.9 seconds at 80 mph	*Motor Trend,* June 1972

NOTE: *SSDI is* Super Stock & Drag Illustrated magazine

GRAN FINALE

With its high price and singular focus—to pop eyeballs out of heads—Buick's GSX never really had a chance to qualify as a hot seller, even after it was made available with all Gran Sport V-8s (not just the 455) in 1971. Only 678 were built for 1970, followed by 124 in 1971 and a mere 44 in 1972. One simple paragraph's worth of promotional ink appeared in 1971 sales brochures, while none was found the following year.

After offering only two exterior shades in 1970, the GSX paint palette expanded to 9 in 1971 and 12 in 1972. Those bold black accents carried over up through '72 with one exception: the black paint offered in 1971 was complemented by white-trimmed gold stripes. The familiar hood tach, front spoiler, rear sway bar, and G60 Wide Ovals on 15x7 sport rims—all standard in 1970—were listed as options in 1972.

As in 1971, front disc brakes weren't part of the basic GSX deal when the 350 small-block was installed in 1972 but were mandated at extra cost when one of the two available 455 big-blocks was chosen. Functional ram-air was included in all cases. The norm behind the 350 was a three-speed stick, with a four-speed or TH-350 automatic optional. Again, the choices behind the 455 numbered two: four-speed manual or TH-400 auto.

Buick tried the GSX treatment again in 1974, this time for the Apollo, which shared a platform with Chevy's Nova's from 1973 to 1975. Both a six-cylinder and small-block V-8 were available for the all-show, no-go GSX Apollo.

Only 44 GSX Buicks were built for 1972, some with vinyl tops, some without. Only three featured Sunburst Yellow paint: one with black vinyl, one with brown vinyl, one with no vinyl. *courtesy Mecum Auctions*

FORD

Next to nothing was done to differentiate a 1972 Mustang from its predecessor. And with no more available big-blocks, the hottest pony car options this year were two Cleveland small-blocks: the 351 Cobra Jet and 351 HO.

The rare 351 HO was basically a toned down version of 1971's Boss 351. Led by John Bowers, Ford engineers had hoped to keep the Boss engine alive in a world fueled on unleaded gasoline even if the Boss Mustang itself was no longer around to benefit from their efforts. According to engineer Tom Morris of Ford's Special Engine Group, "the basic guts" of the two HO small-blocks were the same, with different cylinder heads, pistons, and camshaft incorporated in 1972. Perhaps the most prominent difference involved compression, which dropped from 11:1 to 8.8:1. The '72 HO's cam remained a mechanical unit, but it was tamed considerably to work with that lowered compression. Output was 275 horsepower.

Rolling over from 1971, the 351 CJ this time was rated at 266 horsepower thanks to a few emissions-conscious modifications. Curiously the CJ and HO weren't available in 1972 with the optional Dual Ram Induction hood, which was limited to that year's two-barrel Cleveland small-block. Apparently the ram-air four-barrel Clevelands couldn't earn emissions certification, while the tamer two-barrel could while breathing in cooler air. The same situation existed in 1973.

Revised tape stripes appeared for 1972's Mach 1 Mustang. Lower body paint was either black or argent depending on the overall color choice. *Mike Mueller*

A totally new body went atop a full frame in Ford/Mercury's midsize class in 1972, and in place of the Torino GT/Cobra came the sharp-looking Gran Torino Sport, offered in formal-roof or SportsRoof forms.

American Motors' first second-generation pony car was offered in three forms in 1971: base Javelin, upscale SST, and sporty AMX. The choices numbered two the following year: Javelin SST and AMX, shown here. *courtesy National Automotive History Collection, Detroit Public Library*

The easiest way to spot a 1972 Mach 1 involved a look out back, where a pop-open gas cap was no longer included. The base Mach 1 engine again was a 302 two-barrel, which once more could be topped by the "NASA" hood, a no-cost option. This lid was added automatically along with the three optional Cleveland small-blocks.

A definitely new body, now riding on a full frame, appeared for midsize Fords in 1972, and the upscale Gran Torino joined this year's Torino. All Torino models now came standard with manual front disc brakes. And while the GT and Cobra renditions didn't return, the new Gran Torino Sport at least picked up some of the slack, looking particularly sexy in SportsRoof form with that standard hood scoop and dual racing-style mirrors. A formal-roof Gran Torino Sport also was offered and, like its fastback running mate, featured a 140-horsepower 302 two-barrel small-block in base form.

The hottest Gran Torino Sport in 1972 was equipped with the Rallye Equipment Group, which added full instrumentation inside, a competition suspension (with rear stabilizer) underneath, 14x6 wheels shod in G70 raised-white-letter tires at the corners, and a 248-horsepower 351 four-barrel V-8 beneath that scoop. Backing up the Cleveland small-block was a Hurst-shifted four-speed. A 429 four-barrel big-block, rated at 205 horsepower, was optional.

Mercury's midsize Montego GT was available in one body style only for 1972: fastback. Again, the Ford-dedicated Magnum 500 wheels seen here are not technically correct but were added nonetheless by many Merc owners back in the day. *Tom Shaw*

MERCURY

Replacing Cyclone in Mercury's 1972 midsize lineup was Montego GT, a big boat that again shared Ford's Torino foundation. Like Gran Torino Sport, Montego GT also featured dual racing mirrors, a scooped hood, manual front disc brakes, and a 302 small-block in standard form. But only one body-style, a fastback, was offered. Available on the options list (for both Montego GT and Montego MX hardtop) was the Cyclone Performance package, consisting of a functional ram-air hood, Traction-Lok differential, Wide Oval tires, and either a Hurst-shifted four-speed or Select-Shift automatic. Cyclone engine choices numbered two: the 351 CJ small-block or 429 big-block. F70 rubber was included with the 351, G70 with the 429, and power front discs were mandatory in the latter's case. The small-block Cyclone package cost $518.10, its big-block counterpart was priced at $616.60. Reportedly only 29 Montego GTs and 1 MX were released with the Cyclone option. Of those GTs, 20 featured the 429, 9 the 351.

A Cougar GT appeared one last time for 1972 but no longer featured an available big-block. This year's Cougars were limited to three 351 small-blocks, including the 266-horsepower Cobra Jet.

AMC

The "base" Javelin" was dropped for 1972, leaving the SST and AMX renditions to promote the American way. Although AMC's 150-horsepower 304-cid V-8, fitted with a two-barrel carb and single exhaust, was now standard for AMX, the 220-horsepower 360 and 255-horsepower 401 four-barrel engines were still around on the options list, as was the coveted Go Package. New on that list was a Chrysler-supplied, Torqueflite-based automatic transmission, called "Torque-Command," in place of the old "Shift-Command" auto supplied by Borg-Warner. An optional, unmistakably flashy interior, done by French designer Pierre Cardin (see page 223), also debuted this year.

MOTOR OF THE YEAR: 1972 DODGE/PLYMOUTH 340

Type	LA-series OHV V-8
Displacement	340 cubic inches
Bore	4.040 inches
Stroke	3.31 inches
Horsepower	240 at 4,800 rpm (275 @ 5,000 from 1968 to '71)
Torque	290 at 3,600 rpm (340 at 3,200 from 1968 to '71)
Compression	8.5:1 (10.5:1 from 1968 to '71)
Fuel delivery	750-cfm Carter Thermo-Quad 4-barrel (650-cfm Carter AVS 4-barrel uses before 1971)
Air cleaner	single-snorkel
Ignition	transistorized
Cylinder block	cast-iron
Crankshaft	forged-steel w/2.5-inch journals
Connecting rods	forged-steel
Pistons	cast-aluminum
Cam	hydraulic w/268 degrees duration on intake, 276 degrees on exhaust, 44 degrees of overlap
Rocker ratio	1.5:1
Cylinder heads	cast-iron
Valve sizes	1.88-inch intakes, 1.60-inch exhausts (2.02-inch intakes from 1968 to '71)
Valve lift	0.429 inch, intake; 0.444 inch, exhaust
Exhaust system	cast-iron "log-type" manifolds (streamlined header-type cast-iron manifolds used before 1971)

CHAPTER 10

1973 ONE LAST GASP

PONTIAC BRINGS BACK ITS SUPER DUTY

Pontiac officials initially announced in July 1972 that their 455 Super Duty V-8 would be available for GTOs, Grand Ams, and Firebirds, but this was before a changing of the guard at the division. In October that year, Martin Caserio stepped into the general manager's office after Jim McDonald stepped out, and among the new g.m.'s first moves was cancelling the Super Duty altogether. He later relented, but only in the F-body's case. Both Trans Am (shown here) and Formula were treated to SD-455 power in both 1973 and 1974. *Jim Schild*

While rival engineers were concentrating on fuel efficiency and contaminant counts, Pontiac people continued building real excitement into 1973 and '74. Environmental Protection Agency restrictions and overseas oil embargo be damned, the same folks who introduced midsize muscle in 1964 also signed off on Detroit's last great factory hot rod 10 years later. A coincidence? We think not. Plain and simply, Pontiac saved some of its best work for last, probably to prove once and for all that no one else did it better back then. And as a suitable exclamation point, PMD officials also dusted off a legendary name for this curtain-closer: Super Duty.

Like the 421 Super Duty of 1962–63, the LS2 SD-455 V-8 was bad to the bone. But there was one big difference: while the original SD was an uncivilized beast never meant for civilized operation, its 455-cube successor was amazingly traffic-friendly, as well as emissions-legal, thanks mostly to its certainly mild compression and modest

UNDER THE HOOD: 1973's HOTTEST V-8s*

MODEL	CID	BORE & STROKE	CR	HORSEPOWER	TORQUE
Pontiac Firebird (SD)	455	4.151 x 4.210	8.4:1	290 @ 4,000	395 @ 3,200
Pontiac GTO	455	4.151 x 4.210	8.0:1	250 @ 4,000	380 @ 2,800
Chevrolet SS	454	4.25 x 4.00	8.5:1	245 @ 4,000	375 @ 2,800
Chevrolet Z28	350	4.00 x 3.48	9.0:1	245 @ 5,200	280 @ 4,000
Olds 4-4-2	455	4.125 x 4.250	8.5:1	270 @ 4,200	370 @ 3,200
Buick GS (Stage 1)	455	4.3125 x 3.90	8.5:1	270 @ 4,400	390 @ 3,000
Dodge/Plymouth	440	4.320 x 3.750	8.2:1	280 @ 4,800	380 @ 3,200
Dodge/Plymouth	340	4.04 x 3.310	8.5:1	240 @ 4,800	295 @ 3,600
American Motors	401	4.165 x 3.68	8.5:1	255 @ 4,600	345 @ 3,300
Ford/Mercury (CJ)	351	4.00 x 3.50	9.0:1	266 @ 5,400	301 @ 3,600

NOTE: *CID is cubic-inch displacement; CR is compression ratio; bore/stroke in inches.*

** Discounting Corvette*

cam. Even so the LS2 still could've easily blown away most of Detroit's unfettered, smog-spouting rivals had it debuted five years earlier. In 1973 and '74 it surely reigned supreme at a time when most market watchers agreed that the end of the road had come for four-wheeled fun. "Just when we had fast cars relegated to the museum section, Pontiac has surprised everyone and opened a whole new exhibit," claimed a 1973 *Car and Driver* report on the 455 Super Duty.

Everything about the LS2 was super-duper, beginning with its new beefy block, burly nodular-iron crank, and bulletproof forged-iron rods. A Rochester Quadra-jet four-barrel delivered the fuel/air, while free-flowing cast-iron headers hauled away spent gases. But the real stars of the show were the cylinder heads, which were lovingly massaged by the horsepower hounds at Air Flow Research to move the good air in, bad air out better than anything Pontiac engineers had ever concocted. The end result was a low-compression, high-powered V-8 that could rev surely and strongly to 6,000 rpm, even on 91-octane fuel, while still remaining kind to the environment. Or was it?

Being clever cusses, PMD engineers noticed going in that required EPA engine testing only ran for about 50 seconds. They then put together an ingenious system that automatically shut off the exhaust gas re-circulation (EGR) valve after 53 ticks. This trick in turn allowed the SD-455 to breathe easier while making 310 net-rated horses. Of course it also meant the LS2 spit out unacceptable emissions, this after supposedly passing its test with apparent flying colors.

Unfortunately those clean-air cops were clever too. They immediately smelled a rat and the ruse was quickly uncovered. Pontiac was then forced to remove its EGR inactivating system and retest the Super Duty by March 15, 1973. To survive this second trial, engineers had to trade their original SD cam (with 0.480-inch lift) for a tamer unit with 0.401-inch lift. Advertised output then dropped to 290 horsepower, still nothing to sneeze at.

The SD-455 was originally introduced, in 310-horse form, to the press by Special Products Group chief Herb Adams in July 1972 at GM's Milford Proving

Most witnesses marveled at Pontiac's 455 Super Duty, which somehow managed to make its way past tailpipe sniffers while still producing 290 real horsepower—and with only 8.4:1 compression, to boot. *Jim Schild*

A luxury showboat, Pontiac's 1973 Grand Am also could take on a high-performance persona by installing any of the GTO's optional V-8s.

A totally new LeMans body served as a base for 1973's GTO, offered in two body styles: coupe (with exposed rear quarter glass) and sport coupe, shown here. Setting the latter apart from the former were rear quarter window louvers borrowed from Pontiac's new Grand Am.

A 175-horsepower 350 V-8 was the Firebird Formula's base engine in 1973. Options included the 230-horsepower L78 400, the 250-horsepower L75 455, and the supreme choice (demonstrated here), the 290-horsepower LS2 SD-455. *Jim Schild*

Ground. Adams promised the Super Duty option would be available by that fall for Grand Am, Grand Prix, LeMans, and both Firebirds—Trans Am and Formula. Those certification hassles, however, helped delay initial deliveries of the 290-horse LS2 until April 1973, and then only for the two Firebirds. One Super Duty GTO test mule did find its way into journalists' hands, resulting in the famous *Hi-Performance Cars* April 1973 cover story (see page 220) touting this awesome A-body as its "Car of the Year." Not so fast.

While intermediate applications were cancelled right after that magazine went to press, at least Pontiac was able to release the two F-body renditions, and these Super Duty pony cars shocked the automotive press. "How it ever got past the preview audience in GM's board room is a mystery, but here it is—the car that couldn't happen," announced *Car and Driver* in a May 1973 road test of a pre-production 310-horse Super Duty Trans Am. "The Last of the Fast Cars comes standard with the sort of acceleration that hasn't been seen in years," concluded that *Car and Driver* report.

Pontiac's SD-455 made an encore appearance in 1974 before rolling off into the archives—along with all of Detroit's last remaining muscle machines.

PONTIAC

New for GM's intermediate lines in 1973 was the "Colonnade" body style, which carried "hardtop" designations in company paperwork despite the obvious B-pillars (or "posts") between side windows. The Colonnade's heavily pillared roof was created to meet yet another federal safety standard, this one involving rollover accident survival rates. In the two-door Colonnade coupe's case, frameless door glass was used to enhance the airy hardtop mirage, to great effect in some minds. Big, heavy impact-resistant bumpers also bookended this safety-conscious shell, which wasn't offered in topless form. No more A-body convertibles.

New as well in Pontiac ranks that year was the aforementioned Euro-style Grand Am, available with two or four doors. Combining Grand Prix luxury and prestige with Trans Am performance, this fresh-faced model featured an exclusive, high-profile nose covered in resilient urethane, to both withstand low-speed collisions and hide those prominent "5-mph" bumpers. Radial tires and GM's RTS (Radial Tuned Suspension) were standard, and options included the GTO's two V-8s, meaning a Grand Am coupe could be morphed into arguably Detroit's best-dressed, most prestigious performance car in 1973.

The GTO option was again available for two LeMans body styles in 1973, coupe and sport coupe, with the latter featuring the Grand Am's stylish rear quarter window louvers. Two NACA-duct hood scoops were standard, as were 15x7 stamped-steel wheels. "Baby moon" hubcaps were included with these rims; adding bright trim rings required spending a few extra bucks. Honeycomb and Rally II wheel options returned and could be wrapped up in raised-white-letter G60 tires supplied by Firestone, Goodyear, or Uniroyal. A new notchback bench seat (that looked a little like buckets) with head restraints was standard inside.

Rated at 230 horsepower, Pontiac's 400-cube L78 V-8 was again standard beneath those NACA ducts. The only optional engine was the 250-horsepower L75 455 HO limited to Turbo Hydra-matic applications only.

TURNING GASOLINE INTO GOLD

Growing safety concerns, coupled with tightening emissions standards, already had transformed the way Detroit went about the business of building cars by the time the 1960s closed. Then along came a newfound need to thoroughly maximize fuel efficiency as the 1970s opened, inspired initially by Mother Nature.

The American winter of 1972–73 was an especially cold one, leading energy producers to concentrate on the distillation of heating oils. This was done at the expense of gasoline and diesel fuel production, resulting in shortages at pumps as 1973 warmed up, a reality some Americans believed was more contrived than market-influenced. Whatever the case, these events represented a handful of many lined-up dominoes on the edge of teetering.

By the early 1970s, increasingly powerful environmentalist factions were inhibiting the exploration and development of domestic energy sources, creating a situation where the United States was growing more and more dependent on oil imports—a potentially volatile mix that presented foreign powers with a political apple ripe for picking. All arguments within these shores concerning whether or not the fuel crisis of the previous winter was fact or fiction were rendered moot on October 17, 1973, when 11 Middle Eastern nations placed an embargo on crude oil shipped to all countries supporting Israel. A thoroughly real emergency resulted. So did long lines at many filling stations and dreaded gas rationing in some areas. In 1974, Washington also instituted a national 55 miles per hour speed limit to help conserve every precious drop of gasoline.

In the meantime, fossil squeezing grew even dearer as prices began to soar, from an average of 38.8 cents a gallon for leaded regular in 1973 to 53.2 cents in 1974. Thanks to Secretary of State Henry Kissinger's diplomatic efforts mediating Egypt-Israel relations, the Arab oil embargo was lifted on March 18 that year, but gasoline continued gaining value. The average gallon of leaded fuel cost 62.2 cents in 1977, 85.7 in '79, 119.1 in '80, and 131.1 in '81. Unleaded was averaging 137.8 cents a gallon in 1981.

While drivers in the 1960s rarely blinked an eye watching their beloved muscle car travel less than 10 miles on a gallon of Sunoco's best high-test, such "economy" became unbearable for Average Joe in the 1970s. "Gas hogs" overnight became the scourge of the marketplace, while Detroit's all-new, truly small compacts—cars like Vega, introduced for 1971—suddenly were all the rage. After selling nearly 400,000 Vegas in 1972 and '73, Chevrolet rolled out about 453,000 more in 1974, by which time some industry-watchers were predicting extinction for America's full-size gas-guzzlers—and perhaps the same for their intermediate running mates.

"The late energy circus precipitated the largest, most rapid disruption of the automotive marketplace since World War II," began Jim Brokaw's explanation of the situation in *Motor Trend's* August 1974 issue. "When fuel was short, nub short, fuel economy was the dominant criteria for purchase. When you can't get gas—at any price—there is no choice but the long-legged little cars." Indeed, fuel-efficient budget buggies—the aforementioned Vega, Ford's Pinto and Maverick, AMC's Gremlin, etc.—did do the hotcakes thing during the 1970s' early years and continued cooking with fire after fuel shortage fears subsided in 1974. But then a funny thing happened on the way to big American iron's funeral.

"Just a few months ago, dealers and salesman alike were lamenting the fuel-inspired fact that the only things automotive that were selling could probably fit into the trunk of an intermediate," continued Brokaw in the summer of 1974. "Now, as W. C. Fields would have said, the worm has turned."

Plainly put, Americans still weren't ready to give up on comfort and convenience, nor the kick of a V-8, not even after gasoline started turning into gold. Many car buyers simply grew accustomed to the elevated expense of traveling from A to B as the 1970s rolled on. Sure, compacts were here to stay. But by no means were bigger cars leaving any time soon.

"Logic, reason, fuel problems and the money crunch all indicate that the full-size sedan is all but done," added Brokaw in an April 1975 *Motor Trend* report. "Yet in the face of all common sense and computer analysis, the two best-selling cars, month after month, by a good margin, are the full-size Chevrolet and Ford." Right behind those two "behemoths" in third was Chevy's good ol' Chevelle, still a major player in the not-dead-yet midsize field following a rather radical redesign for 1973 that had completely resisted any and all downsizing influences.

The days of loading down larger cars with heaps of horsepower, however, were plain and simply done, at least for the moment. Not until engineers learned how to combine miles per gallon with miles per hour , using ultra-precise computer-controlled fuel delivery systems, would Detroit once again start building truly fun cars.

The timing simply couldn't have been better for Joe Oldham in 1965. Fresh out of New York University, newly inked journalism degree in hand, he immediately began freelancing for Big-Apple-based Magnum Royal Publications, home to *Hi-Performance Cars* magazine. "I've always been a car guy," he recalled in February 2015. "I used to read all the car magazines, and I always knew I wanted to do that, to write for a car magazine." His dream not only came true, it morphed into reality just as modern high-performance went on the rise. "I was one of the luckiest people in the world to have lived through those years, to drive all those great cars, to write about them."

A compendium of his favorite road tests, *Muscle Car Confidential* was released by Motorbooks in 2007 to rave reviews. If you don't presently have this one in your library (and you should), get ready to fork over about 100 bucks on Amazon.com for a used example of this out-of-print masterpiece.

Oldham left his Magnum Royal gig behind at the end of 1973 to join the Hearst Corporation, initially contributing to *Motor* magazine, the venerable title first published in 1903. He became executive editor of Hearst's *Popular Mechanics* in the fall of 1981 then editor-in-chief in 1985, a position held until retirement in 2004. Along with his cigars, he presently enjoys the California sun, not to mention reminiscing about his 40-year-long labor of love.

His proudest moments? Producing *Muscle Car Confidential* is a given, but he's by far most fond of the July 1986 copy of *Popular Mechanics*. This 310-page double-issue featured a special section titled "The Building of America," introduced on page 106 by President Ronald Reagan, with following contributions from, among others, James Michener, Tom Wolfe, Isaac Asimov, Eric Sevareid, and Bob Hope. A blow-up print of this epic's cover hangs in Oldham's home today.

But, of course, every coin has two sides, and Oldham can only chuckle about *Hi-Performance Cars'* infamous April 1973 cover story, a report on a Pontiac that never was.

Like *Motor Trend* out west, Magnum Royal's east-coast rival also used to honor a "Car of the Year," predictably concentrating on high-perf models. Editor Marty Schorr's choice for 1973 was a Pontiac, a GTO Colonnade sport coupe depicted artistically on that colorful front flap. That a groovy illustration was used in place of a photo was only right considering the subject was never built, at least not for public consumption. Not with the 455 Super Duty V-8 announced on that issue's cover.

How did this mystery machine win *Cars* magazine's 13th Top Performance Car of the Year trophy? This curious tale dates back to July 1972, when Pontiac engineers Herb Adams and Tom Nell introduced their born-again Super Duty to the press at GM's Milford Proving Ground.

"Tom started talking about this new engine, and I couldn't believe my ears," recalled Oldham, there on assignment as usual. "Here was Pontiac, in the midst of the muscle car's demise, bringing out an all-new kind of engine, something really never seen before. The SD-455 was a very conventional pushrod cast-iron engine. [But] what was different was that it was [Detroit's] first high-performance engine specifically designed to meet the new emissions regulations while running on 91-octane unleaded gas. That's what made it unique."

PMD general manager Jim McDonald also took to the podium that day to announce that this low-compression, clean-running, high-powered marvel would become available in the spring of 1973 for F-bodies, as well as the restyled GTO, with an example of that latter application available for test drives. After taking in all the facts, Oldham took a bronze 455 SD GTO pre-production mule for a ride. While nothing was timed and no actual performance figures were available, the veteran autowriter was sure he'd found a winner. "I had driven the 1972 455 HO Trans Am the year before, and I knew this car felt much stronger, much more responsive. When I got into it, I just knew this was special. Even with that extra weight, with that bigger body, it was moving."

Once back in New York, he told his boss that Pontiac's Super Duty GTO was the only choice for their 1973 trophy. Schorr agreed, and the April issue went to press in January in advance of a March 1 on-sale date. Informed of the upcoming award, delighted Pontiac people also prepared an official presentation, scheduled for the New York auto show in March. Then, as Oldham put it, "the wheels came off."

In October 1972, Martin Caserio took over Pontiac's g.m. chair after McDonald moved over to Chevrolet. Not a "car guy" in the least, Caserio couldn't have cared less about the Super Duty, not when improving fuel economy and enhancing safety were now prime goals. He cancelled the option early in 1973, leaving Schorr and Oldham holding the bag, their magazine already in the works. While Caserio soon relented, allowing Super Duty Firebird production to commence, no SD-455 GTOs were built beyond that "rough-edged, incomplete" (Oldham's words) test vehicle. And nothing could be done about that spurious cover story.

Oldham admitted he did feel vindicated when the Super Duty pony car appeared, but he still knew he had to explain things to his readers, as well as apologize, in a column a couple months after the fact. He can't recall any scathing complaints. "Anyone who was 'dialed in,' who knew how these things work, they simply said, 'Tough call, Joe.' Nobody said 'What an asshole.' Marty also stood by me; he knew it wasn't my fault. [And Pontiac] engineers not only apologized, they were pissed [at their boss]. They were disappointed; they had watched their baby get killed."

Joe Oldham laughs about the whole episode today, and why not? He's holding on to two April 1973 *Hi-Performance Cars* back issues that can't be bought on eBay at any price.

Hi-Performance Cars magazine's 13th annual Top Performance Car of the Year pick ended up going to a machine that never was. After driving a 1973 Super Duty GTO test mule, contributor Joe Oldham advised editor Marty Schorr to honor this hot Poncho. Their April 1973 cover story then went to press before Pontiac cancelled the combo. Super Duty V-8s were only installed in Firebirds that year. *courtesy Joe Oldham*

Left: Chevrolet's Super Sport Chevelle made one final appearance in 1973, this time based on GM's new Colonnade coupe. No convertible was offered. Included in this last Z15 package were G70 tires on 14x7 Rally rims.

Along with the optional 455 Super Duty, available V-8s for 1973's Firebird Formula included the base L30 350, rated at 175 horsepower, and the L78 400 and L75 455. The latter V-8 returned beneath the base Trans Am's familiar hood scoop, which was no longer functional. Quicker steering became standard for the Trans Am in 1973, and G70 radial tires (along with RTS equipment) joined the options list late in year.

The wide center stripe running the length of 1972's T/A body was dropped, but this deletion was offset by a new decal option, code WW7, which added a truly large flaming firebird to the hood. The decal's colors varied according to paint choice. While the bird itself remained black, the surrounding flames went from orange (with Buccaneer Red), to blue (with Cameo White), to light green (with Brewster Green).

Don't ask. Why Chevrolet offered a Chevelle SS station wagon for one year only in 1973 is anyone's guess. Turbine wheels were standard for this gonzo grocery-getter.

CHEVROLET

Chevy's Z15 option rolled over into the Colonnade era for one last fling (in Chevelle ranks; it remained for El Camino into the 1980s), and this time was available for the Malibu coupe and two Malibu station wagons; a six-passenger two-seater and its eight-passenger, three-seat companion. The Z15 deal for 1973 included G70 tires on 14x7 Rally rims, dual sport mirrors, and a special instrument cluster with black bezels. Exterior treatments included a blacked-out grille, color-keyed striping along the lower body sides and wheel openings, bright drip moldings, bright trim for the triangular rear-quarter-windows, and "SS" badges for the grille, fenders, and tail. SS wagons also received a rear stabilizer bar.

Large round Camaro taillights appeared for the last time in 1973, the year the trimmed-out upscale LT model debuted. LT buyers also could add the Z28 or RS packages, or both, resulting in a decked-out Chevy pony car like none seen before.

The available engine list began with the L65 350 small-block, net-rated at 145 horsepower. Next was the 175-horse L48 350, followed by the top-dog LS4 454 big-block, which pumped out 245 ponies.

In 1973 Camaro news, civilized hydraulic lifters replaced the solid units used by all previous Z28 V-8s, meaning optional air conditioning could finally enter the equation. Output for the quieter 350 Turbo Fire was 245 horsepower. RPO Z28 was available this year for the base V-8 Camaro coupe and the new Type LT, which replaced the retiring Super Sport.

Back again for 1973 was Oldsmobile's W-29 Appearance and Handling Package, which converted only base Cutlass and Cutlass S coupes into 4-4-2s.

OLDSMOBILE

Oldsmobile's W29 Appearance and Handling Package returned in 1973, this time converting only base Cutlass and Cutlass S coupes into 4-4-2s. Engine availability also carried over almost identically from 1972 with one major exception—the W-30 455 was gone.

Based on the Cutlass S Colonnade coupe, the Hurst/Olds reappeared as well after a one year hiatus and this time was offered in two color schemes. Familiar was the Cameo White paint with white vinyl half top, gold stripes, and gold Super Stock III wheels. New was Ebony black with a black "wet look" half-vinyl roof and black-painted rims. Also new were Goodrich radial T/A tires and standard swivel bucket seats. In between those buckets was a console that once more served as a home to Hurst's Dual Gate shifter.

GM's Turbo Hydra-matic again was the only transmission mated up to the Hurst/Olds' 455 V-8. Air-conditioned models in 1973 used the 250-horsepower L75 455. Non-air models got a hotter 275-horse L77 V-8.

Color choices, white or black, were new for the Hurst/Olds in 1973. A Landau-style half-vinyl roof was standard, as were dual sport mirrors and swiveling bucket seats. The sunroof seen here was optional. *Mike Mueller*

BUICK

Last seen in 1958, Buick's revered Century nameplate superseded Skylark in 1973. Still rolling on a 112-inch wheelbase, the new Century was some 200 pounds heavier than its predecessor thanks to increases in width, height, and length—not to mention the addition of those 5 miles per hour bumpers. Extra attention to noise insulation also helped tip the scales further to the right. More than one driver lauded the 1973 Gran Sport for its quietness, something not commonly associated with earlier muscle cars. But this was Buick's brand of muscle, "a pleasant blend of performance and elegant luxury," according to one magazine review.

Gran Sport equipment moved to the options list in 1973. Along with appropriate exterior identification, the GS package included heavy-duty suspension with stabilizer bars at both ends. All Century models featured standard front disc brakes.

Something other than a four-barrel made its way beneath a Gran Sport's hood for the first time in 1973 as the base engine this year was a two-barrel-fed 350 small-block rated at 150 horsepower. Next up on the options list was a 190-horse 350 with a four-barrel and dual exhausts. Dual exhausts were included in the deal too when the 225-horse 455 big-block was ordered. At the top was the still-hot Stage 1, now rated at 270 horsepower.

The 1973 Gran Sport's base 350 V-8 featured a first for this bloodline: a two-barrel carburetor. Buick's GS was now based on the new Century Colonnade coupe. *Mike Mueller*

FASHIONABLY FAST

"If you had to compete with GM, Ford and Chrysler, what would you do?" asked American Motors ads in 1971. Build a narrow-niche two-seat rival to Chevrolet's Corvette? Finish your cars in patriotic red, white, and blue schemes? Team up with Hurst to morph a previously mundane Rambler into a Super Coupe? Rebel against the establishment with a Machine? Yes in all cases. And when it became clear that marketing muscle would soon be unfeasible for all involved, those avant-garde guys from Wisconsin also opted to venture where no US automaker had ventured before—the international world of fashion.

First they enlisted Italian cowhidesman Aldo Gucci to dress up 1972's Hornet Sportabout wagon with luxury appointments that even Jackie O might've been willing to wrap herself up in—or not. About the same time, AMC interior design director Vince Geraci also inked a deal with famed French fashionista Pierre Cardin to put his label on the Kenosha company's pony car.

"There are few designers in the same league as Pierre Cardin," announced AMC brochures to no one's surprise. "Maybe it's because he's just as good at thinking as he is at designing—'People should feel like they're sitting in a living room instead of sitting in a machine.' That's why we asked him to take the sporty feeling of the outside of our Javelin SST and carry it through to the inside."

Like the Gucci Sportabout, the Cardin Javelin featured a flashy interior that simply couldn't be described in 25 words or less—"must see to appreciate" surely applied. Pleated stripes in plum, red, silver, and white—set off in basic black surroundings—graced the seats, door panels, and headliner. And just in case witnesses didn't recognize his "ultra-modern abstract" work, the designer's stylized "PC" crest appeared both inside on the door panel inserts and outside on the front fenders. Product planners also ensured "proper coordination" by limiting exterior paint choices to four: Snow White, Stardust Silver, Trans-Am Red, and Wild Plum. As for that upholstery material, it was 100-percent nylon with a stain-resistant silicone coating and was supplied by the automotive interior fabric experts at Chatham Mills.

Left: French designer Pierre Cardin's colorful interior was complemented by four exterior paint choices in 1972: Trans Am Red, Stardust Silver, Snow White, and Wild Plum. Some black AMX renditions also are known.

Above: AMC introduced its Cardin-edition Javelin in 1972. The AMX shown here (done in special-order black) is one of 2,875 Cardin-interior models built for 1973. Apparently at least one more was sold in 1974. *courtesy Mecum Auctions*

AMC interior design director Vince Geraci (left) met with Pierre Cardin (right) in Paris early in 1971 to discuss plans to dress up the Javelin's interior.

"Only Pierre Cardin can make upholstery look so elegant, door panels so classy, and a headliner so chic," claimed AMC promotional people. "And only American Motors can give you a Cardin label at the price of a Javelin." Pegged at $84.95, the Cardin interior went into production on February 1, 1972, officially for Javelin SST applications only. But joining the 1,262 Cardin SST models built that year were 14 special-order Cardin AMXs, created perhaps as demonstrators. Reportedly, at least 12 of these were painted black.

The Cardin interior was specifically listed for both the base Javelin and AMX in 1973, with this year's total count coming to 2,875. Paint choices now numbered six: Snow White, Diamond Blue Metallic, Olympic Blue Metallic, Pewter Silver Metallic, Trans-Am Red, and Fresh Plum Metallic. And apparently special-order black again was possible. Evidence also exists of at least one 1974 Cardin Javelin, bringing the final tally for this short-lived fashion-conscious breed to 4,152.

Calling the Cardin interior "one of the wildest designs ever conceived," *Road Test's* Chuck Koch was predictably surprised by the colorful cockpit found inside the 401-equipped AMX he experienced in the spring of 1973. "Entering the car your eyes are assaulted by red, white and purple stripes arcing over the standard black upholstered bucket seats. Then when finally recovering your senses and sitting down, you see the same striped pattern adorning the roofliner. The entire effect is somewhat startling and always good for some sort of passenger reactions."

Like "I love what you've done with the place," perhaps?

A tame 318-cid LA V-8 was the base Road Runner engine in 1973. Front disc brakes, sway bars at both ends, and 14-inch Rallye wheels were standard.

Plymouth offered Barracuda and 'Cuda again in hardtop form only in 1973—and with V-8s only, too, as the base six-cylinder didn't roll over from 1972. Engine choices included a 318- or 340-cid LA small-block.

PLYMOUTH

"Only the strong survive" was the ad slogan chosen to promote Plymouth's Road Runner in 1973, but let's be real, folks. A mild-mannered 318-cid small-block? Net-rated at 170 clearly lame horses? Strong? At least a four-barrel carburetor and dual exhausts remained part of the standard package. Options included the 340 small-block (240 horsepower) and two big-blocks, the 260-horsepower 400 and 280-horsepower "GTX" 440. The three-speed manual was limited to the base 318, and only the Torqueflite was offered behind the 440 four-barrel V-8. Both the Torqueflite and four-speed manual were available behind the other three V-8s.

Additional standard equipment included front disc brakes and 14-inch Rallye wheels. New stripes—available in black, white, or red—also were standard, running along the top of each body side and meeting on top at the roof's trailing edge. These stripes could've been deleted on request, and additional striping was optionally available for the hood in this case.

Basically everything carried over into 1973 in Barracuda ranks save for new, highly noticeable front and rear bumper guards designed to withstand 5 miles per hour impacts. Two model lines again were home to one body style, the hardtop, but the base six was gone, leaving the 318 and 340 small-block V-8s to keep the power coming. Plymouth's final Duster 340 also remained a decent performer for the money in 1973.

DODGE

Larger, damage-inhibiting bumper pads also helped set Dodge's latest Challenger apart from its predecessor in 1973, and only V-8 power was offered this year as the slant-six was finally deleted in E-body ranks. The Rallye model remained, as did optional hot parts like Rallye wheels, a four-speed stick (behind the 340 only), the Performance Axle Package (also 340 only), and F70 rubber. B-body buyers in 1973 could still opt for the Charger Rallye, which again could be fitted with the optional 440 big-block.

TIME SLIPS: 1973

MODEL	¼-MILE PERFORMANCE	SOURCE
Pontiac Trans Am 455 SD	13.54 seconds at 104.3 mph	*Hot Rod*, June 1973
Chevrolet Camaro Z28	14.69 seconds at 96 mph	*Car Craft*, July 1973
Pontiac GTO (455 V-8)	14.70 seconds at 91 mph	*Hi-Performance Cars*, August 1973
Oldsmobile 4-4-2 (455 V-8)	14.90 seconds at 97.3 mph	*Hi-Performance Cars*, April 1973
Plymouth 'Cuda	15.16 seconds at 94.1 mph	*SSDI*, March 1973
Dodge Charger SE (440 V-8)	15.2 seconds at 92.9 mph	*Motor Trend*, May 1973
Buick GS 455 Stage 1	15.30 seconds at 90 mph	*Motor Trend*, July 1973
AMC Javelin AMX	15.4 seconds at 91 mph	*Road Test*, June 1973
Chevrolet Laguna (454 V-8)	15.7 seconds at 88.4 mph	*Motor Trend*, May 1973
Pontiac Grand Am (455 V-8)	15.7 seconds at 88 mph	*Motor Trend*, May 1973
Ford Gran Torino Sport	16.0 seconds at 88.1 mph	*Car and Driver*, July 1973
Ford Mustang Mach 1	16.3 seconds at 86 mph	*Motor Trend*, July 1973

NOTE: *SSDI is* Super Stock & Drag Illustrated *magazine*

Larger bumper pads appeared for Dodge's Challenger in 1973. Both a base Challenger and Rallye again were offered in hardtop forms only.

Now rated at 240 horsepower, Plymouth's 340 small-block powered the Duster 340 for one last time in 1973. A three-speed manual again was included in the basic package.

BY THE NUMBERS: 1973 PRODUCTION

CHEVROLET CHEVELLE SS

	28,647	(includes Colonnade coupe, El Camino & station wagon)

CHEVROLET CAMARO Z28

	11,574	(all hardtops)

PONTIAC GTO

coupe (400 V-8)	469	(187 w/manual trans; 282 w/auto)
coupe (455 V-8)	25	(all w/manual trans)
sprt cpe (400)	3,793	(926 w/manual trans; 2,867 w/auto)
sprt cpe (455)	519	(all w/manual trans)
total	**4,806**	

PONTIAC TRANS AM

w/L75 455 V-8	4,550	(1,420 w/4-speed manual trans; 3,130 w/auto)
455 Super Duty	252	(72 w/4-speed manual trans; 180 w/auto)
total	**4,802**	(all hardtops)

PONTIAC FIREBIRD FORMULA

w/L30 350 V-8	4,771	
w/L78 400 V-8	4,622	
w/L75 455 V-8	730	(227 w/4-speed manual trans; 503 w/auto)
455 Super Duty	43	(10 w/4-speed manual trans; 33 w/auto)
total	**10,166**	(all hardtops)

OLDSMOBILE 4-4-2

Cutlass coupe	251
Cutlass S coupe	9,546
total	**9,797**

HURST/OLDS **1,097**

BUICK GRAN SPORT

w/350-cid V-8	4,930
w/455 V-8	979
w/Stage 1 V-8	728
total	**6,637**

PLYMOUTH ROAD RUNNER

	19,056	(all hardtops; includes 749 GTX 440-cid V-8)

PLYMOUTH 'CUDA

	10,626	(all hardtops; base Barracuda count was 11,587)

PLYMOUTH DUSTER 340

	15,731	(all sport coupes)

DODGE CHALLENGER

	32,596	(all engines & models, including Rallye)

DODGE CHARGER RALLYE

	6,019	(all hardtops)

DODGE DART SPORT 340

	11,315	(all hardtops)

AMERICAN MOTORS JAVELIN AMX

	5,707	(1,134 w/304-cid V-8, 3,153 w/360-cid V-8, 1,420 w/401-cid V-8)

FORD MUSTANG MACH 1

	35,439	(all SportsRoofs w/302- or 351-cid V-8s)

FORD GRAN TORINO SPORT

"formal" roof	17,090
SportsRoof	51,853
total	**68,943**

MERCURY MONTEGO GT

	4,464

NOTE: *Production data was supplied by various sources, including Christo Datini at the GM Heritage Center, Ford Motor Company & Kevin Marti at Marti Auto Works (www.martiauto.com), Galen Govier (Mopar material) at Galen's Tag Service (www.galengovier.com), and American Motors enthusiast Eddie Stakes at www.planethoustonamx.com.*

Not visible here is the 1973 Javelin's "smoothed-out" roof, which no longer featured the fake T-top look introduced in 1971. With or without that creased sheet metal, AMX remained one of America's hottest looking pony cars.

Although this was the last year for the Montego GT fastback, a Sports Appearance Group was offered in 1974 and 1975 to keep things at least sporty-looking in Mercury's midsize ranks.

Right: Bigger bumpers were fitted to Ford's Gran Torino Sport in 1973 to help meet new safety standards. The hottest option under the hood remained Dearborn's 351 Cleveland small-block.

AMC

"American Motors' [1973] Javelin continues with few changes, and few are needed," wrote *Motor Trend's* Jim Brokaw. The roof was smoothed over (no more faux T-tops), the grille was revised, new rectangular taillights went on out back, and large rubber bumper guards were added at both ends to comply with Washington's impact standards. There was no SST model this year, just the base Javelin and warmed-up AMX. Beneath the hood, an EGR valve was new for all 1973 V-8s, and AMX buyers again could choose between the 360- and 401-cid four-barrel bent-eights. The flashy Pierre Cardin interior remained available, as did the two Go Packages (360 and 401), again for AMX only.

AMC introduced a limited-edition "Trans Am Victory" package for 1973 Javelins built between October and December 1972. The idea was to honor back-to-back SCCA road-racing championships (1971 and '72), and to this end a special commemorative decal was added to the front fenders. Included too were E70 Goodyear Polyglas tires (on 14x6 slotted rally wheels) and a Space-Saver spare. The Trans Am Victory option cost $167.45.

Tape stripes replaced contrasting lower body paint in 1973 for Ford's Mach 1 SportsRoof. The Mach 1's cut of Dearborn's pony car pie that year was a hefty 26.2 percent, a high for the Mustang's sporty sub-series.

FORD

To resist 5 miles per hour collisions, 1973's Mustang was fitted with an impact-absorbing front bumper covered in body-colored urethane. Basically all mechanicals carried over unchanged, as did Mach 1, with the most noticeable update involving tape stripes that superseded the contrasting lower body side paint used in 1972. New for 1973 was an optional 14x6 forged-aluminum slotted mag that replaced the 15-inch Magnum 500 wheel offered previously.

Big 5 miles per hour bumpers also graced 1973's Gran Torino Sport to help add extra weight it couldn't afford to gain—and remain in Detroit's fading muscle car class. Underhood choices (with slightly fewer horses) and standard features rolled over from 1972 with one major exception: a high-profile hood scoop was no longer included in the deal.

MERCURY

Gran Torino's corporate cousin, Mercury's fastback-only Montego GT, also carried over into 1973 with next to no changes, save for similar power shrinkages (due to more compression cuts) and an intimidating 5 miles per hour bumper up front. Though this was the last year for a full-fledged Montego GT model, Mercury did offer a Sports Appearance Group option to midsize buyers in 1974 and '75 made up of most of the GT's features, including the familiar twin-scooped hood.

MOTOR OF THE YEAR: 1973 AMC 401

Type	OHV V-8
Displacement	401 cubic inches
Bore	4.165 inches
Stroke	3.68 inches
Horsepower	255 at 4,600 rpm
Torque	345 at 3,300 rpm
Compression	8.5:1
Fuel delivery	Motorcraft 4,300 4-barrel carburetor
Air cleaner	single snorkel housing w/ram-air induction optional
Ignition	single-point distributor w/vacuum-advance
Cylinder block	cast-iron
Crankshaft	forged-steel w.2.7472-inch main journals
Connecting rods	forged-steel
Pistons	cast-aluminum
Cam	hydraulic w/296.32 degrees duration on intake, 303.55 degrees on exhaust, 68.32 degrees of overlap
Rocker ratio	1.6:1
Cylinder heads	cast-iron w/ "dog-leg" exhaust ports & 58cc chamber volume
Valve sizes	2.02-inch intakes, 1.68-inch exhausts
Valve lift	0.457 inch
Exhaust system	cast-iron "free-flow" manifolds

CHAPTER 11

1974 GET THE LEAD OUT

AMERICAN MUSCLE LOSES ITS GRIP

Pontiac's GTO option for 1974 carried various price tags depending on application. This deal was available for the Ventura coupe or hatchback, both bodies in turn being offered with or without Custom trim. Prices were $452 for the coupe, $426 for the Custom coupe, $440 for the hatchback, and $414 for the Custom hatchback.

Engine output during internal combustion's earliest decades was among other things limited by the feeble fuels pumped in. Simply put, raising compression always has been a key to increased power production, and maximizing those combustion-chamber squeezes always will require high-octane gasoline. But, into the mid-1920s, octane ratings barely surpassed 50, meaning in turn that compression ratios were limited to not much more than 4:1, maybe 5:1 at the extreme. Anything tighter and pre-detonation resulted as the fuel/air mix ignited before its time. Pre-detonation—knocking and pinging to you—not only destroys performance, it's also damned hard on valves, piston, and rings.

UNDER THE HOOD: 1974's HOTTEST V-8s*

MODEL	CID	BORE & STROKE	CR	HORSEPOWER	TORQUE
Pontiac Firebird (SD)	455	4.151 x 4.210	8.4:1	290 @ 4,000	395 @ 3,200
Pontiac GTO	350	3.8750 x 3.750	7.6:1	200 @ 4,400	295 @ 2,800
Chevrolet Chevelle	454	4.25 x 4.00	8.5:1	235 @ 4,000	360 @ 2,800
Chevrolet Z28	350	4.00 x 3.48	9.0:1	245 @ 5,200	280 @ 4,000
Buick GS	455	4.3125 x 3.90	8.5:1	255 @ 4,400	390 @ 3,000
Olds 4-4-2	455	4.125 x 4.250	8.5:1	275 @ 4,200	370 @ 3,200
Ford/Mercury	351	4.00 x 3.50	8:1	255 @ 5,600	290 @ 3,400
Dodge/Plymouth	440	4.320 x 3.750	8.2:1	250 @ 4,800	330 @ 3,200
Dodge/Plymouth	360	4.00 x 3.58	8.4:1	245 @ 4,800	320 @ 3,600
American Motors	401	4.165 x 3.68	8.5:1	255 @ 4,600	345 @ 3,300

NOTE: *CID is cubic-inch displacement; CR is compression ratio; bore/stroke in inches.*

** Discounting Corvette*

This country's postwar horsepower race would've never heated up had researchers not found a better way beforehand to fan the flames. Serious octane-boosting experiments began in 1916, when Dayton Electric Light Company president Charles Kettering asked Thomas Midgley to cure knocking problems in his firm's gas-powered electric generators. Midgley's investigations continued after Kettering opened another business, Dayton Metal Products, which was purchased by General Motors in 1919. Various anti-knock additives were explored (and patented) before Midgley settled on the cheapest, tetraethyl lead (TEL), originally discovered in 1853 by German chemist Carl Jacob Löwig. Reportedly, three cubic centimeters of TEL in a gallon of gasoline bumped up the octane rating by 15 points, which then allowed compression ratios to "soar" beyond 6:1, opening the door to unprecedented power potential.

First tested in GM's Dayton research lab in December 1921, Midgley's "ethyl" gasoline initially went on sale to the public in western Ohio in February 1923. Two months later, Dupont began TEL processing at a prototype facility (also in Dayton) under the direction of the General Motors Chemical Company. Full production followed in September at a Dupont plant in Deepwater, New Jersey, but delivery rates weren't fast enough to suit the bosses back in Detroit. In August 1924, GM teamed up with Standard Oil of New Jersey to form the Ethyl Gasoline Corporation to mass produce this fuel booster, and within five years it began filtering into filling stations from coast to coast. Along with making more punch possible, TEL in gasoline also greatly inhibited valve wear, minimizing the need for those pesky grind jobs.

Chrysler was among the first to exploit leaded gas, introducing its optional "Red Head" engine, with 6.2:1 compression in 1928. Later, immediately after World War II, Kettering's research team experimented with molecule-mashing 12.5:1 compression in an OHV six-cylinder that ran on aviation-quality 100-octane gasoline. Meanwhile, in the real world, the ratio for Cadillac's milestone OHV V-8 in 1949 was 7.5:1, still heady numbers for the day. Breaching the 10:1 barrier came seven years down the road, courtesy of top-shelf Chrysler and Packard V-8s. And by the 1960s many max-performance engines required about three digits worth of octane to run as designed without knocking themselves to death.

The downside to this tale, of course, involved a reality all but forgotten today. No ifs, ands, or profit-driven buts about it, lead is pure poison. Hippocrates, the "father of western medicine," recognized this as early as 400 B.C., as did Charles Dickens, who described the tragic plight of Britain's lead mill workers in 1860 in his *Uncommercial Traveller* series. In 1909, France, Austria, and Belgium became the first countries to ban lead-based paint, initially identified 20 years before as a threat to children who nibbled on chips or furniture, losing their minds (and sometime their lives) in the process.

It was a different story in this country. Pioneering toxicologist Alice Hamilton in 1910 observed that lead industry people in Illinois faced deadly conditions that would force plant closures in Europe. Hell, Thomas Midgley even contracted lead poisoning during his research, but at least he survived—to continue denying the seriousness of the situation. Many who worked with his super-fuel weren't so lucky. Dupont employees in Dayton and Deepwater began suffering horrid deaths immediately after TEL production began, and more fatalities (plus countless illnesses) followed as soon as the Ethyl Corp. plant opened for business in Bayway, New Jersey.

Modern high-performance would've never been possible if not for the development of high-octane gasoline during the 1920s. But the tradeoff involved fouling the environment with toxic tetraethyl lead (TEL). Founded in August 1924, the Ethyl Gasoline Corporation was first responsible for mixing TEL with gasoline, allowing Detroit's automakers to increase compression in their engines to unprecedented highs. Phasing out leaded gas didn't begin until the 1970s, and then primarily because it fouled the catalytic converters scheduled to appear on all American cars in 1975—not because it represented a public health hazard on its own.

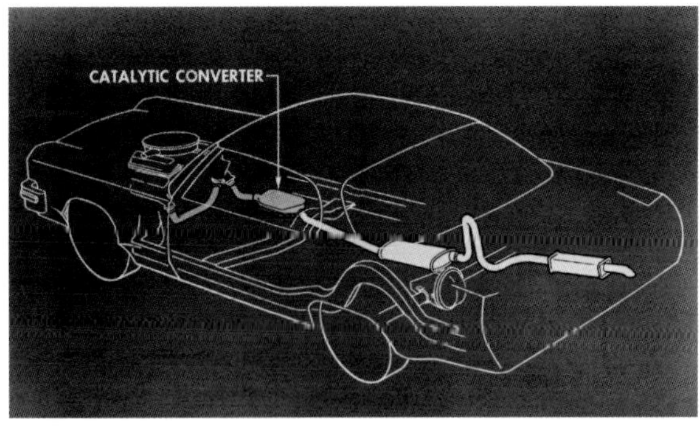

Catalytic converters represented the next logical step on the way to radically reducing automotive emissions, but "cats" and horses initially couldn't peacefully coexist. Back pressure created by typical 1975 exhaust systems (Oldsmobile's is shown here), working in concert with the lowered compression ratios instituted in 1971, choked the last gasps of life out of America's hotter V-8s. Pony-strangling single exhaust pipes were the norm during the catalytic era's early years.

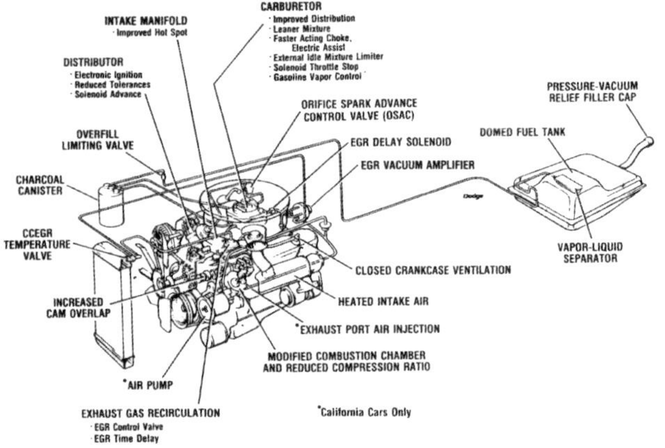

American V-8s were already saddled with a wide-array of pony-killing emissions-control equipment even before catalytic converters started showing up in 1975. According to *Hot Rod*, this Chrysler illustration "shows the amount of pollution BS, aside from low-compression pistons, needed on a '74 auto engine—ridiculous, isn't it?"

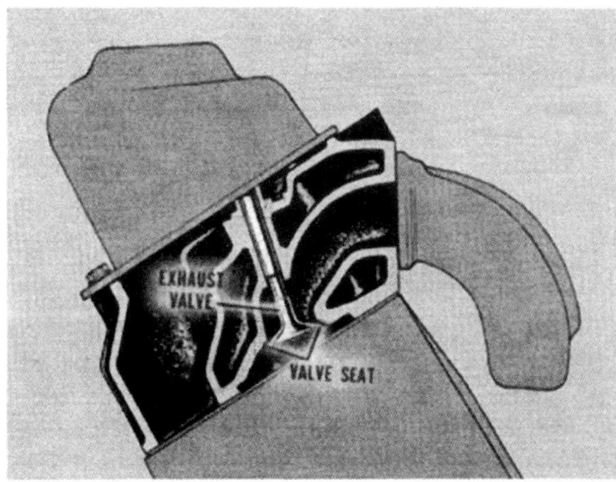

Switching to unleaded fuel left exhaust valves wide open to rapid deterioration, meaning hardened valve seats were required. Valves themselves also were upgraded to make up for the loss of leaded gasoline's "lubricating" benefits.

As early as June 1923, the US Public Health Service was questioning whether or not leaded gas represented a public hazard, and a PHS conference was convened in May 1925 to open a supposedly independent inquiry. Eight months later came a government report claiming that, while continued testing was highly suggested, "no good grounds" existed to support an ethyl ban. Even after more questions later arose concerning the additional dangers of ethyl emissions, further significant investigation didn't occur for another 40 years. PHS officials even approved an Ethyl Corp. request to up the lead content in fuels in 1959.

Awareness of the issue already was on the rebound (thanks mostly to growing air quality concerns in California) when geochemist Clair Patterson published his research paper, "Contaminated and Natural Lead Environments of Man," in September 1965. Hearings before the US Senate followed in June 1966, during which Patterson squared off against Robert Kehoe, Ethyl Corporation's bought-and-paid-for scientist who had been refuting any and all claims of TEL hazards dating back to 1927. Patterson not only attacked the flawed methodology Kehoe used to supply his plainly biased "pro-lead" evidence, he also questioned the agendas of governmental groups, which were supposed to be working in the peoples' best interests.

"It is not just a mistake for public health agencies to cooperate and collaborate with industries in investigating and deciding whether public health is endangered," he said before the committee. "It is a direct abrogation and violation of the duties and responsibilities of those public health organizations." Suffice it say that these hearings inspired further debate concerning needs for both revised regulations and refocused regulatory bodies, leading to the formation in December 1970 of the Environmental Protection Agency, which immediately moved to stamp out lead.

Funny thing, though: Big Three automakers already had beaten the EPA to the punch. GM president Ed Cole made major headlines in January 1970 after calling for the elimination of lead additives, clear irony considering his corporation's role in their creation. In March, Cole announced further that all 1971 GM cars would feature low-compression engines able to operate satisfactorily on unleaded gas, immediately triggering similar promises from Ford and Chrysler. Cole and cohorts' changes of heart, however, had far less to do with lead contamination concerns as they did with keeping up with Washington's latest overriding emissions control mandates, which required the upcoming installation of catalytic converters, long recognized as the only workable solution to the overall smog problem.

TIME SLIPS: 1974

MODEL	¼-MILE PERFORMANCE	SOURCE
Pontiac Trans Am 455 SD	14.25 seconds at 100.9 mph	*SSDI*, June 1974
Chevrolet Camaro Z28	15.4 seconds at 90.54 mph	*Motor Trend*, April 1974
Pontiac GTO	15.72 seconds at 88.0 mph	*Hi-Performance Cars*, May 1974
Chevrolet Laguna S-3	16.2 seconds at 87.0 mph	*Car and Driver*, February 1974
Dodge Challenger (318 V-8)	16.87 seconds at 80.2 mph	*Motor Trend*, April 1974
Pontiac Firebird (400 V-8)	17.05 seconds at 82.1 mph	*Motor Trend*, April 1974
AMC Javelin (304 V-8)	17.3 seconds at 83.05 mph	*Motor Trend*, April 1974

NOTE: *SSDI is* Super Stock & Drag Illustrated *magazine*

Trans Am production more than doubled for 1974, the year Pontiac's pony car was treated to a new slanted nose. *Mike Mueller*

1974 PONTIAC TRANS AM SD-455

CONSTRUCTION: unitized body/frame
MODEL AVAILABILITY: sport coupe
PRICE: $4,446, base Trans Am; SD-455 V-8 cost $578; four-speed manual cost $207; TH-400 automatic trans cost $242
WHEELBASE: 108 inches
WEIGHT: 4,101 pounds
SUSPENSION: heavy duty w/coils in front, leaf springs in back; sway bars at both ends (Radial Tuned Suspension, optional)
STEERING: recirculating ball w/variable-ratio power assist
WHEELS: 15-inch Rally II w/trim rings, std (15x7 Honeycomb rims, optional)
TIRES: F60-15 white-letter, std
BRAKES: power-assisted 11-inch front discs, 9.5-inch rear drums
ENGINE: LS2 455 Super Duty V-8 w/Quadra-jet 4-barrel carburetor
TRANSMISSION: Turbo Hydra-matic automatic or Muncie 4-speed manual
AXLE RATIO: 3.08:1, std w/automatic trans (3.42:1 w/manual trans)

America's high-perf lineup had diminished considerably by 1974, with Ford and Mercury completely out of the running and pony cars making up much of the sporty field. According to a *Hot Rod* magazine preview of this years's upcoming models, the "top drag strip contender" surely would be Road Runner, if only because "Mopar engines, for some unknown reason, seem to perform better than other makes of comparable displacement." Not all others, however. Even with the optional 440 big-block, Plymouth's last true midsize muscle car was plainly no match for Pontiac's Super Duty Trans Am, Detroit's last great muscle machine.

Every bit as amazing as it was the previous year, 1974's LS2 SD-455 still produced 290 emissions-legal horses and remained capable of whipping a PMD F-body down the quarter-mile in right around 14 seconds—with extra-cost goodies like air conditioning, an 8-track stereo, and power windows along for the ride. But, even after a three-fold-plus increase in sales, the second-edition Super Duty Firebird still represented a rarely seen machine, explaining why *Hot Rod's* people didn't bother to give it a nod while sending undue credit Road Runner's way. Some industry watchers simply had no idea that there'd be a Super Duty encore. According to a *Super Stock & Drag Illustrated* report, "Pontiac planned to produce only 40 or 50." The actual 1974 final tally was 1,001.

On its own, Pontiac's latest Trans Am was no slouch in 1974, certainly so from an image-conscious perspective. All that high-profile bodywork repeated, capped this time by a new slanted nose and revised tail that was devoid of the old-school chrome bumper seen in 1973. A beefed suspension was again standard, as were power front discs, variable-ratio power steering, and the Safe-T-Track limited-slip differential. A 225-horse L78 400 V-8 was now the base engine, with the 250-horsepower L75 455 (base in 1973) an option along with the LS2. The L75 was limited to auto-trans installations, while the L78 and SD-455 could be backed by either a Muncie four-speed or TH-400 automatic. Included inside were a Formula steering wheel, a swirl-grain dash, and Rally instrumentation. On the outside were Rally II rims wearing F60-15 white-letter tires. Honeycomb wheels and Pontiac's Radial Tuned Suspension (RTS) were available.

Both a cool cruiser and bad bruiser, PMD's last SD-455 Trans Am served as a suitable send-off for the automotive breed initially conceived by the same company 10 years before. Clearly Pontiac knew a thing or two about building excitement back then.

Pontiac's reality-defying 455 Super Duty V-8 made an encore appearance for 1974 before the fates finally intervened. No way could this muscle motor mix with the catalytic converters waiting right around the corner. *Mike Mueller*

LONE SURVIVOR

Discounting Chevrolet's Corvette, only one hot model managed to run interrupted from the original muscle era up into the latest millennium: Pontiac's Trans Am. Born in 1969, this SCCA-inspired Firebird continued proving it all night even after Chevy opted to drop its F-body counterpart, Camaro Z28, after 1974. Sure, Z28 did return midyear in 1977, but the deed was done, the lineage severed. Trans Am never did look back, never did stop turning heads, at least not until General Motors killed off its pony car pair in 2002. Pontiac itself was shuttered eight years later, just about the time the Bow-Tie boys were bringing Camaro back to life.

From 1969 to 1978, it was a big-cube V-8 or nothing at all beneath a Trans Am hood, which was typically decked out in those "screaming chicken" graphics and pierced by that trademark rear-facing shaker scoop—is there anyone out there not familiar with this image? Maybe some innocent bystanders weren't early on, but even they found themselves sucked in once Burt Reynolds made a Trans Am his tire-smoking, ramp-jumping co-star in Universal's 1977 flick, *Smokey and the Bandit*. Homebodies were further indoctrinated after David Hasselhoff's all-black, computerized T/A—named "KITT," for Knight Industries Two Thousand—picked up where the Bandit left off as one of the main attractions (beside's Hasselhoff's hair) in the television series *Knight Rider*, seen on NBC from 1982 to '86.

Baseball, applie pie, and Chevrolet? By the time the 1970s wound down, the prevailing trendy winds had brought together disco, leisure suits, and Pontiac's Trans Am. And while all that other junk quickly (not to mention thankfully) fell from grace, Trans Am proved itself to be more than a passing fad, initial production counts notwithstanding. Even with its hard-to-miss exterior and top-shelf performance, the second-generation Trans Am, introduced early in 1970, initially stalled in the marketplace, with sales dropping from 3,196 that year to a mere 1,286 in 1972. But the curve started sloping up in 1973, and six years later the annual count surpassed 100,000 for the first time.

Sales then dropped off again in 1980, the year the revered 6.6-liter V-8 was traded for a 4.9-liter. Optional turbocharging also debuted that year, but the forced-induction T/A was a mere shadow of its former normally aspirated large-displacement self. It was then left to a redesigned third-generation platform, introduced in January 1982, to revive things.

Discounting Chevrolet's Corvette—which always had run in a class by itself—the only high-performance model to roll on interrupted from the original muscle car era into the latest millennium was Pontiac's Trans Am, a venerable fun machine that finally retired in 2002. Appearing here is the 1969 original (rear), a 1974 SD-455 rendition (middle), and a 1999 30th Anniversary model. *Mike Mueller*

Fortunately, lukewarm memories of those original Turbo Trans Ams were erased by decade's end after Pontiac engineers released their first V-6 T/A in 1989. Relying on a modified version of the Buick GNX's turbocharged, intercooled, electronically fuel-injected 3.8-liter six, the 20th Anniversary Indy Pace Car GTA emerged to lay claim to the quickest Trans Am ever built. This 250-horsepower screamer could run from rest to 60 miles per hour in a scant five seconds and surpass 160 miles per hour on the top end, leaving even the 1973–74 Super Duty and 1969–70 Ram Air IV renditions behind.

Corvette-class performance pieces began filtering over into GM's F-body lineup in 1982, first in the form of Cross-Fire injection for the Trans Am's 5.0-liter V-8, which was soon superseded by tuned-port injection (TPI). And when another totally redesigned Firebird appeared for 1993, the power choice for the fourth-gen T/A was the Corvette's excellent 5.7-liter LT1 V-8, rated at 275 horsepower when installed in F-bodies. The LT1 was then swapped in 1998 for the LS1, pegged at 305 horses between Trans Am fenders. Introduced the previous year for Chevrolet's plastic-bodied two-seater, the LS1 was advertised at 345 horsepower in that application.

Other notable notes included a convertible Trans Am's return in 1991, the first since 1969. And, along with 1989's 20th Anniversary model, special commemorative Trans Ams also appeared in 1979, 1984, 1994, and 1999. Rumors of this long-running legacy's demise already were running wild when that 30th Anniversary model appeared. That they proved to be too true led to untold tears in 2002.

Along with a high-flying rear wing, Pontiac's last Tran Am came standard in 2002 with the Corvette's LS1 V-8, a 5.7-liter small-block rated at 310 horsepower in GM's F-body platform. Adding the optional WS6 Ram Air package (shown here), upped the output ante to 325 horses.

Borrowing the Buick GNX's awesome turbocharged, injected V-6, Pontiac's 1989 GTA Trans Am represented further rolling proof that the great American muscle car was back in action—better than ever.

French chemist Michel Frenkel had suggested as far back as 1909 that gas-fired emissions could be reduced by instituting "supplementary combustions in the exhaust box, with the aid of a catalytic agent." But it wasn't until mechanical engineer Eugene Houdry opened Oxy-Catalyst, Inc. in 1948 that serious catalytic converter development began, first targeting factory smoke stack pollution. Houdry also earned patents for automotive applications during the 1950s, and then it was left to federal action to force this technology into industry-wide use two decades later.

While various people contributed further advances, the bulk of the credit for creating modern automotive "cats" in the 1970s goes to John Mooney and Carl Keith of the Engelhard Corporation. At General Motors, engineer Robert Stempel was directed by Ed Cole in 1973 to oversee additional development, resulting in regular-production introductions two years later. These first units were of "two-way" design in that they only dealt with carbon monoxide and unburned

Replacing the Super Sport Chevelle for 1974 was Chevrolet's Laguna Type S-3 coupe. Along with its distinctive urethane-covered nose, the S-3 initially came standard with a full vinyl roof. Later models featured vinyl covering only for the roof's front half. Louvers also were optional for the S-3's opera glass.

FAMILY TIES: BUCKET LIST

Bench seats may have worked well at the Saturday-night submarine races, but buckets clearly represented the really cool way to get around during the 1960s. Known primarily to sports car drivers and racers during the 1950s, bucket seats didn't begin gaining real popularity in mainstream American passenger cars (those with back seats as well as fronts) until the following decade. Pioneering limited-edition applications included Pontiac's 1958 Bonneville and Chrysler's 1959 300E, with the latter units adding curious swiveling action to the attraction. The supposedly sporty Monza rendition of Chevy's compact Corvair came standard with bucket seats in 1960, as did Pontiac's certainly prestigious Grand Prix in 1962. And Ford's Mustang and Plymouth's Barracuda established individual front seats as the norm in the pony car field two years later. Standard buckets represented a hit or miss proposition in the muscle car class, with misses occurring more often than not in the best interests of keeping base prices well within the reach of Average Joe. Fortunately, trading out that mundane bench for a pair of butt-planters was always possible—as long as your wallet was just as fat.

Swiveling bucket seats became standard for Chrysler's 300E in 1959. Buckets also had appeared in Pontiac's limited-edition Bonneville the previous year. *Mike Mueller*

Introduced in March 1965, the Mustang's optional Decor Group included specially embossed seat inserts, which inspired this package's "pony interior" nickname. *Mike Mueller*

Standard for the first SS 396 in 1965, Chevrolet's Strato bucket seats were optional for Super Sport Chevelles beginning the following year. The Strato buckets installed in Yenko Chevelles in 1969 featured appropriate stenciling (short for "Yenko Super Car") on their headrests. *Mike Mueller*

Swiveling bucket seats returned in 1973, this time courtesy of General Motors' new Colonnade coupes. A 1973 Hurst/Olds shows off the concept here. *Mike Mueller*

Z28 sales jumped up for 1974, but the decision to end the line was already made by then. Prominent graphics were new that last year.

Buick's last big-block Gran Sport appeared for 1974. The Century GS rolled on into 1975 but only with small-block or V-6 power.

hydrocarbons. They were superseded in 1981 by three-way converters, which minimized nitrogen oxide emissions as well.

One compound catalytic converters couldn't handle was TEL, a fact Eugene Houdry discovered. Leaded gas simply had to go before cats could start working, hence the support for unleaded production supplied by Big Three execs early in 1970. Low-lead and unleaded fuels first showed up in limited supplies the following year, then the stuff really started flowing in 1972, at a slightly higher price compared to leaded regular. Along with 1971's lower compression levels, new engines now also required stronger exhaust valves and hardened seats to compensate for the lost "lubricating" benefits of ethyl-enhanced gas.

In January 1973, EPA officials announced that, by July 1, 1974, every retail outlet across the country "at which 200,000 or more gallons of gasoline were sold during any calendar year beginning with 1971" was required by law to offer unleaded gasoline of at least 91 octane. A full phase-out of leaded gas then began in 1976 and reached complete compliance 10 years later. According to a 1994 study, lead concentrations in American blood fell by 78 percent from 1976 to 1991.

Forgotten, too, these days are all those who suffered and died during the decades when lead contamination was allowed to run unchecked.

PONTIAC

Pontiac rolled out its rare Super Duty F-body one more time before reality finally caught up with this passionate Poncho, a car that also never would have worked with catalytic converters. In many minds, the same company that kicked off the muscle car race in 1964 suitably signaled its end 10 years later with its SD-455 Trans Am. All purported performance machines to follow were obvious imposters, though it should be said that PMD's T/A Firebird did manage to pull off its pretender roll rather ably into the 1980s before re-emerging as a true muscle car. As for the attractive Formula, it remained on the scene until 1982.

That latter pony car was segregated by engine in 1974, with the Formula 350 featuring the 170-horsepower L30 V-8, the Formula 400 the 200-horsepower L78, and the Formula 455 the 250-horsepower L75. Last but certainly not least was the Formula SD-455.

The end of the road also arrived this year for the car that started it all, GTO, now based on the compact Ventura, itself introduced in March 1970 using a familiar Chevrolet platform. When *Hi-Performance Cars* road testers got their hands on a 1974 GTO, they called it "one of the better looking Chevy Novas we had seen in a long time." Pontiac's last GTO option was available for the Ventura coupe or hatchback, which both were offered with or without Custom accoutrements. Bright exterior trim and an upscale front bench seat were included in the Custom package.

Only one engine was offered, the 200-horsepower L76 350, featuring unleaded-friendly 7.62:1 compression. A Trans Am-style shaker hood scoop also was part of the deal, as was a single-muffler exhaust system incorporating dual tailpipes that exited directly behind the rear wheels. Optional items included chrome splitter exhaust tips and Pontiac's Radial Tuned Suspension, consisting of special shocks, revised spring rates, suspension ride restrictors, larger grommets for the stabilizer bars, and FR78x14 steel-belted radial tires featuring either white sidewalls or white lettering. An RTS-equipped GTO also came with an appropriate glovebox badge.

INTO THE SUNSET

By 1974, no way could Mercury and muscle car be used in the same sentence, and much the same also could be said about Ford, which still offered a Gran Torino Sport, but only in ho-hum sport coupe form; no more sexy SportsRoof fastback. Dearborn also no longer had an engine willing to move this two-ton so-called intermediate into the fast lane. Its 460 big-block was nothing more than big, and the diminishing 351 Cleveland small-block, while still comparatively warm, was no match for all that tonnage, nor was the wimpy 400 two-barrel. Most notably, Mustang also lost whatever it had left in its high-performance tank this year after Lee Iacocca opted to turn back the page to 1964.

Iacocca never liked the way his baby grew up after 1966. A bigger pony was by no means a better one in his not-so-humble opinion, and this belief was forged long before an even larger Mustang appeared for 1971. By that time, he wasn't the only one upset. Loyal customers too were letting their feelings known through the mail, with one protesting letter-writer using the term "luxury bus."

As early as November 1969, Iacocca was suggesting a new direction for Mustang, one that would bring it back closer to his original ideal. Success of the compact Maverick in 1970 didn't hurt his cause in the least, and the groundwork was quickly laid for a redesigned, downsized Mustang.

Italy's famed design studio, Ghia, was responsible for creating the first prototype. Ford had bought controlling interest in the Turin firm in November 1970, and within a few months Ghia head Alejandro de Tomaso had turned out a sleek little machine that started the Mustang II project rolling. Eventually based on Ford's Pinto platform, Iacocca's "little jewel" was then officially introduced on August 28, 1973.

Wheelbase was a scant 96.2 inches, down 13 clicks from its 1973 predecessor. Mustang II also was 4 inches skinnier, 14 inches shorter, and some 300 pounds lighter. A 2.3-liter four-cylinder was standard, a 2.8-liter V-6 optional for four models: base coupe, three-door fastback, upscale Ghia, and familiar Mach 1.

Proving that less sometimes is more, the truly small Mustang II set a sales pace nearly as quick as its ancestor had 10 years before. More than 385,000 buyers took flight behind the wheels of Mustang IIs in 1974, a good number of those perhaps jumping on the bandwagon after *Motor Trend* named Ford's downsized pony its "Car of the Year" in January 1974. In *Motor Trend's* words, this new breed stood as "a total departure from the fat old horse of the recent past."

Not happy with the road his beloved Mustang took after 1966, Ford exec Lee Iacocca finally took matters into his own hands, resulting in the downsized Mustang II, introduced for 1974. A true compact with no performance potential whatsoever, Mustang II arrived as the book on Ford muscle cars slammed shut.

Others were not so quick to praise. "While the Mach 1's general concept is enthusiast-oriented," claimed *Car and Driver*, "its poor acceleration, wide-ratio transmission and overweight chassis leave too much of its undeniably sporting flavor unsupported by nourishment." *Car Craft* called the car "regrettably underpowered," then predicted that Ford would probably offer a V-8 version, and soon.

An optional V-8 arrived in 1975, but sales that year still fell by more than 50 percent as the attraction quickly faded. Among other things, many buyers had already grown dissatisfied with the car's cramped quarters. And it seemed soaring gas prices could only compromise a Mustang buyer's standards so far. Sagging demand then signaled the need for yet another redesigned pony car.

While work progressed on this project, Ford made one last stab at pumping up the Mustang II image in 1978. Built for five months, 1978's King Cobra was yet another striped, spoilered, and spatted excuse for a performance car. "With the real muscle-car era now no more than memory, cars like King Cobra are becoming the machismo machines of the late 1970s," wrote *Car Craft's* John Asher.

King Cobras may have looked good parked in front of the local disco, but they never qualified as muscle machines.

CHEVROLET

While Chevelle SS didn't return in 1974, Chevrolet did offer its Laguna Type S-3, called "the kind of sporty car that makes sense today" by company ads. Introduced the previous year, Laguna models were instantly identified by their body-colored, urethane-covered nose, created in part to help hide Chevy's new 5miles per hour crash-resistant bumper system. A special grille featuring Euro-style running lights helped thc Laguna appear much more stylish up front compared to the typical Chevelle facade, dominated by its hefty chrome bumper. Standard S-3 stuff included V-8 power, the Malibu Classic's opera-style rear-quarter windows, 15-inch Rally wheels, swivel bucket seats, a four-spoke sport steering wheel, and a six-dial instrument cluster.

A mild Camaro makeover and new, rather garish graphics made pony car news this year, the last for the original Z28. RPO Z28 components carried over unchanged from 1973 to '74 save for the 245-horsepower 350 Turbo Fire small-block, which was refitted with Chevy's more efficient High Energy Ignition (HEI).

BUICK

The end of the road came for the 455-equipped Gran Sport (and thus the Stage 1, too) this year as Buick's monster mill was limited to full-size models beginning in 1975. Engine availability rolled over unchanged from 1973 with one exception: an optional 455 two-barrel was offered for the last big-block GS. Century Gran Sports

BACK FROM THE DEAD

By 1975, most industry watchers were sure they'd seen their last supercar. Then came news midyear in 1977 that Chevrolet's Z28 Camaro, cancelled in 1974, was returning for an encore performance. A humble 185-horsepower V-8 was standard, inspiring *Car and Driver's* Don Sherman to conclude that "handling will clearly be the new Z28's claim to fame." Horsepower's comeback was still a few years away.

Early attempts to squeeze as many ponies as possible from emissions-legal, low-compression engines involved bolting on exhaust-driven turbochargers, which popped up seemingly everywhere during the 1980s, in most cases at the heart of weak-kneed budget buggies. Exceptions included Pontiac's turbo Trans Am V-8, introduced in 1980, and Dodge's Omni-based GLH and GLHS variants, created with the help of Carroll Shelby. "GLH" stood for "Goes Like Hell," a fair description for the GLHS, offered in 1986 and 1987 with a 175-horsepower turbocharged four-banger. Ford also turned up the pressure in an effort to maximize Mustang performance. Dearborn's Euro-style SVO Mustang, introduced in 1984, relied on a 2.3-liter intercooled turbo four that initially produced 175 horsepower.

While Buick engineers also opted for unnatural aspiration, they added two more cylinders to their bad, black Regal-based Grand Nationals, built from 1984 to 1987. Output for the GN's intercooled 3.8-liter V-6 turbo ranged from 200 to 245 horsepower. Even more impressive was Buick's "Super Grand National," the GNX, created in 1987 with the help of McLaren Engines and the American Sunroof Company (ASC). Featuring 276 pressurized ponies, this limited-edition black beauty could smoke a quarter-mile in a sensational 13.4 seconds, easily the best time slip posted by any 1980s passenger sedan.

Every bit as bodacious as the GNX was Pontiac's 20th Anniversary Trans Am GTA, unleashed in 1989 with another version of Buick's boosted V-6, this one producing 250 healthy horses. Again published quarter-mile times read 13.4 seconds, but in this case the 0–60 clocking was a sensational 4.6 ticks, making the Buick-powered T/A "the quickest sprinter in any US showroom at any price," according to *Car and Driver's* Csaba Csere.

The Cosworth Vega's DOHC four-cylinder pioneered the performance application of electronic fuel injection in 1975. EFI V-8s then emerged during the late 1980s to help mate performance with fuel-saving practicality.

Chevrolet's Z28 Camaro made a triumphant return midyear in 1977. A 185-horsepower 350 V-8 was standard, at least in 49 states. California buyers found a 175-horsepower small-block in there Zs.

Clearly turbocharging played an important role in the rebirth of American high performance, but it by no means represented the main driving force. Also helping both Buick's exceptional V-6 and the SVO four-holer make so many EPA-approved horses from not so many cubes was the 1980s' most historic engineering milestone: electronic fuel injection (EFI).

Pontiac engineers in 1970 were among the first to successfully test EFI V-8s, inspiring *Motor Trend's* Karl Ludvigsen to claim that this advance "could be the vital link in enabling the internal combustion engine to meet stringent emission standards." Volkswagen pioneered EFI applications in America in 1968, and VW's Jetronic "Bugs" were followed by similarly equipped environment-conscious imports from Saab, Volvo, and Mercedes. Detroit's first EFI option was introduced by Cadillac in March 1975, and Chevrolet's limited-edition Cosworth Vega emerged at the same time with an electronically injected DOHC four-cylinder that made 110 horses from 122 cubic inches.

Chevrolet followed that with the 1982 Corvette's L83 350 V-8, a 200-horsepower small-block fed by "Cross-Fire Injection," a high-perf variation on GM's throttle-body injection (TBI) design, introduced in 1980 for Cadillac's Eldorado and Seville. Both Chevy's Z28 and Pontiac's Trans Am also could be fitted with Cross-Fire Injection V-8s in 1982. Then three years later, GM's first true EFI system, Tuned-Port Injection (TPI), appeared for Corvette, Camaro, and Trans Am.

Ford Motor Company entered the modern injected age in 1980, introducing its EFI-equipped Lincoln Versailles. But unlike their GM counterparts, Dearborn officials at first didn't allow their latest, greatest technology to trickle down into pony car ranks, though that wasn't necessarily a bad thing. New for 1982 was Ford's reborn Mustang GT, powered by a 157-horsepower 5.0-liter High Output V-8. Adding a four-barrel carb the following year helped raise the GT ante to 175 horses, then came true dual exhausts and EFI induction in 1986, making the battle with Chevy's TPI Camaro a fair fight—that is until the Bow-Tie boys redesigned Camaro for 1993, fitting it with a 275-horsepower version of Corvette's 300-horsepower LT1 V-8.

It was left to Ford's Special Vehicle Team to re-level the playing field with its Cobra Mustang, also introduced in 1993. Ten years later, the SVT Cobra's 4.6-liter DOHC V-8 was pumping out 390 horsepower. And in 2007, the SVT-badged Shelby GT500 emerged true to its name—beneath its bulging hood were 500 supercharged ponies.

GM's F-bodies by then were moldering in their graves, killed off in 2002. But at least Pontiac got back on track in 2004 with its Aussie-sourced GTO. Based on GM Australia's Holden Monaro, PMD's reborn Goat at first offered 350 horsepower then was refitted with Corvette's 400-horsepower LS2 V-8 in 2005 before re-retiring the following year.

Only 547 GNX Buicks, all painted black and fitted with fender flares were built for 1987. Beneath the hood was a turbocharged EFI V-6 rated at 276 horsepower.

Dodge, meanwhile, was busy readying its own supercar revival. Sure, the narrow-niche Viper had been Detroit's perennial horsepower scoring leader since 1992. But no mainstream muscular models had come out of the Mopar camp during the 1990s, and none with a V-8 since the 1970s. A hint that this wrong was scheduled for righting came in January 2006 when Dodge introduced its Challenger concept vehicle at Detroit's North American International Auto Show. Morphed into regular-production reality two years later, the Challenger SRT8 was teamed up with another old friend, Dodge's Gen III Hemi V-8, rated the same as its 1960s forefather: 425 horsepower.

Chevrolet's decision to bring back Camaro in 2010 made it a three-way race again—just as it was (with apologies to American Motors) a half century ago. As this epic goes to press, Dodge is offering its outrageous 707-horsepower Hellcat Challenger, leaving all witnesses wondering just how high modern muscle cars can fly.

Or how soon they'll fall back to earth.

Ford's Mustang was still running strong in 2015, with 435 horses standard for the new sixth-generation GT, 310 for its EcoBoost turbo four (at right) running mate. While the goal was to roll into the future with their sixth-gen pony car, Ford people simply couldn't help but continue to pay tribute to the past. Especially evident was a return to the true fastback body familiar to Mustang buyers in 1965 and '66. At left here is a 1966 2+2 Mustang, owned by Tom and Michelle Grothouse, of Arlington, Texas. *Mike Mueller*

As in 1973, Oldsmobile's 1974 4-4-2 was created via an appearance package. The 4-4-2 legacy carried on up through 1980 then reappeared from 1985 to 1988 and again from 1990 to 1991.

(some with V-6 power) carried on into 1975, but it just wasn't the same without the Stage 1 around to maximize muscle. A Century GS reappeared in 1986, and a Regal-based Gran Sport was offered from 1988 to 2006.

OLDSMOBILE

Oldsmobile's W29 option again transformed a Cutlass or Cutlass S into a 4-4-2 in 1974 by adding a special grille, body stripes and a heavy-duty suspension, and all Rocket V-8s—350 and 455—were once more available with this package. The 4-4-2 legacy remained alive through 1980, then was reborn from 1985 to '87. A front-wheel-drive Quad 4 4-4-2 also was offered in 1990 and '91.

The Hurst/Olds legacy rolled over almost unchanged into 1974, with the most notable update involving engine availability. Cars sold in California were all fitted with a 180-horsepower 350 Rocket V-8. This engine was optional in all other states and was identified by "W-25" decals on the fenders. A 230-horsepower 455 big-block remained the top choice and changed the exterior identification to "W-30."

Oldsmobile no longer offered a convertible model when the Hurst/Olds was selected to pace the 1974 Indianapolis 500. So Hurst stripped the roofs off two coupes and added padded roll bars. All garden-variety Hurst/Olds built this year were familiar Colonnade coupes.

BY THE NUMBERS: 1974 PRODUCTION

Model	Production	Notes
CHEVROLET LAGUNA S-3		
	21,902	(all Colonnade coupes)
CHEVROLET CAMARO Z28		
	13,802	(all hardtops)
PONTIAC GTO		
coupe	5,335	(2,487 w/manual trans; 2,848 w/auto)
hatchback	1,723	(687 w/manual trans; 1,036 w/auto)
total	**7,058**	
PONTIAC TRANS AM		
	10,255	(all hardtops)
PONTIAC FIREBIRD FORMULA		
	14,519	(all hardtops)
PONTIAC SD-455 FIREBIRD		
	1,001	(included in above totals for both Formula & Trans Am models)
OLDSMOBILE 4-4-2		
Cutlass coupe	245	
Cutlass S coupe	6,959	
total	**7,204**	
HURST/OLDS		
	1,800	(380 w/W-30 455-cid V-8)
BUICK GRAN SPORT		
w/350-cid V-8	2,298	
w/455 2-bl V-8	141	
w/455 4-bl V-8	438	
w/Stage 1 V-8	478	
total	**3,355**	
PLYMOUTH ROAD RUNNER		
	11,555	(all hardtops; includes 386 w/GTX 440-cid V-8)
PLYMOUTH 'CUDA		
	4,989	(all hardtops w/318- or 360-cid V-8s)
PLYMOUTH DUSTER		
	360	3,879 (all sport coupes)
DODGE CHALLENGER		
	16,437	(all hardtops w/all engines, includes Rallye)
DODGE DART 360		
	3,314	(all hardtops)
AMERICAN MOTORS JAVELIN AMX		
	4,980	(all hardtops; 1,884 w/304-cid V-8, 2,320 w/360-cid V-8, 776 w/401-cid V-8)

NOTE: *Production data was supplied by various sources, including Christo Datini at the GM Heritage Center, Ford Motor Company & Kevin Marti at Marti Auto Works (www.martiauto.com), Galen Govier (Mopar material) at Galen's Tag Service (www.galengovier.com), and American Motors enthusiast Eddie Stakes at www.planethoustonamx.com.*

Plymouth's last true midsize Road Runner appeared for 1974 looking essentially identical to its 1973 predecessor. A Fury-based Road Runner debuted for 1975, followed by an F-body Volare rendition in 1976.

A Hurst/Olds again was chosen to pace the Indy 500 in 1974, requiring two customized models for actual on-track duty. With a convertible Cutlass no longer available, the Hurst folks decided to create their own brand of topless travel. The steel roofs were stripped off the two pace cars and large padded roll bars were put in place. A removable hardtop was created just in case weatherproofing was required at the Brickyard on race day.

The pace car's image was replicated on 1974 Hurst/Olds coupes by a stylized band that ran over the roof mimicking that roll bar. Large triangular Cutlass S rear quarter windows replaced the small "opera" glass used the previous year.

PLYMOUTH

Standard once more for Plymouth's all-but-unchanged Road Runner for 1974 was a 318 small-block, rated at 150 horsepower. The options list also again featured one small- and two big-block V-8s, but this time the former was the new 360, rated at 245 horses. Output ratings for the 400 and "GTX" 440 were 250 and 275, respectively.

Cancelling the midsize Satellite platform in 1975 meant moving Road Runner up into luxury-conscious Fury ranks for one final appearance as a distinct model all its own. A Road Runner trim package appeared for the F-body Volare coupe in 1976, and this combo continued on the market until the Volare was discontinued at 1980's end.

No longer coveted by America's no-longer-so-young car buyers, Plymouth's sporty Barracuda made its final appearance in 1974. The only major change that year came under the hood, where a 170-horsepower 360 replaced the 340. A Duster 360 also appeared for 1974, but it plain and simply represented a mere shadow of the performance compact's former self.

American Motors again offered a base Javelin (upper right) and AMX (lower left) in 1974. Like its Mopar rivals, AMC's pony car also rode off into the sunset at year's end.

DODGE

Dodge offered a final Charger Rallye for 1974 before the once-sexy B-body moved on up the following year to become a badge-engineered Cordoba. Challenger, too, showed up one last time in 1974, with minor upgrades including beefier rear bumper guards able to withstand 5 miles per hour impacts, per federal mandate. Challenger Rallye also carried over this year, as did the standard 318 small-block. And like Plymouth, Dodge also traded the optional 340 for the 360 before closing the book on its short, happy E-body tale.

AMC

Like Chrysler, American Motors also gave up on pony car production after 1974, due in part to the fact that a reported $12 million was needed to make a 1975 Javelin comply with even tighter federal standards for impact-resistant bumpers. One more AMX appeared before the axe fell and again could be optionally fitted with 360 or 401 Go Packages, which carried over nearly identically from 1973 with one notable change: functional cowl induction was no longer available. Some later models even were fitted with conventional steel hoods after the supply of fiberglass lids (standard since 1971) ran out well before the end of the line.

AMX fans need not have felt alone, though. All of Detroit's original muscle cars were history by 1974's end.

MOTOR OF THE YEAR: 1974 PONTIAC 455 SUPER DUTY

Type	OHV LS2 V-8 w/non-functional Shaker hood scoop
Displacement	455 cubic inches
Bore	4.15 inches
Stroke	4.21 inches
Horsepower	290 at 4,000 rpm
Torque	395 at 3,200 rpm
Compression	8.4:1
Fuel delivery	800-cfm Rochester Quadra-jet 4-barrel carburetor on cast-iron intake
Air cleaner	large-capacity filter w/cool-air induction ducting through grille
Ignition	single-point distributor
Cylinder block	cast-iron w/reinforced main bearing webs, 4-bolt malleable-iron bearing caps, oil pan baffle & heavy-duty 80-psi oil pump (cast-in provision for dry-sump oiling)
Crankshaft	cast-nodular-iron w/ 3.25-inch main journals
Connecting rods	forged-steel (SAE 5140) with 7/16-inch rod bolts
Pistons	TRW forged-aluminum
Cam	hydraulic w/301 degrees of duration on intake, 313 degrees on exhaust,76 degrees of overlap
Rocker ratio	1.5:1
Cylinder heads	cast-iron w/round exhaust ports, special alloy valve guides & hardened exhaust valve seat inserts; 111cc combustion chambers
Valve sizes	2.11-inch intakes, 1.77-inch exhausts; dual valve springs
Valve lift	0.414 inch
Exhaust system	cast-iron header-type manifolds, 2.5-inch main pipes, transverse-mounted muffler, 2.25-inch tailpipes

INDEX